SKY DANCER

The Secret Life and Songs of the Lady Yeshe Tsogyel

SKY DANCER

The Secret Life and Songs of the Lady Yeshe Tsogyel

KEITH DOWMAN

Illustrated by Eva van Dam

Snow Lion Publications
Ithaca, New York USA

Snow Lion Publications
P.O. Box 6483
Ithaca, New York 14851
tel: 607-273-8519

First published by Routledge & Kegan Paul 1984
Second edition published by Penguin Arkana 1989
This edition published by arrangement with Penguin Books Ltd.

ISBN 1-55939-065-4

Library of Congress Cataloging-in-Publication Data

Stag-śam Nus-ldan-rdo-rje, b. 1655.
[Bod kyi jo mo Ye-śes-mtsho-rgyal gyi mdzad tshul rnam par thar pa gab pa mṅon byuṅ rgyud maṅs dri za'i glu phreṅ. English]
Sky dancer : the secret life and songs of the Lady Yeshe Tsogyel / Keith Dowman ; illustrated by Eva van Dam.
p. cm.
Reprint. London: Routledge & Kegan Paul, 1984.
ISBN 1-55939-065-4
1. Ye-śes-mtsho-rgyal, 8th cent. 2. Yogis--China--Tibet--Biography. 3. Lamas--China--Tibet--Biography. 4. Yoga (Tantric Buddhism)--Early works to 1800. I. Dowman. Keith.
BQ998.E757S713 1996
294.3'923'092--dc20
[B] 96-15585
CIP

HOMAGE TO THE GURU ḌĀKINĪ!

This book is dedicated to the
enlightenment of all sentient beings.

CONTENTS

FOREWORD

TRINLEY NORBU RIMPOCHE

In the profound *sūtra* system, the Ḍākinī is called the Great Mother.

Indescribable, unimaginable Perfection of Wisdom,
Unborn, unobstructed essence of sky,
She is sustained by self-awareness alone:
I bow down before the Great Mother of the Victorious Ones,
  past, present and future.

Thus it is written in the *Great Pāramitā Sūtra*. In the precious tantric tradition, 'desireless, blissful wisdom is the essence of all desirable qualities, unobstructedly going and coming in endless space'. This wisdom is called 'the Sky Dancer', feminine wisdom, the Ḍākinī.

In the *tantra* system, the Three Jewels of the *sūtras* are contained in the Three Roots – Guru, Deva, Ḍākinī. One in essence, these three aspects are the three objects of refuge. Guru is the aspect that bestows blessing; Deva is the aspect that transmits *siddhi*; and Ḍākinī is the aspect that accomplishes the Buddha's *karma*.

In the *tantra*, countless objects of refuge appear spontaneously out of the one essential wisdom. Arising from wisdom as its reflection, all these forms are *nirmāṇakāya*. These forms can appear pure or impure according to the pattern of belief of the individual perceiving them.

Saṃbhogakāya differs from *nirmāṇakāya* in that it is a pure, non-dual *maṇḍala* that cannot be known by limited, individual perception. It can only be attained through pure, sublime, non-dual being.

Dharmakāya is the stainless space constantly pervading the sublime awareness of the *saṃbhogakāya* and the ordinary, individual perceptions of the *nirmāṇakāya*. In the *dharmakāya*'s stainless space Yeshe Tsogyel is Kuntuzangmo, infinite and noble femininity itself. These names and qualities are no more than indications of the nature of the *dharmakāya* which can never be contained in, or identified by, concepts. *Saṃbhogakāya* is the glowing awareness of the *dharmakāya*, where the Five Buddhas and their Consorts appear as unobstructed luminous space–form. As the feminine aspect in the *saṃbhogakāya*, Yeshe Tsogyel is the Five Wisdom-Consorts.

Yeshe Tsogyel is the *nirmāṇakāya*'s multitude of forms; she appears as a Tārā, Sarasvatī, princess, ordinary girl, business woman, prostitute and so on. Also, she was born in Tibet as the daughter of the Prince of Kharchen, as her life story tells.

Tibet's Great Guru, Padma Saṃbhava; possessed countless Ḍākinīs. Appearing like gathering clouds, they accomplished his wisdom action. Among those countless Ḍākinīs five were prominent: Monmo Tashi Khyeudren, Belwong Kalasiddhi, Belmo Śākya Devī and the two supreme consorts, Mandāravā and Yeshe Tsogyel. 'Yeshe Tsogyel is the perfect vessel to contain the essence of the precious tantric teaching,' Padma Saṃbhava declared. And when Trisong Detsen, the King of Tibet, received initiation, he offered Yeshe Tsogyel, his Queen, together with the measureless universal *maṇḍala* to the Great Guru. After that she accompanied him unswervingly, serving him continuously, giving her Body, Speech and Mind completely.

The Guru gave Tsogyel the teaching for the suffering people of this coming degenerate *kaliyuga*. Tsogyel gathered all his speech carefully together, and after systematising it she hid it as secret treasure-troves. She hid it externally in different elements, and internally she hid it in the depths of mind. Each separate treasure included a prediction of the time of its discovery and the person who would find it. Thanks to Padma

Saṃbhava and Yeshe Tsogyel we are using Yeshe Tsogyel's treasures today.

Precious tantric teaching that has the quality of wisdom is naturally, unintentionally concealed – it lies beyond the ordinary, impure and concrete concepts of mind. Tantric teaching is also hidden intentionally to prevent misuse, the misuse that occurs if these precious treasures are used for selfish gain and fame, neglecting appropriate dedication to sentient beings. This creates obstacles to enlightenment. For one man to exploit the teaching is like one person using the electric current intended for an entire city to light his own small bulb – the one bulb is destroyed and perhaps others on the circuit are damaged.

Secrecy is important, but it is especially important for Dzokchen, the Great Perfection teaching, which uses intangible luminous elements to transform the tangible body into a magic rainbow body.

Those who read the biography of the supreme tantric master, Padma Saṃbhava, and his Consort, Yeshe Tsogyel, have the chance to identify with them, and those who cultivate the inner wisdom Ḍākinī, the root Ḍākinī, progress towards becoming the supreme Sky Dancer, incomprehensible feminine wisdom, the lover without motive.

Keith Dowman has translated *The Life of Yeshe Tsogyel* for the benefit of all sentient beings. For this I remain thankful.

May this wonderful history bring the turbulent river of frustrated and neurotic men and women to the attainment of the Ocean of Enriching Wisdom that is Stillness and Bliss.

Trinley Norbu
Mahāṅkāl
Kathmandu
Nepal

TRANSLATOR'S INTRODUCTION

For twenty-five hundred years the Buddhist's goal has not altered – the perfection of man as the Buddha. However, down the centuries, as the faith expanded to include all sections of Indian society, besides other cultures, different schools redefined the nature of the Buddha, and new methods, or vehicles, were developed to traverse the path to Buddhahood. These vehicles differed as much as a tortoise from a hare or a deer from a lion. In the golden age of Śākyamuni Buddha an ascetic path of exalted yet simple self-discipline led through many lifetimes to a *nirvāṇa* of cessation. Later the lay devotee entered the path to strive for the compassionate Bodhisattva ideal, perfecting personal and social virtue, but postponing his final *nirvāṇa* until all beings could accompany him. Then in the mature efflorescence of Indian spiritual genius Buddhism assimilated the cult of the Mother Goddess; in the Buddhist Tantra mysticism and magic, ritual and incantation, characterise the path of the *yogin* who does not abandon the senses and emotions but uses them as the means to attain Buddhahood during his lifetime. The Bodhisattvas acquired consorts, pairs of deities represented every conceivable mode of being; and the mystery of Buddhahood was expressed in terms of the union of sexual duality.

It was tantric Buddhism that the Second Buddha, Padma Saṃbhava, who we shall call Guru Pema, first taught in eighth-century Tibet. The Guru's favourite consort was a Tibetan princess given to him by the Emperor Trisong Detsen. Her name was Yeshe Tsogyel, and in the cult that grew up around her and her Guru, she became the Guru Ḍākinī, the Sky Dancer, the embodiment of the female Buddha. The name of the school that practises Guru Pema and Yeshe Tsogyel's instruction on their path of personal evolution is called the Old School, the Nyingmapa (*rNying-ma-pa*), and in the Old School's innumerable legendary biographies of Guru Pema is contained much of Yeshe Tsogyel's life story. But it was not until the eighteenth century that an inspired tantric *yogin* called Taksham Nuden Dorje revealed a separate biography of Tsogyel, a work that was to become renowned as a masterpiece of this genre of Tibetan literature.

The Secret Life and Songs of the Tibetan Lady Yeshe Tsogyel (Bod-kyi jo-mo ye-shes mtsho-rgyal-gyi mdzad-tshul rnam-par-thar-pa gab-pa mngon-byung rgyud-mangs dri-za'i glu-'phreng) is styled 'secret' (*gab-pa*) because its essential meaning lies on the 'secret' level of tantric analysis. The work reveals Tsogyel's total being as a sphere of non-duality in which Guru and Ḍākinī in union inhabit a pure-land of gods and goddesses; it describes the secret empowerments and vows which accompany initiation into the tantric mysteries; and it elucidates the precepts of the Inner Tantra (*anuttarayoga-tantra*), practical precepts as relevant now as for Tsogyel's own disciples. But in order to give narrative flow to the work, Taksham wove the secret life of Tsogyel into the pageantry of great events that were revolutionising Tibet, events in which Tsogyel herself played a significant role. Thus in recounting the public life of Tsogyel, Taksham relates the history of the Emperor Trisong Detsen's reign, and although his account accords with the legends of the early revealed histories, the inclusion of certain episodes and details makes this a valuable source for historians.

To express his vision of the secret life of Yeshe Tsogyel Taksham employed the conventional literary devices of Tibetan tantric biography (*rnam-thar*): *maṇḍalas*, metaphysics, tantric symbology, twilight language and poetry. With these tools he describes an ideal path of practice that the tantric neophyte can emulate. In her final instruction to her disciples Tsogyel refers them to her biography for direction on the path of Tantra. Although the exigencies of the English language tend to reduce the divine Ḍākinī to human size, it is still evident that a

Buddha's reality is being described from the moment of the Ḍākinī's birth; in the Tibetan text honorific pronominals and verb-forms and the highly specific epithets of the heroine constantly evoke a supra-human reality. Thus the reader will be disappointed if he is looking for humanistic biography. But as an introduction to the Tibetan Tantra this biography is second to none; only *The Life of Milarepa* can compare with it in its power to evoke the spirit of the Tantra and reflect the nature of the path.

Although this secret biography is aimed primarily at practitioners of the Inner Tantra, on an exoteric level it also presents Tsogyel as a subject for deification. Her story provides all the ingredients necessary for devotees of the Outer Tantra (*kriyāyoga-tantra* in particular) to worship her as a goddess. A miraculous birth, flight from persecution and to self-exile, untold ascetic sacrifice to a selfless end, miraculous Christ-like deeds such as resurrecting the dead, healing the sick, feeding the multitude and making a gift of her body to the needy, a profound, ideal relationship with her Lama, and finally the attainment of Buddhahood in a body of light: such material stirs the religious spirit and induces a mind so disposed to take refuge in a goddess who can assuage all life's suffering and offer all life's joys. But Tsogyel warns her disciples on the path of the Inner Tantra against conceiving her as an external entity, a 'person' separate from the perceiver; their aim should not be to propitiate a god or goddess 'out there' capable of bestowing boons upon his or her devotees, whether such favours are the man or woman of their choice or the power (*siddhi*) of flying in the sky. Tsogyel asks these disciples to take her as their consort, either incarnate or metaphysical, so that she can give them the pure pleasure of gnostic awareness; and attaining the ultimate power, every man and woman *is* a Guru and Ḍākinī – a Sky Dancer.

A fact that further enhances the work's extraordinary reputation is that *The Life and Songs of Yeshe Tsogyel* is one of the few texts in the immense Tibetan scriptural literature that treats woman on the tantric path, or indeed, represents woman at all. Perhaps only a dozen women have risen to eminence in Tibetan Buddhism, and of these many were influenced by Tsogyel's crucial metaphysical role in the Old School tradition. The wonderful Machik Labdron, for example, the Ḍākinī Guru of the lineage of 'Severance' (*gcod*), was an incarnation of Tsogyel. But although *The Life* is a veritable treasury of precepts and advice for *yoginīs* on the path, most of the theory and practice is equally relevant to male practitioners; apart from the initiation rites, the third initiation *yogas* described in the text, and certain other special cases, the instruction is applicable to all.

Taksham himself was the kind of man who breathes new life into the traditional rites and doctrines that lineages unthinkingly transmit from generation to generation. Extracting the essential message such an adept can reformulate the teaching and express it in a manner that conveys his existential realisation. Taksham was no doctrinaire scholar; he was in fact seen by his contemporaries as a divine madman (*zhig-po*), a wrathful, though compassionate, crazy saint (*dpa'-bo*). In *The Life*, though he reveals the secrets of Tantra discreetly, endangering neither Guru nor disciple, his existential analysis cuts close to the bone, his vision is always uncompromising and fearlessly honest, and his humour is clever and sharp. His colophon to *The Life* is written in an obscure allusive style as if written by a man half-crazed by a terrible environment and the woes of existence.

Taksham was born in one of Kham's valleys (Lhorong Kham) in S.E. Tibet, 'in a land of impassable narrow defiles', a land of ravines cut by the great rivers of Kham – the Mekhong, Irrawaddy and Salween. Khetsun Sangpo in his *Biographical Dictionary* (Vol. III, p. 804) quotes Pawo Tsuklak's *History of the Dharma* where an unnamed *Thang-yig* is cited: 'a *yogin* called Nuden Dorje will take out the Kham caches of Guru Rimpoche's treasures.' He was prolific in discovery, revealing cycles of treasure-texts for each of the 'three roots' (Guru, Deva and Ḍākinī) and the Dharma Protectors, and much more. His principal cycle concerned a form of Guru Pema called Lama Yishi Norbu (*bLa-ma yid-bzhin nor-bu*), and the Yidam Gongdu (*Yi-dam dgongs-'dus*), a part of Tsogyel's *sādhana* (her personal endeavour), was the chief means of accomplishing this form of the Guru. He also discovered images, *stūpas* and *mantras*. He held the lineage of revealed teaching (*gter-chos*) of the great Knowledge Holder Dudul Dorje, like Longsel Nyingpo, Yolmo Tulku Tenzin Norbu and Katok Tsewong Norbu. Further, he had a strong karmic bond with the Master Choje Lingpa, and it appears that Choje, either reincarnate, or appearing in vision, was his Guru. But it was as a reincarnation of Atsara Sale,

Gyelwa Jangchub, who was Tsogyel's consort, that he gained access to the secrets of Tsogyel's *Life*. Taksham's colophon recounts that he copied out the text of *The Life* 'on a black day, the 29th' in a forest hermitage, but no month or year is mentioned. In fact we know only that he lived in the eighteenth century. His name means Tiger-skin Dynamic Vajra; and he is also known as Samten Lingpa (*bSam-gtan-gling-pa*).

The Life is a revealed scripture, a terma. The nature of termas and the profound doctrine underlying the tradition of revealed texts is discussed in the commentary under the head 'The Nyingma Lineages'. Here suffice it to say that legend records that Guru Pema and Tsogyel hid many treasures of different kinds in innumerable caches throughout Tibet, treasures that were to be revealed by tertons (treasure finders) when the moment was ripe. Further, some treasures were hidden internally, in inner space; this category of terma is called mind-treasure (*dgongs-gter*) and may be considered as direct revelation of Guru and Ḍākinī. The original colophon of *The Life* informs us that Gyelwa Jangchub and Namkhai Nyingpo of Lhodrak wrote down Tsogyel's memoirs *verbatim* on yellow parchment, concealing the completed text in Lhorong in Kham. In the catalogue of prophets (*lung-byang*) in the text, 'a *dpa'-bo* of Lhorong in Kham called Dorje' is mentioned amongst the nine possible tertons who might discover the text. Taksham's colophon tells how he received the text from its protector, Lord of the Black Water (Chu-bdag-nag-po), who in the text's prefatory Protection is called Black Nyong-kha (*sNyong-kha*?) Blazing Lord of Devils (*bDud-rje 'bar-ba*). Gyelwa Jangchub's colophon informs us that Lord of the Black Water, Thousand Beings (?) (*sTong-rgyug*), was instructed to deliver it into the hand of the terton. Although an actual manuscript treasure is indicated here, a study of the manuscript reveals significant variations in style, conflicting historical facts, material relevant to Taksham's era, prophecy up to the seventeenth century, etc. Undoubtedly Taksham had access to ancient material, e.g. the Bon worship of the king, and, perhaps, a biography of Tsogyel written by Gyelwa Jangchub, but the text translated herein was written by Taksham Nuden Dorje. However, since *The Life* is an inspired work that can be said to have its spiritual genesis in the milieu of 'the Guru and Ḍākinī's union in lotus light', certainly it can be classified as a 'mind-treasure'. For the *yogin* such discussion of the authenticity and category of *The Life* is irrelevant; either the power of the Guru's Word illuminates every page, or it does not, and the efficacy of its precepts are proven experientially.

In various passages in the text relating Tsogyel's own experiences the first person singular is employed, and some historical episodes are described from Tsogyel's point of view. Since such passages accord with the colophon's claim that Tsogyel dictated the text herself, and because the use of the first person is effective in creating a more intimate relationship between Tsogyel and the reader as well as maintaining continuity of style, I have taken poetic licence to use the first person throughout. The introductory and concluding sentences of each chapter have been excluded from this.

In translating *The Life* my principal concern has been to convey the precise meaning and feeling-tone of the original in fluent English, rather than to reproduce the peculiarities of the Tibetan style and diction. In order to achieve this aim occasionally I have employed paraphrase. I have solved part of the problem of translating technical tantric terminology by the use of 'symbol words'. Thus words with an initial capital letter contain deeper significance than their face value implies; Awareness (*jñāna, ye-shes*), Knowledge (*rig-pa*), Emptiness (*stong-pa-nyid*), and Body, Speech and Mind (*sku, gsung, thugs*) are attributes or qualities of the Buddha. Where I have used an adjective to describe the nature of these attributes as in 'gnostic awareness' or 'non-referential awareness', the qualifier limits an essentially inexpressible idea.

Although I tried to avoid all foreign words and phrases, I failed. The words *mantra, maṇḍala* and *nirvāṇa* are already included in the Oxford Dictionary, albeit with non-technical definitions, and surely *mudrā* (gesture or posture), *samādhi* (nirvanic state of mind), *siddhi* (success or power), *samaya* (vow or union) and of course Ḍākinī (female Buddha-Guru and goddess) will soon join them. Further, there is no meaningful succinct equivalent for the Tibetan word Yidam (personal deity) or terma (literally 'treasure' or 'cache'). Some English poets would translate 'terma' as 'poetry', 'terton' (treasure-finder) as 'poet' and 'Ḍākinī' as 'the Muse'; some would say that the treasures Tsogyel hid in England are English poetry. Perhaps the most problematic terms for translation are the names of the Buddha's three modes of being (*trikāya*). Rather than employ the Sanskrit terms throughout, I have used admittedly inadequate interpretive translations: 'absolute, or essential, empty being' for *dharmakāya*, 'being of consummate visionary enjoyment', or 'instructive visonary being', for *saṃbhogakāya*, and 'apparitional being' for *nirmāṇakāya*. The Tibetan word gyud (*rgyud*, Sanskrit: *tantra*), has many meanings. In this translation 'Tantra' denotes the practical system of *yoga* and the continuum of enlightened being that results from its practice, while *tantra*, or *tantra*s, denotes a single text, or a corpus of scripture, that treats tantric *yoga*. Another problem in the translation of *The Life* has been to maintain the ambiguity of twilight language (*sandhyābhāṣā*). For instance, when sexual union and mystical union are implied by the same words the translation must not stress one level at the expense of the other; it must contain the same potential for multi-levelled interpretation as the original. Sometimes this proved impossible.

In the text I have rendered Tibetan names in simple phonetic forms approximating the Lhasa dialect, as transliteration is misleading and tongue-tying for the reader with no knowledge of Tibetan. The index gives the transliterated forms. In general, in the notes and commentary I have retained the phonetic forms of proper names used in the text while transliterating other names and technical terms. Another cause of apology to scholars is the inconsistent use of Tibetan and Sanskrit for both names and technical terms. Believing that most students of Tibetan *dharma* acquire a mixed vocabulary I have used whatever form I thought most familiar, or most useful, to them. In the notes I have given the Tibetan equivalents except when the Sanskrit form should be familiar, although sometimes I have given both Tibetan and Sanskrit. Consistency has, therefore, received short shrift, and although some readers will be offended I hope to have helped the student of *dharma*.

This translation and commentary have been several years in preparation. Authorisation to read, study and publish the translation of *The Life* was given by His Holiness Dunjom Rimpoche, the principal hierarch of the Nyingma School; the Tibetan wood-blocks of the text were printed at Dunjom Rimpoche's Zangdokperi Monastery in Kalimpong. The first stage of the translation was to listen to a Nyingma lay scholar, Se Kusho Chomphel Namgyel, rendering the text into English. Then studying the passages on initiation, meditation instruction and the secret precepts in Chapter 8, etc., I was assisted by Khetsun Sangpo, probably the most eminent Nyingma scholar alive. But exegesis of the Dzokchen philosophical view, from which standpoint the text is written, and a detailed commentary upon the difficult passages of tantric precept, I received from Namkhai Norbu, an unorthodox Dzokchenpa with a profound experiential knowledge of the Inner Tantra. I felt his transmission (*lung*) of a vision of the Sky Dancer, the Ḍākinī, to be an informal initiation into the *yoginī-tantra*. Namkhai Norbu, a tulku of Azom Drukpa, is professor of Tibetan Studies at Naples University, Italy; he also teaches practical Dzokchen meditation as a self-contained system of *yoga* in various European and American cities.

When the translation was finished it became evident that the general reader would require commentary to provide metaphysical and historical background to this popular, but abstruse, Tibetan classic. A short foreword couched in the traditional imagery of the Ḍākinī in a metaphysical framework has been written by Trinley Norbu Rimpoche, one of the few remaining Tibetan recipients of Dzokchen precepts possessing both theoretical and experiential understanding who can express Dzokchen for a western audience. The text was annotated with the purpose of elucidating tantric terminology and practices. Concepts and practices and also historical allusions in the text that required greater amplification I have elucidated in the commentarial essays in the second half of the book, although I omitted references to the appropriate page to keep annotation to a minimum. In so short a space it was impossible to treat the tradition comprehensively and no doubt important aspects were overlooked. 'The Path of the Inner Tantra' is a personal view based upon my own experience, observation and the oral transmission. The first part of 'Woman and the Ḍākinī' is a tentative exploration of the means of expression of a crucial aspect of Tantra and a verbal attempt to resolve paradoxes that can only be fully resolved experientially. 'The Nyingma Lineages' deals with Dzokchen's origins, the nature of kama (*bka'-ma*) and terma (*gter-ma*), the relationship between Bon and the Nyingmapa and other fascinating topics relating to the genesis of the Old School. It may increase appreciation of the text if these essays are read first.

In general the historical events described in *The Life* agree with the legends related in the early termas; but several episodes are expanded, particularly the great debate with the Bon, which is not described in other histories. My primary sources for the 'Historical Background' and 'The Nyingma Lineages' (I have reduced references to them to a minimum) are Orgyen Lingpa's *Padma bka'-thang Shel-brag-ma*, Nyima Wozer's *Guru rnam-thar Zangs-gling-ma*, the *Genealogy of Kings* (*rGyal-rabs gsal-ba'i-me-long*), *The Red Annals* (*sDeb-ther dmar-po*), *The Blue Annals* (*sDeb-ther sngon-po*) of 'Gos Lotsawa, *The Ladakhi Chronicles* (*La-dvags rgyal-rabs*), Buton's *History of the Dharma* and Dunjom Rimpoche's *History of the Dharma* (*Chos-'byung*). I relied on Professor Tucci's works (*Tibetan Painted Scrolls* and *Minor Buddhist Texts*), and Hugh Richardson's articles, for knowledge of other early sources such as the Tun Huang chronicles and *The Samye Chronicles* (*sBa-shad*). Eva Dargyay's *Rise of Esoteric Buddhism in Tibet* must also be mentioned. I have accepted much of the Nyingma legend as historical fact, but with discrimination, while rejecting the revisionists who follow Sumpa Khempo, a biased adversary of the Old School. One major history remains ignored; Longchen Rabjampa's *History of the Dharma* (*Chos-'byung*) must one day be accorded its rightful place as the most reliable and authoritative text of the *Chos-'byung* genre, superseding Buton's later work.

It remains for me to thank all those who have helped me in the creation of this book: my Tibetan teachers, His Holiness Dunjom Rimpoche, Khetsun Sangpo, Namkhai Norbu Rimpoche, Trinley Norbu Rimpoche and Chomphel Namgyel, I credit with whatever here is true and consistent with Dzokchen doctrine, and for the understanding they have given me I am infinitely grateful. To Leonard van der Kuijp and Tadeuz Skorupski my thanks for reading the commentary and offering much useful advice. I am indebted to many others who have helped me in many ways during the course of the work, particularly to my wife Meryl for unfailing support and to Mimi Church, Cass Bardwell, Bill Gye and Vikki Floyd for their time and energy. Lastly, my thanks to Eva van Dam for the fine illustrations done out of pure devotion.

Keith Dowman, Kathmandu, Nepal.

THE SECRET LIFE AND SONGS OF THE LADY YESHE TSOGYEL

HOMAGE

NAMO GURU DEVA ḌĀKINĪ JHYA

Obeissance to the hosts of Guru Ḍākinīs!
Homage to Amitābha and Lord Avalokiteśvara,
And to their compassionate emanation Pema Jungne,
Threefold Buddha Exemplar, the Three Jewels, Lord of All Beings,
And homage to the Lamas of the Lineage.
Homage to Dechen Karmo, Mother of the Conquerors past, present and future,
To the Ḍākinī of her absolute empty being, Pure Pleasure Kuntuzangmo,
To the Ḍākinī of her instructive visionary being, Vajra Yoginī,
And to the Ḍākinī of her apparitional being, Yeshe Tsogyelma.[1]

PROTECTION

She who delights the Buddhas past, present and future with her metamorphic dance
She to whom the great Orgyen entrusted his divine authority,
She of infallible memory, matrix of profound hidden treasure,
She who attained supreme power, a rainbow body, a *vajra* body,[2]

Her name is Yeshe Tsogyelma, the Ḍākinī Guru,
Whose cycle of spiritual evolution, activities and legends,
Complete and fragmentary utterances and her Ḍākinīs heart-blood,
Are written here for the benefit of future beings, and concealed.
You Protectors, Black Nyongkha Blazing Lord of Devils,
And Lion-headed Devil Lord, guard this treasure well!

SAMAYA GYA GYA GYA!

GYELWA JANGCHUB'S INTRODUCTION

EHMAHO! The essence of all the Buddhas of the past, present and future, the Mantra-holder, Guru Pema Skull-Garland Skill[3] (Guru Rimpoche), the Great Adept, was miraculously born on the pollen bed of a lotus, uncontaminated by a womb. His deeds were of more significance than those of Śākyamuni Buddha himself, for he was endowed with the power of action of all the Buddhas past, present and future. Specifically, he spread and sustained for a long time the teaching that is most difficult to propagate – the tantric teaching. He converted those who were most difficult to convert – Tibetan barbarians and the demon savages of the South-West; he subdued gods, demons, devils and fanatical extremists merely by entertaining the thought of their subjection. He taught in the most difficult way – showing contrary supernatural forces simultaneously in magical display. And he attained the most elusive of all powers – the power of immortality.

It was this Buddha,then, who served as a skilful means to spread the Tantra. He had a greater number of accomplished mystic consorts than the number of sesame seeds it takes to fill a room supported by four pillars, and all of them came from the Highest Paradise;[4] they inhabited cremation grounds, the heavens, the human world, the great power places, the *nāga* realms and the realm of the celestial musicians. In this world of Jambudvīpa alone – in China, India, Tibet, Gen, Jang, Hor and Mongolia – he had not less than seventy thousand accomplished girls, and among them were the five emanations of Vajra Vārāhī from whom he was never separated. The emanation of Vārāhī's Body, Mandāravā; the emanation of her Speech, Yeshe Tsogyel; the emanation of her Mind, Śākya Dema; the emanation of her Quality, Kalasiddhi; the emanation of her Activity, Tashi Chidren; and the emanation of her essential indefinable individuality, Khandro Wongchang: these six were the aspects of his apparitional being. Of these six, the Indian girl Mandāravā and the Tibetan girl Yeshe Tsogyel were preeminent. The biography of Mandāravā can be found elsewhere. Herein, the stories and activities of Yeshe Tsogyel are recorded in brief.

CHAPTER ONE

TSOGYEL'S CONCEPTION

The Mother of the Conquering Buddhas past, present and future, the apparitional being Yeshe Tsogyel, whose name is known to all, having accumulated vast resources of virtue and awareness in previous aeons, finite and infinite, the veil of ignorance torn away she made this great wave of compassion for the sake of all sentient beings.

During the life-time of the great saint Takngu,[1] when I was the daughter of a merchant, together with five hundred other girls I went for the saint's audience. Introduced to the Buddha's teaching I expressed the supreme, irreversible wish-fulfilling prayer of commitment to Buddhahood. After the transition at the end of that lifetime, I travelled through many Buddhafields of visionary pleasure, and then I took apparitional form as the Goddess Gangā Devī, and at the feet of the Lord Buddha Śākyamuni I absorbed and compiled his sacred word. Returning to the fields of visionary pleasure I was known as the Goddess Sarasvatī,[2] serving all manner of beings.

At that time the Emperor of Tibet was Trisong Detsen, who was in truth an emanation of the Bodhisattva Mañjuśrī. Trisong Detsen invited the Great Master Pema Jungne to come to Tibet to establish the tradition of the Buddha's teaching. This Great Master's being was unborn and undying, because in reality he was the Buddha Amitābha, Boundless Light, come to this world of men. Pema Jungne came to Tibet, and after the Emperor had fulfilled his commitment to build the great monastery of Samye Ling and innumerable other major and minor temples in the provinces and border areas, the light of the Buddha's teaching shone forth like the rising sun.

Then Pema Jungne thought to himself, 'The time has come for the Goddess Sarasvatī to project an emanation so that I can spread the teaching of the Tantra.' Instantaneously, like the planet Mercury falling into the immensity of the sun, Pema Jungne returned to Orgyen,[3] the seat of all his emanation. When it was discovered that the Master had disappeared, the ministers of Tibet whispered abroad that he had been punished, banished to a savage land, Turkhara; the King said that the Master had gone to Senge Dzong Sum in Bhutan, where he was sitting in meditation; and the common people said that he had reconciled the King and Queen and had returned to India.

Meanwhile, in reality, the Guru was coursing through hundreds of Buddhafields of the sphere of apparitional being, and he continued his travelling for the duration of seven human years. Finally, he gathered together Vajra Ḍākinī, the Goddess Sarasvatī, Tārā Bhṛkutī, the Ḍākinīs of the Four Families, the Ḍākinīs of the Power Places and many other Ḍākinīs, and revelling with us all in pleasure, he exhorted us to ultimate pleasure with this song of pleasure:[4]

HRĪ! Through the light-rays of the supreme outflow that is no outflow,
From the Guru's *vajra*, the pleasure of desireless desire,
Into the secret sky of the Ḍākinī, the supreme desire of no desire,
Now is the time to enjoy the profound secret of pure pleasure.

Then from the very centre of the assembled goddesses, I, the Goddess Sarasvatī, arose and answered the Guru:

HO! Buddha Hero, Heruka, Pleasure God!
When you, great dancer, dance the nine dances of life,
The pure pleasure of the sacred lotus is everywhere discovered,
And in the vastness of the *bhaga* there is no anxiety;
It is time to project an emanation into the savage world.

'SAMAYA HO!' exclaimed the Guru. 'The bond is formed.'
'SAMAYASTVAM!' I replied. 'You are the bond!'

'SAMAYA HRĪ!' exclaimed the Guru. 'The bond is all!'
'SAMAYA TISHTHA!' I replied. 'The bond is strong!'
'RAMO HAM!' exclaimed the Guru. 'Let the fire burn!'
'RAGAYAMI!' I concluded. 'We are burning together!'

Thus the Guru's *vajra* and the Ḍākinī's lotus were joined, and we entered a trance of union.[5] The Five Goddesses of the Five Buddha Families, Locanā and her sisters, gave us worship and adoration; their Heruka Consorts expelled malevolent spirits; the Bodhisattvas gave their benediction; the great Takritas defended us from all intruding obstructive influences; the Four Door Keepers kept the mystic circle intact; the Four Vajra Goddesses danced; and the Guardians of the Teaching, the Fierce Lords of the Ten Directions, and the Mamo Ḍākinīs, vowed to defend the teaching. At the same time the great pleasure of we mystic partners caused the elements of the mundane worlds of the ten directions to tremble and quake repeatedly. It was then that from the junction of Guru and Ḍākinī beams of light in the form of a red syllable A surrounded by a circle of white vowels, and the white syllable BAṂ surrounded by a circle of red consonants, shot like the flight of a shooting star towards Tibet, to Seulung in Drak.
Thus ends the first chapter which describes how Tsogyel, having recognised the propitious time for the conversion of all beings, projected an apparitional form.

SAMAYA GYA GYA GYA!

CHAPTER TWO

AUSPICIOUS OMENS AND BIRTH

At the time of the King Namri Songtsen, the last of the royal line of succession from the first Tibetan king, Nyatri Tsenpo, Tibet was ruled as seven independent kingdoms. The heir to Namri Songtsen, The Emperor Songtsen Gampo, and his descendants ruled as emperors of all Tibet. The Emperor Songtsen, whose immortal deeds will be forever remembered, appointed the kings of the seven kingdoms by imperial decree, and those kings were called Kharchenpa, Zurkharpa, Kharchupa, Gongthangpa, Tsepa, Drakpa and Rongpa. Kharchenpa, who established a great coven of Bonpo priests, had a son called Kharchen Zhonnupa, whose son was called Kharchen Dorje Gon; his son was Kharchen Pelgyi Wongchuk. When Pelgyi Wongchuk was fifteen years old he took a wife of the Nub clan called Getso. Shortly afterwards his father died, and he was entrusted the onerous duties of government. To conform to the Emperor Trisong Detsen's desire, and out of his own devotion to the Buddha's teaching, he induced all his subjects to take refuge in the Three Jewels.

One day, when the Prince, my father, was twenty-five years old, while he and his queen, my mother, were enjoying the pleasures of love-making, my mother had a vision. Coming out of the west she saw a golden bee, its hum sounding like a sweet stream of lute music, and it vanished into her husband's fontanelle. The Prince himself saw a vision of his wife with three eyes, and of an eight-year-old girl who appeared holding a lute and singing, 'A Ā I Ī U Ū RI RĪ LI LĪ E Ē O Ō AṂ A' and 'HRĪ HRĪ HRĪ HRĪ HRI!'[1] She came very close to him and then vanished. Immediately the earth quaked, light shone brilliantly around him, thunder rolled, and a long whining hum was heard. A spring beside the castle turned into a lake at this time, and many other portents appeared.

That night the Prince dreamed that an eight-petalled lotus which he held in his hand poured out light in every direction, irradiating every corner of the microcosmic universes.[2] Then, further, he dreamed that a coral *stūpa* emerged from the crown of his head, and that multitudes of people gathered from China, Jang, Hor, Kham, Tibet, Mongolia, Bhutan and Nepal. Some said that they had come on pilgrimage to give respect to the *stūpa*, some to beg for it as a gift, some to carry it off by stealth, and others to take it by force. Then he dreamed that he held a lute in his hand that began to play spontaneously, and the sound reverberated through the millions of microcosmic universes, drawing an inconceivably vast crowd of people from all of these worlds, all of whom listened insatiably. Meanwhile, my mother had a dream, and she dreamed that she received a rosary of coral and conch shell beads. When blood began to pour from the coral and milk from the conch, an inestimable crowd of people came and drank to satiety, but still the blood and milk were not exhausted. All the realms of the earth were flooded with this red and white ambrosia,[3] and it was declared that this source of ambrosia would not dry up until the aeon's end.

The next morning, when the sun shone, a white woman, a god's daughter, the like of whom had never been seen before, appeared. She announced the miraculous event of the Three Jewels in the Prince's house, and then she vanished.

Nine months later the clear sound of the vowels of the Sanskrit alphabet, the mantra HRĪ GURU PADMA VAJRA ĀH and the continual recitation of the *tantra*s in the Sanskrit language were heard in the castle. At sunrise of the tenth day of the monkey month of the year of the bird,[4] Getso, my mother, gave birth painlessly. The earth shook, thunder rolled, and a rain of flowers fell from the sky. The lake increased in size, and on its banks a vast number of different species of flowers bloomed, all flecked with red and white. The palace was covered by a net of rainbow light, a tent of light rays, a miracle to which all present bore witness. Then the sound of music filled the sky, the haunting notes of the lute sounding loud and long, and between the clouds in the sky a host of goddesses appeared who uncovered the upper parts of their bodies and sang these auspicious verses:

HRĪ! Your empty being is the expanse of Pure Pleasure Kuntuzangmo;
Your visionary being is the Ḍākinī Vajra Yoginī;
Your apparitional being is the Conquerors' Mother: may you be happy!
Your empty being is the empty sphere of Vajra Ḍākinī;
Your visionary being is Sarasvatī, Mother of the Conquerors past, present and future;
Your apparitional being is supremely qualified: may you be victorious!
Your empty being is the nature of the plane of Awareness;
Your visionary being is Seven-eyed White Tārā, Mother of Compassion,
Your apparitional being is supreme intelligence: homage to you!

Then sending down a shower of flowers the goddesses vanished into the firmament.

As soon as this apparitional body was born, I recited the alphabet and chanted 'ORGYEN CHEMPO KHYENO!' – 'Homage to the great sage of Orgyen!' Sitting in half-lotus posture with my knees planted on the floor I opened my eyes wide and raised my pupils in adoration. My body was free of the womb's impurities, and my complexion was red and white. In particular, I had a complete set of teeth that were conch shell white in colour, and my hair fell down to my waist. When my mother offered me the customary knob of melted female yak butter, I sang:

I am an apparitional being, a *yoginī*,
And after eating immaterial essences for so long
The memory of coarse food has vanished,
But I will eat to complete my mother's happiness.
I will eat this food as the food of secret precepts,
Swallowing it whole like the whole of *saṃsāra*,
To become replete with Awareness and Knowledge.[5]
Aiyé!

And I swallowed it. Then my father, the Prince, declared, 'Surely this child is superior to others. Either she will become a *mahāsiddha* of the Bonpo or Buddhists, or she will be a queen of the Emperor. We will call her Tsogyel (Ḍākinī of the Ocean), because the lake increased in size at her birth.'

After one month I had attained the appearance of an eight-year-old, and my parents, thinking that it would be harmful to allow others to see me, kept me hidden away for ten years. When I was ten, my body was fully rounded and beautifully formed, and repute of my exquisite loveliness reaching the bounds of the empire, crowds of people, like throngs at a carnival, arrived from Tibet, China, Hor, Jang, Gen and Nepal to catch sight of me.

Thus ends the second chapter in which is described how Tsogyel descended into Tibet, the land that she was to transform.

SAMAYA ITHI!

CHAPTER THREE

DISILLUSIONMENT AND MEETING THE MASTER

When the hordes of suitors descended upon Kharchen, my parents and their officials held council upon the question of my marriage. It was unanimously decided that excepting a claim from the Emperor I should be given to no one, because the disappointment of the unlucky suitors would surely be the cause of strife. This decision was made public, and the suitors dispersed each to his own home.

Soon after, Prince Pelgyi Zhonnu of Kharchu arrived to beg for my hand, bringing three hundred horses and mule loads of gifts. At the same time Prince Dorje Wongchuk of Zurkhar appeared with a similar load of treasure. For my parents to give me to one would leave the other dissatisfied, so I was asked to make my own choice.

'I will go with neither of them,' I insisted. 'If I was to go I would be guilty of incarcerating myself within the dungeon of worldly existence. Freedom is so very hard to obtain. I beg you, my parents, to consider this.'

Although I begged them earnestly, my parents were adamant. 'There are no finer palaces in the known world than the residences of these two princes,' my father told me. 'You are totally lacking in filial affection. I would be unable to give away such a savage as you in either China or Hor. I will give you to one of these princes.'

'My daughter tells me that she is not inclined to go with either of you,' he told the rival suitors. 'So if I give her to one of you and the other disputes it she will stay with me. You are both familiar with competition; when I send her outside whoever lays hands on her first can have her. But the loser must not quarrel. If either of you fight over her, I will petition the Emperor to punish you.'

Then he decked me in fine brocades and gave me one hundred horse loads of chattels and provisions to take with me, and I was involuntarily led out of the house. The instant I stepped outside the rivals rushed towards me, and Kharchupa's official, Śāntipā, reaching me first, caught me by the breast and attempted to lead me away. However, I braced my legs against a boulder so that my feet sank into it like mud. To move me was like trying to move a mountain, and no one succeeded. Then those fiendish officials took a lash of iron thorns, and stripping me naked they began to whip me. I explained to them:

This body is the result of ten thousand years of effort;
If I cannot use it to gain enlightenment
I will not abuse it with the pain of samsaric existence.
You may be the noblest and most powerful in Kharchu
But you lack the equipment to gain a day of wisdom.
So kill me; I care not.

The official called Śāntipā answered me:

Girl, you have a beautiful body that is rotten within;
Your fair skin creates turbulence within the Prince's heart;
Like a dry bean you are smooth on the outside but hard within;
Give up this foolishness and become Princess of Kharchu.

I replied:

This precious human body is hard to obtain
But to gain a body like yours is easy –
Your sinful body is not even human.
Why should I go with you to become Princess of Kharchu?

Then again the officials whipped me with a lash of iron thorns, until my back was a bloody pulp, and unable to bear the physical pain I stood up and accompanied them. That evening the master and his servants camped at Drakda, and out of joy they danced and sang. I was profoundly depressed and wept tears of blood. Although many plans passed through my mind, no opportunity of escape presented itself. My voice breaking with grief I sang this agonised plaint to the Buddhas of the ten directions:

Alas! Buddhas and Bodhisattvas of the ten directions,
  protectors of beings,
The guardians possessing compassion and magical power,
The eye of awareness and magical legions,
Now is the time to fulfil your compassionate pledges.[1]
My pure thoughts whiter than the glacial snows
Have become blacker than the shale of this alien devil;
Take pity on me!
My righteous thoughts as precious as gold
Have now less worth than the bronze of this alien devil;
You protectors with the Eye of Awareness, show
  understanding!
My pure aspiration, a wish-fulfilling gem,
Has less value now than the stone of this alien devil;
You magicians show your magical skill.
I hoped to reach *nirvāṇa* in one body in this lifetime
But this alien devil has pulled me into the mire of *saṃsāra*;
Quickly arrest my fate, compassionate lords.

Even as I made this prayer the men appeared to fall into a drunken stupor and slept. Then I fled, fled faster than the wind. Crossing many passes and valleys, I travelled south. The following morning my former captors were angry and shame-faced. They searched for me fruitlessly in every direction, and having searched Kharchen thoroughly to no avail they returned to Kharchu.

Meanwhile, Pema Jungne had returned instantaneously from Orgyen to Chimphu. Here the fiendish ministers discovered his whereabouts and set out to kill him. On their way to Chimphu they became frightened by the sight of a pillar of fire at their destination, and deterred from their purpose they returned shame-faced to Samye. Approaching the King, they addressed him in this manner:

O World Emperor, Lord of Men, Divine Prince,
The vagrant foreign devil
We banished to Turkhara
Now lives in Chimphu, not in exile.
Should we kill him or banish him again?

The King was secretly pleased. 'The Master possesses instruction through which Buddhahood can be gained without suppressing the passions,' he thought to himself. 'I must now ask him for those precepts.' And he sent three translators with golden bowls for the Master, and an invitation to the palace. Accepting this invitation, the Master descended from Chimphu towards a narrow defile where he knew that the heavily armed ministers were lying in wait for him. He sent the three translators on ahead, while he himself raised his hand in the gesture of threat intoning 'HŪNG HŪNG HŪNG!' and ascended into the sky. He assumed the form of Guru Drakpo[2] inside a flaming mountain of fire that reached to the height of worldly existence, and his adversaries were rendered senseless. Then he appeared before the King in the same form, although to all others Guru Drakpo was invisible, and the terrified monarch lost consciousness. The Master then withdrew his wrathful projection and reassumed the Guru *maṇḍala*[3] of Pema Jungne. The King then regained consciousness and performed innumerable prostrations and circumambulations to the Guru, before preparing a vast *gaṇacakra*[4] feast and making his petition.

'It is not yet the time to reveal the tantric mysteries to you,' the Guru told him. 'Purify your mind on the graduated path of the *mahāyāna* and repeat your offering a year hence.'

After my escape, I, Tsogyel, lived in the valley of Womphu Taktsang, sustaining myself upon fruit and clothing myself with the fibre of the cotton tree. But Zurkharpa, the unsuccessful suitor, heard rumour of where I had gone and sent three hundred men to search for me. They found me and forcibly brought me back to their master.

When Kharchupa, the successful suitor, heard of this development, he sent his letter to my father, Kharchenpa:

Holy Prince, Exalted Pelgyi Wongchuk: You gave me your daughter in marriage, but on the road she vanished

> without trace. I have heard it said, and I wish you to verify this, that Zurkharpa's party has abducted her in a distant land. If this is your design I must fight with you; if not my quarrel lies with Zurkharpa.

After Kharchupa had dispatched this letter, while he was marshalling his troops he received this reply from Kharchenpa:

> Kharchu Dorje Pel, this is my message: Do not villify others in ignorance; I have no knowledge of Tsogyel since she left home. If you make war your defeat is certain.

Having sent this missive to Kharchupa, Kharchenpa marshalled his troops. Then he received another message, this time from Zurkharpa.

> Holy King, Pelgyi Wongchuk: I sought your daughter in a distant border land, and finding her I brought her to live with me here. If I bestow upon you vast wealth and possessions, will you in return give your divine daughter to me?

He soon received a reply:

> According to our binding contract, whoever won the contest would win my daughter; contention would be punished. However, to attain the happiness of us all, let the girl wander freely wherever she will.

But Zurkharpa had no intention of letting me go. On the contrary, he put me in irons, and marshalling his troops he prepared for war. However the Emperor Trisong Detsen was apprised of this situation, and he dispatched this letter to Kharchen Pelgyi Wongchuk:

> Pay heed, Kharchen Pelgyi Wongchuk: Whoever defies the command of the Emperor quickly and certainly faces ruin. You have a superior and divine daughter, a daughter worthy to be my queen. A subject of mine who goes to war shall be punished with death.

The Emperor sent seven officials with this letter, and Kharchen Pelgyi Wongchuk related in detail the sequence of events concerning me, his daughter, to those officials, and he wrote this reply offering me to the Emperor:

> HO! O World Emperor, Holy Lord of Men: My daughter is indeed superior to other girls, so I am happy if you take her to be your queen. Moreover, since I fear to start even a trivial dispute, I am mortally afraid of the World Emperor's hosts.

The King was gratified by this letter, and set out for Zurkhar with nine hundred horsemen. Zurkharpa was terrified. But then Kharchenpa resolved all in harmony. Since he had two other daughters, my sisters, he gave the eldest, Dechen Tso, to Kharchu Dorje Pel, who was contented with her; he gave the second daugher, Nyima Tso, to Zurkhar Zhonnu Pel, who was also satisfied; and when I, Tsogyel, the youngest, was taken by the Emperor for his wife, the rival suitors finally gave up hope of possessing me. Thus war was averted and all lived in harmony.

I arrived in Samye escorted by the King's envoy of welcome, decked in ornaments of precious stones and dressed in silk brocades suited to my new rank. The King celebrated our marriage with a three-month feast. Then due to my faith in the *Buddha-dharma* he appointed me custodian of the *dharma*. Scholars taught me letters and grammar, knowledge of the five arts and sciences, and both secular and religious accomplishments. A mere indication was sufficient for me to grasp whatever I was taught.

One day the King again invited the Great Master Pema Jungne to visit him. He prepared a jewelled-encrusted throne for him, and when the Master was seated he offered him a great *gaṇacakra* feast, piling before him a mountain of material wealth. To make a formal *maṇḍala* offering, he arranged pieces of gold upon a silver *maṇḍala* tray, and pieces of turquoise upon a golden *maṇḍala* tray. The elements of the silver *maṇḍala* represented his empire. He offered the Four Districts of Central Tibet and Tsang as Mount Meru. China, Jang and Kham as the eastern continent and its two satellite islands; he offered Jar, Kongpo and Bhutan as the southern continent and its two islands; and he offered Hor, Mongolia and the Northern Plains (Jang-thang) as the northern continent and its two islands. Further, represented by the turquoise, he offered me, his queen, as an offering of sensual gratification. Then he made this request: 'O Great Guru Rimpoche, in this *maṇḍala* I offer everything within my power. Through your great compassion you

hold in your care all creatures, men and gods, in every form and at all times. Please grant me the special instruction through which I can attain Buddhahood instantaneously, relying upon the effort of this one body in this single lifetime. Grant me the extraordinary teaching of the Tantra, the sacred word beyond *karma* and cause and effect.' And he prostrated before the Guru nine by nine times in supplication.

The Great Guru replied with these verses:

Listen carefully, O Emperor:
From the lotus-fields of pure pleasure, undefiled and undefined,
The Buddha Amitābha, unborn and undying,
Projected his *vajra* Body, Speech and Mind as a ball of light
Into the middle of the oceanic womb, without centre or boundary,
And upon the pollen bed of a lotus, without cause or condition,
Without father or mother and without family lineage,
I, Pema Jungne, this Great Being, miraculously appeared,
Spontaneously manifest, unborn and undying,
With dominion over the hosts of Ḍākinīs,
With knowledge of the supra-causal, most sacred Tantra,
The oral traditions, secret precepts, practices and open-heart methods,
And the vital *samaya*[5] that must never be forgotten;
But the teaching is not to be bartered for material wealth,
Nor even for the gift of the high power of the King.
If I exchange the teaching for wealth, my root *samaya* is broken
And both you and I must suffer retribution, die and fall into hell.
Moreover, the whole world is already in my power.
Your offering is vast, but for your purpose it is improper;
The Tantra requires only a qualified recipient, a suitable vessel;
The snow-lion's milk, the best elixir,
Can only be held in a fine, golden, jewelled bowl,
And any other vessel will break and the elixir will be lost.
The secrets are sealed in my heart.

As he finished speaking the upper part of his body appeared as the realm of desire and the lower part extended to the lowest hell.[6] After creating this illusion he resumed his customary apparitional form on the throne. The King prostrated like a falling wall, and cried out, 'O Great Guru, what karmic irony to be a king yet an unfit recipient of the tantric mysteries!' and he beat his body on the ground and wept noisily. Guru Rimpoche told him to collect himself and to attend, and he continued:

Listen! The tantric mysteries are said to be secret
Not because the Tantra is immoral but because it is closed,
Closed to the narrow-minded adherents of lesser paths.
And there is no irony in your *karma*, O King!
You have intelligence, intuitive insight and a broad mind;
You will not alter your faith or renege on your *samaya*;
And you will attend to the tantric Lama with devotion.
This Great Being is free of any germ of desire,
The aberrations of lust are absent;
But woman is a sacred ingredient of the Tantra,
A qualified Awareness Ḍākinī is necessary;
She must be of good family, faithful and honour bound,
Beautiful, skilful in means, with perfect insight,
Full of kindness and generosity;
Without her the factors of maturity and release are incomplete,
And the goal of tantric practice is lost from sight.
However, throughout this Kingdom of Tibet
There are many practitioners of the Tantra,
But as many reach their goal as there are stars in the day sky.
In view of that, O King,
To you I will open the door of tantric practice.

Completing his address to the King, the Guru assumed the form of Vajradhara,[7] and remained in that state. The King prostrated until his forehead was bruised, and then he offered the five sacred ingredients,[8] including myself, to the Guru, who was exceedingly pleased.

Thereafter, the Guru installed Tsogyel as his Consort and Lady, and gave her initiation and empowerment, and then as mystic partners they went first to Chimphu Geu to perform secret yoga.

Thus ends the third chapter in which is described how Tsogyel recognised impermanence and encountered the Master.

SAMAYA ITHI GYA GYA GYA!

CHAPTER FOUR

INITIATION AND INSTRUCTION

In Chimphu Gegong and Yama Lung, firstly, Tsogyel was inspired to a life of virtue by the teaching upon the Four Noble Truths of the Buddha Śākyamuni. Then she was taught the provisional truths contained in the Tripiṭaka (*the* sūtras *– aphorisms, the* vinaya *– discipline, and* abhidharma *– metaphysics), the inexhorable laws of* karma (*the cause and effect of moral and immoral actions*), *and what she should renounce and what she should cultivate. And she was ordained into the stainless virtue of a* bhikṣunī. *Then having received complete instruction upon the six lower vehicles so that it was deeply impressed upon her mind, what she must accomplish was profoundly imbued, what she had been taught was fully understood, and what she must cognise she already knew.*[1]

At this juncture the goddess Sarasvatī spontaneously appeared to her and bestowed upon her the power of an infallible memory. She gained the ability to see the whole world with her fleshly eye; she gained power to display miracles; and she gained foreknowledge of mundane affairs, together with a divine intuition. The sheer size of The Book of Studies,[2] *Tsogyel's record of what she was taught, filled us with apprehension, and we have not printed it here in full. Here is a shortened account.*

Guru Rimpoche, Pema Jungne, was filled with the Buddha's Word as if it had been poured into him like liquid into a vase. After I, the woman Yeshe Tsogyel, had offered him the three kinds of satisfaction,[3] serving him for a very long time, he imparted that wisdom to me as if he was filling a jug. Soon my mind was completely at ease on the path of virtue, and my sisters and I learnt to distinguish between the nine vehicles[4] which lead to *nirvāṇa*, and to distinguish between what is righteous and what is unrighteous. However, I became aware of a greater reality, the hidden foundation[5] of causality, and conceived a desire for the ultimate, perfect path that transcends *karma* and its inexorable logic. So I made this petition to Guru Rimpoche:

O most revered Apparitional Buddha,
Conceived in the Land of Orgyen,
Supreme Sage of India,
The Buddha's Regent in Tibet,
I am young but not inexperienced
For suffering was revealed to me at the age of twelve
When my parents denied me my request for celibacy
And gave me as a bride in a lay marriage.
My mind was not engaged by the ways of the world
And I fled to the Valley of Womphu Taktsang.
But enflamed by lust, a tormentor sought me,
And powerless, I was captured and submitted to pain.
Then, Lord Guru, through your compassion,
I was delivered by the Emperor,
And enthroned as Queen at Samye
Until at the age of twelve I was offered to you
As the Emperor's offering for the Three Empowerments.
Now, with intuition of the unitary foundation of causality,
I beg for the Sacred Word which transcends cause and effect.

The Guru smiled radiantly at me, and forming his answer in verse, he replied:

So be it, Daughter of Kharchen.
You, a woman of sixteen years,
Have seen the suffering of an eighty-year-old hag.
Know your pain to be age-old *karma*,
And that the residue of that *karma* is erased.
Now you have found pure pleasure,
And it is impossible to revert to a body of bad *karma*.
And now that you know the foundation of cause and effect
It is right to aspire to the unsurpassable apex of the *mahāyāna*.

Then he entered the tantric sphere and recalled the root and branch vows. And he continued:

> Hear me well, Daughter of Kharchen;
> Listen attentively, revered Kuntuzangmo.
> The foundation of the *mahāyāna* Tantra is the *samaya* vows;
> If the *samaya* is broken we both meet disaster.
> Therefore, keep these vows!

After he had spoken I swore to maintain the fundamental, root vows of the Buddha's Body, Speech and Mind, and the twenty-five branch vows. The fundament, the root *samaya*, is the *samaya* of an enlightened mind (*bodhicitta*):[6] the relative *bodhicitta* is sealed by the absolute *bodhicitta*, and in order to maintain this *samaya* so that I would not pass beyond the state where from the beginningless beginning the body is actually a god, speech is the spontaneous vibration of *mantra*, and mind is the intangible, ultimate quality of all experience, first I took the *samaya* of the Buddha's Body. Here I will classify the types of master and spiritual brothers, and then explain the means of sustaining the *samaya*.

There are six kinds of Lama: Lamas in general, the Lama who guides us, the Lama with whom the *samaya* is maintained, the Lama who restores our broken vows, the Lama who liberates us from our personality and thoughts, and the Lama who gives instruction and oral teaching. Then there are four kinds of spiritual brothers: spiritual brothers in general, the close brother (who has the same Lama), the intimate brother (who has the same lineage) and the brother who is both close and intimate (having the same lineage and Lama).

Now to guard the *samaya* of the Buddha's Body, exoterically, the Lama is regarded as Lord and Master, or as parents, or as a loving uncle; esoterically, he is regarded like an eye, the heart, or life itself; and mystically, with body, speech and mind free of hypocrisy and dissimulation, he is identified with the Yidam deity.

To be brief, as far as physical respect is concerned, circumambulate and prostrate before your Lama and his spiritual brothers. Take care of their physical comfort like a servant or maid, and offer whatever may please them, such as food, wealth, body and possessions. To be specific, offer the same amount of respect to the Lama's relatives as to the Lama himself; respect his consort, his sons, his daughters, his parents, his spiritual brothers, *yab, yum,* consorts and attendants and servants: thus the sacred *samaya* is maintained. Accordingly, obey the orders and insinuated injunctions of the Lama; refrain from any disdain towards his young acolytes, monks and patrons who perform physical service; in short, whoever the Lama loves should be respected as the Lama himself – including his horse, his watchdog and his menials. Again, specifically, except when the Lama, or his spiritual brothers, have extended permission, do not partake so much as a sesame seed's worth of their food, wealth or possessions, or even allow the least covetous thought regarding them to arise in the mind. Further, if you overshadow or pass over the Lama's hat, clothes, shoes, seat, bed or couch, or even his own shadow, it is said that such action is equivalent to destroying a *stūpa* or an image of the Buddha. As a further illustration, it is said that you should not fight, kill, steal, or rob within range of the Lama's vision, even if only in jest.

Concerning verbal respect for the Lama and his spiritual brothers, if you relate whatever faults the Lama may have to others, or exaggerate his lack of defects, if you berate him or answer him back, then whatever worship you render to the Sugatas of the microcosmic universes is to no avail, and indubitably rebirth in the *Vajra*-hell follows.

Concerning mental respect for the Lama, do not deceive him, do not harbour malice towards him, ridicule him, hold opinions about him, inwardly accurse him or distrust him. I myself have never once yet failed in as much as the smallest part of a hair of this *samaya* of the Buddha's Body, or failed in these observances of respect to the Lama and his spiritual brothers.

Secondly, the *samaya* of the Buddha's Speech is with the Yidam deity. I will note the three kinds of *mantra* and four kinds of *mudrā* that are aspects of this *samaya*, and then describe the methods of maintaining the *samaya*. There are three kinds of *mantra samaya:*[7] the *samaya* of the root *mantra*, the unfailing cause; the *samaya* of the creative *mantra*, the condition of the deity's appearance; and the *samaya* of the *mantra* that is recited to effect certain *karma*s. Then there are four *samaya*s of union with the four *mudrās*:[8] the *mudrā* of verbal commitment, the *karmamudrā* of Awareness, the *dharmamudrā*, and *mahāmudrā*.

The method of guarding this *samaya* is to sustain union with the *maṇḍalas* of the Lama, the Yidam and the Ḍākinī with body, speech and mind. To sustain this union there are various forms of practice suited to the capacity of the *yogin*. I myself practised the seven hundred thousand *maṇḍalas* of the ultimate *tantras* that my Lama gave me, in the various modes of the superior, average and inferior *yogin*. The highest mode of practice, that of the superior *yogin*, is the Samādhi of Unqualified Pure Pleasure; the intermediate mode, that of the average *yogin*, is the *samādhi* in which light and energy forms appear as gods and goddesses; and the lesser mode, that of the inferior *yogin*, is identity with the Flowing River Samādhi.[9]

On the supreme level of practice the *maṇḍala* is experienced as an unbroken stream, as I experienced the Maṇḍala of Hayagrīva and Vajra Vārāhī. On the intermediate level of practice, the vow to meditate during six periods of seclusion, three in the day and three in the night,[10] is rigidly maintained, as I maintained the practice of Dorje Phurba. And on the inferior level of practice, each complete basic cycle of rites – the recitation of *mantra* with accompanying physical *yogas*, the *gaṇacakra*, etc. – should receive sustained and regular application once every day, as I applied myself to the Sublime Accomplishment of the Eight Logos Deities (Drupa Kabje).[11] Likewise I have never postponed even for a few minutes the practice I pledged to perform in order to sustain my attainment in numerous *maṇḍalas* of other deities, whether it was according to the custom of the superior *yogin* who pledges to perform a prescribed amount of visualisation and recitation at regular times throughout each month; according to the average *yogin* who practises the complete basic cycle of meditation upon a particular deity on the full moon, the dark of the moon, the eighth, tenth, and eighteenth, etc. days of the moon; according to the inferior *yogin* who practises one particular rite once each month; or the indolent *yogin* who practises a complete cycle once a year.

Thirdly, the *samaya* of the Buddha's Mind is the maintenance of Vision, Meditation and Action. I will define these three, and then disclose the methods of keeping this *samaya*: Vision is profound insight; Meditation is accomplished through experiential understanding of the nature of mind; and the Action that meditation induces is uninhibited outer, inner and mystic action.[12]

Then the method of keeping this *samaya* is through secrecy: keeping the four universal secrets, the four intermediate secrets, the appropriate secrets, and entrusted secrets. The four universal secrets are the name of your Yidam, his heart *mantra*, his *karma mantra*, and your signs of mastery. The four intermediate secrets are the place and the time and the allies[13] and the sacred appurtenances of practice. The ritual appurtenances that the *yogin* relies upon in his practice of the ultimate *tantra*s, objects that it is appropriate to keep secret, are the elements of offering, internal and mystic offerings such as *sman* and *gtorma*, etc., manual symbols such as the *bhanda, kīla, khaṭvānga, vajra, ghaṇṭa, māla*, etc., the names of the parts of the *maṇḍala*, the eight adornments of the charnal ground, bone ornaments, etc., and in particular, the *ḍāmaru*, the *kapāla* and the *rkang-gling*. Entrusted secrets are secrets concerning confidential behaviour such as the mystic practices of your spiritual brothers and sisters and the sexual behaviour of men and women in general. In short, all kinds of behaviour that it is proper to keep secret, whether of the Lama, your spiritual brothers and sisters, or of common people, should not be communicated to others.

Since I swore before my master to maintain the ten secret *samaya*s of the Buddha's Body, Speech and Mind, the four *samaya*s of the Buddha's Body concerning the master and spiritual brothers, the *samaya*s of Buddha's Speech – three of *mantra* and four of *mudrā* – and the *samayas* of the Buddha's Mind – the four universal secrets, the four intermediate secrets, the four appropriate secrets and the four entrusted secrets, I have guarded them inviolate, permitting not so much as the smallest deviation equal to a hundredth part of a hair's breadth to appear even for a split second.

Further, these are the twenty-five branch *samaya*s that Pema Jungne taught me; the *samaya*s of the five actions that should be practised – fornication, taking what is not given, false speech, cursing and shouting; the *samaya*s of the five substances that should be accepted gladly – excrement, semen, meat, blood and urine; the *samaya*s of the five realities that should be accomplished – the Five Aspects of the Buddha, the five modes of Awareness, the Five Male Consorts, the Five Female Consorts and the five modes of the Buddha's Being; the *samayas* of the five emotions that should not be suppressed – desire, hatred, sloth, pride and jealousy; and the *samayas* of the five categories of knowledge that should be understood – the five psycho-physical constituents, the five elements, the five sense-organs, the five sense-fields and the five colours.[14] Having taken these branch vows in the light of extended commentary from other sources,[15] since I have never yet come close to deviating from even a single implication of a single one of these vows for even a moment, I have been held perpetually by Orgyen Guru's compassion, remaining within the *maṇḍala* of the ultimate inner *tantra*. And since I realised that initiation and empowerment is the key to the tantric mysteries, and that the *samaya* is the source of empowerment, I have maintained the *samaya* unbroken.

Thereafter, at Samye in Yama Lung, the Guru revealed to me the Maṇḍala of the Tantric Mysteries, bestowing upon me 'the Communion of the Eight Logos Deities: the Ocean of Dharma',[16] and we stayed there together.

At the time of the Tibetan New Year the court and the people gathered at Samye. The ministers noticed that I, Tsogyel, was absent, and they enquired where I had gone. They made exhaustive enquiries as to what had befallen me, but nobody knew. When they asked the King himself where I was, unable to keep the secret, he told them the full story of how he had offered me to Guru Rimpoche as his Consort.[17] The *zhang* ministers, who were implacably hostile to the *dharma*, the great minister Lugong Tsenpo, Takra Lutsen, the Zhang General, Gyud Gyud Ringmo, Mama Zhang, Jarok Gyud, Shen Tago and others opposed to the *dharma*, petitioned the King with one accord and one purpose:

'O great King, O Lord of all the black-topped Tibetans, are you possessed by a demon? Don't skim law and order from the land like cream from milk. Don't let Tibetan heads fall in blood. Don't let Tibetan tails fly in the air. Don't treat Tibetan ministers like dogs. Don't treat the Tibetan kingship like rubbish. Our ancient heritage, the golden yoke that you received from the lineage of god-kings your ancestors, can so very easily be stolen away by this foreign devil, Pema Jungne, this vagrant sadhu,[18] this master of evil spells. Naturally your subjects are pained and downcast. This scion of the Kharchen Clan first created problems for her parents, then she made trouble for her rightful husband, and now she is bringing disaster down upon Tibet. Is this righteous behaviour? Now while your ministers still have breath in their bodies, let each of them voice his opinion. There is a proverb, "So long as the bag of ministerial authority is not rent, even though the king loses his heart there is means of replacing it!" You must take counsel!'

This speech angered everyone, but before the King or any minister had time to speak, Go the Elder addressed the King, 'O Lord, your ministers' discussions are interminable, and since it is said, "Speak briefly before the King", let us deliberate elsewhere.'

All agreed to this, and the ministers assembled outside the council chamber for consultation. Meanwhile the King was much agitated, and straight away sent a secret message of warning to the Guru at Drakmar at Yama Lung. Having received the letter the Guru sent this reply:

O Lord of Men, God-King,
Even now when difficulties have arisen,
I, Pema Jungne, the Lotus Born Guru,
Have nothing to fear in life or death.
How can this supreme *vajra*-like Being
Be affected by any of the eight dangers?[19]
Even if the whole world turns against me
Why should Pema Jungne fear?
If infants are feared by their elders
Who can protect our children?
I am the refuge of all creatures,
And if I cannot protect my dependants
How can I guide indifferent people?
Therefore, Great King, put away anxiety and pray!

This answer calmed the King's mind, and in council he gave this general directive to all of his subjects:

Listen, my subjects, black, white or coloured.
We shall practise the *dharma* and propagate the *dharma*,
And establish the Buddha's doctrine;
The Bon shall not obscure our vision:
Obey this decree of your King, the Dharma-Protector.
In this Land of Tibet, throughout my realm,
The monasteries and meditation centres shall increase and flourish,
The *sūtras* and *tantras* yoked together.
If any individual disobeys this decree,
He shall be punished for opposing the King and his ministers' order.
Further, I advise you to offer hospitality,
Offering and confession, to the Venerable Guru of Orgyen.

Having spoken, the King received this response from Takra and Lugong:

Our only sovereign, Lord of Men, Divine Prince,
Consider well! Take careful account!
Give well-advised counsel, my sovereign!
Do not obliterate the traditions of your ancestors.
Do not flay the law and traditions of Tibet.
Do not destroy the faith of the people.
The happiness of the country depends upon Bon;
Without the Swastika Gods, who will protect Tibet?
To whom can we pray to raise the flag of Tibet?
And where is the best of the King's Consorts,
Who is like the very Daughter of Brahmā?
Where has Yeshe Tsogyel gone?
This foreign barbarian sadhu
Is surely overstepping his limits.
Are you insane, O King? Have you lost your senses?
Is your mind wandering? What is the matter?
If you are mad, your authority cannot last,
And anarchy will prevail.
Therefore keep Tsogyel at home,
And let the law take care of the foreign devil.

'Eradicate those evil spells or loss will dog your footsteps. It is said, "A chronic internal disease is the cause of ceaseless wailing." So catch the foreign devil and turn him over to the law, and if he tries to escape, kill him! These other ministers support my counsel. This is our unanimous advice. If you do not accept this forceful counsel, I will immediately resign my ministerial office. The pig-headed king is bringing ruin upon the pride of lions, his ministers. Because the king's command carries great weight, whatever he ordains must be suffered. But the ministers' advice also carries authority, and that is decisive.'

The majority of the Bon ministers concurred with this counsel, but the ministers sympathetic to the *dharma* – Shubu Pelseng, Drugu Ube, Kaba Peltsek, Chokro Lui Gyeltsen, Namkhai Nyingpo, Langdro Lotsawa, Dre (Gyelwa Lodro), Yung and Nub (Sangye Yeshe) and others – spoke like this: 'This evil time portends the *dharma*'s destruction. An unspeakably heinous crime has been prepared against the Master, the Second Buddha. The Emperor, who is like an ethereal jewel, is being disgraced. The Law will not be propagated, and the doctrine will not be established, and furthermore, following the Bon ministers' advice, we will accrue the *karma* of the five inexpiable sins.[20] Why should we not be ready to die? Therefore, although Tibet may become a desert, we will hold Yeru by force of arms, and whatever happens we will be sure that the Master and his Consort remain safe.' They stopped at that.

Then the Emperor spoke: 'Any minister who fails to show respect or perform service to the Master, who is like the true Vajradhara, and plans this inexpiable crime, will receive punishment nine times as severe as that prepared for the Master. I am the authority in the land.'

Queen Tsepong Za, a daughter of the Tsepong Clan, after inner deliberation sided with the criminal ministers.

Everyone at odds, a bristling quarrel ensued. Then Go the Elder gave the King this advice: 'O God-King, rather than let anarchy loose in Tibet is it not preferable to come to terms with the ministers?'

The King assented, and forthwith he gave this counsel to the evil ministers:

O friends, great ministers of Tibet,
In this world there is no greater king than I.

If the king is great, the ministers perforce are powerful;
If there is no king, what can the ministers do?
So do not try to out-face the king.
Is it not better to settle this matter with civil and wise
discussion?

The Bon ministers agreed. Then the King spoke to the faction of Buddhist ministers:

Alas! Your cause is harmed by your self-centred zeal.
There is no way to atone for a sin accrued for the sake of Truth.
No one can harm the Master's indestructible being,
So is it not best for the King and his ministers to settle this
matter by discussion?

They all agreed with the King, and gathering around him they held an ordered council. They all agreed that for a short time, since it was inopportune for the King to meet with his Master or speak with him, the Master should be sent back to India with a load of gold, and that I, Tsogyel, should be punished by exile to Lhodrak.

We gave the ministers the impression that this would be done, while in fact, we two mystic partners prepared to go to the Tidro grotto in Zhoto. There we would stay unaffected by any malign influences, practising mystic sexual *yoga* in the cave called the Assembly Hall of the Ḍākinīs, the power place of the Goddess of the Destructive Green Bell.[21] Then before we left Yama Lung the Emperor offered us two kilos of gold dust, seven golden bowls and other gifts, and he received blessing and prophetic injunction from the Guru. Descending from Yama Lung, we hid a cache of teaching-treasures to be revealed in the future in the throat of a crag that resembled a crow, and we also prepared a prophetic manifest. And it was there that the Twelve Sisters of the Mountain Passes[22] appeared, blazing in light with a white palanquin of light. After we had seated ourselves within, it rose into the sky and sped away. The King and his ministers who had gathered there all gained faith, and from that time the mountain called Okar Drak (White O Crag) was known as Wokar Drak (Whooshing White Crag).

Instantaneously, we found ourselves in Zhoto, where we

took up residence in the Great Assembly Hall of the Ḍākinīs at Tidro. Here, I, the girl Tsogyel, prepared a conventional *maṇḍala,* and prostrating nine times nine made this request:

O Venerable Lord of Orgyen,
Having attained a Vajra-like Buddha's Being[23]
You have no fear of the devil Lord of Death;
Having attained an Illusion-like Buddha's Being
You have won the battle against the Godling Devil;
Having attained a Rainbow-like Vajra-Being
At one stroke you vanquished the devil Embodiment;
And having attained the Buddha's Being of Creative Samādhi
You have liberated the Devils of Passion as allies.
Immortal Lotus Born Guru,
Now I have found heart-felt, undivided faith
I want to request the ultimate *tantra.*
In Yama Lung spirits of evil oppressed me,
But through your compassion, my Lord,
Flying through the air we have come to this place.
Now through your compassionate understanding,
I beg you to reveal the maturing and releasing *maṇḍala,*
And until I, too, gain enlightenment,
Please grant me unimpeded grace.

The Great Guru replied:

> You are welcome, Daughter of Kharchen.
> The Maṇḍala of the Ultimate Tantra
> Like an *udumbara*[24] lotus flower,
> Rarely appears, and remains only briefly.
> Not all of the blessed encounter it,
> So rare is its blooming. So be glad!
> Now offer your mystic *maṇḍala.*

Then without shame or in the manner of the world, gladly and with devotion and humility, I, Tsogyel, prepared the mystic *maṇḍala* and offered it to my Guru. The radiance[25] of his smile of compassion shone in five-fold rays of light so that the microcosmic universes were pervaded by clear light, before again the beams of light concentrated in his face. Invoking the deity with the ejaculations DZA! and HŪNG! the light descended through his body and his mystical *vajra* arose in wrath and as Vajra Krodha he united with the serene lotus in absolute harmony. Through the progress of our ecstatic dance of delight, the sun and moon *maṇḍala*s of we mystic partners' psychic nerves' eight focal points of energy gradually blazed up into intense light, and the essential energy of each of the eight focal points intensified through the four levels of joy as an offering to the hosts of deities of each of the centres. In a state of sheer pleasure, with an intense feeling of power and realisation that was difficult to bear, the Lama revealed the Maṇḍala of the Ḍākinī's Heartdrop (*Khandro Nying-tik*); he disclosed the personal reality of Mahāvajradhara with the Buddha's Five Aspects in union with their Consorts in the *maṇḍala* of the Guru's Body, and he bestowed upon me the initiation and empowerment of the Guru's Body; the five psycho-physical constituents, intrinsically pure, manifest as the Five Buddhas, and the five elements, intrinsically pure, were their Five Consorts. Thus he conferred upon me the method of accomplishing the Buddha's Five Aspects together with initiation and empowerment.

After the Guru had granted me the means of accomplishing the Buddha's Five Serene Aspects, which are regarded as the Outer Guru, together with the Vase Initiation, and having introduced me to the exterior chalice as an immense insubstantial paradise, and the interior elixir as hosts of gods, he instructed me to apply myself to this practice of identification for seven days.

Even as I was enjoined by the Guru, for seven days I practised identification of the exterior chalice[26] as a divine palace and the interior elixir as gods and goddesses, and without need of effort on my part, indeed, the entire environment arose resplendent as the paradise of a god, and all corporeal forms of interior elixir appeared in variegated colours as the Buddha's Five Aspects in union with their Consorts.

After all appearance, irrespective of day or night, had arisen as the actuality of the Buddha's Five Aspects, the Guru told me that it was time to accord me the inner initiation and empowerment, and that I should prepare to offer the same kind of *maṇḍala* as before, but seven times over. So with joy and devotion I prepared him the *maṇḍala* and offered it to him seven times:

In the Ultimate Maṇḍala of Pure pleasure
The body's tactile sense is the Sacred Mountain,
My four limbs and head are its four satellite continents
And the 'lotus' of pure pleasure is the source of both *saṃsāra* and *nirvāṇa;*
Accept it with compassion for the sake of all beings.

Again the Guru was delighted, and the resonance of his joyful laughter shook the entire three realms,[27] forcefully shaking them up and blowing them apart, and assuming the form of Wong-Drak Pema Heruka, aroused by the terrific laughter of the Heruka's twelve-toned HA HA! HE HE! etc., the Mystic Symbol Heruka himself entered the space of the Lotus Mother. My face became the face of Vajra Vārāhī and the Guru *maṇḍala* became the Maṇḍala of Hayagrīva, the principal Heruka of innumerable Fierce Buddhas: the Maṇḍala of Hayagrīva's Heart-drop was revealed at the coming moment of initiation and empowerment; in the five focal points of the Guru's *maṇḍala* transformed into Glorious Hayagrīva were the Five Buddha Heroes united in harmony with their Ḍākinī Consorts; revealing his personal reality as an iridescent *maṇḍala* he conferred upon me the empowerment of the Lama's Speech. My own body was transformed into the Body of Vajra Vārāhī; appearances were inseparable from Hayagrīva himself; I intuitively realised the meaning of psychic nerves, energy flows and seed-essence;[28] the five passions were transmuted and manifested as the five modes of Awareness: absorbed in the Samādhi of Transcendental Pleasure and Emptiness, I received the Mystic Initiation, attained the eighth degree of enlightenment, and received immediately the means of identifying with the Guru and his Consort in union as Hayagrīva.

So after the Guru had granted me the means to accomplish the Yidam, which is considered to be the Inner Guru, at the same time as the Inner, the Mystic Initiation and Empowerment, and after he had introduced me to my own body as a divine *maṇḍala*, and to psychic nerves, energy flows and seed-essence as deity, *mantra* and *mahāmudrā* respectively, he instructed me to practise for three or seven days.[29]

Obeying the Guru's instruction, sealing my body as a lighted butter-lamp, I applied myself to meditation until Awareness, the value of the initiation, had become strong. Initially, I was oppressed by anxiety, but later the sounds of the syllables in the focal points of the psychic nerves resonated spontaneously; I gained full awareness and perfect control of my vital breath and energy flows, and instinctive and immediate knowledge of how to employ them; I attained intuition of the meaning of seed-essence as *mahāmudrā*; and the potential of the warmth of transcendent delight was fully realised. Thereafter, the capricious movements of karmic energy[30] subsided, the energy of Awareness injected into the medial nerve; and a few signs of mastery occurred.

However, the Guru enjoined me 'not to eat the barley until it was ripe', that my initiations were not yet complete. So with greater faith in Guru Rimpoche than the Buddha himself, I addressed him thus:

> O Venerable Orgyen Rimpoche,
> Superior to the Buddhas past, present and future,
> To myself and other mean and lowly beings
> I beg you to grant the Supreme Initiation.

Then the Guru appeared as the *maṇḍala* of the Red Heruka, and from the syllable HŪNG in his heart extremely fierce beams of red light radiating and again concentrating in his *maṇḍala*, he took up the Absolute Heruka in his hand like a spear, and he replied:

> RAṂ HAṂ[31]
> Listen without distraction, Ḍākinī Tsogyelma,
> Queen Kuntuzangmo, listen attentively.
> If you wish the seed to infuse your inner *maṇḍala*,
> Offer your *maṇḍala* of mystic delight.
> If you speak of this method your *samaya* is broken.

I, the girl Tsogyel, sank beneath mundane appearances, and having slipped into the nakedness of pure pleasure, I annointed my *maṇḍala* of delight with the five sacred substances,[32] and made further petition:

Buddha Hero of Pure Pleasure, do as you will.
Guru and Lord of Pure Pleasure,
With true energy and joy, I implore you to inject
The seed into the inner *maṇḍala*.
And I will guard the secret of the method with my life.

Then with three fingers stirring the pollen dust of the lotus, I offered my *maṇḍala* to the *maṇḍala* of the Guru's Body with an intense snake-like dance. The *maṇḍala* of dynamic space having gathered into itself the nature of the Great Pema Heruka himself by means of the hook of the lower member's focal point, the Absolute Heruka, his magnificent flaming *vajra* in a state of rapacity and violent abuse, his wrinkles uncreased, projecting his full emanation, took command of the lotus throne with a roar of scornful laughter that flooded appearances with glory, transmuting them into pure pleasure. Thus he revealed to me the Maṇḍala of the Blazing Sun of Radiant Inner Space, conferring power upon me.

In this *maṇḍala* of mystic union, Skilful Means and Insight, in this radiant *maṇḍala* of Pure Being and Light Seed – the Pure Being of the Sublime Pure Land of the Four Herukas, the masters of the four focal points, and the Light Seed that is the actuality of a hundred million seed syllables – I was conferred the initiation and empowerment of the four joys.[33]

Out of the bliss-waves of the forehead centre of our union, in the sphere of intense experience of Awareness of joy, arose a white paradise divided into thirty-two lesser pure lands. In each of these pure lands was a white Heruka in mystic union with his Consort surrounded by hundreds of thousands, an incalculable number, of Herukas and their Consorts identical to the principal. In the centre of this vast *maṇḍala* was the Master of all the Herukas, the principal Heruka and Consort into whose Awareness of joy I received initiation. Through this joy the passion of anger was purified, the body cleansed of all traces of habitual action and reaction patterns, insight was gained into the elements of the path of application,[34] and I was enabled to act for the benefit of the seven worlds of the ten directions. At this level I was conferred the secret initiatory name, Tsogyel the White Goddess of Pure Pleasure (Dechen Karmo Tsogyel).

Accordingly, in the throat centre was a yellow paradise divided into sixteen pure lands in each of which was a yellow Heruka in union with his Consort surrounded by hundreds of thousands of identical Herukas as in the forehead centre. In the middle of this *maṇḍala* was the master of all the yellow Herukas, Ratna Vīra and Consort, from whom I received initiation into all the infinite potentialities of superior joy. Thus the passion of desire was purified, all traces of action and reaction patterns were eradicated, and I gained insight into all the elements of the path of accumulation, obtaining the ability to assist the twenty worlds of the ten directions. Here, I received the secret name Tsogyel the Quality Increasing Yellow Goddess (Yonten Gyeje Sermo Tsogyel).

In the same way, in the blue-black paradise of the heart centre comprised of eight lesser pure lands were eight blue-black Herukas in union with their Consorts surrounded by innumerable likenesses as above. In the centre was the master of all the blue-black Herukas, the principal Heruka, Buddha Vīra and Consort, who initiated me into the *mahāmudrā* of supreme joy. Thus all the seeds of passion inherent in the mind were eradicated, and I gained insight into the elements of the path of liberation and the ability to assist the twenty-six worlds of the ten directions. I was given the name, Liberating Samaya Tsogyel (Drolje Damtsik Tsogyel) at this time.

Accordingly, in the red paradise of the gut centre, in the sixty-one lesser pure lands, were sixty-one Herukas in mystic union with their Consorts, surrounded by hundreds of thousands of identical forms, in the centre of which was the principal of them all, the Red Heruka and Consort, into whose Awareness of innate joy I received initiation. Thereby, all traces of emotional clinging and the action and reaction patterns of undifferentiated body, speech and mind were eradicated, and with insight into the elements of the path of utter purity I gained ability to benefit the infinite unbounded universe. Here, I received the secret name, Boundless Awareness Tsogyel (Taye Yeshe Tsogyel).

Then the Guru instructed me to practise in this manner: 'In the Ultimate Maṇḍala of the Four Joys bestow upon yourself the four initiations and empowerments into the four levels of Awareness for seven days. Then visualise the ascent of "love" as Awareness.'[35]

So maintaining unimpaired the progression of the four joys through the love-Awareness that is the value of this initiation, my experience intensified, increasing from height to height. If there is leakage of *bodhicitta*, the Buddha Unchanging Light is slain, and since there is no superior presence to whom such a crime can be acknowledged and thus atoned, such *karma* as that of the Avici Hell results.[36] Therefore, with the power of retraction, drawing up 'love' with the base energy of life-force, I held it in the pot of my belly,[37] and maintaining the recollection of pleasure uncontaminated by lust, divesting myself of mind-created *samādhi* yet not slipping into an instant of torpor, I experienced the ascent of Awareness.

Binding recollection of the *bodhicitta* in the womb's lotus, all ignorance was purified, and suppressing the thousand and eighty movements of karmic energy at the first juncture the Awareness of the dual omniscience of quantity and quality became the path of seeing, and I attained the first degree of enlightenment and certain extra-sensory powers emerged. Then the *bodhicitta* was drawn up and bound in the secret energy centre and motivation and volition were purified, and inhibiting the energy flows of the second juncture I gained the second degree. Then binding the *bodhicitta* between the secret and the gut centres consciousness was purified, and blocking the energy flows of the third juncture I gained the third degree. In the same way, the *bodhicitta* bound at the gut centre, name and form were purified, and when the energy flows of the fourth juncture had been stopped I attained the fourth degree; and the mind capable of both *saṃsāra* and *nirvāṇa*, and Awareness and innate joy, purified, I accomplished the Buddha's essentiality of being.[38] Binding the *bodhicitta* between the gut and the heart *cakra*s the six sense-fields were purified, and the energies of the fifth juncture blocked I attained the fifth degree. Then binding the *bodhicitta* in the heart centre, purifying sensory contact, the energy flows of the sixth juncture were stopped and I reached the sixth degree; ordinary sleeping mind and special joy purified, I attained the goal of the Buddha's absolute, empty being. Between the heart and the throat centres the *bodhicitta* was bound and feeling was purified, and stopping the energy flows of the seventh juncture I reached the seventh degree. Then binding the *bodhicitta* in the throat centre purifying craving and clinging, the energy flows of the eighth juncture stopped I reached the eighth degree; dream and supreme joy purified, I reached the goal of the Buddha's being of consummate visionary enjoyment. Binding the *bodhicitta* between the throat and forehead centres sensual enthralment was purified, and inhibiting the energies of the ninth juncture I attained the ninth degree. Binding the *bodhicitta* in the forehead centre transmigratory existence was purified, and obstructing energy outflow at the tenth juncture I attained the tenth degree; when consciousness of the five sensory doors upon waking from sleep, the body's veins and nerves and Awareness of joy had been purified I reached the goal of the Buddha's stainless apparitional being. Then binding the *bodhicitta* between the forehead and the crown centres rebirth was purified, and the energy flows of the eleventh juncture contained I reached the eleventh degree. Then retracting and binding the *bodhicitta* at the crown centre the entire twelve interdependent elements of *saṃsāra,* including old age and death, were purified, and stopping the twenty-one thousand energy flows of the twelfth juncture, lust, sleep, dream and waking – the four impure states of mind – were purified, and having purified the mind's psychic nerves, energy flows and seed-essence, together with the four joys, I reached the twelfth degree.

Thus I was endowed with the Buddha's Pure Being and all the qualities of Buddha: I was transformed into the Pure Being that functions to imbue all creatures of the infinite universe with the value and meaning of existence, and I gained the innate ability to understand and employ any of the qualities of Buddha at will.

Within six months I had attained the purpose of the three initiations, and my Guru instructed me further:

Human woman and Ḍākinī,
Maiden with perfectly matured body,
A fortunate body endowed with the ten and twice times six
  conditions of ease,[39]
An enduring and courageous body,

Great Mother of Wisdom, Sarasvatī,
Sow-faced Ḍākinī, Mistress of the Mysteries,
Now that the elixir of self and others has brewed,
And the door of the maturing mysteries has been opened to you,
O Great Being, take a consort![40]

But I prepared a *gaṇacakra* offering with my body and possessions, and rendered it to Guru Rimpoche with this petition:

> Venerable Lord of Orgyen, Skull-Garland Skill,
> Stem of the Mysteries, Vajradhara,
> Your vast generosity is beyond gratitude;
> Whatsoever will give you joy
> I swear to give you heedless of body or life.
> Please grant me the final initiation,
> The Word Empowerment of Dzokchen –
> Let the Guru confer the Fourth today!

'The time is not ripe for you to practise the effortless method of Ati,' Guru Rimpoche replied. 'Persist in your practice on the path of the *mahāyāna* mysteries. Now, girl, without a consort, a partner of skilful means, there is no way that you can experience the mysteries of Tantra. It is rather like this: if a pot is unfired it will not bear usage; in an area without wood a fire will not burn; if there is no moisture to sustain growth it is useless to plant a seedling. So go to the Valley of Nepal where there is a sixteen-year-old youth with a mole on his right breast, who is an emanation of the Buddha Hero Hayagrīva called Atsara Sale. He has wandered there from Serling in India. Find him, and make him your ally, and you will soon discover the realm of pure pleasure.'

So, having received my Guru's prophetic injunction, with a golden begging bowl and a pound of gold dust, I set out alone for the Valley of Nepal. In the district of Erong I encountered seven thieves. They sought to steal my gold, and followed me like dogs stalking a deer. I invoked my Guru and visualised the thieves as my Yidam, and conceiving the perfect plan of rendering my possessions as a *maṇḍala* offering, I sang to them inspired:

O seven Yidam of Erong,
It is fortunate to meet you here today.
So that I may attain Buddhahood
And fulfil the wishes of sentient beings
Let karmic misadventure be swiftly transformed.
To discover, fortuitously, the Lama's compassion –
How truly marvellous!
Happy thoughts arising from within
May people find freedom through generosity.

Then placing my hands together in reverence, I arranged the gold in a pile as if it was a *maṇḍala*. The seven thieves, though not understanding a single word, touched by the melody of my song, stood staring at me like statues, transported to the first level of *samādhi*. Then, in the Newar language, they asked, 'Venerable Lady, what is your country? Who is your father? Who is your mother? Who is your Lama? What are you doing here? Please sing us another divine song!'

As they made this request, the hairs of their bodies that had bristled in aggression lay down, a wreath of happy smiles signified their satisfaction, their malicious twisted faces became serene, and their pleasure showed in garlands of teeth. Gathering in front of me they sat down. I had a bamboo cane with three joints in it, and leaning upon it I replied in their Newar tongue:

You seven thieves with whom I have previous karmic connection,
Know that aggression and malice are Mirror-like Awareness itself –
Radiance and clarity have no other source
Than a hostile mind filled with anger and enmity.
Look into your anger
And there is the strength of Diamond Being, Vajrasattva!
Detached from appearances, you are purified in Emptiness.
This maiden's fatherland is Overflowing Joy,
Serene Fields of Emptiness and Visionary Pleasure;
I am no stickler for conventional names and forms
So if your favoured lady's fair land appeals to you,
I will lead you there.

You seven thieves with whom I have previous karmic
  connection,
Know that pride and vain complacency are Awareness of
  Sameness –
Primal purity in meditative composure cannot be found
Except in an ambitious mind that believes itself supreme.
Look into natural purity
And there is a Fountain of Jewels, Ratnasaṃbhava!
Detached from the state of Emptiness, light-form is pure.
    This maiden's father is that source of every gratification,
    He is the wish-fulfilling gem itself;
    I am no glutton for the illusory chattels of wealth
    So if you think you would like the old man
    I will part with him.

You seven thieves with whom I have previous karmic
  connection,
Know that desire and covetousness are Discriminating
  Awareness –
You will find fine sensory distinction in no other place
Than a mind hungering for beautiful things, wanting the
  whole world.
Look into the intrinsic freshness of your desire
And there is Boundless Light, Amitābha!
Detached from radiance, your pleasure is purified.
    This maiden's mother is Boundless Light
    And in her is pure pleasure unlimited;
    I am no votary of the quality of feeling
    So if this old lady appeals to you
    I will give her away.

You seven thieves with whom I have previous karmic
  connection,
Know that envy and alienation are All-Accomplishing
  Awareness –
Efficiency and success have no other source
Than a bigoted mind that is quick to judge and holds a grudge.
Look behind jealous thoughts
And there is immediate success, Amoghasiddhi!

Detached from crass envy and subtle resentments, whatever occurs is pure.
This maiden's Lama is Every Purpose Spontaneously Accomplished,
The Lama whose every action is invariably consummated;
So because I am no slave to the sphere of my work
If you want this Lama
I will abandon him to you.

You seven thieves with whom I have previous karmic connection,
Know that ignorance and stupidity are Awareness of Dynamic Space –
There is no other way to hold fast to the path
Than through ignorance and a dense understanding.
Look into ignorance
And there is Dynamic Visionary Panorama, Vairocana!
Detached from hypnotic states, whatever arises is pure.
This maiden's beloved is Visionary Panorama
And I love that ultimate consort, the Illuminator;
And since I am no adherent of the duality of vision and viewer,
If you desire my service
I will show you the way.

The thieves were filled with undivided faith, and they felt repelled by the wheel of rebirth. They begged instruction and precepts from me, and then gained release from *saṃsāra*. They begged me insistently to come to their country, but I refused and continued on my way.

At the great *stūpa* of Jarung Khashor,[41] which had been built by three Monpa boys long ago, I offered a handful of gold dust and then made this wish-fulfilling prayer:

OM ĀH HŪNG!
In the Valley of Nepal, Pure Land of Conquering Buddhas,
Lord of All Creatures, Symbol of the Buddha's Absolute Being,
Stand for as long as time itself,
Turning the wheel of the ultimate law
To liberate beings from the ocean of confusion.

With your guiding power, O Lord,
Lead all beings, embodied and disembodied,
Out of the land of slavery into the exalted realm of freedom.

The myriad rays of light radiated out of the *stūpa* forming a cloud-like mist, and from within this cloud Guru Rimpoche surrounded by the Abbot Śāntarakṣita, King Trisong Detsen and many Ḍākinīs, spoke to me:

Listen, Daughter of Kharchen!
With exemplary conduct, with forebearance from anger,
Goddess of Great Insight, guiding men out of *saṃsāra*,
Through liberality releasing them, going to the end of endurance,
May you traverse the paths and stages of meditation.
Now do not wander here for long.
Return to Tibet with the consort you need,
And again I will reveal the profound tantric mysteries.

Having delivered this prophetic injunction,[42] the Guru vanished.

Wandering slowly, since I had no precise knowledge of the whereabouts of the object of my search, I found myself in the neighbourhood of the large market-place near the southern gate of the city of Bhaktapur (Kho-khom-han). There a youth boldly approached me. He was handsome and attractive and a red mole on his chest threw out brilliant lustre. His front teeth were like evenly matched slates of conch and his four incisors were like white conches that spiralled clockwise. His intelligent eyes were haloed with a red tint, his nose was pointed and his eyes azure. His thick hair curled to the right and his fingers were webbed like a duck's feet.

'Lady, from where have you come?' he enquired in the language of Serling. 'Have you come to set me free?'

O Listen attentively, charming boy and consort!
I have come from Central Tibet
And I am the Venerable Pema Jungne's Lady.
What is your name? Where is your homeland?
And what are you doing here?

The boy answered:

I am from India, from the village of Serling.
A Hindu sadhu stole me from my parent's bosom
And sold me as a servant to a citizen of this land.
My parents named me Āyra Sale,
And I have lived here seven years as a servant.

While he was speaking a crowd of the town's traders gathered, mesmerised by my face, and then spontaneously they asked me to sing to them, offering me money if I pleased them. So I sang them this song:

NAMO GURU PEMA SIDDHI HRĪ!
In the vast sky of Glorious Kuntuzangpo[43]
The sun of Dzokchen shines in pure space,
Bathing all beings of the six realms, our mothers, in light –
Is this not our father, Pema Jungne?
His space is unalterable *vajra*-fields,
His being is unborn and undying compassion,
His *karma* is neither good nor bad, Buddhahood attained –
Is this not our father, Pema Jungne?
Her home is the Highest Paradise, the Tidro Grotto,
The Ḍākinī inspired by Pema's compassion,
And she bestows delight upon all who relate to her –
Is this not the Lady Yeshe Tsogyel?
To this Land of Nepal, arisen in vision,
A sublime mystic partner has come,
And the boy with fit *karma* must leave with me –
Am I not Tsogyel, the provider?

The crowd could not understand the meaning of my song, but they listened insatiably to the tone and melody, calling me the Ḍākinī of Sweet Song. I accompanied Atsara Sale to his lodging, and that evening, left sitting on the doorstep, I was interrogated by Sale's owner.

'Where are you from? What are you doing here?' she asked me.

I related the relevant parts of my story, and concluded, 'The

Guru Pema Jungne has sent me here to ransom Atsara Sale. So it is propitious for you to let me redeem him.'

'Although Sale is a servant, he is like a son to me,' she replied. 'And since we paid a great sum of gold for him, we will not free him. But if you are so inclined you can stay here together with him. It would be quite satisfactory to me if you both stayed here in service.'

I replied:

> Wherever the sun's *maṇḍala* shines
> Shadows of gloom disappear;
> When the sun has set stars appear
> But tomorrow the sun will shine again.
> Wherever a wish-fulfilling gem is found
> The need for gold disappears;
> Where there is no gem, gold is coveted
> But ever after the gem again is sought.
> Whenever a perfected Buddha appears
> There is no need of a consort;
> When the Buddha has gone depend upon a consort,
> For thereafter Means and Insight should unite.
> When my goal has been reached
> I will no longer have need of Sale,
> But now I need a partner to illuminate the path.[44]
> Therefore, at any cost, I must ransom him.
> Please name your price.

The household – mother, father and son – were captivated by my song, and they invited me inside where they served me a sumptuous meal. 'After you have freed this boy will you marry him? What will you do?' asked my hostess. 'You seem to be a girl of high principles. You are attractive. So if you wish, I will set you up with Sale.'

'Atsara Sale appeared in a vision to Pema Jungne, and he is required for a sacred purpose,' I repeated. 'I have gold for the ransom, and in every way it is propitious for you to set him free.'

'How much gold do you have?' asked Sale's owner. 'I bought him for five hundred gold coins, and now his value is much greater.'

'I will give you whatever you ask,' I replied. 'I must have him.' But when I had weighed my gold dust I found I had no more than the equivalent of one hundred coins. 'Now what should I do?' I asked.

'I will let him go,' the lady said, 'but I must have gold. With such an amount you can't even buy one of Sale's arms. There is nothing you can do except find more gold.'

At this time there was a war in progress in Nepal, and amongst the citizens of Bhaktapur there was a man of incalculable wealth, a merchant called Dāna Ayu whose twenty-year-old son called Nāga had been killed in the fighting. His parents had brought his body home where they paid it inordinate homage. They were bowed with grief, vowing that they would immolate themselves on the same pyre as their son. I felt unbearable compassion for them, and approaching them I said, 'There is no cause for so much grief. In this city lives a youth called Atsara Sale, and if you will give me the large sum of gold that I need to release him from service, I will restore your son to life.'

The couple were overjoyed. 'If you can bring our son back to life we will even ransom a prince for you. But is it really possible?'

After they had agreed to give me whatever gold was required for Sale's ransom in return for resurrecting their son, I took a large white silk cloth, and folding it in half and half again, I covered the corpse up to the chin. Then I sang:

OM ĀH HŪNG GURU SARVA HRĪ!
The universal ground is Kuntuzangpo,
Undeluded, primally pure,
And the path is manifold apparitional form,
Emanation of the six kinds of beings,[45]
Where positive or negative karmic action
Causes certain inevitable results.
Knowing this, why persist in folly?
I am a *yoginī*, Mistress of the Tantra,
Embraced by the compassion of Pema Jungne,
And neither life nor death holds terror for me.
Instantly I can remove the afflictions of others.
Now pray and grace will flow!

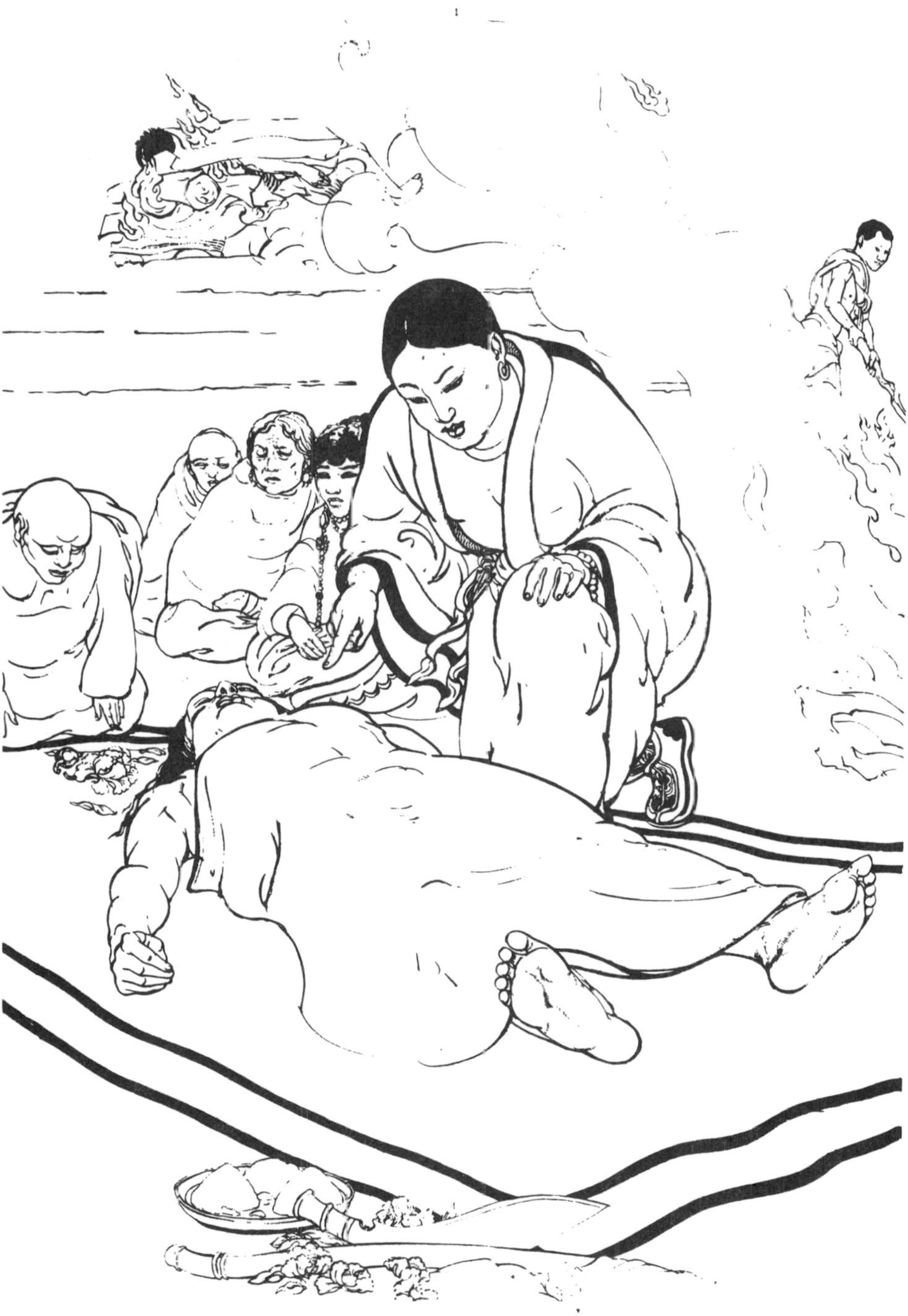

Pointing my finger at the heart of the corpse, it began to glow with increasing intensity, and letting a drop of saliva fall into the dead man's mouth from my own, in his ear I intoned, 'AYU JÑĀNA BHRUṂ!' Then I annointed his deep knife wounds with my hands, and his body was made entirely whole again. The youth's awareness became clearer and clearer, until, finally, he was fully conscious. In delighted astonishment all who were witness to this miracle prostrated before me. The parents in their joy embraced and wept over their son restored to his original strength. With very generous gifts they offered a *gaṇa-cakra* feast to me, and ransomed Atsara Sale for a thousand pieces of gold and presented him to me.

My reputation spread throughout the kingdom. The king himself offered me his hospitality and gave me respect and honour, begging me to remain there as his priestess. But I refused, and departed with my consort for the E Temple in Kathmandu. There we met a spiritual son of Guru Pema called Vasudhara. We offered him a golden bowl and some gold dust, and as an equal I asked him for teaching and secret precepts. Knowing that I was Guru Pema's Consort, Vasudhara was extremely solicitous, giving me all respect and honour. In his turn he asked me for teaching and secret precepts, and I granted whatever he desired.

We then visited Śākya Dema, Jila Jipha and others at Asura and Yanglesho, giving them presents of gold. I sang this song to Śākya Dema:

My Guru's only Consort, sister in the Tantra,
Please listen to Tsogyel of Tibet.
The mind's nature an inexhaustible fountain of every desire,
Impartial dispensation of every requirement,
That is the generosity of Tsogyel of Tibet.
Mind unblemished, free of public and private vows,
With careful awareness that keeps proper conduct,
That is the morality of Tsogyel of Tibet.
Mind unbiased, free of pleasure, pain and indifference,
With patience enduring the good with the bad in every situation,
That is the forebearance of Tsogyel of Tibet.
Mind a continuum like a river's flow,

With continuous endeavour cultivating empty delight,
That is the perseverance of Tsogyel of Tibet.
Mind a union of creation and fulfilment whatever arises,
With fixation upon *mahāmudrā*,[46]
That is the meditation of Tsogyel of Tibet.
Mind a continuum of Awareness, immanent pure pleasure,
Serving a consort of Skilful Means, Insight transcending perfection,
That is the perfect insight of Tsogyel of Tibet.
Well-born Śākya Dema, whatever precepts you possess,
Please share them with me, your sister in truth.

Śākya Dema was rapturous, and answered:

You are welcome, sister, my own Guru's Consort,
But I possess very few secret precepts.
Through Venerable Orgyen Saṃbhava's compassion
I received the secret teaching we need in life and death:
Creative and fulfilment processes united, *mahāmudrā*,
Clear light and magical illusion emanating – such precepts I possess,
And now the womb called the *bar-do* is barren:
That is the instruction of Śākya Dema of Nepal.
I received the secret instruction we need in transition and dying:
Employing the vital breath's energy to purify the medial nerve,
The mystic heat, the syllable A, the blazing and dripping[47] – such precepts I possess,
And now in transition and death I am fearless:
That is the instruction of Śākya Dema of Nepal.
I received the secret instruction using passion as the path:
Using Means and Insight's seed-essence, cultivating empty delight,
To generate the four joys' Awareness[48] – such precepts I possess,
And now I am fearless though legions of hostile passions arise:
That is the instruction of Śākya Dema of Nepal.
I received the secret instruction we need in slothful sleep:[49]
Relying on the teaching of Dzokchen, purifying dream,
To enter the sanctum of clear light – such precepts I possess,
And now I am fearless if engulfed in an aeon of darkness;

That is the instruction of Śākya Dema of Nepal.
I received the secret instruction we need in the experience of ultimate reality:
Utilising the six lamps, cultivating the clear light,
To maximise the four convictions[50] – such precepts I possess,
And now I am fearless though the Buddha turns hostile:
That is the instruction of Śākya Dema of Nepal.
And now I ignore cause and effect, the stages and the paths,
For instant by instant the manifest Buddha is accomplished.
The ultimate attainment is supremely wonderful!
Now whatever instruction you possess, accomplished sister,
Share it with me, this ready vessel.

Then our finite minds united in the Buddha's mind, we exchanged precepts and instruction. Thereafter, I returned to Tibet with my consort.

Leaving Nepal we entered Tsang, and then proceeding to Tidro we stayed in the Assembly Hall of the Ḍākinīs. We were provided for and honoured by the patrons of the district, though a number of gossips maligned me: 'The Lady Tsogyel has been seduced by the devil. She doesn't practise worship such as that of Guru Pema now that she has found this vagrant Indian yogi.'

On the tenth day of the moon I celebrated worship and offering, revealing the Maṇḍala of the Lama's Secret Communion.[51] At the juncture in the rite where I performed the invocation, Orgyen Guru himself appeared, riding on a sunbeam. I was jubilant but touched with guilt, and with extreme emotion I fell down to the ground in homage, before entreating him in this manner:

Alas, O compassionate Guru!
I am an ignorant woman, a creation of delusion,
Lost in negative *karma*. Embrace me with your compassion!
Now cleanse every evil state.
Never leave me, Lord. Be kind!
The object of my journey to Nepal is accomplished –
I found the youth Āyra Sale without mistake.
Now I beg you for entry into the mysteries,
And with compassion dispel the obstacles on my path.

Radiating joy, smiling, the Guru answered:

O Daughter of Kharchen,
Faithful One, listen attentively!
If with your body you wish to cross over
This boundless ocean of *saṃsāra,*
Rely upon a qualified Lama as captain,
Board the boat Oral Transmission,
Hoist the great sail of secret precepts,
Send out the course-setting crow of instruction,
Destroy leviathan obstructions with the conch,[52]
Ballast with lead against adverse winds of *karma,*
Make full sail with the fair winds of faith,
Plug leaks in the pure white *samaya,*
And with the sudden breaking of the wave of maturity and release,
Cast up upon a serendipitous isle,
Enjoy the abundance of whatever you desire,
Delighting in a vision replete with jewels,
Contented in the disappearance of matter and mortality,
Now relaxing in the dawning of permanent pleasure.

And he continued, 'What hardships did you encounter? Did you have an easy journey? How long did it take you?'

I related in detail the vicissitudes of the road, the problem of gold in Nepal and how I restored a man to life to obtain the necessary thousand pieces of gold.

'Good! Good!' said the Guru. 'Whatever hardship you suffered is beneficial. It purifies all kinds of karmic obscuration. You lack the devotion of a woman who loves her husband, so although the price you paid for Sale was high the bargain was fair. You have accrued boundless merit. You are free of the clinging of a lustful woman. But the power to resurrect a dead man and so on is merely mundane *siddhi,* so do not be conceited. Your consort is called Exalted (Āyra) because he is superior to others. And because his price was paid in gold he is called Golden Light.'[53]

Atsara Sale was brought to spiritual maturity through disclosure of the Maṇḍala of the Guru's Blessing.[54] I, myself, was the mainstay of the initiation. Thereafter, Atsara's maturity led to further spiritual development, and established on the path of liberation, having gained emancipating comprehension of both provisional and ultimate teaching, the Guru assigned him to me as my ally and consort. After exhorting us to practise until we had gained mastery of the Tantra, the Guru departed for Lhodrak.

I and my spiritual son ensconced in a corner of the meditation grotto (*which came to be called Tsogyel's Secret Cave*) were completely hidden from view, and for seven months we cultivated the nature of the four joys. At the end of this session I found that I could pass unimpeded through any material object whatsoever, and that my body was unaffected by ageing, frailty or disease, etc. In short I had gained control over the five elements. Further, as the four joys manifest, I gained the Buddha's four modes of being.[55]

Thereafter, the Guru returned and stayed in the great cave at Tidro, for it was time to turn the wheel of the Buddha's teaching. Previously, Guru Rimpoche had initiated the Dharma Protector, King Trisong Detsen, into several tantric *maṇḍala*s, including the Single Yamāntaka, the Single Hayagrīva, the Single Lamp of Yangdak, the Single Tinle Phurba, the Single Dudtsi Tod and the Single Mamo.[56] The King had practised the rites of visualisation and recitation,[57] and various miraculous signs and marks of accomplishment had appeared. He had gained deep faith, and he decided to ask for many of the more profound teachings of the *tantra*s. Therefore he sent Shubu Pelseng, Gyatsa Lhanang and Ma Rinchen Chok with presents of gold for the Guru and his Consort with an invitation for them to visit Samye. Arriving at the Tidro Assembly Hall they approached the Guru and delivered their message:

O Guru and Ḍākinīs, mystic partners,
We are the Tibetan King's speed-walkers.
The sole God-king of Tibet, Trisong Detsen,
Resolved to establish the Tantra, the most profound, ultimate vehicle,
Invites you to Samye.
Consider us with kindness and come quickly.

After offering him the gifts of gold, they waited for his reply:

> Three loyal speed-walkers,
> Three blessed sons, you are welcome.
> I am Pema Jungne,
> My residence is the human world,
> My purpose is the same as the Buddhas,
> And my emanation encompasses the world.
> The Emperor's aspiration is exemplary;
> Now the message of the *tantra*s will spread.

The Guru and Consort, their spiritual son and the three speed-walkers departed for Samye together. At Zhodro the Guru told the three speed-walkers, who would later become translators, to ride on ahead to the King, so that he could prepare a welcome for we three who would follow. The King's three courtiers, arriving at Samye, told the King the story of the Master's coming, and that he was expected to go out to meet him.

The Tibetan ministers, having heard of the Guru's imminent arrival, conferred: 'This man Pema Jungne is like space – he is everywhere but nowhere; he is like a river – weapons cannot harm him; he is like fire – his body glows with lustre; he is like the wind – he cannot be bound; he appears to be a real human being and at the same time he seems disembodied. So for the present we will abandon our nefarious designs and agree with everything that the King proposes. However, when our wretched Queen arrives, if we fail to make an example of her, ultimately the government's authority will be lost.'

Guru Rimpoche was well aware of their intentions. 'What is known as the Tantra implies facility in many, diverse skilful means,' he said. Then straightaway he transformed me, in the minds of others, into a three-pronged trident (*khatvāṅga*). And we proceeded into Tibet proper.

The representative of the King, Takra Gungtsen, with a hundred mounted ministers as envoy of welcome, greeted us at Zhoda, and from there we made our way to Samye. In front of the Great Stūpa the King, his ministers and his entourage gave us a royal welcome. The King prostrated to the Guru and made a gift of a golden pot wrapped in white silk and filled with fresh white chung.

The Guru made this pronouncement: 'At this moment the Tantra has the vital potency of youth. In the future its promise will not be fulfilled. Its practice will be confused and perverted.'

Then we made our way up to the Utse Pagoda where the courtiers remarked that I was absent, and that an Indian sadhu was attending the Guru. 'If Tsogyel is not here, this opportunity to receive the Tantra will be lost,' thought the King. 'She is certainly not here now. I will ask Guru Rimpoche where she is, and because I long to encounter her again, searching for her I will insist upon inviting her.' And aloud he said to the Guru, 'O Great Guru, where is Tsogyel at present? Why has she not come here? Is this Indian sadhu a disciple of yours? What instruction has he received?'

The Guru smiled at him, and replied:

O King and Bodhisattva,
My manifestation has the nature of space,
And a space-master's magical powers are limitless;
Tsogyel has dissolved into the vastness of inner space,
Even now she stands at the junction of *saṃsāra* and *nirvāṇa*.
My manifestation is a fountain of instruction,
My every movement appears as instruction;
Tsogyel has entered the immensity of my empty being,
Her present abode is the realm of Kuntuzangmo.
My manifestation is empty delight
And my desire for any empty illusion is spontaneously fulfilled;
Tsogyel has vanished into the expanse of empty delight,
Her present abode is the Citadel of Delight, the Buddha's three modes of being.

Thereupon the Guru touched his trident[58] which turned into myself. The King was exceedingly amazed. This miracle was seen by the Bonpo Queen Tsepong Za and others. The Queen reported it to the ministers. 'This Indian master is full of surprises. He hid Tsogyel in a trident!' Some ministers were lost in astonishment, but the majority agreed that what the Queen said did not ring true, that it was impossible to contain even one hand in a trident, and although it must have been magical illusion that the Queen saw, it was no less wonderful for that. All that they had been plotting was set aside for the moment, and most of the courtiers gained great faith in the Guru.

Thereafter, the King, twenty-one of his courtiers, thirty-two acolytes, seven Ḍākinī ladies of high birth, and others, totalling three hundred and five, went to the retreat house of Chimphu Gewa. And there the Guru revealed to us one hundred and twenty *maṇḍala*s of the Ultimate Tantra, and confirmed the initiates in spiritual maturity and release. Specifically, he gave us the precepts of the Eight Logos Deities, and of Mamo, Yamāntaka, Phurba, Dudtsi Yonten, The Communion of the Lama's Mind, The Communion of the Yidam's Mind, The Wrathful and Peaceful Deities of Illusory Emanation, The Wrathful and Peaceful Deities of Yangdak's Maṇḍala, and The Wrathful and Peaceful Deities of Padma Sung's Maṇḍala. And again, in particular, sixty-one Heartdrop precepts, the Seven Divisions of Mind Communion, eleven concise and extensive precepts of the Eight Logos Deities, one hundred and two Mind Accomplishment precepts, seventy-six secret precepts and one hundred and thirty direct transmissions of *tantra*. To the King he gave the seven root methods of accomplishment of Dudtsi Yonten and twenty secret precepts, and then he told him to practise them, giving him certain visionary indications. To Namkhai Nyingpo of Nub he gave the methods of accomplishment of the Nine Lamps of Yangdak, and the precepts for the Twenty Black Phurba Demonslayer practices, etc., and instructed him to practise in Lhodrak, giving him visionary direction. To both Sangye Yeshe and Dorje Dunjom he gave the method of accomplishment of Mañjuśrī Yamāntaka primarily through the Six Gods of Overwhelming Mudrā with twenty subsidiary secret precepts, telling them to practise in Yong Dzong in Drak and giving them visionary injunction. To Gyelwa Chokyang of Kung Lung and Gyelwa Lodro of Dre he gave the Three Yogas belonging to the Most Secret Dance of Hayagrīva as the basic method of accomplishment, together with twenty-five subsidiary secret precepts, twelve *tantra*s and the method of accomplishment of the Tramenma Sorceresses, and told them to practise at Chimphu itself, giving them visionary guidance. To both Vairotsana and Denma Tsemang he gave the method of accomplishment of Mopa Drakngak and of Glorious Tobden Nakpo, primarily with the Eight Classes of Spirits and secondarily with the Eighteen Arrogant Spirits, and told them to practise in Yama Lung, showing them visionary indications. To both Kaba Peltsek and Odren Wongchuk he gave the root method of accomplishment of Mamo, the external, internal and secret rites and their ramifications, and told them to meditate at Yerpi Drak, giving them visionary injunction. To both Jñāna Kumāra Vajra and the Mongolian Lhapel Zhonnu he gave the secret precepts of the Secret Yangdak and Phurba and the method of accomplishment and oral transmission of Mahāmudrā Immortality, and told them to meditate at Jemidrak in Nyemo, giving them visionary instruction. To both Pelgyi Senge and Chokro Lui Gyeltsen he gave the basic method of accomplishment of Drekpa, the Garland of the Ten Krodhas, and a subsidiary practice, the Method of Samaya Restoration of the Thirty Chief Drekpa together with secret precepts upon behaviour, and told them to meditate at the cave of meditation on Pelchuwori Mountain, giving them visionary injunction. To both the translator Rinchen Zangpo and Tingzin Zangpo he gave the method of accomplishment of the Mystic Mahākaruṇika, the means to accomplish the Rikdzin Lama, and also the oral transmission of the Supreme Siddhi of the Knowledge Mahāmudrā, and told them to practise at the Uru meditation cave, giving them, also, visionary injunction. To both Langdro Konchok Jungne and Gyelwa Jangchub he gave the method of accomplishment and oral transmission of Jinlab Lama and the method of accomplishment of the Proud Black Horse belonging to the Embodiment of the Secret Hayagrīva, and he told them to meditate at Shangidrak in Yeru, giving them visionary direction. To both Drenpa Namkha Wongchuk and Kheuchung Kading he gave the method of accomplishment of the Wrathful and Peaceful Deities of the Secret Pema Sung and the method of meditating upon the Six Gods in a single deity, the basic Vajrasattva, together with the oral transmission of the meditation of the Thirty-six Herukas, and he told them to meditate at the northern lake of Namtsodo, giving them visionary instruction. To both Ma Rinchen Chok and Gyelmo Yudra Nyingpo he gave the method of accomplishment of Vajrapāṇi, twenty oral transmissions and a hundred secret precepts; in particular he gave them the method of accomplishment, the oral transmission and the secret precepts of the Yoga of Immortality, and he told them to practise in the cave of meditation at Chimphu itself, giving them visionary instruction. To me, Tsogyel, the Guru gave the external, internal, secret and ultimate methods of accomplishment of the Mind of the Guru himself of which the basic practice was the method of accomplishment of Pema Wong, comprising seven dissimilar redactions related to the Guru's *maṇḍala*.[59] In short, he gave me the means of accomplishing the Three Roots (Guru, Yidam and Ḍākinī) in one *maṇḍala*. 'Practise at Womphu Taktsang, Mon Taktsang and Kham Taktsang and in all those places where there is a naturally manifest image of Guru Rimpoche, particularly in Tidro itself,' the Guru instructed me. 'When any difficulty arises pray to me and I will surely come and give you advice. Further, it is forbidden that you should be separated from your partner, Atsara Sale.' Having imparted these instructions he gave me certain visionary indications.

Then the Emperor celebrated as many full *gaṇacakra* feasts as the Guru had given *maṇḍalas*, providing an enormous celebration of thanksgiving to the Guru. Then, offering him a mountainous pile of worldly goods – gold, silk, brocade, – etc., he said:

> We have now received the *maṇḍalas* of the Ultimate Tantra
> That are so very difficult to gain in our aeon.
> Your kindness is overwhelming, and impossible to repay.
> Now until I gain enlightenment,
> Lord, let not your compassion forsake me.
> Upon your distracted and agitated disciples like me,
> Lost in states of uneasiness and confusion,
> We beg you always to look with compassion.

So saying, he poured seven handfuls of gold upon the Guru's body. To each translator and initiate who had been instructed by the Guru to meditate in the various power places he gave a pound of gold dust for his immediate needs and provisions, a golden begging bowl, a piece of white, red and blue brocade, a robe, a horse and a pack animal, and he promised them all the means of their sustenance during the period of their retreat. The Great Guru, radiating happiness, replied to the King:

O Great King, O God-king,
This procedure is correct.
And although I, Pema Jungne,
Have no need for material goods,
To sustain your tantric *samaya*
And to accrue merit for you, the King, I accept them.
Through your generosity your twenty-four subjects
Will achieve their aim free from obstacles.
To promise sustenance is highly meritorious;
That is the activity of a Bodhisattva.
Very good!
My disciples' perseverance and courageous practice,
Pema Jungne's secret precepts and the King's provisions,
These three combined will create inexhaustible virtue.
Through prayers of aspiration, synchronistic circumstances[60]
  and good *karma*,
The infinitude of the Buddha's qualities will be accomplished.

The Guru gave encouragement and advice to each of the twenty-five disciples (but that is not included here – their personal stories are told in separate works), and then they all dispersed to practise in the places that the Guru had indicated. First, Tsogyel went to Tidro, and entered the Maṇḍala of the Union of the Three Roots. In The Book of Studies *is listed a vast number of general and specific* tantras, *which liberate the listener merely by his hearing them, but discouraged by the length of such lists I have not included them here.*

Thus ends the fourth chapter in which is described how Tsogyel requested teaching and instruction from her Guru and how she received initiation and practical precepts.

SAMAYA ITHI GYA GYA GYA!

CHAPTER FIVE

MEDITATION, AUSTERITY AND SPIRITUAL ACCOMPLISHMENT

This is a short account of Tsogyel's methods of spiritual accomplishment, her practice in the Ḍākinī's Assembly Hall at Tidro in Tsogyel's Secret Meditation Cave, and in other places.

At first I lived in a concealed anchorite's cave in a corner of the Tidro Assembly Hall. I was supplied ungrudgingly with provisions by local patrons. Here I diligently applied myself to the method of realising the Serene Guru Pema Jungne in his unconditioned reality. After only a short period of meditation my body assumed a divine form and the Yidam deity appeared before my very eyes. Perceiving my psychic nerves and energy flows as the Ḍākinī's *maṇḍala*, whatever transformative activity I began was automatically accomplished.[1] Favoured by the Lama's empowering blessings, seed-essence, the nature of mind, arose as the Lama's dancing form, and all phenomena appeared as the Lama's pure-lands. Simultaneous with the spontaneous emergence of genuine, non-referential devotion and respect for the Lama, the external *maṇḍala* began to effloresce iridescently, and Buddha Heroes and Ḍākinīs shimmered in union in my sense-fields.[2]

In this vivid vision of radiant light I arrived at a place called Orgyen Khandro Ling, The Land of the Ḍākinīs. In this land the fruit trees were like razors, the ground was plastered with meat, the mountains were bristling piles of skeletons and the clods of earth and stone were scattered fragments of bone. In the centre of this *maṇḍala* was an immeasurable palace built of skulls and wet and dry heads, and the ceilings and door-blinds were made of human skin.[3] At a radius of a hundred thousand leagues the palace was ringed by a circle of volcanoes, a wall of *vajras*, a perimeter of falling thunderbolts, a ring of eight cemeteries and a wall of beautiful lotuses. Within this boundary were flocks of flesh-eating, blood-drinking birds and crowds of demon savages, male and female, and other brutes, all of whom surrounded me glaring at me threateningly, but thereafter they acted with neither hostility nor friendliness.

Then I went up into the palace, and having passed through three successive doorways, I found many Ḍākinīs in human form, carrying various offerings to the principal Ḍākinī. Some cut shreds of flesh from their bodies with knives and preparing the flesh as *gaṇacakra* offering, they made worship. Some let blood from their veins, some gouged out their eye-balls, some cut off their noses, their tongues, or their ears, some cut out their hearts or their lungs, liver, spleen or kidneys, some gave their flesh and some their life blood, some gave their bone marrow and fluids, some gave their life-force or their breath, and some cut off their heads or their limbs. After cutting and preparing their offerings, they presented them to their principal Ḍākinī and Consort who blessed them and distributed them as tokens of faith.

'Why are you pursuing pain like this?' I asked them. 'If you take your own lives, how is it possible to reach the end of the Buddha's path?'

They replied:

O woman with procrastinating mind,
The accomplished Lama, a real Lama,[4]
Instantaneously confers his compassion,
Knowing what pleases him but deferring his pleasure,
Procrastinating, merit is lost –
Delay, and hindrances and obstacles multiply.
In so far as your cognition of ultimate truth is instantaneous,
It is fast as a flash of genuine faith;
If you fail to offer Awareness the moment it dawns,
Procrastinating, merit is lost –
Delay, and hindrances and obstacles multiply.
In so far as your cognition of ultimate truth is instantaneous,

It is fast as a flash of genuine faith;
If you fail to offer Awareness the moment it dawns,
Procrastinating, merit is lost –
Delay, and hindrances and obstacles multiply.
In so far as we have obtained this body for a moment,
Only a moment exists to celebrate the path;
Failing to offer this auspicious body while you have it,
Delaying, hindrances and obstacles multiply.
Inasmuch as the Teacher appears only for an instant,
There is only an instant to enter the door of the mysteries;
Failing to offer the teaching the moment you possess it,
Delaying, hindrances and obstacles multiply.

Hearing this, I felt ashamed.

Simultaneous with the dedication of the merit of the offerings, a Vajra Yoginī appeared in front of each of the Ḍākinī devotees, and at a snap of the thumb and forefinger she dissolved, and all was as before. Then each of the Ḍākinīs asked the principal for instruction before withdrawing into herself for meditation. Thus their offering and meditation periods were repeated twelve times a day. Inside each of the doors to the meditation chamber was a guardian of the gate; in the centre of the *maṇḍala* was Vajra Yoginī standing in a blaze of light so intense that it was almost unbearable to gaze upon.

(*What Tsogyel saw in the vast expanses of other pure-lands is written elsewhere. Disconcerted by the size of these accounts I could not include them here.*)

When Guru Rimpoche visited me again I described the various visions that I had experienced. 'I want to practise something of that kind of austerity,' I told him. 'Please accept my pledge to undertake such a sacrifice.'

'All that was only symbolic vision,' Guru Rimpoche replied. 'It is not necessary for you now to make an actual offering of the flesh. Better than that, practise these austerities.'

Listen to me, you goddess Tsogyelma;
Listen attentively, bewitching lady!
Those who possess this precious human trunk of gold
And who practise meditation always find sustenance,
While those ignorant of meditation go hungry,

And failing to grasp their chance they die of starvation.
It is beneficial to fulfil a pledge to practise these eight great austerities.
Practise austerity of diet: subsist on mineral essences,
Extract the essences of ambrosial medicinal herbs and then eat air.
Practise austerity of dress, wear cotton cloth, then only bone ornaments,
And then go naked, relying on the mystic heat.
Practise austerity of speech: perform recitation and visualisation;
Sing prayers, songs and liturgies, and practise *mantra* and breathing,
And then stay mute; abandon all idle talk.
Practise austerity of body: perform prostration and circumambulation,
Physical *yoga*, and the lotus posture in formal meditation.
Practise austerity of mind: develop the creative and fulfilment processes,
Cultivate the seed-essence of empty delight and abide in the *samādhi* of union.
Practise austerity of teaching: bear the torch of the Buddha's doctrine;
Sustain the tradition, perfect the technique of transforming beings,
And cultivate skill in discourse, debate and composition.
Practise austerity of compassion: cherish others over yourself,
Treating aggressors like your sons and gold and excrement alike.
Practise austerity of benevolence: without concern for body or life;
Cultivate the *mahāyāna* aspiration of selfless service to others.
If you practise these austerities you become one with the Buddha and his teaching;
You attain the unsurpassable, the miraculous and pure pleasure.
If you deviate from this practice to follow self-mutilating asceticism
You become no different from despised fanatics and extremists.[5]
Daughter of Kharchen, take my injunction to heart!

Then I vowed to practise these eight great austerities described by the Guru:

The Buddha's teaching has come to this vicious land;
A lamp of radiant fire-crystal[6] has come to this dark land;
Venerable Orgyen has come to Tibet, the land of demon savages.
You dispense the sacred *mahāyāna* knowledge to insecure beings,
You transform the wretched into the blessed;
I have never heard of such *yoga* as this
Even when the Buddha lived in Vajrāsana.
There is no way that I can repay the Guru's kindness.
Now that I, Yeshe Tsogyel, a woman,
Have entered the most secret tantric *maṇḍala*,
May I die if I fail in a fraction of my pledge.
And further, unconcerned with body, life or social status,
Caring only for the Guru's injunction,
Practising these eight great austerities,
May I die if I infringe this sacred vow in any way.
Come whatever, I swear to practise truly altogether,
Austerities of diet, clothing and food, these three,
Austerities of body, speech and mind, these three,
And austerity for the Buddha's teaching and for sentient beings,
And the austerity of kindness, cherishing others above myself.

I took this vow to practise the eight great austerities three times. The Guru was delighted, and after giving me further advice and prophetic injunction he returned to continue his mission as the Emperor's priest.

First, I practised the austerity of dress by means of the mystic heat. On the mountain peak of Tidro where scree and glacial ice meet, protected by nothing but a piece of cotton cloth I meditated for one year. Initially the warmth of the mystic heat failed to arise within me, and I could hardly bear the piercing wind of the new year blowing about me, together with the frost and snow. Atsara Sale could not endure it, and he left me to serve the Guru as manservant. With my vow as witness I continued my meditation. Blisters erupted all over my body, convulsive pains wracked me within, I began to hiccough incessantly, and I came close to death. Then evoking my Guru I prayed:

Orgyen, Master of Truth, Lord of Beings,
Compassionate sun, shine on me.
This friendless, solitary, naked girl
In her scree house that beckons the wind,
I am an ice-maiden when the blizzards blow.
Frozen between the four slates of my bed and roof,
All activity forgotten, sitting like a heap of earth and rocks,
Here is no outside, inside or golden mean
And I am no White Cotton-clad Ḍākinī.[7]
Now, with the sunlight of your compassion,
Bless me. Ignite the fire of mystic heat and help me.

From a slight respiratory movement brought about by karmic energy, the warmth of mystic heat was generated. Finding even greater certainty and faith in the Lama than before, I sang:

When the real Guru bestowed
The elixir of potent grace
Of the mysteries, the *vajrayāna*,
Then Vajrasattva's Awareness,
The four joys, arose within me.
The White Cotton-clad Ḍākinī assumed her proper place
Giving me the warmth of bliss
And now I am utterly happy.
Still, I ask you to show me your favour.

And as I spoke Lama Orgyen himself appeared in a vision in the guise of an Heruka and gave me a skull-cup of chung[8] to drink before vanishing like a dream.

'In this continuous visionary state my pleasure is real pleasure, warmth is real warmth, and happiness is spiritual joy,' I sang.

Then my frost-bitten, blistered skin was sloughed off like the skin of a snake, and thinking that the time was propitious to practise the austerity of bone ornaments, I cast away my cotton cloth and decked myself with the various bones.[9] That year I practised the austerity called 'the three precepts in one'. For the entire year I had nothing to eat, not even a single grain of barley; for food I relied upon stones and for drink upon water. Thus I sustained my meditation. After some time my previous perception of the nature of mind, and its accompanying insight, had waned. My legs could not bear my body, my body could not support my head, my breathing from the mouth and nose ceased, and my mind seemed totally enervated. My condition grew worse, and finally, coming close to death, I prayed to my Lama, cried from the depths of my heart to my Yidam, and visualised an unbroken stream of offerings to the Ḍākinī:

From the first my body has been offered to you;
You know its happy and sad deeds, Lama.
From the first my speech has followed the Buddha's path;
You know what my stream of breath creates, Lama.
From the first my mind was stirred to virtue;
You know its merits and vices, Lama.
From the first this body was the citadel of the Yidam;
You know the nature of his residence, Lama.
From the first nerves and energy flows were the Ḍākinī's
courses;
You know what these currents create, Lama.
From the first seed-essence was the nature of the Sugatas;
Should I pass into *nirvāṇa* or turn the wheel of the teaching?
Look at the madness of sentient beings, my mothers!
Whatever appears in *saṃsāra* or *nirvāṇa* is adequate sign for me.

Then I had a vision of a red woman, naked, lacking even the covering of bone ornaments, who thrust her *bhaga* against my mouth, and I drank deeply from her copious flow of blood.[10] My entire being was filled with health and well-being, I felt as strong as a snow-lion, and I realised profound absorption to be inexpressible truth.

I decided that the time was ripe to go naked, depending upon the air for sustenance. So for a further year I meditated without any cover for my body with only the air I breathed for food. At first my respiration was easy, and various distinct visionary experiences occurred through the unimpeded play of Knowledge. Later an influx of doubt brought adversity. Respiratory movement ceased, my throat and gullet became extremely parched, my nose was as if stuffed with cotton wool, my bowels were filled with shooting pains, and my intestines shrivelled. It seemed as though I would die. Then taking courage, marshalling my remaining strength, I sang this song to exhort myself to persevere, and then called Guru Rimpoche from afar off:[11]

You girl, out of eternity, took a body and roamed in *saṃsāra*,
Spinning upon the wheel of birth and death,
Suffering in the lower realms,
Enduring heat and cold, hunger and thirst,
Slaving as a beast of burden.
Now the essence of the meaningful human situation,
The direct path of the tantric teaching,
Is quickly traversed by austerity –
For this reason endure whatever occurs.
There is nothing else to do.
Death is no alternative. Take courage Tsogyelma!
KYEMAHO!
Apparitional being, miraculously born in the pollen heart of a lotus,
Spontaneously manifest Lama, Sage of Orgyen,
Lord of Compassion in human form,
Rainbow *maṇḍala*, supreme *vajra*-being,
Look with compassion upon embodied beings,
Save this girl with an ordinary body,
Do whatever you will with this mortal.
Wherever you are, look upon me with loving compassion.

And instantly the Guru appeared in a ball of light, smiling radiantly, and from the distance of a man's height in the sky in front of me, he admonished me thus:

Listen, Daughter of Kharchen,
Royal daughter, infatuated with your own beauty and pleasure,
Ever wont to be intolerant of unpleasant situations,
Now is the time to employ both joy and pain as the path.
Turn whatever suffering arises into the path of pure pleasure,
And be less desirous of an easy life, faithful, virtuous consort.

Listen, Daughter of Kharchen,
King's consort, youthful and vain,

Ever wont to be bound by wantonness and self-will,
Now is the time to abandon futile self-indulgent pursuits.
Meditate upon impermanence, ponder the pain of the lower realms,
And be less ambitious, faithful, virtuous consort.

Listen, Daughter of Kharchen,
Lama's consort, conceited and proud,
Ever wont to consider yourself superior,
Now is the time to reveal your faults.
Do not hide your latent vices, lay bare your inadequacies,
And be less desirous of fame, faithful, virtuous consort.

Listen, Daughter of Kharchen,
Sanctimonious nun and hypocrite,
Ever wont to be over-extended in deceit,
Now is the time to throw off hypocrisy and dissimulation.
Expose your secret self and take courage,
And be less boastful, faithful, virtuous consort.

The Guru then descended to earth, sat upon a rock and continued, 'You are too repressed and too fervent in your practice. You should use essential elixirs of herbs and shrubs to cultivate the play of your intelligence and restore your body to health.'

'Now I, Pema Jungne, can do nothing more for beings here. It remains for me to conceal the ultimately inexhaustible treasures of the sacred teaching (terma)[12] for discovery in the future for as long as *saṃsāra* is not emptied of beings. After these treasures have been hidden, I must go again to Ngayab, to the Land of the Ḍākinīs. You, Tsogyel, will be the custodian of these profound treasures. In the near future, after I have disclosed to you many more of the *maṇḍala*s of the Tantra, the time will be ripe for you to begin work for the sake of others. So prepare yourself!' After granting me extensive instruction, he departed.

Then I took Atsara Sale and a girl called Dewamo to Senge Dzong Sum in Bhutan, where we practised meditation. First, arriving at Senge Dzong, I extracted the essences[13] of various medicinal herbs and shrubs and used them in an alchemical metamorphosis of my psycho-organism. Secondly, I imbibed the essences of minerals. Discovering that the mineral chongshi[14] was 'the essence of all stones', I used it in my continued practice of the alchemical metamorphosis of my body-mind. Then my body became like a *vajra;* it could not be pierced by weapons. My voice gained the quality and tone of Brahmā's sweet voice, so that even a proud tigress hearing it would be pacified and obedient. My mind became set in the *samādhi* that is like an immaterial *vajra.*

Then with sublime purpose I thought that the time was propitious for me to practise the most pure austerity. In the first place, in order to purify the defilements of my speech, I practised approach and identification;[15] through recitation and visualisation the deity invoked approached, and through meditation on Emptiness of the deity I attained union with that deity; and performing liturgical rites without respite I repeated *mantra* in a perpetual stream of sound. First, I practised knowledge *mantra*s and extended *mantra*s (*dharāṇi*), such as the One Hundred Syllable Mantra of Vajrasattva, making atonement by practice of the three classes of *kriyāyoga-tantra.* Second, I recited the extended *mantra*s of the *maṇḍala*s of *upayoga-tantra* and *yoga-tantra,* such as those of the Buddha's Five Aspects and Three Aspects.[16] Finally, applying myself with vigour to the very end, I recited the verbal confessions and vows of the *sūtra*s, the rules and regulations of the *vinaya* discipline, the practices of the Buddha Boundless Life, Amitāyus, and the treatises upon language and logic, etc., of *abhidharma* metaphysics that cultivate the intellect.

At first my voice developed a stammer, quantities of blood and pus oozed out of a rent in my neck, my throat became twisted, parched and paralysed, and various swellings of blood and pus erupted.I came close to death. But finally, however much I used my voice, there was no discomfort. My enunciation was distinct, and the sweet tones of my voice were mellifluous. Whether I spoke loudly, moderately or in a whisper, slowly, conversationally or swiftly, however I spoke I had perfect control. In short, I had been endowed with the sixty elements of speech, and I had gained the seven supports of a retentive memory.

In the second place, according to the procedure of *mahāyoga,* I disclosed the *maṇḍala* of the Sublime Accomplishment of the

Eight Logos Deities. I recited *mantra* with visualisation until all the deities approached in visible form, and then, through absorption in Emptiness, I continued until I had gained union with them. Sitting in lotus posture with hands folded in meditation position, firstly, when the deities appeared, many signs such as blazing light arose and various qualities were generated in my mind. Secondly, I received instructive vision of the Yidam together with his authorisations, and mundane *siddhi* – the eight great *siddhis*,[17] and ultimate realisation in the Bodhisattva's *samādhi* that is like a *vajra*.[18] And finally, I received a prophetic vision indicating liberation into the matrix of Kuntuzangmo.

In the third place, I opened the *maṇḍala* of the Communion of the Lama's Mind according to the procedure of *lung anuyoga*. Training myself in *mantra*, control of vital energies and *samādhi*, I created the *maṇḍalas* of the Mind Communion in the focal points of my psychic nerves, and free of dichotomising concepts I apprehended the reality of psychic nerves, energy flows and seed-essence. At first my nerves ached, my vital energy flows were reversed, my seed-essence was paralysed, and the horror of death's proximity overcame me, but I continued to practise indifferent to these reverses. After some time the deities manifested themselves and I gained control over psychic nerves, vital energy flows and seed-essence; the flows of the four rivers of birth, old-age, sickness and death were dammed; and I was granted the title 'Siddha'.

Then the thought arose in my mind that I was without the means to repay Guru Rimpoche's kindness to me, so I sang this song:

Lord Guru, Pema Jungne, I bow to you!
This pile of dust accumulated from beginningless time,
You, Lord Guru, have transformed into the Sacred Mountain,
And now this mountain of mind will serve others.
Virtuous Indra, come here and be my patron!
Let luckless inhabitants of the valleys be as Great Kings
And all the heavens shall be contented.
This ocean of accumulated droplets gathered from beginningless time,
You, Lord Guru, have transformed into the Seven Lakes of Enjoyment,

And now this Lady of the Lake will serve others.
Virtuous Ānanda, come here and be my *nāga* patron!
Let luckless frogs and fishes of the ponds be as the Eight Great *Nāga* Kings
And all the *nāga* realms shall be contented.
To this Munīndra replete with merit gathered from beginningless time,
You, Lord Guru, have given inexhaustible quality,
And now this Munīndra will serve others.
Lord of Men, Great King, come here and be my patron!
Let luckless barbarian savages be as monks
And the whole world shall be contented.
The reward of virtue collected from beginningless time,
You, Lord Guru, have transformed into this precious human body,
And now this girl will serve others.
Fortunate spiritual sons, come here and be my patrons!
Opinionated, guilty people ignorant of the teaching,
Tibetans having gained faith, this whole land shall be contented.

After I had finished this song in which I expressed my gratitude to the Guru as commitment to selfless service, I extracted and consumed the essences of one hundred and eight psychotropic substances and medicinal shrubs. Then the Four Divine Great Sages[19] appeared surrounded by four hundred and eight goddesses of medicinal substances, each holding a vase containing a different ambrosial panacea, and they sang these verses of praise to me:

KYEMAHO!
Human girl who has discovered the Supreme, the Miraculous,
In the past you were our goddess, our sister,
And wise aspiration brought you great wisdom,
Leading the celestial musicians with the sound of your lute:
We adore you as the Goddess Sarasvatī.
Later, when Munīndra was turning the wheel of the teaching,
Through pure aspiration you became a disciple, a *bhikṣunī*,
Leading all beings with your compassionate eye:
We adore you as the Goddess Gangā Devī.

Now, when Vajradhara as Padma Jungne,
A *vajra*-master, is turning the wheel of the teaching,
You open the door of the mysteries and absorb *mahāyāna* precepts:
We praise you, ascetic Tsogyel, suffering for the sake of others.
All manner of things spring up in the vastness of your mind;
Extracting the essences of medicines and poisons you revel in ambrosia;
In your immortal, youthful body, the ideal marks are complete:
We adore you, mother of beings past, present, and future.
You have cured the chronic diseases of rebirth and death,
Nourishing yourself on the elixir of immortality:[20]
You are the source of all the Buddhas' qualities, Medicine Goddess.
In you, Tsogyel, all these forms are embodied.

Through a synchronistic coincidence of external events and inner needs, a human girl called Khyidren visited me and offered me a large quantity of honey. Consuming it, I began my practice of physical austerity. At first I practised circumambulation, and then, without respite or concern for the passing of day and night, I practised prostrations. But bones began to protrude through the wounds on my forehead, the soles of my feet and the palms of my hands, and a stream of blood and pus ran out of them. I continued regardless, practising countless different purificatory exercises of the body (*the majority of which can be found in various manuals of instruction*). At first my body became fatigued, exhausted, worn out. Then the seed-essence at the joints of my limbs turned to lymph, and feverish, aching, twisting, swelling, my tendons split apart, my muscles slackened, and my body lost its vitality. However, after the poisonous seed-essence separated from the pure, my consciousness expanded; permanently my seed-essence became the nature of Awareness, the knots in my tendons, veins and nerves were united, their flaccidity became tension, their weakness was cured, their worn-out patches were restored, their breaks rejoined and their splits mended. Thus a basis for the accomplishment of the Tantra was established.

Then in the extremely isolated meditation cave of Nering Senge Dzong and other places, after I had sworn an immutable commitment, I continued my physical austerity. I sat in mute *samādhi*, never relaxing the important points of posture,[21] sitting immovable in lotus posture, my eyes set in a fixed gaze. The malicious local gods and demons, however, could not endure my *samādhi*'s glory, and created magical illusions, threatening me with seductive and fierce, embodied and disembodied, phantoms. First they projected themselves as various delectable foods, and repeatedly appeared in front of me. Then they transformed themselves into all manner of material objects, clothes, horses, oxen and every possible necessity and luxury that this world can offer. I overcame all these temptations with my *samādhi*'s radiance. Through my insight into the nature of the world as illusion, inasmuch as I felt profound disgust for attachment to worldly things, some of these phantoms dissolved; by changing earth and stone into dung by the power of my *samādhi* I rendered some repulsive; and some vanished after my wish that they became that district's future store of food and wealth was fulfilled.

On another occasion these demons projected themselves as charming youths, handsome, with fine complexions, smelling sweetly, glowing with desire, strong and capable, young men at whom a girl need only glance to feel excited. They would begin by addressing me respectfully, but they soon became familiar, relating obscene stories and making lewd suggestions. Sometimes they would play games with me: gradually they would expose their sexual organs, whispering, 'Would you like this, sweetheart?' and 'Would you like to milk me, darling?' and other such importunities, all the time embracing me, rubbing my breasts, fondling my vagina, kissing me, and trying all kinds of seductive foreplay. Overcome by the splendour of my *samādhi*, some of them vanished immediately; some I reduced to petty frauds by insight into all appearances as illusion; by means of the Bodhisattva's meditation that produces revulsion, I transformed some into black corpses, some into bent and frail geriatrics, some into lepers, some into blind, deformed, dumb or ugly creatures, and without exception they all vanished.

Then these malicious gods and demons demonstrated their violent devices. The earth moved beneath me, shaking and quaking, emitting an empty roar louder than the bellow of a

thousand dragons, with the intolerable banging of black lightning, the roaring of white lightning, the swishing of red lightning, the knocking of yellow lightning, the baying of blue lightning, the shimmering of iridescent lightning, and the blazing of the light of the sky. Likewise, I was threatened by a terrific display of weapons, various knives, sharp-pointed daggers and spears, all glistening steel-blue, bristling menacingly, jostling for space. I dissolved these apparitions with my *samādhi* of divine assurance.

Another day I was besieged by phantom herds of ferocious beasts. Tigers, leopards, bears, yetis and other carnivores appeared, roaring above and outside the cave entrance. From my right and from my left, animals attacked from every direction, howling in their various styles, their mouths gaping ravenously, snarling in rage, beating their tails, their paws scratching at me, shaking their bodies, hackles risen, hair bristling. From the assurance I had gained from abandoning attachment to my body and love of myself, arose compassion for all these beasts, and they vanished. Then, leaving me with no respite, a vast army of billions of different insects and worms led by spiders, scorpions and snakes inundated the area. Some slipped through my sensory doors, some bit me, some stung me, some scratched me, some climbed over me, some jumped upon me, some fought each other, ate each other and left piles of carcasses scattered about. There was no trick that these insects failed to use to frighten me. I shuddered a little, yet I found pity in my heart, but the insects became increasingly terrifying and loathsome. 'Since I have often vowed that I will in no way be attached to any form of body, speech or mind,' I thought to myself, 'why should I now be afraid of such illusory tricks of spirits, the activity of sentient beings – insects – that is karmic manifestation? Because all behaviour is determined by positive or negative concepts, I should understand that whatever occurs, good or bad, is a mental construct, and so keep a level head.' With this thought I regained my assurance, and I sang:

> All 'phenomena' are only tricks of the mind;[22]
> I see nothing to fear in inner space.
> All this is nothing but clear light's natural radiance;
> There is no reason at all to react.

Since all activity is my ornamentation
I should remain in mute meditative absorption.

And so saying, I entered the *samādhi* of universal identity in which there is no discrimination or evaluation, and the apparitions vanished.

Again a variety of shapes and forms appeared. Many limbs without bodies hung in space before me. Many exceedingly repulsive forms flashed in and out of my vision, writhing around in spectral configurations in space. An enormous head without a body, its upper jaw lost in the clouds and its lower jaw resting on the ground its tongue lolling in between, its fangs gleaming white, approached closer and closer. Other violent forms also appeared: within a castle the size of a mustard seed many men struggled and fought; fires blazed, floods poured forth, landslides hurtled down, trees fell, gales blew, etc., but always I would sit unmoving in *vajra*-like *samādhi*, and the forms would vanish.

'We are the legions of gods and demons, Khatra and Kangtra,[23] come hither from the southern lands lying between E in Nepal and Ja in Bhutan,' pronounced a voice, and these demons proceeded to threaten me with various sounds. Some wept, some raged, some wailed and some roared. Then thunderbolts fell from above, fire blazed up from below, and in between rivers flowed backwards. Blizzards of various weapons swirled about me. In this manner they strove to obstruct my meditation. But with my intuitive understanding fully charged, my awareness expanded, my insight's nerves opened, attaining irreversible faith, I sang:

Since I entered the dimension of dynamic space,
Reaching the Mind of the Great Mother, absolute, empty being,
The heart of the ten transcendental perfections,[24]
Enjoying profound and perfect insight,
I am not to be cowed by visionary experience.
Every situation is a play of empty being,
The magical illusion that is the Lama's compassion:
Now stir my creativity still more!
Since I entered the dimension of spontaneity,
Reaching the Mind of Lama Kunzang,

The heart of Vision, Meditation and the Goal,
Enjoying the unstructured quality of every occurrence,
I am no coward in the face of my thought-forms.
Every event is a display of mental projections,
The thought-forms that are the Lama's compassion:
Now excite my creative skill still more!
Since I entered the dimension of pure pleasure,
Reaching the Mind of the Lotus Born Guru,
The heart of all-encompassing Ati,
Enjoying the mind's immaculate nature,
I no longer possess a sense of impurity.
The welter of defilements are the stuff of reality,
The forms of vision that are the Lama's compassion:
Now inspire my creative expression still more!
Since I entered the arena of mystic practice,
Arriving at the heart of the *mahāyāna* mysteries,
Enjoying the identical flavour of pleasure and pain,
I have no preference for good or bad.
Both good and bad are lifts to peak experience,
To the visual experience that is the Lama's compassion:
Now arouse my creative potential still more!

At the end of my song legions of Indian, Nepali and Tibetan gods and demons again rose up. With three of their number – the red, blue and black – appointed as leaders, they attempted to create obstacles through many different devices, but they were in no way successful. Then they induced human beings to tempt me. Through these gods' and demons' machinations a thick black fog blanketed the land of Bhutan so that the day was as night. Thunderbolts and hail blighted the fields, blizzards swept down, pestilence struck, and confusion reigned in the land as these and other calamities struck the people.

'Who is harming us?' they asked one another. 'Why is this happening?'

A Bhutanese hunter had happened to catch a glimpse of me in my cave. 'There's a dumb Tibetan woman up there in the Nering Drak Cave,' he told them. 'She must be the cause. Why look any further?'

They all agreed with him, and forming a lynching mob they came up to the cave to kill me. 'You starving Tibetan corpse!'

they cried. 'You have been practising black magic. Now our land of Bhutan is enshrouded in darkness. Thick fog has descended upon the country. Thunderbolts and hail have laid waste our fields, and pestilence and other disasters have befallen us. Remove your curses! If you refuse, we will kill you immediately!'

'It seems that the malicious devices of these gods and demons have harmed the local people,' I thought. 'There is nothing positive that I can do. I will account whatever occurs a creation of my mind and meditate upon it. Come what may I will not break my vow.' And refusing to answer them I kept still with my gaze fixed, staring at the nature of my mind.

'She's paralysed by guilt,' said some. 'Perhaps she can't hear us,' said others. So they threw ashes into my eyes and poked knives into my ears. I sat where I was, totally detached, thought-free. 'She must be a yeti!' they cried, and then they proceeded to shoot their arrows at me, beat me with their clubs, stab at me with their spears and slash at me with their knives. But no matter in what way they attacked me or with what weapons, they caused absolutely no harm to my body. They gave me the name Invulnerable Tibetan, and not knowing what to do they dispersed to their homes.

Then the girl who had previously brought me honey returned. She was the daughter of a Bhutanese king, and she possessed great power and wealth. Filled with high faith she prostrated before me, and then departed. Thereafter, from time to time, she would bring me buffalo milk and sometimes honey, serving me in every way that might please me.

Not long after, led by devils, local demons and *nāgas*, all the gods and demons who had previously threatened me with their illusions came to offer their lives to me. The devils, local demons and *nāgas* in particular, vowed to protect my *dharma* and to destroy my enemies:

> EH HO HO!
> Only Consort of Guru Pema Skull-Garland Pleasure,
> Ḍākinī Heruka, unvanquished heroine,
> We confess our devilish crimes.
> Now as your entourage, we offer you our very lives,
> Faithfully vowing to obey your every command.

Then, individually, they offered their lives to me, and departed.

Similarly, all the great and terrible gods and demons of Tibet – Rahula, Dorje Lekpa and others – offered their lives, and promised to protect the teaching. Then the men and women who had previously tried to harm me gathered there, and confessing their faults they paid homage to me. In particular, King Hamras of Bhutan came in a state of wonder and credulity. I asked him to give me his beautiful thirteen-year-old daughter, who had all the marks and signs of a Ḍākinī, and who was called Khyidren (Leader of Dogs). With strong faith and devotion the King presented her to me, and I conferred the name Tashi Chidren (Fortunate Guide of Mankind) upon her. I then took her to Paro Taktsang.

At Paro Taktsang I began the last austerity to be practised for my own benefit. This was the austerity of 'the seed-essence of co-incident pleasure and Emptiness'.[25] With my consorts Atsara Sale, a Bhutanese boy called Sale and Atsara Pelyang, all three invigorated by nutritious herbal elixirs, I disciplined myself in the cultivation of creative skill to its full potential for seven months through day and night without respite. At first, shaking and trembling, my body was enervated and my mind was stunned and intoxicated. Lymph saturated my whole body, above and below, and diseased, aching, feverish and trembling, I came close to death. But later, all the lymph was transmuted into the nature of seed-essence and pleasure flooded my entire body. Initially this pleasure was contaminated by passion, but soon it became a field of Awareness and finally an unremitting flow of Awareness. Red and white seed-essence gradually blended into an homogenous mixture, and the resulting seed-essence was not capable of evolving into dualistic vision. After placing my psycho-organism into the Conqueror's *maṇḍala*, through offering pleasure and worshipping in pleasure the full potential of pleasure was aroused and sealed in the body of pure pleasure. Red radiance suffused my white body, and retaining the appearance of a charming, sixteen-year-old maiden, my body was transformed into the pure being of an Heruka Ḍākinī Heroine (Vajra Vārāhī). At the same time I had a vision of Amitāyus' *maṇḍala*, and in the immutable being of a *vajra*-body I accomplished the Immortal Knowledge Holder[26] who is free of ageing and infirmity. At that time I received a prophecy that I would live for 225 years in this world; Glorious Hayagrīva and Vajra Vārāhī exorcised obstructive spirits; the Five Buddha Heroes and the Five Ḍākinīs became my constant companions, accompanying me like shadows and performing whatever magical transformation was necessary with unimpeded efficiency; the Bodhisattvas gave auspicious benediction; and since I was now a Knowledge Holder with power over my life-span I was given the name Radiant Sky-blue Mistress of Life (Tsedak Tingwo Barma).

Thereafter, I and my five companions went to Womphu Takstang where Guru Rimpoche was staying. When we met him I prostrated, and greeting me he said, 'So you have come, Ḍākinī Heruka! What a surprise! I thought that you would have lost heart!' And he continued:

O *yoginī* who has mastered the Tantra,
The human body is the basis of the accomplishment of wisdom
And the gross bodies of men and women are equally suited,
But if a woman has strong aspiration, she has higher potential.
From beginningless time you have accrued merit from virtue
  and awareness,
And now, faultless, endowed with a Buddha's Qualities,
Superior woman, you are a human Bodhisattva.
This is you I am speaking of, happy girl, is it not?
Now that you have achieved your own enlightenment,
Work for others, for the sake of other beings.
Such a marvellous woman as you
Never existed in the world before,
Not in the past, not at present,
Nor in the future – of this I am certain.
Yeshe Tsogyel, a la la!
Hereafter, in the future, at the end of your time,
You will project five emanations,
And the Buddha's doctrine will survive 30 more years.
Specifically, in a place called Lab in the Land of Dak[27]
A woman will appear known as Drolma
And imbibe the essences of the Great Mother's precepts;
She will spread the Zap-chod Doctrine, Profound Severance,
And her teaching will produce the highest good of beings.
At that time Atsara Sale will appear as a monk called Topa,

And as the Ḍākinī's Consort he will open your secret door;
The Bhutanese girl, Tashi Khyidren, will be your only daughter;
This Bhutanese boy, Sale, will be your spiritual son
And act in the manner of a crazy saint;
Atsara Pelyang will appear as a monk called Drapa Ngonshe,
And after becoming the Ḍākinī's mystic consort
He will achieve his own and others' supreme purpose.
Then I, Pema Jungne, named Dampa of India,[28]
Coming from Lato, will preach Zhi-je, the Doctrine of Peace,
And after you and I, Lady, have encountered each other,
Circumstances beneficial to the Tantra will arise;
The Doctrine of Zhi-je, the profound path of skilful means,
Will bring temporary comfort to the world.
After that you will not stay long;
Thereafter, in supreme fields of lotus light,
You and I will unite,
And serve beings through the body of visionary enjoyment.

After the Guru had given this prophecy, he reassured me further, and again I sang a song of thanksgiving:

Vajradhara, Stem of the Mysteries,
Amitāyus, free from death and free from causality,
Heruka, Master of Magical Power:
These three are united in you, Pema Jungne, alone.
And since I have depended upon you, finding no other,
Out of your kindness, Supreme Guide,
I attained the *siddhi* of the Tantra:
I accomplished the miraculous powers of the eight great *siddhi*s,
And I became master of both *sūtra* and *tantra*.
My birth was low but my merit was great;
Now my body has been transfigured
And ordinary vision has permanently vanished;
The *samādhi* in which all is illusion has arisen,
And I control the five elements.
Now my speech has become *mantra*
And useless, vacant gossip is a thing of the past;
The *vajra*-like *samādhi* has arisen,
And intuitively I know and use the modes of *sūtra* and *tantra*.
Now my mind has become Buddha,

And my ordinary thoughts have vanished into empty space;
The *samādhi* of a Bodhisattva has arisen
And my Mind is identical to Vajradhara.
What great kindness, Lord Guru!
While there is time, form, rebirth and life,
If I would forsake your lotus feet
I could never find another Guru such as you.
So never deprive me of your compassion.
Such great kindness as yours I can never repay.
If in the past, overwhelmed by unknowing,
I have been in conflict, even in part,
With your Body, Speech, Mind, Qualities or Action,
I acknowledge it. And I promise that hereafter
I will avoid every conflict, even in the slightest degree.
Now, for the sake of all beings, out of your great kindness,
I beg you to turn the wheel of the tantric teaching.

Then I related in detail how I had performed my austerities, how I attained *siddhi*, in what manner the illusory devices of gods, demons and men arose, and most particularly, how through my experience of the Tantra at Paro Taktsang I had seen the deities of the *maṇḍala* of Amitāyus. Radiating satisfaction, the Guru placed his right hand upon my head, 'In your present state it is propitious for you to practise the Yoga of the Immortal Knowledge Holder. Your experience in Paro Taktsang was merely an indication that if with the Guru's compassion you practise in such a way, then a certain result will occur. I will reveal to you the *maṇḍala* of Amitāyus and grant you initiation and empowerment, and then you must find a consort who will act as mainstay in the long-life practice.

'Also, this Bhutanese girl, Khyidren, has all the marks and signs of an Awareness Ḍākinī, a vajrakarmakī, and if you give her to me I will employ her as the consort of Dorje Phurba, fulfilling the need to spread the secret teachings of Dorje Phurba. Otherwise in this dull land of Tibet the Tantra will stagnate, and *yogin*s will be unable to protect even their own lives. The many gods and demons throughout Tibet who are hostile to the spread of the tantric doctrine will cause obstacles, and they will prevent the doctrine's propagation. Even if the doctrine spreads, it will soon wane.'

I prostrated, and as a thanksgiving offering, I presented a plate of gold and turquoises, together with Tashi Khyidren, to the Guru. Then I made this request: 'O Great Guru, I thank you for your offer to give me the secret instructions upon the Yoga of Immortality. What kind of consort is required as an aid in this practice? Is not Atsara Sale qualified? It is exceedingly magnanimous of you to reveal the *maṇḍala* of Dorje Phurba, so I offer you the girl Khyidren. Embrace her with your compassion, and please, please, reveal the tantric mysteries to her.

'Inadequate women like me with little energy and an inferior birth incur the whole world's hostility. When we go begging the dogs are hostile. If we possess food or wealth then thieves molest us. If we are attractive we are bothered by fornicators. If we work hard the country people are hostile. Even if we do nothing at all the tongues of malicious gossips turn against us. If our attitude is improper then the whole world is hostile. Whatever we do, the lot of a woman on the path is a miserable one. To maintain our practice is virtually impossible, and even to stay alive is very difficult. Therefore, I beg of you to give me the secret instructions upon Dorje Phurba also.'

The Guru thought for a moment, and then replied, 'The practice of the Yoga of Immortality is like a general, while Phurba is like a protecting escort. It is certainly of great importance, no matter what your principal tantric practise, to cultivate Phurba, the Remover of Obstacles; but it is of more relevance that your personal deity is Phurba, so I will initiate you.' And then he continued, 'No matter whether you practice Phurba or the Yoga of Immortality, you need a partner for practice. Go to Uru in Central Tibet, and there you will find a fourteen-year-old boy of *caṇḍāla* cast whose father's name is Lhapel and whose mother's name is Chokroza. You will undertake practice with him, and you will accomplish your deity.'

I found the boy according to the Guru's prediction, and together we returned to Pema Jungne. The Guru said:

This boy is a Knowledge Holder who has Phurba's *siddhi*;
Possessing indestructible life-force he is invulnerable.
The Deity named him Devil Destroying Buddha Hero (Dudul Pawo),

And since he appeared as a lion at his initiatory
 enthronement
The name Lhalung Pelgyi Senge was conferred upon him.

Upon Pelgyi Senge's induction into the *maṇḍala* of the tantric mysteries, he gained spiritual maturity.

Then the Guru's five 'root' spiritual sons – Lhalung Pelgyi Senge, Namkhai Nyingpo of Lhodrak, Ma Rinchen Chok, Dorje Dunjom and I, Tsogyel – together with the girl Dewamo, were assigned roles in the initiatory rite of Dorje Phurba by the Guru. Dewamo, who was renamed Chonema, the Glorious Priestess, was appointed the Vajra Hostess (Dorje Jenmo); Atsara Sale and Atsara Pelyang were appointed Vajra Dancers (Dorje Gingpa) and renamed Karma Dondrub and Karma Tarje; the Bhutanese boy Sale was appointed Vajra Attendant (Vajrakarmaka); and then, at the beginning, he made me the 'root consort' and Tashi Khyidren the 'liberating consort'. Then after the Guru had revealed the forty-two etram *maṇḍala*s associated with the *Dorje Phurba Tantra Byitotama,*[29] and the *maṇḍala*s of the seventy-eight Phurbas, the Guru and we two mystic partners practised for seven days. All the signs and marks appeared to perfection. The gods attendant upon Dorje Phurba manifested to the eye, and the symbolic phurbas, the sacred ritual daggers, bounced, danced and flew, and shining brightly they became redolent with perfume. The evening that these miraculous signs appeared, the Guru himself was transformed into Dorje Trollo (Adamantine Sagging Belly) with myself as Ekajaṭī (The Crone with One Hair Knot) joined in union with him, and Tashi Khyidren as our mount, the tigress, to subject the gods and demons of the microcosmic worlds of the four quarters of Tibet. Riding upon the back of the girl Khyidren transformed into a tigress, the Guru and his mystic partner absorbed in the *samādhi* of Dorje Phurba, holding a nine-pronged *vajra* in his right hand and rolling a phurba of bell-metal in his left hand, the Guru projected countless fierce, terrifying beings in forms identical to himself. In particular, one of these forms called Blue-black Vajra Wrathful Phurba (Tingnak Dorje Trophur) flew directly to Paro Taktsang, and there he subjected gods, demons, wrathful Ḍākinīs, and demon savages and the three eight-fold classes of spirits[30] of the barbarian borderlands and beyond – Bhutan,

Nepal, India and Lho – and bound them to serve the *dharma*. Another emanation called Purple Vajra Wrathful Phurba (Muknak Dorje Trophur) flew as far as the second Taktsang, in Kham, and subjected the gods, demons and demon savages and the three eight-fold classes of spirits in the barbarian lands of Kham, Jang, China and Hor, binding them to serve the *dharma*, taking away their life-essence.

At that time a venomous *nāga*-serpent who lived in an inlet of Lake Mānasarovar escaped from the Purple Vajra Wrathful Phurba, and transforming himself into a red ox he begged for sanctuary at the Emperor's feet. This red ox appeared to the Emperor with feet bound by an iron chain, a deep wound in his head out of which seeped blood and brains, his tongue distended and his eyes bulging. The Emperor asked him who had afflicted him so, and the ox answered, 'The savage wretch from the borderlands (Mon) called Pema Jungne is systematically exterminating both the gods and men of Tibet. Just now he has been scourging even innocent gods and demons, and I have come to you, the Emperor, for refuge.'

The Emperor, moved to pity, told the ox that sanctuary was granted, but at that very instant the red ox vanished into thin air. The Emperor was pondering the meaning of this strange occurrence when the Guru's voice echoed in his ears:

Your sympathy is sadly misplaced, O Emperor!
Now in all your future existences
Siddhi will always be fraught with obstacles.
The Buddha's future followers will have short lives and ill-luck;
In the third generation, this red-ox demon,
Transformed into a prince called Ox (Langdarma)
Will kill his brother and establish an iniquitous regime,
Eradicating even the names of *sūtra* and *tantra*.
However, this is *karma* and cannot be deflected.

At that Pelgyi Dorje prayed, 'May I be able to destroy this Ox King!'

'So be it! So be it!' said the Guru, and ordained through prophecy that indeed Pelgyi Dorje would kill the Ox King. He gave him initiation and empowerment, and it was then that he conferred upon him the name Pelgyi Dorje. He also gave him detailed predictions and personal advice written upon a scroll. The Guru then granted him the practice of the rites of the Twenty Mahāśākti Kīlayas,[31] who are endowed with great magical powers, instructing him to practise them immediately.

Then I, the woman Tsogyel, with the youth Pelgyi Senge, achieved identity with Dorje Phurba, and very soon we had a vision of the deities of Phurba's *maṇḍala* and gained Phurba's *siddhi*. Then the Guru gave us the method of accomplishing auto-initiation, the personal practice and the general practice in assembly of Phurba Chidu, which is associated with the subsidiary cycle of *Dorje Zhonnu*. The *Phurba Chidu* has two sections: the upper part contains the means of obtaining enlightenment through the peaceful method of practice associated with Vajrasattva, and the lower part contains the means of effecting particular *karma*s, such as killing, through the liberating *karma* of the Poisonous Black Phurba (Dukphur Nakpo) associated with the Son Kīlaya. When he had given us this empowerment the Guru said, 'I, Pema Jungne, possess nothing more profound pertaining to Dorje Phurba than this teaching. Practise it and extract magical power from it. You should transmit part of this cycle as oral teaching of the pronouncement lineage and part of it as treasure to be revealed in the future.' Then he gave us visionary indications.

Later, he gave us the *maṇḍala*, precepts and method of accomplishment of the Garland of Light of Immortal Amitāyus, the Vajra Garland, the Communion of All Secrets, the Communion of All the Conquerors, the Hundred Thousand Gods in One, the Sixty-two Gods of Long-life,[32] and others. Pelgyi Dorje and I, brother and sister, practised without an instant of inertia, and, the deities manifesting themselves, we accomplished the Immortal Knowledge Holder in happiness.

At this time Tsogyel annihilated the heretical Bon-shamans, but that is related below together with a description of the practice of her final austerities.

Tsogyel practised meditation throughout Greater Tibet in a way that is beyond the mind's power to grasp: below Tise (Kailāś) and above Jampaling, on twenty-five mountain peaks, in eighteen great forts, a hundred and twenty-eight minor power spots, twelve great hidden valleys, seven places of miracles, five secret power spots, and seven million spots where treasures were concealed. Some of these places are mentioned below. The details are not given here due to fear of the immense length.

Thus ends the fifth chapter in which is described how Tsogyel practised meditation and performed her austerities.

SAMAYA GYA GYA GYA!

CHAPTER SIX

SIGNS OF SUCCESS AND PROOFS OF POWER

An extensive account of the evidence of Tsogyel's success in some meditation practices has been included above. Here is her own short description in verse.[1]

At Tidro, inspired by the Ḍākinīs' symbolic indications,
I practised austerity, and evidence of success appeared.
Where shale and snow met, I found the mystic heat's inner
  warmth
And I took off my samsaric clothes.
In the Assembly Hall, possessing the warmth of the four
  empowerments,
I transformed the visual world into the Lama's ideal form.
In Nepal, I resurrected the corpse of a dead man,
Ransoming Atsara, my Skilful Means, by skill in means.
I attained the *siddhi* of zap-lam's nectar:
My voice gained Brahmā's quality and tone,
My body became a sky-dancing rainbow body,
And my mind, the Mind of Buddhas past, present and future.
At Senge Dzong, I drank alchemical, medicinal elixirs
And received a visitation of the gods of medicine.
At Nering, I subjected the legions of devils,
And temptation overcome I gained *siddhi*.
Accomplishing each Yidam I invoked and seeing his face,
I easily gained the *siddhi* of each with pleasure.
At Paro Taktsang, I practised on the profound path of zap-lam[2]

With three partners, pure pleasure Herukas:
I gained control of nerves, seed-essence and energy flows
And controlling the five elements I gained self-control;
My body, speech and mind became the Buddha's three modes;
I received Amitāyus' visionary prophecy;
I became inseparable from Vajra Vārāhī herself;
I became the chief Ḍākinī of all *maṇḍalas*.
At Womphu Taktsang, Dorje Phurba was accomplished,
And I took the life-essence of the microcosmic worlds' gods
and demons;
I saw the divine host of Amitāyus' *maṇḍala*,
The Immortal Knowledge Holder was accomplished
And my body became inviolate, indestructible like a *vajra*.
In Upper and Lower Tibet and the areas in between,
Innumerable power-places witnessed my practice
And I blessed them all,
Neglecting never a handful of earth.
The future will gradually reveal this truth
For each treasure discovered will be evidence of it.
And in numerous minor power places
Rocks were marked with my hand and foot-prints,
And *mantras*, seed-syllables and images were placed there,
Left as articles of faith for the future
With prayers that qualified devotees will discover them.

(*Details of Tsogyel's destruction of devils and heretics, signs of her* siddhi, *follow later*.)

Through intuition of the reality and manipulation of the five
elements[3]
I filled the earth below with treasures;
Through my attainment of an infallible memory
I absorbed the pronouncements of Pema Jungne;
Through the achievement of fearless conviction
I predicted the future, strengthening the destiny of the
fortunate;
Through identification with all the Buddhas,
Perfectly, I performed the deeds of Sugatas past, present and
future.
And thus I gained these ornaments of spiritual power:

My mundane *siddhis*, in brief, are control of phenomena,
Speed-walking, the eye-salve of omniscience, the healing pills of everlasting life,
And the *siddhis* of sky-dancing, dancing through matter and the mystic dance.
And my supreme *siddhi*: possessing the three *samādhis*,[4]
Dynamic Mind, the vast expanse of Kuntuzangmo,
Reality is disclosed as an ornamental display.
I have no hope for higher states nor fear of the hells,
But my vision is not nihilistic, not extreme,
For I possess the conviction of profound Emptiness;
I have reached the goal, Dzokchen's pure potential,
Where all pervasive Ati is spontaneously accomplished.[5]
My mind is co-extensive with space,
My compassion is more radiant than the sun,
My blessings are more extensive than an immense cloud
And my *siddhi* falls faster than gentle rain.
So you of the future with faith,
Pray! and reading the language of synchronicity
You possess the answer to your ultimate prayer.[6]
I will guide you out of the lower realms:
If you deny that, you deny all the Conquering Buddhas.[7]
False views and opinions cause you to suffer,
But again my compassion will not forsake you,
And *karma* exhausted, you become my converts.

Thus ends the sixth chapter in which Tsogyel describes in verse the evidence of her success in meditation and the nature of her siddhi.

SAMAYA GYA GYA GYA!

CHAPTER SEVEN

ESTABLISHING, SPREADING AND PERPETUATING THE TEACHING

The Buddha's teaching has no other purpose than the welfare of mankind. The well-being of mankind is the only object of a Buddha's activity. Therefore there are three parts to this chapter that describes the way in which Tsogyel served all living beings. The first part *describes the manner in which she firmly established the precious tradition of the Buddha's teaching, exorcising evil spirits and converting diabolists and unbelievers.* The second part *describes how having established the tradition she disseminated the teachings of* sūtra *and* tantra, *thereby expanding the monastic communities and sustaining them. And* the third part *describes how she concealed an inexhaustible wealth of apocalyptic teaching-treasures to be revealed in the future so that the Word of the Conquerors would not disappear but increase until* saṃsāra *is emptied of worldly desire.*

Nyatri Tsenpo, descended from the Śākya Clan of India, was enthroned king of all Tibet. He propagated the Bon religion. The last of his line was Lhatotori, in whose reign the Buddha's teaching was introduced into Tibet. The name of Indian Śākyamuni became well-known in the Four Districts of Central Tibet, and the people received transmission of the practice of the ten virtues.[1] At this time the doctrines of Reformed Bon were propagated widely. The practice of these doctrines was in accord with the Buddha's teaching. The Reformed Bon believed that the Buddha Śākyamuni and the Bon Master, Shenrab, were two forms of one essence, and painted scrolls depicting this relationship became popular. This new movement became known as The New Translation of Zhang-zhung.[2] During the lifetime of the Buddhist Emperor Songtsen Gampo, who was an emanation of Arya Avalokiteśvara, two images of the Lord Buddha were brought to Tibet and installed in the Lhasa and Ramoche Temples, which the King had built for that purpose. He raised one hundred and eight other temples that were instrumental in the conversion of the Four Districts and the borderlands.[3] Many clay and cast images, and painted scrolls depicting the gods, all of Nepali or Chinese design, became popular.

When the naturally manifest image called Jowo Zhalzema (Tārā) miraculously appeared in Trandruk, the astonished King built a particularly sublime temple for her. The sacred name of the Three Jewels as Deity, the practice of the Six Syllable Mantra (OM MAṆI PADMA HŪNG), and the image of Great Compassion (Mahākaruṇika – Tujechembo), spread throughout the Land of Tibet as far as the Chinese border. Both the Buddha's teaching and reformed Bon spread, existing together free of prejudice. There was no distinction made between the values of different practices. Thus it was said regarding circumambulation, to ambulate anti-clockwise indicated Dzokchen, to ambulate clockwise indicated *mahāmudrā*, and to make prostration indicated Umachembo (*mahāmadhyamaka*). The King established a law based upon the ten virtues. Tonmi Saṃbhoṭa translated many *tantras* of Tujechembo, extensive, abridged and concise, and the King, his ministers, courtiers and queens, lived strictly according to their commitments and pledges to that deity.

Twenty-five years after the God-king died, the influence of the heretical Bon-shamans increased, and both the Buddha's teaching and Reformed Bon were bitterly persecuted. The followers of Reformed Bon were muted even as they are today. Some were banished to Kham, some to Jar and other outlying places, until none remained in Central Tibet. When the Buddha's teaching was threatened with eradication, the King and his ministers were at odds, but influence prevented further persecution, although faith remained at a low ebb. The religion of the misguided Bon-shamans corrupted the country, so that later, at the time of the Buddhist Emperor Trisong Detsen, conditions had been created that made propagation of the Buddha's teaching very difficult.

The religion of the Bon-shamans with its deviant metaphysics held that there were no such places as pure-lands. Their gods were spirits – gyalpo, gongpo and others of the eight-fold classes of spirits – and country gods and earth-lords, and Cha and Yang, Gods of Chance and Fortune, and other mundane entities. Their religion prescribed exchange of daughters for marriage to sons, and elaborate wedding celebrations. Their teachings were transmitted as inspired fables and legends. It was believed that Cha and Yang, the Gods of Chance and Fortune, could be propitiated by dance and song. In autumn they performed a blood sacrifice of a thousand wild asses. In spring they performed a rite in which the legs of a hind were offered to the gods as ransom for new life. In winter blood sacrifice was made to the Bon-god (Bon-lha), and in summer they killed an offering and made sacrifice to the Bon Master (Shen-rab). Thus they accumulated the *karma* of the ten vicious actions and the inexpiable sins. Concerning their metaphysical vision, the universe was held to be immaterial mindstuff in the form of gods and demons, so whatever the mind conceived was a god or demon. Their highest goal was rebirth in the sphere of utter nothingness; failing that rebirth in the sphere of infinity; or at least rebirth in limbo where there is neither existence nor non-existence.[4] The sign of success of their rites was actual manifestation of the god propitiated, who at best would eat the flesh of a sentient being or drink its blood, or at least appear as a rainbow. The common people with little intelligence were impressed by such signs, and believing in the philosophy of the Bon-shamans were led to disaster. Anyhow, this perverse religion of the Bon-shamans pervaded the country, patronised by the majority of the *zhang* ministers. At this time the sacred Buddhist paintings and sculpture disappeared, the Buddha's teaching was no longer taught, the Lhasa and Trandruk temples fell into ruins and the provincial temples were destroyed.

Tibet was in a state of anarchy when Āyra Mañjuśrī incarnated as the Buddhist Emperor Trisong Detsen in order to restore the traditions of the Buddha's teaching. The King invited many scholars from India, amongst whom was the Bodhisattva of Zahor, Śāntarakṣita. The temples of Lhasa, Trandruk and Ramoche, which had been built in fulfilment of the sacred pledge of the Emperor Songtsen Gampo, were repaired and reconsecrated. Then preparation was made for the construction of the Samye Temple, but the Tibetan gods, men and Bonpos caused so many obstacles that construction was postponed. The Abbot, the Bodhisattva Śāntarakṣita of Zahor, gave this prophetic injunction: 'No man embodied, nor god nor demon disembodied, can ever harm one who has attained an immutable *vajra*-body. Invite the Lotus Born Master of Orgyen here, otherwise you and I, priest and patron, will face obstacles at every turn.'

Acting upon this advice the King sent three of his trustworthy courtiers, who had studied language, to India to invite Orgyen Guru Rimpoche to Tibet. The three translators arrived at the feet of the Guru without incident, and having delivered their invitation they returned with him to Tibet. The King, his ministers courtiers and queens were involuntarily seized with faith. An envoy of distant welcome was sent as far as Zhongda; the second envoy of welcome met him at Lhasa; and the King himself with his entourage welcomed him in the Ombu Grove. Leading his guest's horse by the bridle to Samye, the King and patron gained an immediate rapport with his Guru and priest. The King, his ministers, courtiers and the queens all gazed at the Guru with devotion, and overwhelmed by his splendour, the radiance of his being, they were impelled to obey him without hesitation. The Abbot also prostrated before him, and passed some time with him in religious discussion.

After the King, his ministers and their entourage, together with the Abbot, Master and translators, had come to Samye, the Guru examined the site of the projected temple and made his prognosis.

'During the lifetime of my ancestor Songtsen Gampo,' said the King, 'one hundred and eight temples were constructed. But because they were scattered it was not possible to attend to them, and they fell into ruin. I would like to build a like number of temples within the confines of a single wall.'

The Guru agreed, and out of his *samādhi* he magically projected a vision of four temples each with two satellite temples surrounding a central pagoda temple within a confining wall, a spectacle that all beheld. This design represented the *maṇḍala* of Mount Meru with its surrounding continents and satellite islands. 'Great King, if we create this vision in wood and stone, will it please your heart?' asked the Guru.

The King was delighted. 'This is inconceivable! Surely it is impossible to fulfil such a dream! If we indeed succeed, this temple complex shall be called Samye, The Inconceivable.'

'Widen your horizons, Great King!' the Guru replied. 'Act! and nothing can stand in your way. As you the King have dominion over human beings, the embodied beings of Tibet, and I control the formless, disembodied gods and demons, why should we not succeed?'

So Samye was constructed. The outer shell completed and purified, the temples were filled with receptacles of the Buddha's Body, Speech and Mind – images, books and *stūpas* – piled up high. Then the monastic community was assembled. One hundred and eight brilliant translators, who were karmically favoured, were chosen according to the Guru's intuitive judgment. Further, three thousand men were assembled from the thirteen principalities,[5] and of these three thousand, three hundred were ordained as monks by the Abbot. The Guru became their master (*vajrācārya*). But when the translators began their work on the scriptures, the Bon ministers who were hostile to the Buddha's teaching and the Bon-shamans referred to above, began to create obstacles. On several occasions translators were banished separately to border areas through the machinations of these diabolists. After the translators' work had been stopped for a third time, the King was forced to accord the Bon religion equal status with the Buddhist, and it was decided that the Bonpos should found the monastery called Bongso in Yarlung.

After the King and his ministers had been reconciled, twenty-one scholars were invited at once from India.[6] The hundred and eight translators who had been dispersed were reassembled at Samye, and three thousand candidates for orders gathered from the thirteen principalities to be ordained simultaneously. From Zhang-zhung and other Bon areas seven Bon scholars and seven Bon magicians were invited to Ombu. The King sent three courtiers to meet and to escort the great translator Drenpa Namkha Wongchuk; to Guru Rimpoche, who was living with me in Womphu Taktsang, he offered a magnificent horse named Nine Galloping Garudas;[7] and to all the other translators and candidates he dispatched a horse and a pack animal. In this way we all arrived at Samye quickly.

The Guru insisted upon a detour to Lhasa, where he augured seven good omens portending success in the establishment of the Tantra. The Jowo image of Śākyamuni in Lhasa spoke at this time, predicting an auspicious outcome. The Guru returned to Samye in stages and was met by an envoy of welcome in front of the stone flask at Zurkhar.

On the Yobok Plain near Samye a high throne was raised. When Guru Rimpoche took his seat upon it, the twenty-one scholars from India, and the Tibetan translators, made obeisance, and the twenty-one scholars all said the same: 'A la la! Just this once we are favoured to meet the Guru of Orgyen, Pema Jungne, in person! A la la! This is the fruit of many aeons of accumulated merit!' And gazing at the face of the Guru, they wept. In particular, the meeting of the Guru and Vimalamitra was attended with great joy, like the reunion of a father and his son, and later, hand in hand, they strolled to the Utse Pagoda Temple.

In the first floor shrine room of Utse, the King, his courtiers and the Abbot made prostration, and then they ascended and sat down in the upper shrine room, the abode of the Buddha Vairocana. Here the Guru announced that to facilitate the increase of the Buddha's teaching three rites of consecration should be celebrated at Samye, and three rites of fire sacrifice should be performed to subdue devils. The consecrations were celebrated, but due to the King's distraction he neglected to petition the Guru to conduct the third fire sacrifice, and the Guru omitted to perform it. 'Now if you ask about the future,' the Guru said later, 'the Buddha's teaching will certainly spread, but the power of tempting devils will increase proportionately.'

During the final moon of the year, at the festival known as Loze Daze,[8] both Buddhists and Bonpos converged upon Samye to celebrate the rites of worship of the Tibetan King. The five Bon scholars, who had been personally invited to Samye by the King, did not recognise the sacred symbols of the Buddha's Body, Speech and Mind, and they did not accept the ethic of the ten virtues. They made no prostrations or circumambulation whatsoever, sitting down in a row with their backs to the images. The King and the majority of his ministers were offended. Early the following day the King encountered the Bon in front of the image of Vairocana in the Utse Pagoda. 'O God-king, what does this naked figure and his entourage of eight naked men represent?' asked the Bon scholars. 'What is its purpose? Where did they come from? Are they not Indian pundits?'

'The central, principal figure is an image of the Buddha Vairocana, and his circle of attendants are eight great spiritual heroes,' replied the King. 'We consider the image to be the actual Body of Buddha, so we prostrate to it and worship it. Our vicious *karma* is eradicated and merit is accumulated thereby.'

'What are those two horrible forms at the door? Are they not murderers?' the Bon asked further. 'What are they made from and what is their purpose?'

'Those two door-keepers are Glorious Lekden Nakpo, the Great Raging One, Master of All Magical Power,' said the King. 'He is the executioner of vow-breakers, but he is an ally of those who follow the *mahāyāna*. These images of him were made from various precious stones by divine sages and blessed by the great Indian sage, Pema Jungne. This deity performs the very necessary function of spreading the Buddha's doctrine and purifying the defilements of sentient beings.'

'What can come of clay statues fashioned by skilful men?' the Bon asked scornfully. 'You have been deceived and beguiled, O King. Tomorrow we Bon will perform a spectacular rite for you, a sacrifice that will completely renew your spiritual resources.'

Later, while walking outside for recreation and observing the many *stūpa*s, the Bon asked the King, 'What are those monuments over there that have a pile of vulture droppings on the top, rolls of fat around their middles and a pile of dog manure as their base?'

'Those are called "Sugatas' reliquaries" or "symbols of the Buddha's absolute, empty being". The meaning of these names is self-explanatory', replied the King. 'There is no representation of the Buddha's visionary being, but because the *stūpa*'s apparitional form, this deceptively concrete edifice, is the receptacle of offerings of all beings, it is also called "place of worship" or "receptacle of offerings".[9] Of the components of its superstructure, the thirteen discs indicating the thirteen wheels of the teaching's propagation are adorned with the canopy and crowning ornaments symbolic of the Buddha's eighty ideal marks and signs. The dome indicates the four boundless qualities of absolute, empty being – loving kindness, sympathetic joy, compassion and equanimity. And the base, decorated with lions that are at once a vehicle and a throne, represents a treasure house of wealth and wishes fulfilled.'

'This monument built with so much hard work is totally useless,' said the Bon. 'It is useless as a barricade for courageous warriors and it is useless as a hiding place for cowards. It is most strange. Some evil Indian has bewitched the King.'

At this the hearts of the King and his ministers shrank.

Then the Bon gathered in the three Lady Temples (Jowo Ling) to perform the rite of worship of the King.[10] The Bon priests stayed in the eight small temples and the scholars in the Tamdin Temple (Tamdin Ling).[11] 'Because this rite is for a great king,' said the Bon priests to the King, 'we will need a stag with fine antlers, a hind with a turquoise halter, a thousand male and a thousand female yaks, sheep and goats, and a complete outfit of royal robes.' The King quickly supplied them. 'We need specimens of all things existing in the world,' they then demanded, and the King quickly supplied them. 'We need eight kinds of wine and nine kinds of grain,' they told him, and it was granted.

Then the King and his entourage received a formal invitation to witness the rite of the Bon, and King, queens, ministers and courtiers arrived to find nine Bon scholars sitting in a central line, and in lines to the right and left of them nine magicians and other Bon priests. The many slaughterers called Servants of the Sacrifice each carried a knife; the many Purifier Bon brought water in golden ladles which they sprinkled upon the deer and other sacrificial beasts to purify them; and other shamans called Black Bon threw grain upon them. The shamans called Petitioner Bon asked questions and received answers from the gods and demons that surrounded them. Then the slaughterers, crying 'Here is a stag!' cut the throat of the animal in sacrifice. Three thousand yaks, sheep and goats were sacrificed at the same time in the same way. Next the four legs of a hind were severed in sacrifice. Crying 'Here is a she-dri!' 'Here is an ewe!', 'Here is a she-goat!' as they took each kind of animal, the slaughterers flayed the limbs of three thousand living animals. Horses, oxen, zo, mules, dogs, birds and pigs were sacrificed in different ways. After the killing the stench of burning hair permeated Samye as the various kinds of flesh were offered up. After the roasting a shaman called the Butcher Bon cut up the meat; a shaman called the Sorter Bon divided the meat and distributed it to the various functionaries; and the Diviner Bon made calculations. Then the Blood-letters, having already filled the copper bowls with blood, arranged them on skins while other priests piled the meat upon more skins. Their work completed they all chanted invocations. As the King, his ministers and queens watched with apprehension the copper bowls of blood began to steam and boil, and from the steam rainbow-like wraiths shone and sparkled, and various evil disembodied voices sounding shrill or drunken, with heavy breathing or with raucous laughter, could be heard. 'These are the voices of the Swastika Gods, Cha, the God of Chance, and Yang, the God of Fortune,' cried the Bon priests jubilantly. The flesh and blood was then offered to us to eat and drink.

'Does this bloody rite have any virtue in it?' asked the King.

'It is good for the King,' they answered, 'but it is of little benefit to us. Isn't your heart full, O King? Aren't you amazed?'

But the King was depressed, and the others were filled with confusion and doubt as they returned to the Utse Pagoda. All the scholars and translators who had witnessed the rite were unanimous in their opinion. 'One doctrine cannot have two teachers,' they said. 'If the east is down, then naturally the west is up. Fire and water can never be allies. No purpose is served by mixing the Buddha's doctrine with the tradition of these extremist fanatics. The wise man abhors evil companions. We will not accompany these fools for a moment. We will not drink the water from the valley in which these vow-breakers live. Rather we will seek peace and happiness in the border areas.' Then they sent this ultimatum to the King, and presented it to him nine times over, 'Either the teaching of the Buddha is exclusively established in Tibet, or Bon is permitted to flourish. It is absolutely impossible for them to co-exist.'

On the ninth occasion of presentation of this petition, the King called his ministers and court before him, and addressed them: 'Tibetan ministers and subjects, please listen to me! As the customs of the Buddhists and Bonpos are like the palm and the back of the hand and mutual recrimination abounds, who can sustain confidence in either? You Indian scholars, Tibetan translators and newly ordained monks who have given me such uncompromising counsel, what is to be done?'

The Bonpo *zhang* ministers replied, 'O God-king, when the river and its water-course are the same size there is harmony. Previously when this problem arose, it was necessary to banish many translators. If you follow the same course of action now, both Bonpos and Buddhists can sleep in their own beds, and there will be peace.'

Then Go the Elder demanded silence. 'When Bon is on the increase, then the King is disconsolate and full of doubt and fear. When Buddhism spreads the ministers lose their confidence and their purpose wavers. When Bon and Buddhism are given equal status, like fire and water, they become deadly enemies. It is evident that this agony must finally cease. Truth shall be separated from falsehood in a court of law. The relative validity of the two doctrines shall be weighed by the pebble procedure. If the real is distinguished from the unreal nothing at all remains to be done. Therefore, tomorrow, with the King presiding, the ministers and courtiers in the front row, the Buddhist faction in a row on the King's right and the Bon in a row on his left, a contest will be initiated. By metaphysics shall you be judged. Truth shall be given recognition by the customary cup of wine, and fraud shall receive just punishment. Further, the rivals must demonstrate miraculous power as evidence of their righteousness, their creative skill fully potentiated through psychic strength. Then if the Buddha's doctrine is proven valid, it will be preserved and strengthened and Bon will be eradicated. If Bon is validated, then Buddhism will be destroyed and Bon will be established. A decree to this effect shall be promulgated. Whoever disobeys this decree, whether it should be the king, ministers, queens or subjects, he will be delivered up to the law. All must vow to abide by it.'

This was found acceptable to the King, ministers, queens and courtiers, all of whom vowed to obey the decree. The Bonpo ministers advised concurrence, believing that in such a contest the Buddhists could not possibly rival the magical powers and craft of the Bon.

Then the King sent this reply to the scholars' petition:

Pay heed, O you gods, masters of wisdom and power!
Buddists and Bonpos treat each other as executioners,
And as neither gives credit to the other
The King, ministers and queens are full of distrust for both;
Both Buddhist and Bonpo are overcome by doubt and fear.
Therefore, tomorrow, you will compete with the Bon priests,
Rivalling them in signs of truth, proof of power, in magic and psychic strength.
Whichever *dharma* inspires confidence in the King and his ministers
In that *dharma* shall we place our trust, and that *dharma* shall we follow.
The false and untrustworthy shall be utterly rejected,
And they shall be banished to barbarian tribal borderlands.
This the King and ministers have ordained. Reflect and act wisely.

The scholars were delighted to receive this communication, and they sent this response:

So be it, Lord of Men, sacred God-king!
This is the method of all just kings.
The righteous shall vanquish the unrighteous;
The truth will certainly defeat these devils and rebels.
As all the great sages and adepts are present here,
More devils will perish than in Vajrāsana.
Often before has our *dharma* defeated fanatical extremists,
So why should we fear these common Bon?
Whoever is defeated should be punished by the victors,
And it is just that the losers should be banished.

The King was very pleased by this reply. He then explained the terms of the contest in detail to the Bon, and told them to prepare. The Bon sent assurance that their nine scholars would win the contest, informing him that their nine magicians were unrivalled in magical power.

On the fifteenth day of the new year, in the middle of the great plain of Yobok near Samye, a high throne was raised for the King. The scholars and translators took their seats on his right, the Bon on his left and the ministers and courtiers in rows in front of him. Behind them milled a vast throng wearing red or black, assembled from the Four Districts of Central Tibet. First the King made this pronouncement: 'HO! People of my Land of Tibet, gods and men, Buddhists and Bonpos, ministers, queens and courtiers, please pay attention. Formerly the kings permitted Buddhism and Bon to co-exist. Then the Bon gained ascendency. I have tried to establish Buddhism and Bon in equality like my ancestor Songtsen Gampo, but Buddhism and Bon are inimical, and mutual recrimination has created doubt and suspicion in the minds of the King and his ministers. Now we will compare and appraise their metaphysics and whichever system gains our trust will be adopted as a whole. Whoever refuses to embrace the winners' doctrine the law will destroy. The adherents of whichever of these two systems, Buddhism or Bon, proves false will be banished to the borderlands, so that even the name of their doctrine will be forgotten in this land. This official decree warrants that the vanquished will receive their just deserts. To the victors we shall accord all praise, and all will adhere to their doctrine.' The King repeated this decree nine times over, and the ministers corroborated it by repeating it from their law scroll, and all were agreed.

Then the Great Orgyen himself levitated to the height of a palm tree and addressed the contestants: 'It is right to distinguish the metaphysics of Buddhism from Bon. First, since it is the preface to all formal debate, sharpen your wits with the customary exchange of riddles.[12] Then with gems of exegesis lay bare the heart of your tradition, because there lies the joy of every lineage. At last, your arguments, their premises and conclusions will be judged, because authentic polemics are the mark of a sound metaphysique. Thereafter, you will demonstrate evidence of your *siddhi,* because magical skill inspires confidence in the King and his ministers.' After this announcement he manifested the essence of his Body as Śākyamuni, Lord of the Śākyas, and the King, his ministers and the Bonpos were overwhelmed by his aura; he manifested an emanation of his Speech in the form of Padma Saṃbhava,[13] the leader of the hosts of scholars, and the translators and scholars were given courage and inspiration; and an emanation of his Mind took the form of Dorje Trollo, vanquishing the opinionated, and showing miracles contrary to nature so that even the Bonpos gained undivided faith and praised him.

Then Atsara Pelyang and a Bon engaged in the exchange of riddles, and the Bon won. The Bon entourage worshipped their god, raising his flag. The King presented them with the ceremonial cup of wine, and the Bonpo ministers were contented, giving their contestants in riddles generous gifts. The King was anxious. 'Early morning food is a presage of imminent pain,' said the scholars. 'They have won the contest in riddles, but riddles are not part of Buddha's teaching. Now the Bon must discuss religion with the scholars.'

The Great Sage Vimalamitra arose at the head of his row:

> All phenomena arise from a cause,
> And that cause was explained by the Tathāgata.
> What effects the cessation of that cause
> The Great Ascetic explained in these terms:
> Do no evil whatsoever
> And cultivate virtue in full measure;
> Your own mind is thus fully disciplined.

And sitting in lotus posture in the sky, his aura glowing, he snapped his fingers thrice. The nine Bon magicians fainted away, and the nine Bon scholars were struck dumb. They sat stunned without an answer. Then, likewise, the twenty-five Indian scholars and the hundred and eight translators each expounded an essential passage of scripture, and taking a topic of contention each demonstrated miraculous, authentic evidence of his realisation. The Bon were struck dumb, enshrouded in gloom because they were unable to perform any genuine miracles.

'You must win this debate,' urged the Bon ministers. 'Show your magical powers. These monks have astonished the gods and men of Tibet with their miracles. They have argued convincingly. Their demeanour and behaviour is a delight to the mind, and they radiate benevolence and joy. It seems that our expectations have been betrayed. Now if you have any skill at all, whether it is in evidence of *siddhi*, magical powers or evil spells, use it quickly.' And their minds disturbed, they became angry and bitter, exhorting their priests with terrible curses.

'These Indian barbarians have insulted our Bon Swastika Deities,' said the Bon. 'We will not debate with these scholars. Later we will kill them by magic. We will only debate with the translators, because they are Tibetans.'

Meanwhile, praising the scholars, the King gave each of them a pound of gold dust, a yellow begging bowl and a robe of brocade. The flag of the *dharma* was unfurled, the conch was blown and an actual, miraculous rain of flowers fell upon them. From the sky the gods proclaimed their homage in verse, and revealed themselves in reality. At that all the Tibetan people were amazed, and their tears of faith in the Buddha's teaching fell like rain. But upon the ranks of the Bon fell hail and stones. 'The gods are indicating the genuine signs of achievement,' said the Bonpo ministers, and they paid homage to the Buddha's teaching, placing the feet of the scholars upon their heads, and acknowledging their misdeeds to the translators. Mañjuśrī himself appeared to the King showing him the difference between true and false *dharma*.

'The Buddhists already hold the victory,' most of the people agreed. 'Their marvellous *dharma* is superior. We shall all practise the Buddha's teaching.' And they began to disperse.

'Stay!' commanded the King. 'The translators must debate with the Bon.'

First the great translator Vairotsana debated with the Bon Tangnak. Then Namkhai Nyingpo debated with Tongyu. Likewise each translator debated with a Bon and not a single Bon could rise to the height of his rival. The King counted out a pebble for each valid statement or action and a black pebble for each inauthentic statement or action. Vairotsana accrued nine hundred of the white pebbles and Tangnak accumulated five thousand of the black. The translators relaxed in relief, and the sacred flag was again unfurled. At the end of his debate Namkhai Nyingpo of Nub had accrued three thousand white pebbles of truth and Tongyu had acquired thirty thousand black pebbles of falsehood. Again the translators unfurled the flag. I, Tsogyel, debated with the Swastika Bon *yoginī*, Bonmo Tso of the Chokro Clan, and I was victorious. I demonstrated my magical powers, which I will describe later, and Bonmo Tso was struck dumb. Likewise one hundred and twenty translators were victorious. Even the nine leading Bon sages were defeated.

Struck dumb, their tongues shrinking, their lips paralysed, their faces perspiring, their legs shaking, they were unable to utter a word.

Then the time arrived for the competition in evidence of *siddhi*. Vairotsana held the three realms in the palm of his hand. Namkhai Nyingpo, riding on the sun's rays, demonstrated many miracles. Sangye Yeshe summoned malevolent spirits with a gesture of his phurba, slew his enemies with a movement of his phurba, and pierced a stone with a thrust of his phurba. Dorje Dunjom ran like the wind, encircling the four continents in a flash, and offered the King seven different kinds of treasure as proof of his feat. Gyelwa Chokyang projected Hayagrīva, the Horse-necked, from his fontanelle, instantaneously filling the microcosmic universes with the sound of his neighing. Tsangri Gompo conquered the three realms in an instant, and offered the god Brahmā's nine-spoked wheel as proof of his feat. Gyelwa Lodro walked on water. Denma Tsemang conclusively defeated the Bon in religious debate, explaining the *Kanjur Rochok*[14] from memory, projecting the forms of the vowels and consonants into the sky. Kaba Peltsek enslaved the legions of arrogant spirits. Odren Zhonnu swam like a fish in the ocean. Jñāna Kumāra drew ambrosia from a rock. Ma Rinchen Chok ate pebbles, chewing them like dough. Pelgyi Dorje moved unimpeded through rocks and mountains. Sokpo Lhapel summoned a female tiger in heat from the south by means of his hook-*mudrā*, his *mantra* of summons and his *samādhi*. Drenpa Namkha summoned a wild yak from the north. Chokro Lui Gyeltsen invoked the manifest forms of the Three Lords of the Buddha's Three Aspects in the sky in front of him. Langdro Konchok Jungden brought down thirteen thunderbolts at once, and despatched them like arrows wherever he wished. Kyeuchung caught and bound all the Ḍākinīs with his *samādhi*. Gyelmo Yudra Nyingpo disciplined the Bon in grammar, logic and science, and overpowering external appearances through the penetrating insight of his *samādhi*, he effected many transformations. Gyelwa Jangchub levitated in lotus posture. Tingdzin Zangpo flew in the sky, his vision encompassing the four continents simultaneously. In this manner all of the Twenty-five Mahāsiddhas of Chimphu demonstrated evidence of their *siddhi*. Furthermore, the Eight Siddhas of Yerpa, the

Thirty Tantric Priests of Sheldrak, the Fifty-five Recluses of Yong Dzong, etc., all showed a particular dissimilar sign of *siddhi*. They transmuted fire into water and water into fire. They danced in the sky, passed unimpeded through mountains and rocks, walked on water, reduced many to a few and increased a few into a multitude. All the Tibetan people could not help but gain great faith in the Buddha, and the Bon could not help their defeat. The Bonpo sympathisers amongst the ministers were speechless.

Concerning the details of my contest with the Bon in evidence of *siddhi* the Bon were defeated. But afterwards they wove nine evil spells called The Magical Odour of the Skunk, Flinging Food to the Dog, Snuffing the Butter Lamp with Blood, Black Magical Leather, Projection of Pestilential Spirits and Projection of Devils, etc.[15] With these curses they struck down nine young monks at once, but I spat into each of the monks' mouths, so that they stood up fully restored, showing greater skill in the play of wisdom than before. Thus again the Bon were defeated. Then pointing my index finger in gesture of threat at the nine magicians, and incanting PHAT! nine times over, paralysed, they lost consciousness. To restore them I intoned HŪNG nine times. Levitating in lotus posture, etc., I demonstrated my full control over elemental forces. Spinning fire wheels of five colours on the tips of the fingers of my right hand, I terrified the Bon, and then ejecting streams of five-coloured water from the tips of the fingers of my left hand, the streams swirled away into a lake. Taking a Chimphu boulder, breaking it like butter, I moulded it into various images. Then I projected twenty-five apparitional forms similar to myself, each displaying some proof of *siddhi*.

'These Bon cannot even defeat a woman,' said the people of Tibet, becoming contemptuous of them.

'Tomorrow our nine magicians will each call down a thunderbolt simultaneously, and reduce this Samye to a pile of ashes,' said the Bon. And they went to Hepori and called down their thunderbolts, but I wound them around the tip of my index finger, holding a gesture of threat, and flung them upon the Bon settlement of Ombu, which was demolished. After I had called down thirteen thunderbolts upon the heads of the Bon, they returned to Samye repentant.

When the Bonpos were to be banished, having been defeated in magical skill as described above, the ministers Takra and Lugong and others swore that they would not go into exile. They returned to Ombu where they made elaborate preparations to ruin Tibet by unleashing the efficacious magical powers of the ninefold cycle of the minor *karma*s and then the ninefold cycle of major *karma*s of Pelmo, through imprecations cast into fire, into water, into the earth and into the air by means of a flag and so on. The King fully explained this matter to the translators and scholars, asking them for means to repel the evil. Guru Rimpoche, assuring them that all would be well, instructed me to protect them. Then I went to the Utse Pagoda where I revealed the *maṇḍala* of Dorje Phurba, and practised Phurba's rites, until after seven days the deities of the *maṇḍala* appeared. The *siddhi* obtained in this practice was the power to make enemies their own executioners. Thus the Bon destroyed themselves. Both Takra and Lugong, together with five other Bonpo ministers implacably hostile to the *dharma*, died at once, and of the nine magicians eight died, only one remaining. Thus the Bon covens became empty, all defeated by magic.

The Emperor immediately confined all the Bonpos at Samye, where they suffered some chastisement. Guru Rimpoche decided their fate. 'Since the Reformed Bonpos have a faith that is in accordance with the Buddha's doctrine, they may sleep in their own beds. The Bon-shamans, however, all fanatical extremists, shall be banished to border countries. No purpose is served by killing them.'

The King, acting in accordance with the Guru's command, classified Bon books into Reformed and Shamanist categories, casting those of the Bon-shamans into fire, while the books of Reformed Bon were concealed as hidden treasures for future revelation. The Reformed Bonpos were sent back to Zhang-zhung and the provinces, while the Bon-shamans were sent to Treulakchan in Mongolia.

Thereafter, the King, his ministers and courtiers, all the King's subjects, both Tibetan and foreigners, were bound by law to refrain from Bon-shaman practices, and to practise the Buddha's teaching alone. Due to this law all of Central Tibet and Kham as far as the Throne Gate of China became filled with the teaching of the Buddha and the community of the

Sangha, and many monasteries and meditation centres and academies were founded.

Then after the King had promulgated this second decree, at Samye the drum of the teaching was beaten, the conch of the teaching was blown, the flag of the teaching unfurled, and the throne of the teaching was prepared. The twenty-one Indian scholars took their seats upon nine brocaded cushions. Great Orgyen Pema Jungne, the Bodhisattva Abbot of Zahor and the Kashmiri Sage Vimalamitra took their seats on great golden thrones furnished with nine brocaded cushions. The translators Vairotsana and Namkhai Nyingpo each took his seat upon more piles of nine brocaded cushions, and the other translators were seated upon piles of two or three brocaded cushions. Then to each of them the King gave generous gifts of gold and other presents. To each of the great Indian scholars he presented nine bolts of brocade, three golden bowls, three pounds of gold dust, etc., so that the offering created a mountainous pile. To the three priests, from Zahor, Orgyen and Kashmir, he presented a plate of gold and turquoises and a heap of brocade, etc., gifts of immense honour. Then he entreated them all to propagate the teaching of both *sūtra* and *tantra* in Tibet. All the scholars were delighted to accept, smiling their approval, and the Abbot, the Vajra Master and Vimalamitra gave their solemn word that they would stay to strengthen the teaching of the Buddha until the King's ambitions were fulfilled.

Thereafter, seven thousand monks entered the academy at Samye, and nine hundred entered the meditation centre at Chimphu; a thousand monks entered the academy at Trandruk, and a hundred monks entered the meditation centre at Yong Dzong; three thousand monks entered the academy at Lhasa, and five hundred monks entered the meditation centre at Yerpa: the new monks were ordained at these three pairs of institutions within a year. Furthermore, monasteries and meditation centres were established at Langtang in Kham, Rabgang in Minyak, Gyeltam in Jang, Jatsang in Mar, Rongzhi and Gangdruk in Kham, Dongchu in Powo, Ronglam in Barlam, Buchu in Kongpo, in Chimyul, at Danglung in Dakpo, at Tsuklak in the Four Districts of Central Tibet, and at Takden Jomo Nang in Tsang. On Everest, etc., throughout Tsang, Tsangrong and

Ngari, monasteries and meditation centres were established in great numbers.

The Second Part to Chapter Seven describes how in her benevolence Yeshe Tsogyel strengthened the Religious Community.

The Buddha's teaching, monastic communities, tantric colleges and the exegetical tradition spread and increased in the land of Tibet without opposition. Then the Indian, Chinese and Nepali scholars, laden with gold and provisions offered to them as a thanksgiving offering, returned to their own lands full of happiness. The Bodhisattva Abbot the Vajra Master and Vimalamitra remained in Tibet turning the wheel of the teaching of *sūtra* and *tantra,* and soon the ambitions of the Emperor had been completely fulfilled. King Trisong Detsen's authority and sovereignty was higher than the sky; aggressors in the four border areas were subdued and the Bon-shamans had vanished. Not even a fraction of his life's work remaining undone, the King appointed Prince Mune Tsenpo to the throne, while he himself was totally free of the suffering of even the most trivial anxiety. Thus in a state of mind that would pass from bliss to further bliss, at twilight on the day before his passing, he gave final advice to the Prince, the queens, his courtiers and ministers. At midnight he offered flowers of consecration in all the temples, and he gave benediction. Before first light the following morning, he chanted the liturgy of his practice of the creative process of meditation upon his Yidam, and at daybreak he dissolved into the plenum of clear light in Āyra Mañjuśrī's heart, and vanished.

Soon afterwards the Prince Mune Tsenpo was assassinated when a queen administered the poison of calumny. His brother, Mutri Tsenpo, was appointed to the throne in his place, and crowned king. The queens were very hostile to the Buddha's teaching at this time, and incited two religious communities to quarrel. With skilful means and compassion I brought the two groups together and reconciled them. Thereafter, quarrelling within the Community was prohibited. It was at this time that the woman Bonmo Tso of the Chokro Clan, an adherent of Reformed Bon living at Hepori near Samye, who I had known well since I was a child, presented me with a subtly poisoned elixir to drink. I drank it knowingly, saying:

O listen, friend of my heart,
This ambrosial elixir is delicious!
Myself, yes this immaterial *vajra*-body,
Ambrosial in essence,[16] has become pure essence.
Is it not wonderful!
While your ambition remains unfulfilled,
My aspiration has been consummated.
Do not be jaundiced in jealousy;
Practise Bon and Buddhism with no bias;
Pray to the Yidam deity;
Cultivate a pure vision of your friends and sisters in truth.
Compassionate One, give up your power-play,
And give faith and devotion to Lord Guru.

And my body became a mass of radiant, rainbow light, and every pore of my body was filled with a *vajra*. The Bon *yoginī* was ashamed and, unable to stay there any longer, she went to another country.

The queens, full of vindictiveness, banished me to Tsang. In Tsang I stayed first at Kharak Gang, and three hundred monks gathered in the Kharak retreat centre I established there. Later this place was to become known as Jomo Kharak. Thirty-nine of the three hundred monks in the Kharak meditation centre gained *siddhi*, attaining the ability to display miracles, and of these thirty-nine, there were twenty with the capacity to serve others, and seven who were equal to myself and whose accomplishment for the sake of others was immeasurable. Then I meditated at the place that was later to be called Jomo Nang because I practised internal meditation there, and of the one thousand nuns who gathered there, a hundred gained the ability to give ultimate meaning to the lives of others,[17] seven were my equal, and five hundred attained *siddhi*.

Then continuing to Sangak Ugpalung, I recommenced my labours, and my reputation spread throughout Tsang. A thousand tantric priests and monks and one thousand three hundred nuns assembled there. I brought all these to spiritual maturity and release through the Ultimate Tantra, some becoming unalterably set towards their goal. Seven became known as the Seven Blessed Sages of Tsang, and a further eighty became known as the Eighty Mahāsiddhas.

Specifically, I taught all these initiates in Tsang through the lineage of the oral transmission of the pronouncements.[18] In Jomo Nang I taught the secret precepts of the whispered transmission, and in Ugpalung I established the scriptural tradition. Many *siddhas* appeared in Kharak and Jomo Nang.

Then I went to live in Shampo Gang, and it was there that seven bandits robbed me of my possessions and raped me. Afterwards I sang them this song of introduction to the four joys:

NAMO GURU PADMA SIDDHI HRĪ!
My sons you have met a sublime consort, the Great Mother,
And by virtue of your resources of accumulated merit,
Fortuitously, you have received the four empowerments.
Concentrate upon the evolution of the four levels of joy.

Immediately you set eyes upon my body-*maṇḍala*,
Your mind was possessed by a lustful disposition,
And your confidence won you the Vase Initiation.
Apprehend the very essence of lust,
Identify it as your creative vision of the deity,
And that is nothing but the Yidam deity himself.
Meditate upon lustful mind as Divine Being.

Uniting with space, your consort's secret *maṇḍala*,
Pure pleasure exciting your nerve centres,
Your aggression was assuaged and loving kindness was born,
And its power won you the Mystic Initiation.
Apprehend the very essence of joy,
Mix it with your vital energy and maintain it awhile,
And if that is not *mahāmudrā*, nothing is.
Experience pleasure as *mahāmudrā*.

Joined to your consort's sphere of pure pleasure,
Inspired to involuntary exertion,
Your mind merged with my mind,
And that blessing won you the Wisdom Initiation.
Undistracted, guard the very essence of pleasure,
Identify pure pleasure with Emptiness,
And that is what is known as immaculate empty pleasure.
Experience pure pleasure as supreme joy.

United at your consort's blissful nerve,
Our two nectars fused into one elixir.
The phenomena of self and others extinguished,
Awareness won you the Initiation of Creative Expression.
Guard the natural purity in the world of appearances,
Identify your love and attachment with Emptiness,
And that is nothing other than Dzokchen itself.
Experience innate joy as no-joy.

This is extraordinary, exalted secret instruction;
To consciously practise this method brings a fall,
But discovered by chance it gives miraculous release.
You attained the four empowerments at once,
And your success was matured by the four stages of joy.

As soon as I had spoken the seven thieves gained simultaneous spiritual maturity and release. They gained energy control and knowledge of the evolution of the four joys. Without leaving their bodies these seven Mahāsiddhas, who were thieves, arrived in the Land of Orgyen and served other beings to immeasurable purpose.

Thereafter, having gained seven new disciples, I arrived again in the Valley of Nepal, where my previous patrons and the King of Nepal, called Jila Jipha, supported me, and I propagated many of the Guru's secret precepts. Here in Nepal a fourteen-year-old girl called Ḍākinī, daughter of Bhadana and Nāginī, became my disciple. I conferred upon her the name Kalasiddhi because she would gain the *siddhi* of the Tantra in the incarnate family of Ḍākinīs. Then from Khosho we travelled in stages to Mangyul, where I revealed the *maṇḍala* of the Tantra Lama, and for one year Kalasiddhi, Lodro Kyi, Dechenmo, Selta and others, applied themselves to their meditation, and through my instruction they gained *siddhi*. As many as two hundred faithful people gathered there, and although the Buddha's teaching had made little headway in that country before, after my visit both lay men and women at least knew the essential doctrine of karmic causality.

While I was still in Mangyul the King Mutri Tsenpo sent three of his courtiers to invite me back to Samye. Leaving the nun Lodro Kyi as my representative in Mangyul, I departed for

Tibet with twelve disciples. Kharak, Jomo Nang and Ugpalung offered generous hospitality, honour and worship on my way to Samye. The King arranged a wonderful welcome, and a procession of rejoicing monks accompanied me to the Utse Pagoda. The ministers, courtiers and translators were overjoyed to see me, greeting me as if I had returned from the dead, but as soon as I was able I went to the *stūpa* enshrining the remains of the Great Abbot Śāntarakṣita. I made an offering of seven handfuls of gold dust and nine pieces of silk in a *maṇḍala,* and weeping profusely I said:

Alas! alas! O Best of Teachers, Holy One,
The sky is vast and the stars are many,
But now that the Seven-horsed Sun has gone
Who can dispel the gloom of our ignorance?
Where is the shining lamp in this Tibetan isle of darkness?
Where is the stainless globe of fire-crystal?
Now that the beams of your compassion no longer sustain us,
Who will lead the blind who stare like statues?

The king's treasury may be filled with wealth,
But now that our wish-fulfilling gem has gone,
Who will grant us our hearts' desire?
Who now is the deliverer of our land of hungry ghosts?
Where have you gone, precious Wish-fulfilling Gem?
Now that the fountain of our desires no longer sustains us,
Who can protect the lame who have legs they cannot use?

The microcosmic worlds may be full of kings,
But without a universal emperor who will protect us?
To whom can we look for refuge in this savage Tibet?
Where have you gone, universal emperor and lord?
Now that a teacher of discipline no longer sustains us,
Who will protect the dumb who have tongues they cannot use?

There are many saints and sages in Magadha in India,
But without you, Great Abbot, who will bear the torch of the
  doctrine?
Where have you gone, exalted regent of the Buddha?
Now that a teacher of *sūtra* and *tantra* no longer sustains us,
Who will protect these corpses who think and move?

Alas! alas! O great sage and scholar, Śāntarakṣita,
Bodhisattva, god of gods,
Lord, through your compassion, may I and all living beings,
Walk the path in every lifetime, and with ease
Gain maturity and release through the teaching of *sūtra* and *tantra*,
Achieving the good of all beings through the four principles of fellowship.[19]
Perfecting, completing, the activity of the Bodhisattva,
May I become the leader of the teaching and teachers;
Raising the doctrine's banner to remain for ever,
In human form crossing the ocean in the boat of the doctrine,
May I be Lama of beings, the captain of the boat.

Then from the upper part of the *stūpa* a disembodied voice intoned:

OM ĀH HŪNG!
Performing the actions of Buddhas, past present and future,
Your activity will spread co-extensive with the sky;
Spreading root and branch of the Buddha's teaching, embracing the ten directions,
All-embracing Mother of Buddhas past, present and future, be blessed.

All those assembled there heard the same sound and were happy.

Then I became the King's priestess and remained in Chimphu for eleven years, living with my Guru, spreading the Buddha's teaching in theory and practice. Drawing out the tantric teaching and secret precepts contained within the Guru's spiritual treasury, he bestowed them all upon me, retaining nothing, just as the contents of one vessel are poured into another. Of particular importance, Guru Rimpoche told me this: 'Very soon the time will come for me to go to Ngayab Khandroling, the Land of the Ḍākinīs. I must leave behind me inexhaustible teaching, immense in its profundity,[20] throughout the entire Tibetan Empire. You must carefully assimilate and compile and prepare my teaching as treasure to be revealed in the future. Also, as the girl Kalasiddhi has realised the meaning of her name, having gained the *siddhi* of the Tantra in the family of incarnate conch-like Ḍākinīs, she must be my consort in the task of engendering many profound, secret precepts of the Tantra that are not found elsewhere, and which I wish concealed as apocalyptic treasures.'

I presented the girl Kalasiddhi to him as he requested. Then I revealed the *maṇḍala* of the Communion of the Lama's Mind,[21] and brought the King Mutri Tsenpo to maturity and release, and thus he continued in his ancestral stream of the Buddha's teaching.

Then all the teaching that Guru Rimpoche had given and which was to be concealed as treasure for future revelation (terma) was written down. Namkhai Nyingpo who was pre-eminent at speed-writing, Atsara Pelyang pre-eminent at calligraphy, Denma Tsemang pre-eminent at spelling, Chokro Lui-Gyeltsen pre-eminent at clarity, Yudra Nyingpo master of grammar and logic, Vairotsana master of every skill, and myself endowed with an infallible memory: all the twenty-five disciples and many acolytes assisted in the work. Some wrote in Sanskrit, some in the Ḍākinī script, some in Newari, some in letters of fire, some in letters of water, some in letters of air, some in Tibetan script in either long hand or capitals, with either long hooks or short hooks, with illuminated letters on black paper, in the scripts of 'Bru and Gilgit, in kong-seng or khyi-nyal styles, with long leg or short leg, all correctly punctuated. We wrote a million cycles of Mind Accomplishment, a hundred thousand Heart-drop cycles,[22] *tantra*s, commentaries, secret precepts, all of immense profundity, some extensive but of great import, some short but complete, some easy to practise but great in grace, some profound but quickly endowing whatever is required. All these texts were reduced to manifests, lists of twice concealed texts, concise lists and prophetic catalogues, etc.[23] to inspire trust, and then they were all arranged in order.

The Guru and Ḍākinī, mystic partners, having identical ambition, serve all beings with skilful means and perfect insight; with the same activity of Speech we expound the *sūtra*s and *tantra*s; with the same apparitional projections we control the phenomenal world; with the same knowledge and talents we work for the good of the teaching and all living beings; with the same karmic activity we utilise the four *karma*s of transform-

ation[24] at will. Ultimately Pema Jungne and Yeshe Tsogyel are identical to Kuntuzangpo and Kuntuzangmo (Kunzang yab-yum): our Body, Speech, Mind, Activity, and Quality are co-extensive with all-pervasive space.

From Chimphu we went from place to place on foot, blessing all the power spots of Greater Tibet. First we went to the three Taktsangs. In Paro Taktsang in Bhutan we disposed the treasures separately and left prophetic catalogues. 'This is the place of the Guru's Mind,' prayed the Guru. 'Whoever practises here will attain *mahāmudrā siddhi*. When the Guru dwells in The Highest Paradise (Ogmin) these symbols of his Body, Speech and Mind will spontaneously manifest.' Then he made wish-granting prayers and made benediction upon an image of Dorje Trollo, a naturally manifest *stūpa* and the spontaneously manifest Six-syllable Mantra. Then we went to Womphu Taktsang in Central Tibet, where the Guru coerced the Lords of Hidden Treasure, enjoining them to protect the treasures that he entrusted to their care, and he disposed concise lists. 'This is the power place of the Guru's Body. Whoever meditates here will gain the power of long-life. When the Guru is born on the Dhanakośa Lake these symbols of his Body, Speech and Mind will manifest naturally.' Then, as before, he made prayer and gave benediction upon the images, the Three Seed-syllable Mantra, the Nine Seed-syllable RULU Mantra, a *stūpa* and a *vajra*. At Taktsang in Kham, having concealed the treasures individually, he extorted a vow and promise from the Lords of Hidden Treasure to protect them, making prophecies and disposing manifests. 'This is the power place of the Guru's Speech. Great renown and great blessing will accrue to those meditating here, but great opposition will arise to those who have no *samaya*. Both mundane and supreme *siddhi* can be attained here. When the wheel of the teaching is turned, devils subjugated and opinionated unbelievers converted as at Vajrāsana, Sarnāth, etc., the Buddha's three modes will naturally manifest, and the Six-syllable Mantra, the Three Seed-syllables and the Twelve Syllable Mantra will appear together with a *stūpa*.' And he then said prayers and gave benediction.

(*To discover details of the Guru and Consort's activity in many other power spots look into the biographies of Guru Rimpoche and other tomes.*)

Then the Guru and his Consort, we mystic partners, returned to the Utse Pagoda as priest and priestess of the Tibetan Emperor. After bestowing oral instruction, prophetic catalogues of treasures and their discoverers, and extensive personal advice upon the King, his ministers, queens, courtiers and translators, on the tenth day of the tenth month of the monkey year,[25] the Guru departed, riding on the rays of the sun to the Island of Ngayab in the South-West. For the sake of the King, and because I was the Superior of the three pairs of religious communities, I remained behind, working for the welfare of beings, filling the earth with the treasures of the Guru's teaching.

As the short distance escort of honour, the King, patrons and their entourage carried the Guru on their shoulders up to the Gungtang Pass. There they entreated him for final advice and prognostication, and then depressed in spirits they returned to Samye. Riding on the sun's rays I accompanied him as far as the Nepali border at Tsashorong, where we descended into the Secret Cave of Tsashorong for twenty-one days. Here the Guru revealed the *maṇḍala* of Dzokchen Ati Khyabdal[26] and initiated me. The priestess Chonema was accompanied by an ill-omen that indicated her doubt and equivocation, and to her the Guru said: 'The teaching of the Tantra has spread in Tibet, but Ati, the supreme teaching of the *mahāyāna* has become a cause of dispute. Spiritual release has not been attained through it as much as through the lineage of the oral transmission of the pronouncements or the lineage of revealed treasure. Furthermore, its practitioners have no inclination to serve other beings. The conditions of its practice, and indeed the Tantra in general, are conducive to a quick rise and fall in limited power and capability.' Thus he refused Chonema initiation. But to me he granted it in full, exhaustively, leaving nothing out. 'Now you are ready to be given the precepts of the extraordinary vehicle which make the analytical view redundant. This teaching must not be given too early or too late, at an inopportune juncture or to someone who is unprepared, because like setting the seeds of a crop that after ripening cannot remain in the fields, after the goal is attained there is no way that existence in this world can be prolonged. On this path there is no good or bad *karma*, no superior or inferior beings, no acuity or dullness, no youth or old age – the goal is total immersion in the dynamic space where all reality is extinguished.[27] If this teaching had been given to someone like you too early, to enter upon the career of selfless service for embodied beings, propagation of the Buddha's teaching, and concealing profound treasures for the good of all beings, would have been rendered very difficult. And why? Because your mortal body would have been immediately consumed. Now you should immerse yourself without a moment of forgetfulness in the vision of reality manifest,[28] and retaining your body you will quickly attain Buddhahood. After I have gone immerse yourself in meditation at Zapu and Tidro and such places; after three years the intensity of your visionary experience will have increased; and after six years you will have attained optimal, non-referential Knowledge. At that time you will conceal the remaining treasures for future revelation, and through transmission of secret precepts you will complete your duty to others. Then you will go to Kharchu in Lhodrak to continue your practice, and then showing magical transformation contrary to nature, appearing first as one form and then as another, you will assist specific individuals as their need determines. After two hundred years in all your body will vanish, and you will meet me in the macrocosmic realm of Awareness in Ngayab Khandro Ling, the Land of the Ḍākinīs, where indivisibly united we will work for the welfare of others as an infinite expanse of purity.'

After giving me these visionary predictions he prepared to ride away on the sun's rays, but bowing down to him I offered this urgent plaint:

Alas! alas! Lord of Orgyen,
Here one moment, gone the next,
Surely this is the impermanence of birth and death.
How can I arrest the process of birth and dying?

Alas! alas! Lord of Orgyen,
We have been together so long
And now in a flash we are separated –
This is surely what is meant by meeting and parting.
How can I remain with you always?

Alas! alas! Lord of Orgyen,
In the past you have pervaded the whole of Tibet
But now only the imprint of your presence remains –
Surely this is what is called impermanence.
How can I arrest the winds of *karma*?

Alas! alas! Lord of Orgyen,
In the past your advice has strengthened Tibet
But now we have only legend to listen to –
Surely this is what is called change and becoming.
How can I gain unshakable conviction?

Alas! alas! Lord of Orgyen,
Until now I have been your constant companion
But now the Guru is vanishing into the sky
Leaving this woman in her bed of bad *karma*.
Who will give me empowerment and blessing?

Alas! alas! Lord of Orgyen,
Your words have been full of profound instruction
But now undying you dissolve into space
Leaving this body-bound woman behind you.
Who can I ask to dispel obstacles and inspire me?

Alas! alas! Compassionate One,
Please grant me three simple words of advice.
Look upon me always with compassion,
Please remember Tibet in your wish-filling prayers.

Then I threw thirteen handfuls of gold dust upon the Guru's Body, and while I was still keening in distress, the Guru, riding upon the rays of the sun, spoke to me from the height of an arm span above the ground, answering my questions:

O listen, daughter, Ocean of Talent,
Pema Jungne is leaving to befriend and convert demon savages.
This skilful act of the totally perfected Buddha's three modes
Cannot be compared to the bursting of human bubbles.
If you are afraid of birth and death, assimilate the Buddha's teaching,

And when you control your energy flows and creative and fulfilment processes,
You arrest the process of birth and death in the most superior way.

O listen, most virtuous, faithful consort,
Pema Jungne is leaving for the good of all creatures.
All-embracing and undiscriminating compassion
Cannot be compared to humanity's veil of delusion.
To be with me always, practise Guru Yoga,
And idealised appearances will arise as the Lama;
There is no better way to avoid meeting and parting.

O listen, enticing, captivating Lady,
Pema Jungne is leaving for selfless conversion of others.
This supreme, immaculate being in whom matter has dissolved
Cannot be compared to human beings driven by bad *karma*.
I have filled Tibet with disciples and *siddhas*;
Meditate upon *mahāmudrā* to gain insight into impermanence,
And the phenomenal world, *saṃsāra* and *nirvāṇa*, is free as it stands:
There is no better way to arrest the wind of *karma*.

O listen, faithful, eternally youthful maiden.
Pema Jungne is going to teach in the realms of demon savages.
This supreme *vajra*-body, immune to change,
Cannot be compared to disease-stricken human being.
I have filled Tibet, above and below, with the Buddha's teaching
And if you preach and meditate the teaching will not be lost,
Study, contemplation and meditation sustaining the Buddha's doctrine.
The good of self and others is spontaneously accomplished;
There is no more profound way to avert change and decay.

O listen, faithful girl of Kharchen,
Pema Jungne is leaving for fields of lotus-light.
Inspired by the ambition of Sugatas past, present and future,
I cannot be compared to human beings hounded by the Lord of Death.
You woman, after attaining *siddhi*, possess a 'super-body';

So ask your superior mind for empowerment and blessing:
There is no higher regent of Guru Pema.

O listen, Yeshe Tsogyelma,
Pema Jungne is leaving for the place of pure pleasure.
This immortal god, dwelling in a body of Emptiness,
Cannot be compared to human beings with split body and
mind.
Tsogyel has been liberated by profound secret precepts;
Meditate upon Dzokchen Ati to extinguish corporeality,
And through meditative absorption and prayer dispel
obstacles and gain inspiration:
There is no better way to remove obstacles to the Lama's
compassion.

O listen, accomplished Blazing Blue Light,
I have given you much advice and instruction in the past,
All of which is compressed into this final injunction –
Practise this Guru Yoga:
One span above your head on a lotus and moon,
In an expanse of rainbow light,
Sits Pema Jungne, everyone's Guru,
With one face and two hands, holding *vajra* and skull,
Wearing a vest, a waistcoat, a skirt and a shawl,
An outer shawl and a loose robe,
Indicating his perfect completion of the six vehicles of practice,
Adorned with a hat, vulture feather and ear-rings,
In lotus posture, radiating light,
Endowed with the eighty ideal marks and signs,
In the midst of shimmering Ḍākinīs of five-fold rainbow light,
Shining, glowing, clear as the light of the mind.
When this vision is distinct, take the empowerment and
remain in absorption;
If the vision is unclear, meditate with diligence.
Then count the essential and quintessential GURU SIDDHI
Mantras,
And finally, integrate the Lama with your three doors,
Share the merit, and pray to attain the nature of the Lama
himself,
And bathe in the Dzokchen seed-sphere of pure potential.[29]

There is nothing better than that Tsogyelma.
And there is no waxing or waning of my compassion;
It is impossible to break my beam of compassion shining upon Tibet;
I am always present before my sons who pray to me;
I am never separated from the faithful;
To opinionated people I am veiled though physically present;
Continuous compassion strengthens my sons with clear vision.
Thus in the future on the tenth day of the moon
Pema Jungne will come riding on the Lord of the Day,
In peaceful, enriching, dominating and destructive forms,
During the four successive quarters of the day,
To give corresponding *siddhi* to my spiritual sons.
In the same way, I will appear on the tenth day of the waning moon,
To accomplish, in particular, all dominating and destructive acts;
On the fifteenth of the moon, riding the rays of the moon,
I will stir the depths of *saṃsāra* with my compassionate prayer,
Emptying the lower realms without exception,
Working perfectly with power for the sake of beings.
On the eighth of the moon, after nightfall and before dawn,
At sunset and sunrise, riding my all-wise steed,
Travelling through the power places of the world,
I will bestow various *siddhis*:
In the land of the vicious demonesses I will turn the wheel of the teaching;
For all beings of the twenty-one barbarian islands
And the thirty most savage lands,
To pacify, enrich, dominate or destroy,
Emanating as fire, wind or water,
As sky, as rainbow, or earthquake or thunder,
I will despatch a million apparitional forms to guide them to happiness;
There will be no interruption to my work for beings.

You, woman, hereafter, will live for more than a hundred years
To achieve the happiness of all beings of Tibet.
After a hundred years plus one, you may come to Ngayab Ling,
And inseparable from Pema Jungne, protect your disciples.

The Knowledge Holder Blazing Blue Light[30] will be your name,
And forever your Body, Speech and Mind will be one with me.
The process of birth and death arrested, the winds of *karma* suppressed,
You will project emanations for the good of future beings.
In the Land of Tibet your emanations will continue forever,
Without fatigue or regret, working for the welfare of beings.
So be composed, Tsogyelma!
You and I will never part.
But on the relative plane, Farewell!
And through my compassionate prayer, may Tibet be happy.

After he had ceased speaking, the firmament was filled with Buddha Heroes and Ḍākinīs making music and song, carrying canopies, victory banners, pennants, tubular parasols, square parasols, *mṛdang* drums, silk tassels, double-faced drums, yak tail fly whisks, yak tails, banners, fans, flags, throne canopies, tapestries, cymbals, phem, drums, conches, trumpets, thigh bone trumpets, *ḍāmarus*, great drums, lutes, stringed instruments, kettle drums, tingcha, war, tsel and piwi.[31] From the centre of this vast cloud of offerings, this celestial orchestra, shone beams of beckoning light into which the Guru vanished. I was utterly unable to bear his departure, and cried out, 'O Guru Rimpoche! One and only Buddha Exemplar! Our only father and saviour! One and only eye of Tibet! My only heart! You have no pity! Why do you torture me so! Alas! O lack-a-day!' And so on, begging him to return, wailing and lamenting, doing full prostration continually. Then he turned around one last time and gave me his first testament,[32] before again vanishing into the burgeoning fields of pulsating light with his face set towards the South-West. And again I threw myself upon the ground, tearing my hair, scratching my face, and twisting and turning, rolling over and over like a baby, and besought him, 'Alas! O misery! Lord of Orgyen, will you leave Tibet in a vacuum? Will you withdraw the light of your compassion? Will you have the Buddha's teaching aborted? Will you shamelessly reject the Tibetan people? Will you leave your Tsogyel without refuge? Be compassionate! Look now!' and I continued to weep and wail until his disembodied voice spoke in response in clear and pure tones, giving me his second testament. Then again the sky was filled with light engulfing the earth in its radiance, and the mass of patterned pulsating light took the form of a Ḍākinī whose brilliance faded little by little until she finally vanished. Again I beat my body on the rocks, tearing off pieces of flesh and letting streams of blood, offering flesh and blood to him as a *gaṇacakra* offering, and with fervent tormented prayer I called to my vanished Guru:

> Alas! alas! Matrix of Compassion!
> The Guru's activity is co-extensive with space,
> But today Tibet's Guru's story is completed.
> The black-topped people have their various destinies,
> But today all of Tibet has met its inexorable fate.
> To each being his own private happiness and woe,
> But today real misery has befallen me.
> Alas! O misery! Quickly show your compassion!

In response a voice said, 'Tsogyel, look!' and looking round a ball of light as large as my head fell out of the sky before me. Within was the Guru's first legacy of his *parinirvāṇa*.[33] Then the light which had engulfed Tibet became concentrated into a ball, which vanished, radiating brilliantly into the South-West where the Guru had gone. Again, utterly incapable of bearing my grief, I cried out in entreaty, 'Venerable Orgyen, do not withdraw your compassion! Please do not leave me!' And as before a voice directed me where to look, and immediately a casket of light as large as my fist, containing the second legacy of the Guru's *parinirvāṇa*, fell down before me. Then the light of day and the light of the sun itself concentrated and was absorbed into the South-West. In the remaining half-light I awoke as if in a dream to the memory of the Guru surrounded by his Ḍākinīs, and in extreme agitation of mind, my eyes overflowing with suppressed tears, yearning for my Guru, I sang this song with a distraught, keening melody:

Alas! O venerable Orgyen Rimpoche,
Only father and protector of Tibet,
Now you have gone to Khandro Ling
And Tibet has become empty.
Essential jewel, where are you now?

In truth there is no coming or going,
But today you left for the realm of Orgyen.
Behind the head of each man and god a sun has set,
Who will warm the unclothed and naked?
From the brow of every man an eye has been plucked,
Who will lead the blind with their fixed glazed stares?
From the breast of every man his heart has been torn,
Who will guide these thinking corpses?
You came here for the sake of all beings,
So why not stay here for ever?
Alas! O misery! Orgyen Rimpoche!
A time of murk and gloom has befallen Tibet,
A time when the hermitages remain empty,
A time when the Throne of the Dharma is vacant,
A time when the Vase of Empowerment is empty,
A time when Mind's revelation is mixed with conceit,
A time to turn to books for instruction,
A time when we can only visualise the Lama,
A time to rely upon symbolic paintings and sculptures,
A time to look to dreams for pure vision:
These are the portents of this unfortunate time that befalls us.
Alas! O woe! Venerable Lord of Orgyen!
Look upon us with compassion, Orgyen, Master of Truth!

After praying like that, a casket of light no bigger than a finger joint appeared at the end of a single ray of light shining from the South-West. Within it I found the third legacy of the Guru's *parinirvāṇa*, and at once I gained indomitable confidence. The nest of hopes and fears hidden deep within me was destroyed; the torments of emotional confusion were assuaged; and an intuition of the eternal immanence of the Lama arose.

Then with the utmost devotion, I revealed the *maṇḍala* of the Lama's Mystic Communion, and after three months of practice I met with the Guru during the six periods of day and night, receiving from him much visionary instruction, advice and whispered transmission.

Thereafter, in order to allow Dewamo to restore her full vision of the Guru, with the Guru's permission I compiled the liturgical rite called *Yang-Phur Drakma*,[34] the higher part of which consisted of a liturgy of confession associated with the basic rite of

Yangdak and the lower part associated with Dorje Zhonnu, the Remover of Obstacles. It was taught to many of the faithful, particularly Dewamo, and then transmitted through both the lineages of the oral transmission of the pronouncements and the lineage of hidden treasures.

Thereafter I returned to Mangyul, where my former monks and students and the devoted nun Lodro Kyi, with great joy, celebrated my return with a *gaṇacakra* feast. They requested me to settle there permanently, but I remained only a month, giving them much ultimate instruction, dispelling obstacles, giving personal advice and developing meditation by leading them to recognition of their achievement. Then I went up to Tsang. Wherever I went in Tsang the country people told me: 'Though Guru Rimpoche went to the land of the demon savages, you returned, and for that we are grateful.' They gave me the same devotion as they had given to Guru Rimpoche himself, blocking the road with their faith. I gave them initiation and instruction, assisting them all without preference or bias.

Then I came to Zurpisa, where I stayed for a year. Nyen Pelyang, Be Yeshe Nyingpo, Lasum Gyelwa Jangchub, Odren Pelgyi Zhonnu the younger, Langlab Jangchub Dorje and Dacha Rupa Dorje who was a child of seven years, I found to be suitable vessels and took them as my disciples, bringing them to maturity and release. From Zurpisa I went to Shang, where I lived in the Pama Gang caves for three years, and worked extensively for the sake of beings. From Shang I went to Zapu, where I remained in meditation upon the reality of the effortless peak (Ati) of the *mahāyāna*, and after one year my visionary experience had intensified, and I found vast resources of energy and new strength of commitment. I hid thirteen caches of treasure there. From Zapu I went on to Tidro in Zho where I remained six years. By the end of that six years I had attained optimal Knowledge, penetrating to the core of Dzokchen.

(*The story of how Tsogyel served many Ḍākinīs and travelled through sixty-two pure-lands is concealed elsewhere.*)

It was during this period that I performed my final austerity – 'the exchange of my *karma* for that of others'. The fiendish official, Śāntipā, who had previously caused me so much pain, had been reborn in the hell of extreme heat, and energy that grew out of my pity for him extricated him from his hell.

(The exact manner in which Tsogyel emptied the depths of the various hells of their inhabitants, beings with whom she had previous karmic association, and beings for whom she had disinterested affection, must be sought elsewhere.)

Further, I gave my body to ravenous carnivores, I fed the hungry, I clothed the destitute and cold, I gave medicine to the sick, I gave wealth to the poverty-stricken, I gave refuge to the forlorn, and I gave my sexual parts to the lustful. In short, to benefit others I gave my body and life. And because even when my sense-organs were required I gave willingly without attachment or concern for myself, both the god Indra and the *nāga* Ānanda sent spies to test me.

Thus it was at Tidro that a lame man, carried by three porters in turn, approached me. 'Where are you from? Why have you come?' I asked them.

'We come from Ombu in Central Tibet,' replied the lame man. 'I have been wrongly punished by the King, and both my knee-caps have been removed. The wise physicians of Tibet have told me that there is a method of transplanting the knee-caps of a woman to a man. Otherwise there is no possible remedy. I have heard that you, Lady, will give whatever is asked of you, and I have come here to beg. Is it possible for you to grant my petition?' and he sighed long and deep.

'I will give you whatever you need,' I replied, with pity welling up within me. 'I promised my Guru that I would assist beings with my Body, Speech and Mind. So take what you want.'

'It is necessary to inflict great wounds to take out the bones,' they said, taking up the knife. 'Can you endure the pain?'

'Whatever happens, do what you must,' I told them.

They cut a cross on each of my knees and tore out my knee-caps with the sound of 'Kak!' 'Kak!', and, finally, they placed the bloody, grisly discs in front of me. At that point my spirit temporarily left me. Recovering consciousness, I told them to take the knee-caps away, and they left happily.

After some time, when my knees had healed, a leper with his disease in a far worse state than other lepers, his entire body dripping with pus and blood, his nose rotted down to its root leaving a gaping wound, a foul odour spreading all around him from between his rotted lips, came to me, just crying and crying.

'Why cry?' I asked him. 'The present is the effect of your previous actions, and this crying will not help. It would be better for you to recite *mantras* and visualise the Yidam deity. That would be beneficial.'

'To be stricken with disease is indeed the curse of *saṃsāra*,' the leper replied, 'but I am the victim of something worse than mere disease.'

'What could be worse than that?' I inquired.

'I was stricken with this plague by a pestilential spirit; but I had a wife who like you was the daughter of a god. She fled to the company of another man when she lost her desire for me, and finally she threw me out of my house. So I thought that since you had devoted your entire life to others you might possibly become my wife,' and he started crying again.

'Don't cry!' I told him, compassion welling up within me. 'I will be obedient to your every wish.' And thereafter I lived together with the leper, fulfilling the duties of a model wife.

In similar ways I solved many people's problems. Seven Bonpos came begging for my skin which they said was needed as a ransom for Yang, the God of Fortune. I had myself flayed and gave them the skin. Many other people came begging, and I gave them whatever they required: my eyes, my head, my limbs, my two feet, my tongue and so on. I made a wish-granting prayer of encouragement for each of them.

After some time Indra himself came and presented me with the riches of the gods, the five divine silk robes, a vase of ambrosia and the seven divine precious things, praising me in these words:

Human girl, miraculous, superior being,
Acting like the Bodhisattvas of the past,
Willingly sacrificing your body and life for others,
Compassionate Mother, I take refuge in you.
Most marvellous being, I adore you.
From now for as long as the aeon lasts,
Divine queen, whatever teaching-wheel you turn,
I will support and inspire you.

So saying, he vanished, and my body became whole once more.

Furthermore, the leper my husband became transformed into the serpent Ānanda, who piled before me the inconceivable wealth of the *nāgas*. Folding his hands in devotion, weeping, he said:

Guru Yeshe Tsogyelma!
You are the mystic key to Pema Jungne!
Through pity you gladly accept others' suffering,
You are free of the concepts of 'clean' and 'unclean',
Your self love is hidden deep:
Mistress of the Teaching, Mother of Buddhas, I bow to you.
Guru Pema Skull-Garland Skill is my Lama;
So, sister, think of me with kindness.
Source of the ocean of teaching, every *tantra*,
Source of the meaning of Pema's profound oral and revealed transmissions,
You alone are responsible for their propagation and increase.
For as long as I live I will follow you,
Sustaining and protecting you,
Promoting your welfare and averting aggression.

So saying he vanished into the ground in his true form.

When the God-king heard that I was in Tidro, he invited me to Samye, and I lived in Chimphu for six years. The translators, courtiers, ministers and queens led by the King, Mutri Tsenpo, all paid me honour and served me with humility. Since the previous ordination of monks, the numbers at the meditation centres of Chimphu and other places had decreased slightly, the *mahāsiddhas* who had attained their own enlightenment dispersing in all directions to serve other beings, while others grew old and attained *parinirvāṇa*. By the King's grace fifteen hundred new monks were ordained at one time, and he appointed the Indian sage Kamalaśīla as the new Abbot. I gave instruction to the newly ordained monks, and they went to Chimphu to begin their meditation, which bore nothing but positive results. Many of them attained *siddhi* and were able to show evidence of their attainment.

It was at this time that the Tonmin and Tsemin[35] began to quarrel. The teacher called Hashang propounded a philosophy of false views, and repudiating the orthodox teaching he was bent on its destruction. The monastery at Samye was divided in two, the Master Kamalaśīla holding the Tamdin Temple (Tamdin Ling) side and Hashang holding the Jampa Temple (Jampa Ling) side.[36] The two factions fought a little. At this point I came down from Chimphu with a retinue of a hundred monks to effect a reconciliation. I met with disobedience, but I demonstrated many supernatural signs of accomplishment and both Tonmin and Tsemin gained faith in me. Thereafter, a religious decree enforced the practice and philosophy of the school of Kamalaśīla, and Hashang and his attendants were suffered to return to China, their own land, laden with gold.

The Emperor richly endowed the religious communities of Lhasa, Samye, Trandruk and others. Thirteen thousand new monks were ordained. Living in Chimphu I became the source of instruction and spiritual practice of the Guru's original disciples, the new monks, my own family of disciples, those who more recently had gained faith in Guru Rimpoche, in Ngari, Mangyul, Purang, Bhutan, Tsang, Jar, Loro, Kongpo, the Four Districts of Central Tibet, the Four Northern Provinces, and the Gang-druk of Dokham, and China, Jang, Hor, Minyak and other lands. Thus the sphere of my selfless activity became co-extensive with the sky, and the lineages of my disciples embraced and filled the whole world.

The Third Part of Chapter Seven describes in brief how Tsogyel concealed the 'Foot Treasures' of the Guru's teaching: how for the sake of all beings without prejudice she went on foot to the minor power places, the secret valleys and the districts concealing treasures.

Then I, Tsogyel, thought to myself, 'I have now fulfilled my ambition of promoting the teaching and the good of all beings. Half of the life-span predicted by the Guru has passed. My Knowledge has achieved its optimal potential. My action has reached full maturity. Therefore I must go into meditation in all the power places previously blessed by Guru Rimpoche to conceal the Foot Treasures, giving benediction and broadcasting my wish-fulfilling prayers.'

After determining my course of action, I went first to Tidro where I stayed for one year and seven months, concealing ten caches of treasure, and praying that whoever had the good fortune to relate to the Guru or myself in that place would achieve his end, I gave my benediction. Then I moved on to Sheldrak in Yar Lung where I concealed five caches of treasure, and having lived there for thirteen months I made wish-fulfilling prayers. At Yong Dzong I stayed one year, concealing ten caches. At Yerpa I stayed one month concealing ten caches. Then moving slowly eastwards to Tsari Gang, I stayed there for one year and four months, concealing thirty great caches of treasure; in the land of Kongpo I concealed one hundred and fifty caches in all. Then in the south, in the Mountain Range of Central Nepal, I stayed thirteen months, concealing thirty-five caches. In the west, in the Lachi Mountain Range, I stayed four months and seven days, concealing eight caches. In the north, in the Noichin Mountain Range, I stayed three months and five days, concealing three caches. In the south-east, in Kempa Lung in Gyel, I stayed one year and a half month, concealing ten caches. In the south-west, in Draphu Lung, I stayed five months and ten days, concealing seven caches. In the north-west, in Jakma Lung, I stayed one year and five months, concealing nine great caches. In the north-east, in Droma Lung, I stayed eleven months, concealing five caches. In the Yarbu Mountain Range I stayed one month and ten days, concealing three caches. Likewise in the Selje Mountain Range I stayed one year, concealing ten caches. In the Yu Lung Mountain Range I stayed three months, concealing three caches. In the Drongje Mountain Range I stayed ten days, concealing three caches. In the Yul Lung Mountain Range I stayed three months, concealing four caches. In the Jomo Mountain Range I stayed five months, concealing ten caches. In the Nyewo Mountain Range I stayed five months, concealing four caches. In the Dzayul Mountain Range I stayed twenty-one days, concealing one cache. In the Nanam Mountain Range I stayed seven days, concealing five caches. In the Lhorong Mountain Range I stayed three months and seven days, concealing thirteen caches. In the Rongtsen Mountain Range I stayed seven months, concealing fifteen caches. In the Sheldrang Mountain Range I stayed two months and ten days, concealing five caches. In the Gampo Mountain Range I stayed one year and one month and one day, concealing twenty caches. In the Jephu Mountain Range I stayed one month, concealing fourteen caches. In the Bubol Mountain Range I stayed twenty-one days, concealing three caches. In the Sengtom Mountain Range I stayed seven days, concealing two caches. In the Tsonak Mountain Range I stayed nine days and half a month, concealing one cache. Likewise, in the east, in Makung Lung, I stayed one month, concealing thirteen caches. In the south, in Bachak Śrī, I stayed one year, concealing seven caches. In the west, in Drangmen Lung, I stayed one month, concealing three caches. In the north, in Semodo, I stayed three months, concealing four caches.

Furthermore, in the highland Tsari Dzong, in the mid-land Kharak Dzong, in lowland Gere Dzong, in Phari Dzong in Bhutan, in Buchu Dzong in Kongpo, in Bakyul Dzong in Puwo, in Dorje Dzong in Den, in Nabun Dzong in Cham, in Nering Senge Dzong, in Yari Drakmar Dzong, in Kaling Sinpo Dzong, in Lhari Yuru Dzong, in Pelbar Dzong in Tola, Bumo Dzong in Rekha, in Drakmar Dzong in Ling, in Lhadrak Dzong in Dri, in Kongme Drakar Dzong, and in other places, I stayed some months and days, making a firm connection with each power place, and hiding treasure in every one.

Likewise, I went to the Eight Great Hidden Valleys:[37] the Dremo Shong in Central Nepal, Pemako in Lhoyul, Zapu Lung in Shang, Gowo Jong in Me, Gyelmo Mudo Jong, Lhamo Ngulkhang Jong, Gyellung Jokpo Lung and Budum Lung in Bhutan. I stayed a year in each of them, concealing many caches of treasure according to the importance of the power place.

Thus I went to the Twenty-five Mountain Ranges, the Four Blessed Power Places, the eighteen power places of the Eighteen Great Forts (Dzong),[38] and the one hundred and eight power places where Guru Rimpoche meditated, where I myself meditated for years, months or days, concealing caches of treasure and making wish-granting prayers and benediction.

Again, in particular, in the area of Dokham, upon the eight power places of the eight names of Guru Rimpoche blessed by the Guru himself, upon the five power places of the Five Aspects of Skull-Garland Skill, upon the twelve power places of miraculous *karmas*, upon the three power places blessed by prophecies (*just as appears elsewhere in extensive manifests*) I bestowed my blessing, and there I concealed caches of treasure. *Thus Tsogyel hid the Guru's treasures in the one hundred and five major power places and in the one thousand and seventy minor power places of Greater Tibet. Although there are millions of places that*

could be mentioned, their names, significance and their number would consume too much space in this text. Further, the manner in which the treasures were hidden in Greater Tibet, and particularly in Samye, Lhasa and Trandruk, may be seen in the manifests of treasure and in the extensive biographies of the Guru.
Thus ends the seventh chapter which describes Yeshe Tsogyel's work for all beings.

SAMAYA GYA GYA GYA ITHI GUHYA KHA-THAM MANDA ZAB GYA!

CHAPTER EIGHT
FRUITION AND BUDDHAHOOD

After I, Tsogyel, had blessed the great power places of the world and concealed caches of the Guru's treasure for future revelation, I returned to Chimphu as the Emperor's priestess. I remained there for some time, working with even greater zeal for the welfare of all beings. In the temple of Karchung Dorying I bestowed many unsurpassable maturing and releasing practices, immense in their profundity, to seven worthy recipients, including the King Mutri Tsenpo, Prince Murum Tsenpo and Ngangchung Pelgyi Gyelmo. I revealed the *maṇḍala*s of the Communion of the Lama's Mystic Word, the Communion of the Yidam's Mind and the Communion of Dzokchen Ati.[1] Granting the initiates empowerment I brought them to maturity and release.

After I had revealed the *maṇḍala* of the Communion of the Lama's Mystic Word, we immersed ourselves in meditation, and before dawn on the seventh day, while we were performing the invocation at the beginning of the rite, reciting the Seven Line Prayer[2] –

> In the north-west of the land of Orgyen,
> Born in the pollen heart of a lotus flower,
> Endowed with the most miraculous *siddhi*
> You, the Lotus Born Guru, appeared
> Surrounded by a host of attendant Ḍākinīs.
> So that we may follow in your footsteps
> We beg you to come here to bless us –

the Guru himself, surrounded by his attendants, appeared from the South-West. Accompanied by the sound of music, the smell of incense, sweet melodies, beautiful dancers and the song of mystic experience, shining resplendently, he entered into the middle of the *maṇḍala*. I told the King to prepare a throne for the Guru, but the King had fainted away overwhelmed by the fervour of his devotion, and the throne was not made ready.

Then the Guru spoke to the King: 'It will not be long now before the appearance of the Divine Prince's savage nephew, when the Emperor's dynasty will lose its ancestral throne. However, through the power of your faith, you need not take another karmic body. The power to serve other beings through emanation, and your realisation and liberation, will occur simultaneously.'

Prince Murum then prepared many thrones for the Guru and his attendants, and entreated them to be seated. The King Mutri Tsenpo prepared a hundred *maṇḍalas* of gold and turquoises, and offering them to Guru Rimpoche he made this request:

O Venerable Orgyen Pema, Apparitional Buddha,
Only father of all the Tibetan people,
We who are ground down by the weight of bad *karma*
And sucked down by the mire of distraction,
Through compassion never abandon us, always protect us.
Out of your great kindness you are here with us today,
Now tell us that you will stay here forever,
Turning the wheel of the teaching again.

The Guru replied:

Listen to my words, Righteous King, God-king.
Field of great faith, fully endowed and virtuous,
Through the Lama's blessing may you mature spiritually;
By the opening of Tsogyel's secret door may you find release;
Knowing your own mind as *mahāmudrā* may you gain
realisation;
In the matrix[3] of Body, Speech and Mind, may you gain
mastery.

The Guru placed his hand upon the head of the King, and immediately he gained simultaneous realisation and release.

Then Prince Murum Tsenpo performed prostration and circumambulation; and piling up a mountain of offerings including an effigy of a deer made of gold, thirty large copper tubs full of turquoise – the principal piece was the great turquoise 'The Open Door of the Sky' – and much more. Then he made this request: 'I, the mere semblance of a prince, in my great pride, indolence and distraction, I delight in vice, warfare and enforcing the law. Whatever I do is a sinful game. Please give me instruction that is profound and concise, easy to understand and easy to practise, a teaching that confers great blessing and quickly leads to *siddhi,* and that will erase my faults and restore my wasted mind. This I beg of you.'

The Guru replied:

So be it! So be it! Conqueror's Son!
Your aspiration is pure, your *karma* is pure,
With faith, holding fast, on trial you are firm.[4]
After seven rebirths from now
You will not take a karmic body
But teach others through emanation.
Your mind will be one with the Buddhas past, present and future,
And after the passing of an aeon
You will become the Buddha Starlight.

The Guru then revealed the *maṇḍala* of Yangdak, the deity who is quick to grant *siddhi,* and he gave the Prince the special instruction called The Self-liberating Understanding of the Profound Path of the Wrathful and Peaceful Deities,[5] which brought him to spiritual maturity and release. He was instructed to conceal this teaching upon the mountain peak of Dakpo Dar so that it could be of great benefit to beings of the future. Furthermore, the Great Guru granted him the special means of identifying with the Lama called Lama Jewel Lotus Garland and other teaching, instructing that it should be concealed in the Ramoche Rock.

Later, the Guru consecrated the Karchung Dorying temple, and remained there a week before preparing to leave for

Orgyen. Before dawn on the seventh day, before the Guru's departure, I made this prayer:

O Lama, in your great compassion draining the bog of emotion,
Immediately liberating even sinful people
Who see you, hear you, think of you or touch you,
Pema Jungne, Messenger of the Conquering Buddhas,
Now and forever look upon the Land of Tibet with compassion.
Now that I have finished my work of conversion
I implore you, Lord, to grant my prayer
To remain with you always, never to leave you for a moment.

The Lama replied:

O Listen, Daughter of Kharchen.
The ball of fire-crystal blown by the wind
Creates day and night and the four seasons in due order;
Neither sun nor sky has any control.
When the harvest ripens the rice grains spill out;
The farmer can do nothing to prevent it.
Now that your Awareness has expanded,
The residual germs of passion lie impotent;
Your limitless body, its impurity dissolved,
Cannot remain, though grasped by a finite mentality.
You have realised the creative, fulfilment and Dzokchen meditations
And you cannot remain, despite the imagination of your disciples.
Karma exhausted, reality extinguished, transformation complete,
Corporeality consumed, now the five sense-fields and the five elements vanish
And wondrously you arrive at the state of *nirvāṇa.*
After the passing of fifty years, on the eighth day of the bird month,
Tsogyel will pass into lotus light.
A galaxy of Ḍākinīs and Buddha Heroes will meet you,
But until then, employ your abilities for the sake of others.

So saying the Guru vanished.

Then I, Tsogyel, went to the Phukmoche Cave at Kharchu in Lhodrak, where I inspired Namkhai Nyingpo to reach the goal of his energy control practices, granting him the *siddhi* of immortality. The Gelong also gained both mundane and supreme *siddhi*.

Thereafter, I entered into meditation with understanding of the pure potential of Dzokchen, and the vision of reality extinguished arose. Sentient beings, who were to be transformed, identified me as a variety of different appearances emanating for their benefit. To the starving I appeared as a mountain of food, bringing them happiness; to the poverty-stricken I appeared as all kinds of wealth, bringing them happiness; to the naked I appeared as various kinds of clothes, bringing them happiness; to the childless I appeared as sons or daughters, bringing them happiness; to men desiring women I appeared as attractive girls, bringing them happiness; to women desiring husbands I appeared as handsome men, bringing them happiness; to those who wished to perform miracles I granted the eight great *siddhi*s, bringing them happiness; to those afflicted by disease I appeared as medicine, bringing them happiness; to those afflicted by anxiety and frustration I appeared as their inner needs, bringing them happiness; those tormented by the law I brought back into the land of harmony and loving fellowship, bringing them happiness; to those paralysed by fear of wild beasts and spectres I appeared as the various deterrents of their persecutors, bringing them happiness; those who had fallen into the abyss I rescued, bringing them happiness; to those afflicted by fire I appeared as water, and to those afflicted by any of the five elements I appeared as the appropriate antidote, bringing them happiness; to the blind I manifested as eyes, bringing them happiness; to the lame I manifested as legs, bringing them happiness; to the dumb I manifested as tongues, bringing them happiness; to those trembling in fear of death I granted immortality, bringing them happiness; the dying I set on the path of transference to a pure-land, bringing them happiness; to beings wandering in the *bardo* I appeared as a Yidam deity, bringing them happiness; beings wandering in hell suffering from heat I cooled, bringing them happiness; those suffering in hell from cold I warmed, bringing them happiness; and wherever and from whatever the denizens of hell suffered I transformed myself into the means of assuaging their suffering, bringing them happiness; savage people living an evil existence I turned back from the path of error, bringing them happiness; to beings wandering in the realm of the hungry ghosts I appeared as all sorts of food and drink, bringing them happiness; beings wandering in the jungle as beasts I liberated from the suffering of stupidity, insensitivity and servitude, bringing them happiness; those born as anti-gods and titans I freed from war and strife, bringing them happiness; those born as gods I freed from knowledge of their impending discomfiture, death and ignominious rebirth, bringing them happiness; I saved beings from their torment no matter what their discomfort, bringing them to happiness.

In short, wheresoever is human emotion, there is sentient life; wheresoever is sentient life, there are the five elements; wheresoever are the five elements, there is space; and in so far as my compassion is co-extensive with space, it pervades all human emotion. Appearing first as one emanation and then as another, I remained in Phukmoche for twelve years.

Then it was that the former consort of Guru Rimpoche, an Awareness Ḍākinī, the Queen of the Siddhas, the Knowledge Holder Dungmen Gyelmo, known also as the Divine Consort, the Flower Mandāravā came from India. Emerging from the sky with her six disciples, she greeted me. She stayed with me for thirty-nine human days, and we exchanged and tightened our precepts, making endless discussion on the *dharma*. In particular, Mandāravā asked me for the twenty-seven secret precepts, special teaching, which the Guru had not given in India, and I asked Mandāravā, who was a Ḍākinī of Long-life, a Lord of Life, for the seven secret precepts upon the Accomplishment of Long-life, and thirty-three further secret precepts concerning Hayagrīva and other deities. All these teachings I concealed as treasures to be revealed in the future. Then I offered these verses to Mandāravā:

OM ĀH HŪNG! O Ḍākinī, you have attained an immortal
  vajra-body –
Your body dances in the sky like a rainbow
And with skill you move unimpeded through concrete form.
You have destroyed the devil Lord of Death

And conquered the devil Embodiment;
You are liberated from the bondage of passion
And you have annihilated the Godling Devil:
You are surely a Ḍākinī Mistress of Life.
You have attained the Body of Pure Pleasure by means of all the best elixirs
In the three realms beneath the Highest Heaven.
Mandāravā, Magnificent Symbol of Emptiness,
Mother of beings, to you I bow down.
To human beings with the constant *karma* of rebirth and death,
Treading the waterwheel of continual delusion,
You close the door of descent;
May this prayer to emulate you be fulfilled.
Karma exhausted, worldly pleasure at an end, all taint of delusion erased,
The three realms and all of *saṃsāra* extinguished, and all fictional projection withdrawn,
Sealed by pleasure in the sphere of pure pleasure,
May we be one with Kuntuzangpo's pure pleasure.

After this I made many wish-fulfilling prayers and requested the various teachings that had not been heard previously in Tibet. The Divine Consort, Queen of Siddhas, Mandāravā, replied in this way:

O Sky-dancer, you have mastery of the Tantra;
O shape-shifter, you have dissolved your corporeal impurity in immaculate space;
You drank the nectar of Pema's precepts, gathering essences:
Surely you are the Great Mother of Perfect Wisdom!
You entered the path of seeing the truth of the teaching;
You repudiated the eight petty preoccupations of this life;[6]
You performed the austerity of extracting and consuming essences,
And reduced the universe and its energy to sameness:
I bow down to you, Tsogyel, immaculate maiden.
Through your skill in ascetic *yoga* you have liberated beings,
Sinful beings, blown by the storm of *karma* and slaves to endless *saṃsāra*!
You have established the Buddha's teaching,

Destroying Bonpos of demonic form and distorted vision:
May I be one with you, Mistress of Powerful Magic.
Hereafter, purity suffusing the sphere of purity,
In your field of lotus-light,
You and I will project emanations of Buddha's *karma*
As light-forms of Guru Pema Skull-Garland's compassion:
May we empty the depths of the three realms of *saṃsāra*.

Having made this wish-fulfilling prayer, she disappeared into the firmament.

Thereafter, I, Tsogyel, with Be Yeshe Nyingpo, Ma Rinchen Chok, Odren Pelgyi Zhonnu, Langlab Gyelwa Jangchub Dorje, Darcha Dorje Pawo, Surya Tepa of Central Tibet, the Bhutanese girl Tashi Chidren, the Nepali Kalasiddhi, Jangchub Drolma of Khotan, Dorje Tsomo of Shelkar, Zhonnu Drolma of Kharchen, these eleven root disciples together with seventy-nine acolytes, went to the Zapu Valley in Shang. After I had been there for ten years in all, serving my disciples, I composed myself in the *samādhi* that brings all things to extinction.[7] But six of my karmically favoured spiritual sons led by Be Yeshe Nyingpo, with the faithful 'Khon and others, implored me to stay to turn the wheel of the teaching rather than to pass into *nirvāṇa*:

Great Mother Transcendent, endowed with the signs of empty being,
When your sun and moon's lustre is absorbed into inner space
Who can we two-footed earth-bound creatures trust?
Please stay to reveal to us still the *maṇḍala* of perfect insight.
Transcendent Conqueror whose visionary being is a provident raincloud,
When your ambrosial secret precepts are absorbed into inner space
Who can we earth-bound seedlings and young shoots trust?
Please stay to shower us still with the ambrosia of your teaching.
Tsogyel, our refuge and exemplar of apparitional being,
When your signs and marks of Buddhahood are absorbed into inner space
Who can we pathless dependants trust?
We entreat you for spiritual maturity and release.
Take pity on us, exalted Tsogyelma!

Thus they prayed to me fervently. I replied, 'Prepare a great *gaṇacakra* feast, my sons and daughters, and after I have revealed to you the *maṇḍala*s of many, most profound *tantra*s, I will give you instruction. After the eighth day of this month only Tsogyel's name will remain here in Tibet.' Then, despondent and somewhat hysterical, they prepared an extensive *gaṇacakra*. The disciples, all brothers and sisters on the path, sat down around me with long faces, weeping as they gazed at me. After some time I spoke to them:

Listen carefully, you people of my community,
Lend your ear and mind to the sound.
There is no need for despond, take heart!
Since life is a conditioned state, it is transitory;
Since the objective world is light-form, it is insubstantial;
Since the path is delusive, it has no validity;
Since *saṃsāra* is Emptiness, it is unreal;
Since the mind is its conflicting thoughts, it has no foundation:
I have seen nothing whatsoever that is ultimately real.

You faithful brothers and sisters assembled here,
Pray unequivocally to me, your Mother,
And I will bless you with the pure pleasure of dynamic space.
There can never be any meeting or parting –
Those forming karmic connection with me automatically have my guidance,
And others will be saved by my impartial compassionate emanations.
Your Mother is free of the anxiety of death and transition
So there is no reason for sadness, brothers and sisters.

I have completed direct conversion of my circle on this plane.
According to the prophecy of venerable Śrī Orgyen,
In this life two hundred years were allotted for conversion.
Not only two hundred but more have passed
And I have sustained Tibet for a very long time.
At the age of 13 I became the Emperor's Queen;
At the age of 16 my Guru's compassion embraced me;
Reaching 20 I gained full initiation and practised austerities;
At 30 I gained realisation and worked for others' welfare;

At 40 I identified with my Guru's mind;
At 50 I vanquished devils and defended the teaching;
At 60 I propagated the scriptures and enlarged the community;
At 70 I discovered the nature of reality;
When I reached 80 my Guru departed for the South-West;
At 90 I saw the face of reality as its essence;
At 100 my Knowledge reached optimal fullness;
At 120 I became the Emperor's priestess;
At 130 I travelled throughout the whole of Tibet;
At 150 I concealed treasures and worked for others;
When I was 160 King Mutri Tsenpo died;
And at 170 I liberated my remaining disciples;
At 180 I projected apparitional forms in Lhodrak;
At 190 I met my only elder sister, Queen of Siddhas,
And receiving the supreme precept, attaining the *siddhi* of long-life,
The marks of rebirth and death spontaneously dissolved.
Now 211 years have passed;
Surely that is sufficient protection for Tibet,
And surely all the gods and men are grateful,
My partners in happiness and sorrow.
Now when I have gone it will seem that we have parted
But do not be depressed, my friends;
Pray with penetration and concentration.
Immerse yourselves in the pure potential of Dzokchen
For there is no other way to transcend the misery of existence.
Instruction in Dzokchen is the heartblood of Orgyen Pema.
He gave it to me
And now I must transmit it to you.
Practise it and attain *siddhi*.
You may transmit it to all suitable recipients,
But deny it to those who lack the capacity to contain it.
Swear to keep it out of the hands of vow-violators
And seal it away from opinionated people.

Then swearing them to secrecy, to my eleven root disciples I revealed the *maṇḍala* of Dzokchen Ati, bestowing upon them the hundred secret precepts which are like my heart, and in an instant they gained release. (*This was the final propagation of Tsogyel's whispered transmission.*)

I was residing in the uppermost cave of Pama Gang when on the third day of the bird month of my 211th year I announced to my disciples that we all should leave for the Zapu Peak to view a spectacle that would take place there on the eighth day of that month, and that we should all stay there on the Copper-coloured Mountain.[8] With my eleven most favoured disciples and about fifty acolytes I started out for the Zapu Peak. On the seventh day of the month, at the waist of the mountain, I found a cave shaped like a *namaste mudrā*, and we settled there for the night. I gave my disciples twenty-nine short teachings, and then, having enjoyed a great *gaṇacakra* feast that creates identity with the Lama, my disciples gathered in front of me.

'Mortality is the essential characteristic of humanity,'[9] I told them.

Then Tashi Chidren offered me a golden plate and made this petition:

Most generous Mother, Lady Tsogyel,
Only mother of all the beings of the three realms,
When you no longer sustain your spiritual sons,
Although those with co-ordinated hand and mouth can survive,
How will the clutch of naive idealists manage?
O great golden jewel of the firmament,
When you no longer enlighten the darkness of beings,
Although those with the eye of wisdom can follow the path,
Your bubble-eyed dependants will fall into the abyss.
O specially qualified regent of the Buddha,
When you no longer guard your devout Listeners,
Although exalted *arhats* can protect themselves,
Who will take care of the little monks, hard of hearing?
O Ḍākinī endowed with the voice of Brahmā,
When you no longer protect this community,
Although the translators, scholars and adepts will survive,
Who will lead the masses of common people?
Alas! accomplished lady,
Still look upon this circle with compassion.
If you must leave this community of brothers and sisters
We implore you first to grant us the ambrosia of your lips.

Tashi Chidren prostrated repeatedly, and then sat down. I replied:

Listen, faithful Daughter of Bhutan.
I, the Lady Tsogyel,
Tirelessly working for the people's welfare,
Have sustained the whole of Tibet with my vibrance,
And as many as 200 years have passed.
Now that my work of conversion is certainly complete,
Without means to remain, to postpone my departure is impossible,
Just as it is for sentient beings who must pass over at death.
However, I will leave behind a few words of testament.
Please listen to me, brothers and sisters here assembled.

There are innumerable black-topped people in this world
But those who cherish the teaching can be counted;
You practitioners of the Community are far fewer,
And *siddha*s are as rare as stars in the day sky,
While these days no-one attains Buddhahood.
So remember this maxim, 'Live the *dharma*!'
Although it is said that there are eighty-four thousand methods,
Innumerable paths that lead to the one goal,
In essence they are reducible to the nine vehicles,
And the nine vehicles reduce to the threefold Ati;[10]
The substance of Ati is contained in this unsurpassable teaching,
This teaching upon Vision, Meditation, Action and Goal:
Vision is freedom from analytical mentality;
Meditation is experiential knowledge of primal purity;
Action is characterised by imperturbable relaxation;
And the goal is natural expression of the Buddha's three modes.
This, then, is the quintessence of the teaching.

When your public behaviour conforms to the strictures of the *vinaya*,
The aberrant strains in others are automatically suppressed.
When inner spiritual practice is in accordance with the *sūtra*s,
Since like breeds like, virtue and merit automatically accrue.
When metaphysical vision is in accordance with the *abhidharma*,

Doubts and over-evaluated ideas are automatically eradicated.
Vinaya, sūtra and *abhidharma* are the bedrock of the teaching,
And there is no other way to bear the torch of the doctrine.

Purificatory practices performed according to the rubric of *kriyā*
Eradicate the germs of negative proclivities.
Cultivating the mind according to the rubric of *upayoga*
Automatically induces familiarity with the *dharma*.
Training vision according to the rubric of *yoga-tantra*
Automatically induces the blessings of compassion.
Practice of invocation and accomplishment in *mahāyoga*
Automatically produces Vision, Meditation and Action.
Practice of energy control in *anuyoga*
Automatically grants power and *siddhi*.
Purifying seed-essence as Ati itself
Accomplishes Buddhahood instantaneously.

No more instruction than this is necessary.
All who would emulate me
Should rely upon techniques described in this biography
And the fulfilment of one's own and others' aims – the final goal – is achieved.

After I had finished, the Nepali girl Kalasiddhi performed many prostrations and circumambulations and then made this request:

Mother, when you have vanished into inner space,
What should we zap-lam initiates of the Tibetan mysteries do?
Who will dispel obstructing spirits and stimulate our meditation?
Still sustain Tibet with your compassion!

I answered her:

O listen Ḍākinī, well-born lady,
Mantra-born maiden with *siddhi*,
You who show the path of virtue
With a well-endowed body's selfless aspiration.
This community and future travellers on the zap-lam path,

Must first find a Lama especially qualified,
And from the Lama possessing every spiritual sign,
You must request initiation and pledge fulfilment of your vows.
Then train your energy flows until you gain self-control,
And after receiving the three superior initiations,[11] cultivate ensuing desire,
To perfect the nature of the four levels of joy,
For six months or until signs of achievement appear in the body.
Unite male (solar) and female (lunar) energies,
Developing the method of mixing higher and lower energies,
Female assisting male and male assisting female,
The principles of each being separately practised.
Intensify and elevate your practice, broadening the horizons of your pleasure;
But if pleasure and Emptiness are not identified,
Profitlessly you stray from the path of Tantra:
Apprehend the intrinsic unity of pleasure and Emptiness.
Guard the *samaya* of Guru and Ḍākinī like your eyes;
In various skilful ways enjoy the five sacred substances;
Practise to perfection the skill of retaining your seed-essence;
Be attentive to obstacles and hostile powers;
If the *samaya* is impaired strive to restore it.
About the body: do not let it slip into old habits
Or you will become like ordinary men and women;
With the confidence of the deity, meditate charged with power
And inform your focal points of energy as a principal and his circle of deities.
About speech: concentrate upon *mantra* and energy flows –
Without energy control your sexual activity is fornication;
Properly execute the exercises of 'drawing up' and 'saturating'
And with the nails of your imagination apply an hermetic seal.
About mind: identify the conditioned mind with seed-essence itself;
If seed-essence is lost in actuality
The *karma* of slaying a Buddha is incurred;
At all costs gain self-control.
Absorb yourself intently in the experience of desire,
For without it the mysteries have no meaning;
Desire as pure pleasure is the goal fulfilled.

Preserve constant cognition of the primal purity of experience;
Protect the *samaya* like your body and life,
For if it is broken there is no authority to restore it.
The foregoing is advice upon meditation practice.
All you initiates into the tantric mysteries
Should bury your ambition and conceit in a pit,
Pour your sanctimony and pride into a river,
Burn your obsessive lust and infatuation in fire,
Cast your selfish aggression and perverse behaviour on the wind,
And dissolve your shamelessness and deceitful lies in space.
Protect your secret sexual practices from prying eyes;
Do not be loose with your sexual organs, bind them fast;
Do not flaunt your signs of success;
Rely upon the Yidam deity as the indivisible three roots;[12]
Maintain regular torma offerings[13] and *gaṇacakra* feast rites;
Preserve the seed of kindness for the sake of other beings;
Do not break the flow of formless benediction.
The foregoing is general instruction upon Action.

With that understanding fixed in your heart, O Siddhi,
You and I are essentially one,
And through emanation we will give purpose to beings of the future.

Then Be Yeshe Nyingpo made this request:

O Yeshe Tsogyelma!
I beg you to give oral instruction
For me and those like me.
Still with your compassionate waves of grace
Never leave us, always protect us.

And I replied:

O listen, Yeshe Nyingpo.
Ask your Lord and Lama for his blessings;
Ask the Four Ḍākinīs for their powers of magical activity;
Then reveal your signs of power at the opportune moment:
That is an indication of meditation in action.

Listen further, Yeshe Nyingpo:
Through the *vinaya*, maintain the noble image of your order
And others will appreciate it and emulate you.
Apply yourself to tantric meditation
And you will quickly gain realisation.
Strive in your spiritual practice according to the essence of the *sūtra*s
And the scriptural tradition will become strong.
Diligently practise invocation and accomplishment of the Yidam deity
And you will quickly attain whatever *siddhi* you desire.
Rid yourself of over-evaluated ideas by reference to the *abhidharma*
And you will become free from hesitancy and doubt.
Exert yourself in meditation upon psychic nerves, energy flows and seed-essence
And signs of success will be quickly perfected.
Purify yourself according to the techniques of *kriyā*
And unclean habits will be quickly eradicated.
Penetrate the reality of Vision, Meditation and Action,
And your own enlightenment will be firmly established.
Meditate upon the goal, the pure potential of Dzokchen,
And reality extinguished, mental processes cease.
Offer impartial wish-fulfilling prayers
And measureless advantage will accrue to sentient beings.

Then Ma Rinchen Chok made his petition:

> Lama, Lady Tsogyelma,
> When you have gone to the Land of Orgyen
> How should we of this community act?
> How should we pray?
> Please tell us how we can remain with you.

And he wept. I replied:

O listen, *yogin*,
You who have gained mastery of the Tantra,
Your concern for others is admirable.
I, a woman, Yeshe Tsogyelma,

Have been blessed by the Guru's compassion
And now my goal is fully realised;
Tomorrow I go to the Land of Orgyen.
Pray and you will be blessed.

Brothers and sisters of this assembly,
Concentrate upon the teaching to serve your highest interest,
And without conceit, guard the interest of others.
Liberate yourselves through Vision, Meditation and Action;
Mount your prayers on the vibrance of Buddha Speech,
And despatch them with bone deep assurance and devotion.
Meditate upon the Lama just as the radiance of Knowledge
And when the peak experience of immense space dawns,
When centrifugal diffusion and centripetal re-absorption are one[14]
Remain in that state.
If you recognise me, the Ḍākinī Queen of the Lake of Awareness,
The principal of the whole of *saṃsāra* and *nirvāṇa,*
You know that I live in the minds of all sentient beings;
I project myself as the elements of body-mind and the sense-fields
And by secondary emanation I appear as the twelve interdependent elements of existence.[15]
Though certainly we are ultimately inseparable,
Failing to recognise me, you objectify me as an external entity.
But when you finally discover me,
The one naked mind arisen from within,
Absolute Awareness[16] permeates the universe;
Pleasure in primal purity is contained like a lake;
And the golden-eyed fishes of heightened perception multiply.
Sustain that consummation of visionary experience and pleasure
And on the wings of perfect creativity you cross to the other side;
Running and jumping in the meadows of visionary appearances
You fly into the sky-matrix and vanish.
In the immense space of absolute Awareness
The seed-essence of pure pleasure stands thick like a lake,
Pure being and seed-essence glister and pulsate

And seed-syllables and light-garlands sparkle and shimmer.
The vision of reality manifest expands, intensive visionary
  experience increases,
The castle of optimal Knowledge is seized
And reality is extinguished as you vanish into primal space.
That is the way to remain inseparable from me.

Then Odren Zhonnu Pel made this petition:

> O Yeshe Tsogyelma!
> When you go to the Land of Orgyen
> How should we incorrigible common creatures
> Practise Vision, Meditation and Action?
> I beg you for a little advice.

In response I gave this instruction:

Listen, faithful Zhonnu Pel.
The fledgling Ḍākinī-bird nesting in a crag
Could not conceive how easy was flight
Until her skill in the six vehicles was perfected;
But her potential realised, wings beating with hidden strength,
Breaking the back of even the razor-edged wind,
She arrived at whatever destination she chose.
It was like that with me too, the girl Tsogyel;
Although I longed for Buddhahood I was forced to wait
Until I had perfected my skill in meditation practice.
Practising to perfection the creative and fulfilment processes
  and Dzokchen,[17]
This corporeal bundle dissolved in light,
And now I go into the presence of Orgyen Guru.
But I will leave you with these few words of testament.

'Vision' is but a quality of all meditative existence;
Yet absorbed in reality, experiencing its nature,
You find not Emptiness for there is Knowledge and radiance,
Yet nothing permanent for it is intrinsically empty.
That essential insight is called 'Vision'.
What are the modes of Vision?

When you practise radiation and re-absorption, it is
compassion;
When you practise the fulfilment process, it is *mahāmudrā*,
The essence without permanence or flux.
Turn your eyes inwards upon your own reality
And you see yourself, but you see nothing:
That visionary perception in itself,
That is what is designated 'Vision'.

'Meditation' is the basis of all meditative existence;
When absorbed in reality, experiencing its nature,
Intent upon seeing the essential Vision,
Focusing an unwavering attention free of any limitation,
That is called meditative absorption.
And what are the modes of meditation?
Whether you practise the creative or fulfilment process
Peak experience shows you the ineffable reality –
You may practise any of the innumerable modes of meditation.
In truth, whatever your technique, the creative or fulfilment
process,
In a condition free from depression, torpor and mental fog,
Registering undistracted silence,
If you focus upon universal sameness, you practise 'Meditation'.

'Action' is the dynamic form of meditative existence;
When absorbed in its reality, experiencing its nature,
Sure in clarity of Vision, Meditation an ineradicable habit,
In a state of imperturbable relaxation,
You will see yourself perform a variety of actions.
What are the specific modes of Action?
Whatever the variable form of your activity,
Based in primal purity there is no conflict with meditative
experience,
Which is intensified and elevated.
In truth, working, sleeping, coming, going,
Eating, sitting – in the performance of every activity
Is the quality of 'Action'
Because Action is an integral function of meditation practice –
Creative and fulfilment processes and Dzokchen, etc.
There is nothing else to say.

Although I am going to Ngayab Ling,
I leave Tibet saturated with precepts.
All you who have faith must pray!

Then Dorje Tso of Shelkar made this request:

O Mother of this entire land of Tibet,
And especially lord of this dependant,
Because there is no one to replace you
Do not forsake me, do not withdraw your compassion,
Please take me with you into lotus-light.
But if my heavy load of *karma*
Prevents me from following you there,
Please give me plenty of instruction and secret precepts.

Choked by her tears, Dorje Tso fainted away with emotion. When she revived I answered her:

Listen, faithful Daughter of Shelkar,
Awareness Ḍākinī, Dorje Tso!
Your body is a thing of flesh and blood,
An inferior body, a slave to matter –
Practise energy control and become a Sky-dancer.
When you gain control of your energy flows and mind
You become nothing if not a *siddha*.

Your slippery mind, possessed by the five poisons,
Orchestrates a coarse personality,
An obstinate train of ordinary crass thoughts.
If you desire to obtain Buddhahood, purify your mind,
Composing yourself in *mahāmudrā*.
When Emptiness and Awareness are set free,
You are nothing if not a Buddha.

This dissimulating corporeal bundle,
This body is the seat of all good and bad.
If you wish to obtain a rainbow body, dissolve corporeality,
Absorbing yourself in the continuous peak experience of
  Dzokchen Ati.
When you arrive at the extinction of reality

There is nothing but the spontaneity of pure potential.
There is no other way to dance in the sky.

In the meantime, while you purify your gross body,
There is a secret way to enter lotus-light.
So listen to this instruction.
Pray to your root Guru;
Without even a moment's thought of equality with him,
Pray to him with pure vision, devotion, respect and faith,
Asking him for the blessings of the four empowerments;
Then admitting no separation from him,
Visualise him as light radiating from the centre of your heart;
Uniting your body, speech and mind with his,
Stay in the meditative composure of *mahāmudrā*.
Then in subsequent cognition along the path, sustain your heightened perception;[18]
To inspire your meditation, try to cultivate the play of empty pleasure,
And continue on your way detached from objects of desire;
With conviction practise Dzokchen
And enter the place where Ati ends.

After this, for eleven successive lives,
You will show skilful means in training the people of Tibet,
And then you will arrive in lotus-light.
When you are known as Dorje Dechen Pema Tso,
You will project an apparitional form
And join with Gelong Namkhai Nyingpo
In a union of Means and Insight.
Training a billion alienated beings,
The vicious hosts at the edge of the world
Your selfless activity will be beyond expression.
Namkhai Nyingpo will be named 'Ching'
(called Che-'jing mir-gon)[19]
And you will be his divine consort
And live for 130,000 human years.
After that, in a nimbus of lotus light,
You will become inseparable from your Guru and Lord.

After I had made these prophecies, I gave Dorje Tso much

further advice. Then Lasum Gyelwa Jangchub peformed innumerable prostrations and circumambulations, and having prepared a plate of seven turquoises, the chief of which was a life-protection amulet called 'A Thousand Blazing Lights', he presented it to me and made this request:

Endowed with an infallible memory, the Keeper of Pema's
  Secret Word,
Mother of Great and Perfect Insight, Voice of Puṛe Pleasure,[20]
Only sun in this dark land of Tibet, Tsogyelma,
Now if you are truly leaving for the South-West,
Please grant me a few concise words that will bestow great
  waves of bliss,
Precepts of profound import, framing a practice sharp and
  quick,
Instructions in the accomplishment of Buddhahood in this
  lifetime.
And please tell me how many rebirths I must take after this,
And when I will meet you, the Sky Dancer, the Ḍākinī.
Still bathe me in your compassion!

In response to Gyelwa Jangchub's first request, I taught *The Heartdrop of the Apparitional Sky Dancer*, which was divided into three parts – outer, inner and secret. The outer part was in conformity with the *sūtra*s, and consisted of ten topics; the inner part was in conformity with the *tantra*s and consisted of eleven topics; the secret part, in the form of secret instruction, consisted of thirteen ultimate precepts. [*The text then lists the topics dealt with in each part of the* Khacho Tulku Nying-tik.[21]] Upon the conclusion of this instruction, the seven members of the initiatory circle, Gyelwa Jangchub and his brothers and sisters, having gained the final relief of freedom into the clear light, leaving no mortal remains behind, attained spiritual release. Then I gave Gyelwa Jangchub this advice and prophecy:

Listen attentively, Gyelwa Jangchub,
Hear me well, Guardian of a Virtuous Mind.
O Buddha Hero of Skilful Means, Āyra Sale,
When you were known as Atsara Sale
You and I related as Skilful Means and Perfect Insight,

And the requisite constituents of many profound *tantras* were synchronised.
Thereby you were blessed, and you will gain release in this lifetime.
However, at times you were over-familiar with me,
And sometimes doubting me, you abused me and derided me within.
In all future lives, in later incarnations,
Although you will have gained mastery of the Tantra,
Obstructive influences will certainly impede you,
Much malicious boastful talk will haunt you
And your attempts to serve others will be fraught with difficulty.
Remember that whatever obstacles arise are the result of your past actions,
And pray to Pema Jungne and Tsogyel indivisible.
Hereafter, for thirteen lifetimes, you will continue selfless service to others,
And then you will reincarnate in a rough inhospitable land.
To the west of this sacred mountain you will appear as Namkha,
In a *vajra* body, heroic and fierce, called Taksham,
And as Taksham in three successive lives
You will still the wind of *karma* and appear in lotus light.
Then inseparable from me, in a union of Means and Insight,
We will project emanations until the current of reincarnation is exhausted in all beings.
Then will powerful aspiration reach its fulfilment;
Then will the essences of many profound *tantras* spread;
Then will the fruit of deep meditation practice ripen;
Then will the full potential of creative and fulfilment processes evolve;
Then will the just deserts of meritorious *karma* be served;
Then will a great cloud of profound blessings waft across the sky;
Then will the rain of deep compassion fall;
Āyra Salewa will gain *siddhi*,
Gyelwa Jangchub will gain true realisation.
Now pray with fervour, meditate intensely!

Upon the evening of the eighth day the twelve kinds of Devil Ḍākinīs[22] from the Ḍākinī Land of Orgyen appeared, proclaiming themselves to be twelve million in all (12000000). Around midnight the twelve kinds of man-eating Ḍākinīs arrived – life-suckers, breath-thieves, flesh-eaters, blood-drinkers, bone-chewers, etc., proclaiming themselves to be five million, five thousand, five hundred in number (5005500), so that the earth and sky were filled with carnivores. In the small hours hosts of Mundane Ḍākinīs and Ḍākinīs of the Twelve Divisions of Time, twelve million, one hundred and twenty thousand in all (12120000) announced themselves, coming riding upon lions and various other beasts, different birds such as the Garuḍa, various domestic animals such as the elephant, and other jungle animals like the deer and the rhinoceros; their forms were of different sizes and shapes and their faces were covered with masks of human beings and various other kinds of creatures. During the hour before dawn more Ḍākinīs appeared, proclaiming themselves as the Ḍākinīs of the Four Directions of Orgyen and as Ḍākinīs of the Twelve Island Continents. These hosts of Ḍākinīs were differentiated by colour into white, red, green, blue-black and yellow legions – of the white legion some were fully white, some partially red, some partially green, some partially blue and some partially yellow, and likewise the red, green, yellow and blue-black legions were particoloured. Accordingly, they held different symbolic emblems in their hands, various kinds of weapons indicating their nature. Wearing silk scarves, bone ornaments, tiaras, mantles covering the upper part of their bodies and skirts covering their lower parts; they carried small tinkling bells, thighbone trumpets, skull drums and any of a million different kinds of musical instruments difficult to classify or enumerate. There were five million, two hundred thousand (5200000) of these Ḍākinīs. Between first light and sunrise the Ḍākinī of the Sixty-eight Maṇḍalas and their principal, the Beautifully Proportioned Queen of the Lotus Dance (Pema Garwong Lhundze), announced themselves. The sky was full of shimmering rainbow light, redolence of incense permeated the earth, and the air in between was full of Ḍākinīs. Between noon and evening all the Ḍākinīs of the Thirty-two Lands, the Ten Heruka Power Places, the Eight Great Cemeteries, and the Pīlava, the Chandoha and their subsidiary power places[23] fully manifest themselves, each performing her particular dance, each demonstrating her personal gesture, each playing her unique musical instrument, each singing her own song and with her own style of entertainment, each with her special skill, each with her different mode of worship and her precious offering, all worshipping and praising me, filling the earth.

Then I gave a vast *gaṇacakra* feast for them. Through my magical powers, with a single piece of pure molasses, I fed to satiety all the assembled humans, and to the Ḍākinīs I distributed an even greater amount. Next, with just one full skull-bowl of chung, I satisfied both men and Ḍākinīs. Then I pronounced the secret symbol empowerment of the Ḍākinīs,[24] and simultaneously the assembled human crowd became possessed with an intense feeling of consummate intercourse with the Ḍākinīs; I brought them to the level of ultimate irreversibility.

It being the evening of the ninth day, I ascended with my disciples from the Heart Cave at the waist of the Zapu Mountain to the peak, which resembled the Copper-coloured Mountain, Zangdokperi. At the third hour of the tenth day I revealed the *maṇḍala* of the rite of *Accomplishment of the Lama's Mind through a Single Syllable*,[25] and simultaneously myriads of savage demons, an inconceivable number, appeared. There was a three-headed faction, a one-headed faction, a headless faction, a five-headed faction, a six-headed faction, a hundred-headed faction and so on, countless factions with any number of heads and feet from one to a hundred thousand. 'Guru Pema has sent us to escort the Queen of the Demon Savages, the Ḍākinī Blazing Blue Light,' they said, gathering around.

At daybreak, after I had celebrated a *gaṇacakra*, Gyelwa Jangchub and the eleven faithful, all the human beings, Buddha Heroes, Ḍākinīs, demon savages, gods and demons, devoutly bowed down to me. With tears of grief running down his face, Gyelwa Jangchub addressed me in this manner:

Alas! Awareness Ḍākinī,
Human Guru, Yeshe Tsogyelma,
You, Tibet's only Mother, are dissolving into space.
What shall we intellectual babies do without your support?

We beg you to sustain Tibet for a long time yet.
If you must go, if you cannot remain by any means,
Tell us of the future ebb and flow of the teaching in Tibet.
Please tell us the names of the torch-bearers of the doctrine.
Tell us how the destructive, diabolic emanation will come,
And what will augur reversal of catastrophe.
In particular, tell us what your emanations will be,
What will be their names, their purpose, their location,
Their activity for others, and the nature of their teaching.
Without concealment, secrecy or symbols, but clearly,
We implore you to tell us this, Omniscient Queen.
And particularly, your extensive, abridged and concise biographies,
The Heartdrop of the Apparitional Sky Dancer
And the set of *Higher and Lower, Mother and Son, Whispered Transmission*,
How should we transmit them? through the oral or revealed transmission?
And to what fortunate beings should they be entrusted?
Where should they be concealed if they are to be hidden treasures?
What treasure-finders will come, and what signs will appear to them?
Please give us detailed instruction and extensive manifests.
And what should this community of brothers do now?
Where should we place our confidence, hope and trust?
Who will pray for us upon death and dispel obstacles in the *bardo*?
O take pity on us, and help us quickly!

(*For a full account of Tsogyel's answer look into* the Great Register of Prophets:[26] *this is a short summary of her reply*.)

Listen attentively, Tibetan men and gods;
Listen closely, faithful, fortunate beings.
I, this Supreme Being, Yeshe Tsogyelma,
I have served Tibet for 211 years, and hereafter
King Tri Repachan, the Dharma Protector, an emanation of Vajrapāṇi,
Shall universalise the doctrines of *sūtra* and *tantra*.

His younger brother, the diabolic emanation Ox (Langdarma), will conspire with the ministers,
And after assassinating his elder brother, Ox will rule the kingdom
And erase even the memory of the monasteries and the scriptures.
He will establish a law inimical to the Buddha's teaching,
Based upon the ten vices and the five inexpiable sins.
The most devout practitioners of the Faith will be killed,
The lesser banished, the least enslaved,
But the tantric *vajra*-brothers of the villages will keep the teaching alive,
While Lhasa and Samye are despoiled and fall into ruin.
When Pelgyi Dorje remembers his Guru's prophetic injunction,
He will assassinate the diabolic king and flee towards Mekham.
Mar and Yo will restore the pure *vinaya* teaching;[27]
Ten monks will assemble at Lang-thang Drolma, in Kham,
And the bright light of the doctrine will be re-established in Central Tibet and Tsang.
A devout Tibet will promote the teaching,
And through the energy of the sages the Tantra will encompass the earth.

However, much disorderly conduct and some immorality will occur.
An emanation of Orgyen's Speech, Śāntarakṣita's final emanation,
Called Atīśa, will propagate the *sūtra*s and *tantra*s.
I, Tsogyel, called Jayākara,
I will be the attendant of the translator of the Dom Family.[28]
When average lifespan is seventy years, the teaching will increase,
And the world will be white-washed by *sūtra* and *tantra*.

Thereafter, when lifespan has declined to sixty years,
Sa,[29] an emanation of King Trisong Detsen, will bear the torch of the teaching;
Upon the weakening of his royal line, the Tartars will patronise the Lamas.

Drokmi, an emanation of Pema Jungne's Body, will appear,
And propagate The Path as the Goal, re-establishing the scriptural tradition of *sūtras* and *tantras*;
His advent will be comparable to the coming of peerless Śākyamuni.

Thereafter, when the Sakya power disintegrates,
Phak's teaching[30] will gain sway, and average lifespan will be fifty years.
The Old Tradition re-established, the Law will be as strong as it is today.
From Lhorong an emanation of Pema Jungne's Mind will appear,
And his name will be Marpa and the teaching of the Tantra will increase.
I, Tsogyel, will become Marpa's consort and support.
Mila will practise austerity and gain mastery;
An emanation of Pema Jungne's Quality will appear in Dakpo;
Dri, Tak, Kar and Druk will rush forth like streams from Tise.
This ocean of teaching will remain 'til the end to guide beings to happiness.

When average lifespan declines to forty years, the teaching will be fragmented.
Sustained by barbarians like the Tartars the teaching will be coarse:
The country of Tibet will be divided into small autonomous states
And the world will be covered with ulcer-like excrescences.
At that time Pema Jungne's Activity will be projected as Karma,[31]
And the teaching will spread in Tibet, prolonged for a further thirty years,
And the sacred sound of MAṆI will echo throughout the kingdom.

Thereafter, when average lifespan is thirty years, the Virtuous Doctrine[32] will appear.
An emanation of Pema Jungne's essence will come from Central Tibet,

And Tibet will become a paradise of pleasure and delight.
The teaching of the king of the barbarian dynasty of Zahor
Will be established in Central Tibet, Tsang and Kham.

[*Here the text has a single line in the Ḍākinī script beginning with the word 'Thereafter', but otherwise cryptic.*]

An unhappy Tibet will fall into anarchy,
And everyone will depend upon the Tartars for support.
When average lifespan is twenty years, an emanation of Pema Jungne's Speech
Will come from Lhodrak to bring happiness to all beings.
A king with a mole on his shoulder will appear in Khotan,
And his teaching will last until the end. Then lifespan will decrease to ten years,
And then at the aeon's turn, through emanation the earth's essence will be reabsorbed,
And Black Devil Slayer (Dunjom Nakpo) will reign over a dark aeon called Gyachu Mulkal,
Culminating in the advent of Maitreya and resurrection.
These prophecies give only general indications.
For the means to avert errors in transition consult Pema Jungne's pronouncements;
It is not possible for the word of truth to beguile.

In reply to your specific question about my emanations:
I, this Supreme Being, Yeshe Tsogyelma,
I will never withdraw my compassion from Tibet.
Radiating the light of skilful means through emanation,
I will guide all beings of the future to happiness.
In particular, five emanations of Body and five of Speech,
Five emanations of Mind, five of Quality and five of Action –
These twenty-five emanations will constantly sustain Tibet.
Each of these twenty-five will project five secondary emanations,
And each of these will project tertiary emanations, etc.,
Until all sentient beings are apparitional beings,
United with the blissful Great Mother,
Gathered into the matrix of delight, Kuntuzangmo's clear sky.

To be brief, five hundred years from now,
When Tibet is one vast fort bristling with spears,
And the valleys and peaks are covered with castles,
An extremist she-devil will lead beings down a false path.
When her perverse teaching of Severance (gcod) has beguiled the land,
An emanation of my Body will project an emanation of Speech called Drolma;
A Body emanation of my Body called Kunga Zangmo will appear;
A Mind emanation of my Body called Pelmo of Central Tibet will shine forth;
A Quality emanation of my Body called Spiritual Son will appear in Yeru;
And an activity emanation of my Body will appear in Tamyul in Kham.
Thus the scriptural tradition of the profound Tantra will be reasserted;
The perfect esoteric doctrine of Severance will be re-established;
The spiritual sons' Four Leonine Blessings will convert beings.

Thereafter, the Tibetan state is quickly devoured by the Sakyas and Mongols.
The Governor of Central Tibet and Tsang is like the fixed eye of a dice;
The Buddha's teaching is like the flame of a brimming butter lamp;
The malign influences of perversion are like harsh dust storms.
At that time the hundred treasure-finders of Pema's prediction will come,
And the treasures of the Tantra will bring peace to the world.
When spurious revelations, unlike those of the hundred treasure-finders, are forged,
And destructive sourcerers' black magical revelations proliferate,
A Body emanation of my Speech will appear in Ngari
And this famous name will separate true from false revelations;
A Speech emanation of my Speech, a nun, will appear in Central Tibet
And she will be called Orgyen and found a meditation centre

And evince signal powers of mastery of the Tantra;
A Mind emanation of my Speech will appear in Tasho
And he will be called Pema, subject to profound revelations,
Granting *siddhi* to karmically related, purposeful people;
A Quality emanation of my Speech will appear in Kongpo
And this spiritual son will give relief to common people,
And remove all hindrances encountered by treasure-finders;
An Activity emanation of my Speech will appear in Tsang
And known as Jomo she will found a Phakmo meditation centre
And the rites of Pig-face will embrace the world.

Thereafter, foreign armies invade, rising like summer lakes;
Sakya and Drigung quarrel and curdling spreads from the border;
Each holds his own philosophical view;
Adherents of the old and new traditions begin passionate factional strife;
And the distinction between the religious and the secular becomes blurred.
At that time a Body emanation of my Mind will appear from Nyaksa
And he will be called Orgyen and increase the *siddhas*' experiential understanding;
A Speech emanation of my Mind called Sonam Peldren,
Affecting a common manner, will appear in the north;
Covertly granting *siddhi* to the fortunate,
His intelligent disciples leaving behind signs of achievement at death;
A Mind emanation of my Mind called E of Central Tibet
Will lead closely related disciples to the Sky Dancer's Paradise,
Teaching the path to liberation to many *yogin*s practising energy control;
A Quality emanation of my Mind will appear in Lhodrak
And whoever relates to his shape-shifting is established in bliss;
An Activity emanation of Mind will appear in Central Nepal
Where he will establish many people on the path through skilful means.

Thereafter the Emperor's emanations are divided into five;
In Tsang the regent is like a firefly;

The forts of Tramo are like illusory villages;
Good news sounds like songs of the Celestial Musicians;
Bad advice of sages is like sugar-coated poison;
The doctrine's teachers are like dying butter-lamps;
Hor and Mongolia become priest and patron, their cushions touching.
At that time a Body emanation of my Quality, a Ḍākinī, will come from Central Tibet;
A speech emanation of my Quality, called Ḍrolma, will come from Kham;
A Mind emanation of my Quality, a tulku, will appear in Nyemo;
A Quality emanation of my Quality will appear as a teacher in the north;
An Activity emanation of my Quality will appear in Tsang-rong:
Whoever relates to their unpredictable shape-shifting, their miraculous display,
And various extra-sensory powers, are led to Pure Pleasure (Sukhāvatī).

Thereafter, all of Upper and Lower Tibet fragments;
The powerful grab the passes, valleys and gorges, and land is redistributed;
Families are registered and communal land is restricted;
All wealth is concentrated in Hor, and everyone wears Tartar dress;
The devout go to war and armies led by monks increase;
Monks ride camels in the army;
Nuns become coolies, and laymen expound the teaching;
The lot of infants is painful labour.
Then Lhasa is destroyed by water, Samye by fire,
Trandruk falls and the Four Districts are destroyed.
At this time a body emanation of my Activity will come to Chimphu;
A Speech emanation of my Activity will show form in Ngari;
A Mind emanation of my Activity will come to Puwo;
A Quality emanation of my Activity will be projected into Dokham;
An Activity emanation of my Activity will appear as a female leader from Central Tibet:

All these, too, through their various manifold forms,
Guide beings to the paradise of finite infinity,
And lead whosoever relates to them to the Paradise of Pure Pleasure,
And project different tertiary emanations into the Hidden Valleys,
Serving all those with auspicious *karma*, and removing obstacles.

Remember that from the present day until *saṃsāra* is emptied,
Innumerable primary and secondary emanations will appear continually.
And remember in the future that whosoever practises energy control,
The best will see my reality manifest, the average will see signs in vision,
And the mediocre will see my form in a dream.
Either I will be one with your own nature, or appear as your *mudrā*.
For those who maintain the *samaya*,
I will remove obstacles and inspire meditation,
So that the warmth of pleasure, together with *siddhi*, is swiftly generated.

Regarding my extensive, condensed and concise biographies,
Hide the extensive version here on Zapu Peak,
Conceal the concise version at Namkechan in Lhodrak,
And conceal this, the abridged version, in Lhorong Kham.
Concerning *The Higher and Lower Whispered Transmission* and *The Ḍākinī's Heart-drop*,
It is best if you scatter the prophetic manifests separately.
The discoverers will be Jangchub and Ma,[33]
And they will fulfil separate purposes in the future.

Particularly, about this biography, there are nine sets of auspicious circumstances:
First, if it is revealed by one called Chowong,
Its fame will travel throughout the kingdom for the good of beings,
And, finally, reaching China, converts will appear there.

If that opportunity is missed and the treasure remains
concealed,
Someone called Tashi will come from Lato,
And if it is retrieved by him wearing his hair in a knot,
It will embrace converts in Central Tibet, Tsang and Kham for
the good of beings,
And finally it will enlarge the Community in Central Nepal.
If that opportunity is lost and it remains concealed,
A man named Dorje, a Pawo,[34]
Will appear in the south in the Lhorong Mountain Range;
If he retrieves it, it will become well-known throughout
Dokham,
And finally it will make converts in Hor.
Failing that, a man called Rāja of the Shampo area,
A crazy saint, will discover it.
Otherwise a certain Dorje of Puwo
And a certain Kunga from the east may retrieve it:
Each will write half of it for the good of beings.
If they fail to discover it, the final opportunity will occur
To three women – or it will naturally manifest itself.
In this last case it will become known only in the area in which
it is found.

When in the future the paths of these nine spiritual beings cross
The teaching will burgeon and blossom.
In particular, at a place called Katok to the east,[35]
The source of the teaching of Guru Senge Dradrok,
Where Pema Jungne celebrated thirteen consecrations,
There is a mountain shaped like a lion with his head held high,
And in the throat of this mountain are concealed the most
profound treasures.
Two thousand five hundred years hence
Certain omens will augur retrieval of these treasures;
Pema Jungne and his Consort will enrich this area, serving
others;
Dampa Gyeltsen and Tsogyel will emanate there;
The supreme doctrine of Tantra will remain there to the end,
And though sometimes it will degenerate
The blessed will appear in due season;
The conversion of my last disciple will occur there.

And that ends my advice and instruction to you.
Now I am unable to stay much longer.
Pray aloud together, and remain composed in meditation.
This community and future disciples
Must take my advice and my prophecies to heart.

[*The remainder of Tsogyel's story is related by Atsara Sale – Gyelwa Jangchub – the scribe, and the origin of the emanation Taksham, who was the treasure-finder.*]

Then with her left hand Tsogyel touched the Bhutanese Tashi Chidren, who was transformed into an eight-petalled blue *utpala* lotus, each petal and the centre marked with the syllables HŪNG PHAT, and the lotus was absorbed into Tsogyel's right breast. Then with her left hand Tsogyel touched the Nepali Kalasiddhi, who became a sixteen-petalled red lotus with a vowel sign and the syllable HRĪ inscribed upon each petal, and this red lotus was absorbed into her left breast.[36]

Late on the eve of the tenth day, an escort of the Four Guardian Kings leading the outer, inner and secret oath-bound hosts, and the eight and the twelve classes of spirits, appeared. 'The complete escort from Ngayab Ling is now assembled. Please come, O Knowledge Holder Ḍākinī Blazing Blue Light,' they implored her.

The gods and men of Tibet begged her nine times over and over to postpone her departure, just as is described elsewhere, and after their attempt to dissuade her from parting had failed, Dorje Lekpa of Tsang, Machen Pomra from the East, Rongtsen Mebar from the South, Tsomen Gyelmo from the North, Gangzang Hao from the West, Lijin Harlek of Central Tibet and Thanglha Gangtsen of the pestilential demons, and all the Great Lords of the Earth and the pestilential demons without number, each with his own entourage, gathered around her. In particular, she gave them *Answers to the Questions of the Tenma Protectors: the Oracle of Gods and Demons*,[37] amongst other tomes, the size of which dissuades me from including any here.

As the first flicker of light dawned on the tenth day, a palanquin of the light of four Ḍākinīs in the form of an eight-petalled lotus descended like a shooting star before Tsogyel. And then, transformed into the resplendent form of Vajra Yoginī, holding a *ḍāmaru* drum in her right hand and a skull-cup in her left hand, Tsogyel mounted the palanquin. At this point the human throng began to weep and wail uncontrollably. 'What can we tell Tibet? What can we do?' they cried. Tsogyel answered them:

For pity! Listen to me, O my faithful Tibetans!
Tell the people I am absorbed in inner space, the omnipresent ground,
And the aches and pains of corporeality have ceased.
Tell them that the mortal Tsogyel has finally attained an immaculate state,
And that the agony and ecstasy of embodiment is over.
Tell them that the illusory body of flesh and blood has been transfigured,
And the need for diagnosis, prescription, *mokṣa*, bleeding and hot needles, has gone.
Tell them that when the truth of impermanence is finally made plain
The seemingly concrete and permanent must vanish.
Tell them that the end of the way is a body of light,
And this black corpse, this bag of water and mucus must pass.
Tell them that Ama Tsogyel has melted into the primordial A,
And cries of anguish have ceased.
Tell them that outside and inside, mother and son, have united,
And the material superfluity, flesh and blood, has vanished.
Tell them that the Lama's compassion never fails;
His apparitional hosts of welcome encompass the universe.
Tell them that this incorrigible woman, this wanton uninhibited woman,
This woman has achieved the impossible nine times over.
Tell them that this Daughter of Tibet, this unlovable spinster,
Now is Queen of Kunzang's absolute, empty being.
Tell them this woman, over-extended in vanity and deceit,
Successful in her final deceit, has gone to the South-West.
Tell them this passionate woman, repeatedly fallen in her maze of intrigue,
Through intrigue has vanished into the sphere of inner space.
Tell them that this widow of Tibet, rejected by Tibetan males,
Has captured the state of Buddhahood.
Now do not despair! Pray for waves of grace!

Tsogyel will never leave the faithful!
I will certainly appear to you at the time of your supplication.
So my friends, return home and pray!
May your happiness and good fortune increase!

When she had finished speaking, radiating blinding rainbow light she dissolved into a sesame seed-pod-like sheath of shimmering blue light,[38] and she vanished. The four Ḍākinī lotus petals began to move, and in a blaze of light the lotus ascended, higher and higher, until it vanished from sight. The onlookers with one voice and one strain wailed:

Alas! alas! Yeshe Tsogyelma!
How pitiless you are! How little your compassion!
If you do not continue to help Tibet
In whom can we miserable people trust?
You, our Mother, have gone to a pure-land,
But who will save this deeply defiled land of Tibet?
You, our Mother, have entered an immaculate sphere,
But who will guide us at the final outcome of our negative *karma*?
You, our Mother, have gone to a Land of Pure Pleasure,
But who will guide us wanderers in samsaric suffering?
You, our Mother, have vanished into lotus-light,
But who will guide us through Tibet's narrow defiles?
You, our Mother, have arrived in Pema's presence,
But who will save the outcaste who has nowhere to turn?
Alas! alas! still show us your compassion!
Please leave us a short wish-granting prayer for Tibet's happiness!
Please leave a few words of testament for the whole of Tibet!
How can we of this community assuage our pain?
Mother, Lady, still sustain us with your compassion!
Please lead us to the field of all-embracing lotus-light!

After addressing this half-crazed plaint to our now far distant Guru, we threw our bodies on the ground, weeping and crying out. Then out of an abiding blaze of light a disembodied voice spoke:

O pity! Listen you faithful, sad Tibetan people!
This Supreme Being is the Ḍākinī Queen of the Lake of
Awareness![39]
My defiled body has been absorbed in immaculate inner space,
And I am a Buddha in the lotus-light of dynamic space;
I tell you you need not be anxious, be happy!
People of Tibet afflicted with infinite anxiety,
Laden with behaviour patterned by negative *karmas*,
When you see that your personal pain is self-inflicted,
The Three Jewels is your refuge from suffering.
Pray to a single hope and support!

This Supreme Being is the Ḍākinī Queen of the Lake of
Awareness!
After purifying defiling elements I have passed into the sky,
And now I serve beings through miraculous emanation;
Do not make yourselves miserable, be optimistic!
When you see this body with its weight of bad habits
As the seat of passionate responses, and the cause of negative
karma,
Knowing Buddha's teaching to be the way to positive,
personal evolution,
Strive to apply your instruction on the ten virtues.

This Supreme Being is the Ḍākinī Queen of the Lake of
Awareness!
I have gone to the space which is the white evolutionary goal,
Leaving behind an inextinguishable impetus of exemplary
activity;
Do not despair, be joyful!
When you see that your many forms of behaviour,
Negative *karmas*, are leading you eventually to hell,
Fasten your body and speech to virtue to purify the lower
realms,
And integrating body, speech and mind, travel the path of
virtue.

This Supreme Being is the Ḍākinī Queen of the Lake of
Awareness!
I have gone to the unsullied Land of Pure Pleasure,

After teaching the receptive the method of irreversible release;
Do not despair, make song!
When you become aware of the subconscious tendency towards painful, paranoid vision
That is the boundless ocean of suffering in *saṃsāra,*
A Real Lama has the skilful means to release you from anxiety.
Finding a qualified, unerring mentor, obey his injunction.

This Supreme Being is the Ḍākinī Queen of the Lake of Awareness!
I have vanished into fields of lotus-light, the plenum of dynamic space,
To be born in the inner sanctum of an immaculate lotus;
Do not despair, have faith!
When you have withdrawn attachment to this rocky defile,
This barbaric Tibet, full of war and strife,
Abandon unnecessary activity and rely on solitude.
Practise energy control, purify your psychic nerves and seed-essence,
And cultivate *mahāmudrā* and Dzokchen.

This Supreme Being is the Ḍākinī Queen of the Lake of Awareness!
Attaining humility, through Guru Pema Jungne's compassion I followed him,
And now I have finally gone into his presence;
Do not despair, but pray!
When you see your karmic body as vulnerable as a bubble,
Realising the truth of impermanence, and that in death you are helpless,
Disabuse yourself of fantasies of eternity,
Make your life a practice of *sādhana,*[40]
And cultivate the experience that takes you to the place where Ati ends.

O listen, and cease your lamentation!
My compassion will never alter.
Your behaviour is precisely the response of eternalists.
I am not dead, I have not forsaken you, I have not gone elsewhere;

Pray, and I swear I will show you my reality,
And to those of single-minded devotion I will give whatever *siddhi* you desire,
From this time forth until the last of the human race.

As Guru Pema's field of conversion,
Tibet has matured into the pure-land of Lokeśvara,[41] the Great Compassionate Lord;
With Ārya Mañjuśrī acting as Master of the Doctrine,
And through the brilliance and magical power of Vajrapāṇi, Lord of the Mysteries,
The ocean of the teaching should remain forever constant.
Free from the mischief of fanatical, foreign extremists,
All demons and demonic powers laid to rest,
The *sūtra*-class academies should hold the torch of the doctrine;
And the masters of Tantra attaining magical energy
The whole of Tibet should be covered with meditation centres.
The people of Central Tibet, in this and later lives,
Should keep the Three Jewels as witness to their pleasures and pains,
Striving to practise the ten virtues, forsaking the ten vices.
Question the scriptures about both outer and inner activity;
As to right and wrong, obey the Word of Guru Pema implicitly;
About secular and social mores, conform to the laws of the king;
Base the secular law of the Four Districts upon *dharma*.
Subdue foreign aggressors with magical power –
With compassion the gods and the Three Jewels will certainly force their retreat;
Students in the monasteries should study according to the scriptural tradition.
Lay men and women should cultivate an ideal vision on the path;
With boundless humility and reverence, respect your superiors,
And distribute the surfeit of your goods amongst your inferiors;
All should tell beads, reciting the Six-syllable Mantra for the sake of others;
And confidently pray to Pema Jungne, our Lord.

This community should take the four empowerments with heartfelt devotion;
Pray aloud, calling out the name of Tsogyel,
And receiving the four empowerments, your mind is united with mine;
Without a thought in your head, remain in constant meditative absorption.
For the majority of future inhabitants of Tibet,
Pema Jungne is the Lama,
And everyone should strive to identify with him.
All transformed as the body of Guru Pema,
Blessings of superlative compassion will arise.
Practise according to the extensive or concise rites of *Accomplishment of the Lama's Mind*,
And I promise you Buddhahood in one lifetime.
Tell the quintessential GURU SIDDHI *mantra;*
On the 10th and 25th and on the 8th and 15th days of the moon,
Celebrate the *gaṇacakra* feast and make offerings –
A single celebration closes the door of rebirth to the lower realms,
And I swear that it will carry you to the level of irreversible release.
Take that as a solemn promise.
Recited in reverse the GURU SIDDHI is the Lama's essence:
HŪNG is the vitality common to all Buddhas past, present and future;
DHI is the *siddhi* of all the Yidam deities and the Conquerors;
SID is the magical activity of the Ḍākinīs and Oath-bound Lords;
MA cuts away the delusions of all beings;
PAD is the past, present and future Buddhas' supreme pure-land;
RU shuts the door on the winds of *karma;*
GU confers the power of Awareness and Compassion;
JRA is the indestructible Emptiness of *mahāmudrā;*
VA indicates the ultimate spaciousness of every specific;
HŪNG is apparitional being, emanation transforming mankind;
ĀH is the epitome of the consummate visionary richness of the path;
OM is absolute, empty being, the primally pure Kuntuzangpo.

If these twelve quintessential seed syllables of Pema Jungne
Are chanted with the tongue in this reverse order,
One hundred thousand recitations erase disorders of body, speech and mind;
Two hundred thousand recitations extinguish negative *karma* of the past, present and future;
Three hundred thousand bring you to the level of irreversibility;
Seven hundred thousand ensure a meeting with Pema Jungne in this life;
One million accomplish the four *karma*s of Buddha;
Six million empty the depths of *saṃsāra;*
Ten million identify you with the Buddha Amitābha himself
And indubitably you will gain whatever *siddhi* you desire;
The benefit of further recitation can be known by experiment.
The normal order of recitation is the way to obtain *nirvāṇa*:
OM is the epitome of the Five Buddha Aspects and all the Sugatas;
ĀH is the epitome of the Five Buddhas' *mantra*s and all Heart *mantra*s;
HŪNG is the epitome of the Five Buddhas' Mind and the essentiality of being;
VA is indicated by the gesture of indestructibility;
JRA is the *vajra*'s compassionate, magical activity;
GU is the Lama Herukas of the past, present and future;
RU is the drop of elixir of maturity and release;
PAD is the entrance to the pure-lands of pleasure;
MA is spontaneous entry into pleasure's womb;
SID is the spontaneous play of fully potentiated compassion;
DHI is the *siddhi* that gives you whatever you desire;
And HŪNG attains the highest level.
Thus this *mantra* is like a wish-fulfilling gem;
It fulfils whatever wish enters your mind.
Further, since it purifies the twelve elements of *saṃsāra,*
It is the Great Mother, the nature of the ten transcendental perfections;
If this *mantra* fulfils whatever wish enters the mind,
All those present here and all beings of the future
Should practise this Heart Mantra with diligence.

Now, for a while, until your split minds are whole,
Parting will seem like separation. Be happy!
When your split minds are one, you and I will be reunited.
May good fortune and happiness be everywhere!

With this farewell she ended, and light, shimmering, sparkling iridescently in splendid vivid colours, streamed towards the South-West and vanished from sight. All of us who witnessed this final departure prostrated countless times after her, praying our wish-fulfilling prayers. Then our minds full of grief, our hearts heavy, our stomachs in our mouths, our tears flooding the path, staggering, unable to control our bodies, panting and heaving, we returned to the meditation cave in the heart of Zapu, where we spent the night.

Then Be Yeshe Nyingpo, Lasum Gyelwa Jangchub and Ma Rinchen Chok revealed the *maṇḍala* of Guru and Ḍākinī, and after applying ourselves to practice for seven months we accomplished the union of Guru and Ḍākinī, receiving prophecy and authorisation.

It was at that time that the Tibetan King, Tri Repachan, the Dharma Protector, promulgated his first decree, ordering the translators to assemble. At this convocation some people reported different versions of Tsogyel's *parinirvāṇa*. Some people said that at Mutik Pama Gangbuk, Tsogyel attained the vision of reality extinguished and left her nasal membrane, her teeth, finger-nails, hair and body-hair behind her on her bed. These became relics that would give material support to the faithful. Furthermore, these people maintained that when Tsogyel's body vanished, she gained Buddhahood. Others said that on the eighth day of the bird month of the bird year she gave her final testament; on the evening of the tenth she subdued evil spirits; at midnight she turned the wheel of the teaching; after midnight she entered a meditative trance; in the early hours of the morning she gained enlightenment; and at daybreak her body straightened and she passed into *nirvāṇa*. Her body turned into a heap of relics which could be held in the palm of one hand, and the Dharma Protector, ordering them to be brought to him, put them in an urn. In truth, I, Gyelwa Jangchub and Be Yeshe Nyingpo, Ma Rinchen Chok, Odren Pelgyi Zhonnu, Dacha Rupa Dorje Pawo, Surya Tepa of

Central Tibet, Liza Jangchub of Khotan, Dorje Tso of Shelkar, together with not less than one hundred other fortunate beings who observed the scene, corroborate the version that I have described here.

Thus ends the eighth chapter which describes how Yeshe Tsogyel's aspirations were finally fulfilled, and how she gained Buddhahood in the sanctum of dynamic space.

ITHI GUHYA EVAM MANDA[42]
SAMAYA GYA GYA GYA![43]

I, Gyelwa Jangchub, who was blessed by Tsogyel and attained *siddhi* in one lifetime, together with Namkhai Nyingpo of Lhodrak who is indivisible from the Great Master Pema Jungne, he who is free from the characteristics of birth and death, wrote down Tsogyel's narrative on sheets of yellow parchment without addition or subtraction and without any exaggeration. Then we entrusted the text to the hand of Chudak Nakpo Tongyuk, exhorting him to deliver it into the hand of a Spiritual Son who Tsogyel herself had foretold, an order which he vowed to fulfil. May this text find its way into the hands of a being of the future endowed with auspicious *karma*.

DHA THIM ITHI ZAB GYA TE GYA!

NOTES TO THE TEXT

Homage, Protection and Gyelwa Jangchub's Introduction

1 Consult the index for the transliterated Tibetan form. The initial formula of homage, invoking and worshipping the three roots (Lama, Yidam, Khandroma; *Guru, Deva, Ḍākinī*), is like the quintessential mantric form of the text's meaning. The following verses elaborate that *mantra* in a *maṇḍala* form, the *maṇḍala*s of Guru Pema and Tsogyel's *trikāya*s. Since Dechen Karmo is given primacy, the *yoginī-tantra* is indicated.

2 *'Ja'-lus*, and *rdo-rje lus*: these existential modes, the goal of Tsogyel's endeavour (*sādhana*), indicate that Dzokchen *atiyoga* is the path herein described. The rainbow body is achieved by realising the impure material body as a body of light.

3 sNgags-'chang Padma thod-'phreng-rtsal. The skill or spontaneous effusion (*rtsal*) of this *mantradharin* (*sngags-'chang*), '*mantra*-holder', 'tantric priest', he whose words (*mantra*) actualise their own meanings, lies in his capacity to realise spontaneously the succession (*'phreng*) of point-instants (*klong* or *chos-nyid*) of experiences as Emptiness (*stong-pa-nyid*), as symbolised by the skull (*thod*), or as the *maṇḍala* of the *trikāya*.

4 *'Og-min, Akaniṣṭha*: the supreme *nirmāṇakāya* Buddhafield where absolute reality is perceived as a multi-dimensional phenomenal panorama. Guru Pema's girls appeared in all shapes and sizes but his most beloved five were Orgyen Ḍākinī Buddhafield emanations.

Notes to the Text

Chapter 1: Tsogyel's Conception

1 rTag-ngu, Sadāprarudita, 'Always Weeping', the name of a Bodhisattva whose story is related by Śākyamuni to Subhuti in the *Aṣṭasāhasrikā-prajñāpāramitā-sūtra*, Ch. XXX, illustrating diligence. In the *Sadharmapuṇḍarīka*, Ch. XIX, he is called Sadāparibhūta.

2 dbYangs-can-ma, Sarasvatī, is the *saṃbhogakāya* consort of Mañjuśrī, called Vākīśvarī, 'Lady of the Word', the Muse, the expression of *dharma*, Awareness of Speech, and as such she is the beloved of tertons, the Revealers of the Guru's Word; she is Goddess of Sound conferring learning, wisdom, memory, musical accomplishment, poetic inspiration, etc. As Akṣobhya's Consort in the *vajra* family she is dbYings-kyi-dbang-phyug-ma (Dhātīśvarī), the primal purity of consciousness, the element space, and anger. She may also be the White Cloaked Lady (Gos-dkar-mo) who is the Ḍākinī of the Mystic Heat.

3 'O-rgyan, Oḍḍiyāna, is the ancient kingdom of the Swat Valley in northern Pakistan. Before the Muslim invasion it was a centre of tantric practice, and as Guru Pema's birthplace it became known as the Ḍākinī Paradise, a *nirmāṇakāya* Buddhafield (O-rgyan mkha' – 'gro gling).

4 The language of this song mixing concrete imagery with sublime abstraction is specifically 'tantric'; it is the verbal device used to express the inexpressible, the unitary field of non-dual reality. The songs simply describe the union of *vajra* and *bhaga* (or 'sky'), male and female, on the *saṃbhogakāya* level, to conceive a *nirmāṇakāya* emanation.

5 With the consummation of the Guru Ḍākinī union the entire *maṇḍala* of the Five Buddhas and their Consorts is generated, which means that the powers of their psycho-organisms were potentiated to the uttermost, and the realisation of Emptiness was accompanied by ecstasy.

Chapter 2: Auspicious Omens and Birth

1 Sarasvatī, who holds a lute (vīṇa), can mean Vowel (dbyangs-can) Goddess besides Sweet-voiced Maiden in Tibetan, and the Sanskrit vowels invoke the Goddess while the consonants invoke Mañjuśrī. HRĪ is the seed-syllable (bīja-mantra) of Tārā and an exclamation destroying attachment and proclaiming freedom.

2 *sTong gsum*, lit. '3000'. The three dimensions of microscopic universes containing a thousand worlds each are entered through the

lotus in the begging bowl in Śākyamuni's *dhyānamudrā*. In each grain of pollen on each pistil of this lotus are world systems like our own, and in the centre of each sits a similar Buddha with a similar lotus also containing Buddhas and lotuses, to three dimensions, indicating inner space.

3 The 'red and white' appear repetitively in these dreams; they are the colours of the female and the male sexual fluids, and of the 'airs' (*rlung, prāṇa*) that run in the right and left (*lalanā* and *rasanā*) psychic veins. Red connotes relativity, passion and thought, karmically created seed-consciousness (*kun-gzhi rnam-shes*) and, when purified, the ambrosial energies of the Ḍākinī; white connotes the absolute, the subjective pole, the life-force (*srog-rlung*), creative and procreative energies, and, when purified, the ambrosial skilful means of the Guru.

4 The year of the bird was probably AD 757. The 10th day of the monkey month (the 10th lunar month) is the anniversary of the Guru's departure for the South-West. The symbology of the bird as the Ḍākinī casts doubt upon the actual year of Tsogyel's birth.

5 *Ye-shes rig-pa*. Both these nominals denote the non-dual field of reality; *ye-shes* (*jñāna*) is non-dual reality, the Ḍākinī of gnostic awareness, while *rig-pa* describes the same reality stressing the content, the Guru's skilful means. 'Awareness/Knowledge' is the literal translation.

Chapter 3: Disillusionment and Meeting the Master

1 *Thugs-dam* = *thugs-kyi-dam-tshig*. The Bon gods and demons (*lha-'dre*) pledged their troth to Guru Pema that they would protect the teaching, while those with the eye or awareness (the third eye) pledged the Bodhisattva Vow.

2 Guru Drag-po, a wrathful form of the Guru in *saṃbhogakāya*; he holds a *vajra* and a scorpion.

3 *dKyil-'khor*: besides the common definitions of *maṇḍala* – (1) a simple symmetrical *yantra*; (2) an external, symbolical, ideal representation of the mind; (3) an internal, visualised palace with principal deity and retinue – *maṇḍala* can also denote: (4) the body-mind of the Guru or Ḍākinī, etc.; (5) the female organ (*bhaga*); (6) an offering plate; (7) a globe, sphere or disc. The defining characteristics of a *maṇḍala* are its centre and circumference.

4 *Tshogs-'khor*: (1) a circle of devotees and/or gods and goddesses assembled for an offering sacrament; (2) the essential, tantric sacramental rite of offering itself; (3) the accumulation of offerings for the sacrament. The elements of the rite: (A) the deity is invoked

and worshipped; (B) the offerings are blessed, transformed into the nature of the deity as *amṛta* and offered up; (C) voluntary *samaya* restoration, confession, etc., before the deity; (D) the offerings are consumed by the participants thereby re-establishing the *samaya* of the deity; (E) remnants of the offerings and the dishwater, etc. are rendered to spirits, *pretas*, etc. In the context of a *yoginī-tantra* the five ambrosias (*pañcāmṛta*) are offered. Various elements of the rite are capable of both literal and figurative interpretation, and in different lineages and cultures, and in various historical periods, one or the other has been preferred. Atīśa decried the Old School Tibetans for an unthinking literal interpretation; the British of the Raj denounced the Śākta-cult Bengalis for odious sexual orgies; though ritualism dominates in Nepal, literal interpretation was the norm; in Tibet the mode varies according to the lineage, but in general the literal mode is associated with the lower *tantras*. In *The Life* it would appear that a feast, or even an ordinary meal, was transformed into a *gaṇacakra* rite; and when offerings were to be made it was always an occasion for a *gaṇacakra*. The figurative mode of *gaṇacakra* shows a striking parallel with the Catholic eucharist; and the literal, non-ritualist, informal mode is comparable to a Dionysian orgy.

5 *Dam-tshig, samaya*: vow, commitment, integrity, union. This word is, for some, the single most important word in the tradition; the relative *samayas* (vows) sustain the absolute *samaya* (union).

6 The Guru transforms himself into Yama, Lord of Existence (*srid-pa'i-bdag-po*) or Lord of Dharma (*chos-kyi-bdag-po*) who holds the wheel of existence (*srid-pa'i-'khor-lo*) between his teeth and his thighs. The upper part represents the realms of men, gods and anti-gods and the lower the realms of beasts, hungry ghosts and denizens of hell.

7 rDo-rje 'chang: the Guru as Adi-buddha, the first or primordial *dharmakāya* Buddha, arrayed in *saṃbhogakāya* ornaments, coloured blue, sitting in *padmāsana*, holding bell and *vajra*, his arms crossed at his heart centre.

8 *Dam-rdzas lnga*.

Chapter 4: Initiation and Instruction

1 Of Tsogyel's preliminary training, the four noble truths (*bden-pa bzhi*) that Śākyamuni taught in his first sermon at Sarnāth are (1) the truth of suffering; (2) the truth of the cause of suffering; (3) the truth of the cessation of suffering; (4) the truth of the path to *nirvāṇa*. The *Tripiṭaka* contains the provisional, indirect or leading

truth (*drang-don*) while the *mādhyamika* teaches ultimate truth (*nges-don*). The six lower vehicles are enumerated below (n. 4).

2 *gSan-yig*: many initiates compile a catalogue of their instruction.

3 *mNyes-pa gsum*: the Guru's satisfactions derived from receiving offering of (1) respect and honour; (2) food and drink; (3) the disciple's meditation practice and accomplishment.

4 *Theg-pa dgu*: the vehicles (*yānas*) of (1) *śravaka*, (2) *pratyekabuddha*, (3) *Bodhisattva*, (4) *kriyāyoga-tantra*, (5) *upayoga-tantra*, (6) *yoga-tantra*, (7) *mahāyoga*, (8) *anuyoga*, (9) *atiyoga*. 1–2 belong to the *hīnayāna* or lesser vehicle; 3–9 are *mahāyāna* or great vehicle paths; 4–9 are *vajrayāna* or tantric paths; 4–6 are outer tantric vehicles; 7–9 are divisions of the *anuttarayoga-tantra*, the inner, supreme or ultimate *tantra*. The outer tantric vehicles are stages of increasing introversion and mind-*yoga* and decreasing concern with ritual acts, ritual cleanliness and dualistic worship of a deity. This nine-fold division is a Nyingma formulation; the other Tibetan schools count only the first six.

5 *mTshangs*: here the 'hidden foundation' is the universal ground (*kun-gzhi*), Emptiness; but it can also denote a 'nest' of confusion, deceit and limitation.

6 *Byang-chub-sems*: the thought of enlightenment, the Bodhisattva's aspiration, enlightened mind, the Bodhisattva's Vow; the seed of compassion, semen virile, 'the milk of human kindness'; the red and white elixirs of the left and right channels. Without *bodhicitta* Tantra easily becomes the manipulation of power, often with a sexual slant.

7 The three kinds of *mantra*: (1) *rgyu ma-nor-ba rtsa-ba'i sngags*, the seed-syllable that is the deity's euphonic essence (e.g. Vajrasattva's *bīja-mantra* is HŪNG); (2) *bskyed-pa rkyen-gyi sngags*, the mantric form that is the condition of the deity's visitation (e.g. Vajrasattva's creative *mantra* is OṂ VAJRASATTVA HŪNG); (3) *bzla-ba las-kyi sngags*, the *karma-mantra* recited repetitively to realise the deity's specific powers (Vajrasattva's 100 Syllable Mantra – *yig-rgya*).

8 The four kinds of *mudrā*: (1) *thugs-dam-tshig-gi phyag-rgya*, *samaya-mudrā*; (2) *ye-shes las-kyi phyag-rgya*, *jñāna-karma-mudrā*; (3) *chos-kyi phyag-rgya*, *dharma-mudrā*; (4) *phyag-rgya-chen-po*, *mahāmudrā*. The first is verbal commitment to sustain the root and branch *samaya*s; the second is commitment to union with the Five Ḍākinīs' modes of Awareness embodied in the Guru's Consort; the third is commitment to practise hand gestures and postures; the fourth is commitment to Buddhahood itself. See also pp. 255f. *Mudrā* (*phyag-rgya*) can be translated as: (1) seal, (2) commitment, (3) symbol, (4) hand gesture, (5) posture, (6) Ḍākinī or consort.

9 The three modes of *samādhi*: (1) *bde-chen samādhi*; (2) *snang-srid lha dang lha-mo'i samādhi*; (3) *chu-bo rgyun-gyi samādhi*.

10 Six periods of 3 hour meditations (*thun*) with hour-long breaks (*mtshams*) is customary.

11 sGrub-pa bka'-brgyad: the eight principal Yidam deities of *mahāyoga* treated in *bka'-ma* and *gter-ma* literature, introduced into Tibet by Guru Pema, relate to the five qualities of Buddha's being and to three qualities of *mantra* in mundane *tantra*: 'Jam-dpal gshin-rje-shed (*sku*) (Mañjuśrī Yamāntaka), Padma gsung or rTa-mgrin (*gsung*) (Hayagrīva), Yang-dag Heruka (*thugs*), bDud-rtsi yon-tan (*yon-tan*), rDo-rje phur-ba or rDo-rje gzhon-nu (*phrin-las*) (Vajrakīla or Vajrakumāra), Ma-mo rbod-gtong, 'Jig-rten dregs-pa, Dregs-sngags dmod-pa. Che-mchog Heruka, who combines the first five, or Rig-'dzin bla-ma, or sPhyi-dril-snying-po, are sometimes added to the eight.

12 *lTa-ba zab-mo / sgom-pa nyam-myong-gi sgo-nas / spyod-pa ta-na-ga-na phyi-nang-gsang spyod-rnams-so*. These three precepts belong to the Dzokchen *mkhregs-gcod* tradition and may be given as the one basic, all-embracing, crucial *samaya*.

13 *sGrub-pa'i grogs*: mystic partners, or servants or helpers of any kind in a *tantrika*'s *sādhana*.

14 The first *tantra*, the root *tantra* of all *tantras*, the *Guhyasamāja-tantra*, taught the five-fold *maṇḍala* of the *Dhyāni*-Buddhas; the correspondences of the Five Buddhas are basic to the entire *vajrayāna*.

Correspondences of the Five Buddhas

Five Buddhas	Vairocana rNam-par-snang-mdzad	Amitābha 'Od-dpag-med	Akṣobhya Mi-skyod-pa	Ratnasambhava Rin-chen-'byung-ldan	Amoghasiddhi Don-yod-grub-pa
Five Consorts	Locanā Sangs-rgyas spyan-ma	Pāṇḍaravāsinī Gos-dkar-can	Dhātīśvarī dbYings-kyi-dbang-phyug-ma	Māmakī Māmakī	Samaya Tārā Dam-tshig sgrol-ma
Five Modes of Awareness	Omnipresent A. (*chos-dbyings*)	Discriminating A. (*sor-rtog*)	Mirror-like A. (*me-long*)	A. of Equality (*mnyam-nyid*)	All-accomplishing A. (*bya-grub*)
Five Families	Buddha (*sangs-rgyas*)	Padma (*padma*)	Vajra (*rdo-rje*)	Ratna (*rin-chen*)	Karma *phrin-las*
Five Modes	Body (*sku, kāya*)	Speech (*gsung, vāk*)	Mind (*thugs, citta*)	Qualities (*yon-tan, gūṇa*)	Action (*phrin-las, karma*)
Five Psycho-physical constituents	Name and form (*rūpa, gzugs*)	Ideation (*samjñā, 'du-shes*)	Consciousness (*vijñāna, rnam-shes*)	Feeling (*vedana, tshor-ba*)	Volition (*saṃskāra, 'du-byed*)
Five Emotions	Sloth (*moha, gti-mug*)	Lust (*rāga, gdod-chags*)	Anger (*[?]veśa, zhe-sdang*)	Pride (*agra, nga-bdag*)	Jealousy (*īrṣyā, phrag-dog*)
Five Elements	Earth solidity	Fire heat	Sky spaciousness	Water fluidity	Air motion
Five Sense-Organs	Eyes	Mouth	Ears	Nose	Touch
Five Colours	White	Red	Blue	Yellow	Green

15 Particularly Nāgārjuna and Candrakīrti's commentaries upon the *Guhyasamāja-tantra* (recommended by Khetsun Sangpo). See also *Lam-rim Ye-shes-snying-po 'grel-ba* of bLo-gros mtha'-yas f. 104ff.

16 *bKa'-'dus chos-kyi-rgya-mtsho*: a *gter-ma* of Orgyan-gling-pa.

17 *gZungs-ma*, 'she who supports or holds', *phyag-rgya* (*mudrā*) and *rig-ma* (*vidhyā*) all describe the Ḍākinī as an embodied consort.

18 Atsara, properly *ācārya*, a teacher, was a derogatory appellation of tantric Indian ascetics (like today's 'sadhu').

19 *'Jigs-pa rnam-par brgyad, aṣṭabhayatrāṇa*: lions, elephants, fire, snakes, robbers, the king, floods, demons (*senghe, glang-chen, me, sprul, rkun-po, rgyal-po, chu, sha-za*).

20 *mTshams-pa lnga*: paricide, matricide, letting the blood of the Guru, stealing from the Community, destroying a *stūpa*.

21 Thar-byed dril-bu-ljang-mo: a form of sGrol-ma, Tārā.

22 brTan-ma bcu-gnyis: the twelve local protectresses guarding the pass-gates to Central Tibet were subjected by Guru Pema at Yang-lesho, in Nepal. brTan-ma is often spelt *bsTan-ma*, guardian.

23 The four modes of being (*sku, kāya*) subjecting the four devils (*bdud bzhi*): the *rdo-rje lta-bu'i sku* subjects the *'chi-bdag bdud*, the *sgyu-ma lta-bu'i sku* subjects the *lha-bu bdud*, the *'ja'-lus rdo-rje' i sku* subjects the *phung-po bdud* and the *ting-'dzin rtsal-gyi sku* subjects the *nyon-mongs bdud*.

24 *Udumbara'i me-tog; ficus clomerata*, a beautiful blue lotus flower, the Buddha of flowers that blooms once every *yuga*; the so-called thousand-petalled lotus; an immense blue lotus blossom.

25 The Vase Initiation (*bum-dbang*) into the Guru's Body (*sku*) begins with the Guru's radiance (*mdangs*) purifying the sensual realm, and then the serene union of Guru and Ḍākinī creates the *maṇḍala* described in Taksham's own terma, the *mKha'-'gro snying-thig*. The four levels of joy (*dga'-ba bzhi*) that arise in each of the four *cakras* of each of them as *kuṇḍalinī* ascends the medial nerve are joy, (*dga'-ba*), supreme joy (*mchog-dga'*), no-joy (*dga'-bral*) and innate or spontaneous joy (*lhan-skyes-dga'*). Mahāvajradhara is the unitary totality in the *mahāyoga* scenario, and the Five Aspects (Amitābha, Vairocana, etc. – see n. 14 above) and their consorts (Pāṇḍarāvasinī, Māmakī, etc.) are the primal purity of the subjective functions and the objective energy forms of the sensual dimension.

26 The chalice or vessel (*snod*) is the environment, phenomenal appearance, or the *dharmadhātu*, and the elixir or contents (*bcud*) is sensual-being experienced as the primal purity of its perceptions or stimuli; thus 'chalice and elixir' is a way of saying 'Emptiness and form'.

27 The Mystic Initiation (*gsang-dbang*) into the Guru's Speech (*gsung*) begins with the resonance (*gdangs*) of the Guru's Speech purifying

the realms of sense, form and formlessness. dBang-drag Padma Heruka, his *vajra* termed gSang-rtags-kyi heruka, in compassionate wrath unites with Padma Yum and creates Taksham's *rTa-mgrin snying-thig maṇḍala*, in which Hayagrīva (rTa-mgrin – Horse-neck, or Padma gsung) is in union with Vajra Vārāhī (rDo-rje phag-mo – the Vajra Sow-faced Ḍākinī), while in their five *cakras* are the wrathful forms of the Five Buddha Aspects called the Five Herukas or the Five Ḍākas (*dpa'-bo*, Buddha Hero) and the Five wrathful Ḍākinī consorts.

28 *rTsa, nāḍī; rlung, prāṇa; thig-le, bindu*. These describe the *saṃbhogakāya* Ḍākinī in the dimension of sound, vibration, subtle energies and feeling. 'Psychic nerves' denotes the energy structure, and 'energy flows' are the 'motions' or 'vibrations', 'airs', 'winds', or energies themselves, while 'seed-essence' is the empty nature of such energy. The Guru's skilful means are the modes of Awareness (see n. 14 above) that are the primally pure nature of the five passions. Thus in this *anuyoga maṇḍala* Vārāhī is the energy of dynamic space, Hayagrīva is the gnostic awareness inherent in passion, and their *samādhi* is pure pleasure.

29 The precept that Guru Pema gives Tsogyel for her post-initiation *yoga* practice is instruction in the fulfilment process of meditation in which *mantra* resounds in the focal points of energy and purifies the passions associated with the various kinds of energy. The Yidam deity describes the grand structure and form of energy, and his retinue describes the details; the body-mind is informed as a *maṇḍala* of deities. *Mahāmudrā* is the absolute truth of Emptiness self-cognised in relativity.

30 *Las-rlung-gi 'gyu-ba*: karmic energies are emotional and conceptual impulses conditioned by previous experience dependent upon a sub-conscious belief in a substantial, discrete ego; they are derived from the focal points of energy, each dominated by a passion and controlling a specific field of activity; the left-hand nerve carries the seeds of these energies as 'seed-consciousness' (*ālaya-vijñāna, kun-gzhi rnam-shes*).

31 RAṂ (the *bīja-mantra* of fire) lights the Ḍākinī's fire in the gut centre that burns the HAṂ in the head centre destroying limiting concepts of substance and duality and distilling the elixir that drips into the heart centre purifying the entire body. Here a symbiosis of male and female principles gives rise to the four joys.

32 The five sacred substances (*dam-rdzas lnga*) that Tsogyel annoints her *bhaga* are the five *amṛtas* (*bdud-rtsi lnga*).

33 The Wisdom Initiation (*shes-dbang*) introduces the initiate to the Awareness and pure pleasure of the *dharmakāya* and the Guru's

Pure Being (*kāya*). The Guru becomes the Wrathful Red Heruka, the Great Lotus Heruka (Padma Heruka-chen-po), and Tsogyel is his Padma family, wrathful Ḍākinī. The Guru's *vajra*, his Absolute Heruka (Don-dam-pa'i Heruka) is galvanised by *bodhicitta* withdrawn from his psychic nerves, and his 'seed', or 'nuclear' or 'radiation energy' (*dwangs-ma*), is then injected into the Ḍākinī's *yonī maṇḍala*. The resulting *maṇḍala* (*klong-gsal nyi-ma'i 'bar-ma*), the *maṇḍala* of mystic heat (*gtu-mo'i dkyil-'khor*), is described in terms of skilful means (Pure Being, *yab*) and perfect insight (Light Seed – *thig-le, yum*). Pure Being in its four modalities (*kāya*s) comprise the sublime pure-land of the Herukas, the nature of which is Light Seed: self-cognitive seed-essence in the *dharmakāya*, seed-syllables in the *saṃbhogakāya*, and in the *nirmāṇakāya* it is the Light Seed which is described as 'a hundred million suns'.

34 *sByor-lam*, whose elements, or phases, are 'warmth', 'peak heat', 'acceptance' and 'supreme heat'. The remaining four of the five successive paths to Buddhahood are the path of accumulation (*tshogs-lam*), path of seeing (*mthong-lam*), path of utter purity (*yongs-byang-lam*), and path of liberation (*sgrol-lam*). See H. Guenther, *Kindly Bent to Ease Us* (pt 1, p. 94ff.).

35 *rJes-chags, anurakta*. In this *yoga* 'love', or 'attachment' or 'after-glow', can be conceived as the spiritual partner. After initiation, since desire has become Awareness (*ye-shes*), Awareness is the nature of the *bodhicitta* (or *kuṇḍalinī*) as it rises up the medial nerve.

36 *mNar-med-pa, avīci*: the *vajra*-hell ends only with the destruction of the world system.

37 'Life-force' (*srog-rtsol-kyi 'og-rlung*) is the procreative and creative energy of the genital centre. *Yogins* (*goms-chen*) practising energy control (*rtsa-rlung*) over a number of years gain enormous stomachs (*bum-pa*, pot-belly) caused by holding air in the bottom of the lungs.

38 *Ngo-bo-nyid-kyi-sku, svabhāvikakāya*: the integrated *trikāya*, or 'the existential essence of being', the fourth mode of a Buddha's being relating to the gut centre.

39 *bCu drug drug-ldan dal-lus-ma*: this line must refer to the positive conditions governing 'the precious human body' (*mi-lus rin-po-che*); but these are usually enumerated as 18: freedom from rebirth as a denizen of hell, a hungry ghost, a beast, a god, a savage, or a dumb man, and freedom from false views and from rebirth when no Buddha's teaching is known (8); rebirth as a human being, in a central place, all senses fully functional, free of inexpiable sin, with confidence in the *dharma* (5), and rebirth in a world where a Buddha has lived, taught the doctrine, that has endured, and that can be practised, under guidance of a teacher (5). These constitute freedom

from the eight unfavourable conditions and the 2 × 5 conditions of ease; but the 10, 6 and 6 may have different meanings.

40 *dPa'-bo, vīra* or *ḍāka*: in this context 'consort', a rendering of *ḍāka*, the male counterpart of Ḍākinī, is more appropriate than 'Buddha Hero'. Like a Ḍākinī, a *dpa'-bo* can be either embodied or supernal.

41 For references to the holy places of Nepal see K. Dowman, 'A Buddhist Guide to the Power Places of the Kathmandu Valley', *Kailash*, Vol. VIII (2–3), 1981.

42 *Lung-bstan-nas*. As a substantive *lung-bstan* connotes a perfectly clear state of mind in which a vision of the past or future can be reflected. The Guru's vision of a disciple's future is an implied injunction to proceed in a particular way and can be, therefore, a self-fulfilling prophecy, or 'visionary instruction', 'guidance', etc. This unusual verbal form denotes the phrase's literal meaning: 'to demonstrate meaning', 'to instruct'.

43 *Kun-tu-bzang-po mkha'-klong-che*: the primal space of Kun-tu-bzang-po, the vast sky, *vajra*-fields, is the reverse aspect of Guru Pema's manifest, *karma*-less, compassionate being (*kāya*): the nature of the Guru's compassionate emanation is empty space.

44 Here Tsogyel unequivocally states her motivation. In the *dharmayuga* passion is slight and peace and happiness facilitate the simple *hīnayāna* means to Buddhahood; thereafter, although Means and Insight are always indissolubly united, the nature of mind is veiled by strong passion, and the tantric method alone is efficacious in the *kaliyuga*. The consort embodies either skilful means or perfect insight, and through this externalisation passion can be employed to illuminate the darkness.

45 *'Gro-ba rigs drug*: gods, anti-gods, humans, hungry ghosts, beasts, and denizens of hell.

46 *Rang-sems rang-shar bskyed-rdzogs zung-du-'jug / phyag-rgya-chen-por bsam* . . . This context defines the creative process of meditation (*bskyed-rim*) as perception of phenomenal appearances (*snang-ba*) as magical illusion (*sgyu-ma*), and the fulfilment process of meditation as insight into the clear light of Emptiness (*stong-pa-nyid*). *Mahāmudrā* is achieved by perceiving whatever arises in the mind as illusion and Emptiness simultaneously. The phrase 'the union of creation and fulfilment' could be replaced by 'the union of phenomena and Emptiness' (*snang-ba dang stong-pa-nyid*) without loss of meaning, except the implication of a dynamic function. In *atiyoga* creative and fulfilment processes must be simultaneous; in *mahāmudrā* there is no duality of good and bad, night and day, *yoga* practice and existential praxis. The above precept is repeated in Śākya Dema's reply: *bskyed-rdzogs zung-'jug phyag-rgya-che* –

'*māhamudrā* is the simultaneity of creative and fulfilment processes', and to amplify the next line, 'and the clear light (*'od-gsal*) and magical illusion (*sgyu-ma*) are the undivided content of *mahāmudrā*'.

47 The syllables A and HAṂ have the same potency as RAṂ and HAṂ (see n. 31 above). *Kuṇḍalinī* rises in the life-force (n. 37 above) to the gut centre where her flame arises to melt the HAṂ in the head centre, elixir dripping to the heart centre. The formula AHAṂ signifies a symbiosis of male and female principles, clear light and Awareness.

48 See nn. 25 and 34 above, and pp. 41f., 85, 118–19, 155–7, 249f.

49 In this important Dzokchen *yoga* the seed-syllable A, the euphonic corollary of the pure potential of Dzokchen, or the *tathātagarbha*, or primal purity of dynamic space, is visualised before sleep, so that Awareness of the clear light is maintained through the dream state until waking. If this practice is sustained in sleep then gnostic awareness is easily maintained as the wheel spins in daily praxis.

50 The six lamps (*sgron-ma drug*) and the four convictions (*gding bzhi*) refer to six kinds of insight (*shes-rab, prajñā*) and four aspects of confidence which are a result of togal (*thod-rgal*) meditation. The experience of reality alluded to here is awareness of the nature of all things (*chos-nyid, dharmatā*), the absolute reality of awareness inherent in the relative field of transforming illusion; the Ḍākinī's nature is this reality and her form is magical illusion.

51 *bLa-ma gsang-'dus-kyi dkyil-'khor, Guru-guyhasamāja-maṇḍala.*

52 *Dung, śaṅkha*. The conch is a natural symbol of the process of emanation of the *maṇḍala* from the central point of Emptiness to the Emptiness of the circumference, from the conch's point to its empty mouth. Realisation of the Emptiness of this spiral process destroys the threat of every monster (*bar-chad*); further, it is a Tibetan belief that the mariner best defends himself from a sea monster by throwing a conch into the fish's mouth.

53 *gSer-'od;* but Sale (*gsal-le* pronounced *sa-le*) means 'clear light' and the epithet 'atsara' (*ācārya*) means 'Buddhist sādhu'.

54 *Byin-rlab bla-ma'i dkyil-'khor.*

55 *sKu bzhi*: *dharmakāya* (*chos-sku*), *saṃbhogakāya* (*longs-spyod-sku*) *nirmāṇakāya* (*sprul-sku*, pronounced tulku) and *svabhāvikakāya* (*ngo-bo-nyid-sku*). Although these four are one and indivisible, their specific characteristics are experienced separately in the four superior focal points of energy.

56 *gShin-rje e gcig, rta-mgrin dpa'-bo cgig, yang-dag mar-me gcig, phrin-las phur-ba gcig, bdud-rtsi thod gcig, ma-mo khram gcig*. In simple *bKa'-brgyad mahāyoga* practices the deity is visualised alone without a consort.

57 *bsNyen-sgrub*: this term has a general and technical meaning: (a) it denotes the creative stage (*bskyed-rim*) practice of visualisation and recitation, etc. and (b) *bsnyen* denotes the 'approach' of the deity through visualisation and recitation and *sgrub* denotes the accomplishment of the deity, identifying with his reality and becoming one with him.

58 *Khatvāṅga*: a trident with three heads – male, female and a skull – and crossed *vajras* (*viśvavajra*) on a shaft. The Guru's song describes the *khatvāṅga* as symbolic of inner space (*dbyings*), empty being (*dharmakāya*), the realm of Kuntuzangmo, empty delight (*bde-stong*), and the *trikāya*, which is evidently Emptiness itself. Iconographically in *mahāyoga* the Guru's *khatvāṅga* represents his consort, Tsogyel.

59 *sGrub-chen bka'-brgyad / ma-gshin-phur-ba / bdud-rtsi yang-dag / bla-ma dgongs-'dus / yi-dam dgongs-'dus / sgyu-'phrul zhi-khro / yang-dag zhi-khro / padma zhi-khro sogs / snying-thig drug-cu-rtsa-gcig / dgongs-'dus bye-brag bdun-po / bka'-brgyad rgyas-bsdus bcu-gcig / thugs-sgrub brgya-dang-rtsa-gnyis / mang-ngag bdun-cu-rtsa-drug / rgyud-kyi dgongs-pa brgya-dang-sum-cu sogs. . ./. . . rgyal-la bdud-rtsi yon-tan-gyi sgrub-thabs rtsa-ba bdun/man-ngag nyi-shu. . ./. . . nam-mkha'i snying-po-la yang-dag mar-me dgu-pa / bgegs-'dul phur-nag nyi-shu sogs. . . / sangs-rgyas ye-shes dang rdo-rje bdud-'joms gnyis-la jam-dpal gshin-rje gshed rtsa-ba phyag-rgya zil-gnon lha drug-gi sgrub-thabs sogs / man-ngag nyi-shu rtsa-ba rgyal-ba mchog-dbyangs dang / rgyal-ba blo-gros-la / rta-mgrin yang-gsang rol-pa / rtsa-ba yoga gsum-gyi sgrub-thabs / . . . Bairotsana dang ldan-ma rtse-mang-la dmod-pa drag-sngags-kyi sgrub-thabs / dpal-stobs-ldan nag-po rtsa-ba sde brgyad / yan-lag dregs-pa bco-brgyad-kyi sgrub-thabs. . . / ska-ba dpal-brtsegs dang 'o-bran dbang-phyug-la ma-mo rtsa-ba'i sgrub-thabs phyi-nang-gsang gsum. . . / Jñānakumāra bajra dang sog-po lha-dpal-la yang-phur gsang-ba 'i man-ngag chig dang / phyag-rgya-chen-po tshe'i sgrub lung. . . / dpal-gyi senge dang cog-ro klu'i rgyal-mtshan-la / dregs-pa rtsa-ba sgrub-thabs khro-bo bcus brgyan-pa dang / yan-lag-gi sgrub-thabs dregs-dpon sum-cu'i bskang-thabs / las-kyi man-ngag. . . / rin-chen bzang-po dang ting-nge-'dzin bzang-po-la thugs-rje-chen-po gsang-ba'i sgrub-thabs dang / rig-'dzin bla-ma'i sgrub-pa'i thabs dang / rig-pa phyag-rgya-chen-po mchog-gi dngos-grub-kyi lung. . . / lang-gro dang rgyal-ba byang-chub-la byin-rlabs bla-ma'i sgrub-lung dang / rta-mgrin gsang-ba kun-'dus / rta-nag dregs-pa'i sgrub-thabs. . . / khye'u-chung dang dran-pa nam-mkha-la / padma zhi-khro gsang-ba'i sgrub-thabs dang / rdo-rje sems-dpa' rtsa-ba lha drug / dpa'-gcig bsgom-pa'i thabs / heruka sum-cu-rtsa-drug bsgom-pa'i lung. . . / rma dang g-yu-sgra snying-po-la phyag-na rdo-rje gsang-ba'i sgrub-thabs / . . . yoga tshe'i sgrub-lung man-ngag. . ./bdag mtsho-rgyal-la rtsa-ba gsum dkyil-'khor gcig-tu bsgrub-pa'i thabs.*

60 *rTen-'brel*. This word has a general and a technical meaning: (a)

saṃyoga; 'circumstances combining to found a judgement or prognostic' (C. Das, *Dictionary*, p. 573); and since every point-instant of experience is a combination of inter-related, portentous factors, every instant constitutes an omen (*rten-'brel*) from which the past or future can be read; (b) *pratītyasamutpāda*: interdependent origination, the field of relativity; this basic doctrine, a pillar of all Buddhist philosophy, affirms that there is no one first cause but that all things in space and time are inter-related and mutually dependent. This field, or better, continuum, of relativity composed of length, depth, breadth and time has the nature of the primal purity of dynamic space (*dharmadhātu*).

Chapter 5: Meditation, Austerity and Spiritual Accomplishment

1 *'Phrin-las*: the Guru's transformative *karmas* performed by the Ḍākinī, internally and externally, upon herself and others, are pacification, enrichment, control and destruction. Motivated by the loving desire to give the pure pleasure of ultimate *siddhi*, karmic energies subsided, with utter detachment, and perfect control over the subtle energies of the body-mind, their structure and direction, the Ḍākinī performs her tranformative activity.

2 This paragraph describes the results of Tsogyel's meditation upon the three roots. The Ḍākinī is understood as structural patterns of energy (*rtsa*), the dynamic energies that play within that structure (*rlung*), and ultimate non-dual awareness (*thig-le*). The Yidam's visitation is a projection and reification of divine qualities; the meaning of his symbolic values are existentially realised. The nature of 'own mind' (*rang-sems*), which is the seed-essence of non-dual awareness, is seen as the Lama's dance (*bla-ma'i rol-pa*) in which his pure-lands (*bla-ma'i rnal-'byor*) are the visual appearances of his Body, all sound his Speech and all consciousness his Mind. The external *maṇḍala*, is that of Mahāvajradhara in the Vase Initiation.

3 In this *nirmāṇakāya maṇḍala* vision, the symbols of death indicate Emptiness, the skull and bones of existential being. Death is immortality and life on the wheel of existence is a series of deaths from moment to moment. When the wheel accelerates there is an illusion of continuity; when the wheel slows the *bar-do* is endured at the conclusion of every micro- and macro-cycle. Release from the wheel is immortality in a continuum of metamorphosing illusion.

4 *mTshan-ldan bla-ma dam-pa*. Sympathy, lack of prejudice, equanimity, knowledge and power are some of the hall-marks of a good Lama; but 'instantaneous compassion' and absolute non-discrimination are the qualities of a 'real Lama', the 'root' Lama, who will

become the unconditioned Lama, a ubiquitous reality inseparable from the *yogin*'s mind.

5 *Mu-stegs rgyang-'phen, tirthika chārbbāka* or *lokayata*: this sect of extremist, self-mutilating ascetics who cursed their bodies for its passion were condemned by Buddhists and Brahmins alike.

6 *Me-shel, sūryakāntamaṇi*: a kind of rock crystal supposed to emit heat when exposed to the sun.

7 Gos-dkar-mo, Pāṇḍaravāsinī; Amitābha's Consort, the primal purity of desire and attachment (see ch. 4, n. 14); the Ḍākinī of Mystic Heat (*gtu-mo mkha'-'gro*), the primal purity of the element fire and the psycho-organic power of heat. White cotton cloth is the garb of the *ras-pas*, the emulators of Mi-la Ras-pa.

8 *Chang kapāla*. In tantric rites the white *bodhicitta* (semen) can be represented by white barley liquor; the female receptacle (*bhaga*) is the human-skull cup (*thod-pa, kapāla*). Thus the relative contains the absolute; Tsogyel quaffs the elixir of life.

9 *Rus rgyan*: the Ḍākinī's bone ornaments representing the five modes of Awareness are: *cakra* on the crown (*chos-dbyings*), ear-rings (*sor-rtog*), short necklace (*mnyam-nyid*), bracelets, armlets and anklets (*me-long*), girdle (*don-grub*).

10 *Khrag, rakta*: the red *bodhicitta*, the essence of the Ḍākinī; it carries the seeds of passion, thought and samsaric action that provide the modes of Awareness of Emptiness.

11 *bLa-ma rgyang-'bod mgur*: this genre of liturgical song contains fine devotional Tibetan poetry.

12 *Ye-nas mi-zad-pa'i dam-pa'i chos-gter*. In the first reference to termas (*gter-ma*), revealed texts, a clear indication of their mystical nature is given by 'ultimately inexhaustible'. In most passages concerning termas, as indeed in the entire text, literal and figurative meanings are not distinguished.

13 *bCud-led mdzad-pa. bCud-len, rasayana*; lit. 'the extraction of essence or nectar', hence 'alchemy', both chemical and metaphysical, although again no distinction is made between the two in 'Ḍākinī talk'. Indian *rasayana* employed psychotropic and regenerative drugs and poisons, and sought (and often found) the ultimate philosopher's stone, also called *rasayana*.

14 *Chong-zhi*: a crystalline form of calcium used by naturopaths and ayurveds as a panacea, particularly for throat ailments; it is commonly used by fasting yogins. C. Das (*Dictionary*, p. 385) has '=*cung-zho, soma*, the *soma* plant said to be useful in diarrhoea, in phlegm and fever'. *Soma* is also identified with the *ephedra* plant, the *amanita muscaria* mushroom, the alchohol of fermented fruit, etc.

15 See ch. 4, n. 57.

16 *Rigs lnga rigs gsum*: for the Five Aspects, the Dhyāni Buddhas, see ch. 4, n. 14; the Three Aspects are Body, Speech and Mind – Vajrapāṇi, Saḍakṣarī Avalokiteśvara and Mañjuśrī, the Bodhisattva protectors of the three doors.

17 *Grub-chen brgyad*: speed-walking (*rkang-mgyogs*), the eye salve of omniscience (*mig-sman*), infallible memory (*mi-brjed gzungs*), prescience (*pra-se*), the power of subjection (*dbang-sdud*), transformative powers (*rdzu-'phrul*), the wisdom of unbounded knowledge (*shes-bya thogs-med-kyi shes-rab*) (from Chos-gling's *Lam-rim Ye-shes snying-po*).

18 *rDo-rje ltar dpa'-bar 'gro-ba'i ting-nge-'dzin*, 'the *samādhi* that is as strong as a *vajra*'. See ch. 6, n. 4. *Samādhi* is not concentration; on the contrary the mind is relaxed. *Samādhi* in most Buddhist contexts can be defined as 'identification with Emptiness'.

19 *Lha'i drang-srong-chen-po sde bzhi.*

20 *Chi-med bdud-rtsi sman*. Interpreted literally, this medicinal substance (*sman*) in the form of small, brown coagulated droplets is created by the Lama in a highly controlled, ritual, alchemical process (*bcud-len*) out of various ingredients prescribed by the formulae that accompany different *tantra*s. The power of the *bdud-rtsi* (*amṛta*) lies as much in the alchemical transmission of the Lama's power in the ritual process as in the innumerable ingredients. (For a recipe see Dudjom Rimpoche's *'Chi-med srog-thig*). 'Immortality' (*'chi-med*) implies (a) longevity or control of a very long life, and (b) the deathlessness of the *dharmakāya*.

21 *Lus gnad*: Vairocana's seven points of posture are lotus posture, straight back, tongue turned up and back, chin down with the neck and spinal column in line, eyes open and focused one yard (approx.) before the nose, hands in *dhyānamudrā*.

22 *sNang-srid bya-ba sems-kyi cho-'phrul tsam*: *cho-'phrul* denotes illusions of a low order, or hallucination, whereas *rdzu-'phrul* (*ṛddhi*) is illusion created for a Bodhisattva's purpose.

23 *kLo-yul kha-khra dang rkang-kra*: the Striped-mouths (*kha-khra*) seem to have been non-humans (*mi-ma-yin*) who became humans upon their conversion. Identified by some as the savage hunters of N.W. Assam, to the Tibetans they are the archetypal border barbarians (*kla-klo*). See M. Aris, *Bhutan*, pp. 58, 143. The Striped-feet are not identified.

24 *Pha-rol-tu-phyin-pa bcu*: moral action, perseverance, patience, generosity, meditative absorption, perfect insight, skilful means, higher aspiration, psychic power and Awareness.

25 *bDe-stong zung-'jug thig-le'i dka'-sbyad*: this is a Third Initiation *yoga*. See pp. 249ff.

26 *rDo-rje'i sku-la bsgres-rgud-med-pa tshe'i rig-'dzin* = *tshe'i dbang-la rig-'dzin*. The other three of the four kinds of *Rig–'dzin* (*vidhyādhara*) are: Knowledge Holder of Manifold Maturity (*sna-tshogs smin-pa'i rig-'dzin*), K.H. of Spontaneity (*lhun-grub-kyi rig-'dzin*), the *Mahāmudrā* K.H. (*phyag-rgya-chen-po'i rig–'dzin*).

27 Ma-gcig La-phyi sgron-ma (Lab-sgron) was born in La-phyi in Tsang (west-central Tibet) and only moved to Dwags-po (Dak) after she had achieved notoriety by cohabiting with the teacher Thod-pa Bhadra (or 'Ba'-re) at the great monastery of Grwa-thang founded by her master, Grwa-pa mNgon-shes. Her eldest son Grub-pa was a thief until at the age of thirty-two he received his mother's teaching; her younger son Grub-se was ordained young and later became a respected crazy yogin (*zhig-po*); her daughter was named Grub-chung-ma. Her first teacher was Grwa-pa (1012–1090), abbot of Samye, a famous *gter-ston*, who revealed the medical works *rGyud bzhi*, and who died while having lymph sucked from his heart up a golden straw by a disciple. During Lab-sgron's ritual initiation into Dam'pa's lineage she left the temple to receive initiation directly from the Goddesses Mahāmāyā, Prajñāpāramitā and Tārā. Pha-dam-pa Sangs-rgyas was her most important teacher. *Zab-gcod* (profound severance), taught by Dam-pa, is a path to *mahāmudrā* through evocation of demons and spirits in terrifying situations, abandoning attachment to the body-mind and identifying with the clear-light. This practice is an example of the homeopathic tantric principle *similar similibus curator*, 'like cures like', passion is passions' remedy. *gCod* can also be applied in medicine; provoking the spirits of disease then identifying with their essential primal purity, the disease is destroyed with the spirit. Ma-gcig's principal *gcod* practice involved destruction of her four devils – attachment to sense objects and thought, delight in achievement, and egotism – offering flesh and blood to the devils (*bdud*) to feed on, detached from body-mind. Dam-pa's teaching affected her in a way that motivated her to associate with outcastes, and to renounce her family and wander, living in caves.

28 Pha-dam-pa Sangs-rgyas, born in S. India, ordained young, was taught by many of the famous scholars and *siddhas* of his day. He travelled to the Eight Knowledge Holders' Śītavana Cremation Ground, to Swayamabhu in Nepal, and five times in Tibet, where he stayed in Kham, Ngari, Central Tibet, but mostly in Tsang and particularly Tingri. His school was called 'zhi-je' (*zhi-byed*), the Pacifier, and, including *gcod*, this was based on the *prajñāpāramitā*; he also taught the *Kālacakra-tantra* and *karmamudrā yoga*. He taught the direct method: 'Your best teacher is your own mind!' This story

of his disciple, So-chung-pa, illustrates the method. So-chung-pa took his disciple begging. All day, whenever they reached a house, he would say, 'No, this is not the one.' His disciple became angry. Then, later, returning home, he entered first, loudly whispering to a stranger, 'Hide your things, a thief is entering!' The disciple overheard, and enraged he took a knife and rushed at the Guru, who slipped into a locked room, saying, 'Look into your anger at the nature of your mind!'

29 *rDo-rje phur-ba'i rgyud Byitotama*: a large collection of Phur-ba *tantras*. The 42 *e-khram maṇḍalas* belong in this collection.

30 *Lha-ma-srin sde brgyad = lhadang 'dre dang ma-mo dang srin-po dang sde brgyad*. The Bon deities, spirits, etc., like earth-lords (*sa-bdag*), mountain gods (*gnod-sbyin*), spirits of disease (*theu-rang*), etc., were classified into three groups of eight, without any apparent method.

31 *Nus-pa-che-ba kīlaya nyi-shu'i sgrub-thabs*.

32 *Tshe-dpag-med 'chi-med 'od-kyi phreng-ba/rdo-rje phreng-ba/gsang-ba kun-'dus / rgyal-ba kun-'dus/lha-gcig bum gcig/tshe-lha drug-cu-rtsa-gnyis-kyi dkyil-'khor*.

Chapter 6: Signs of Success and Proofs of Power

1 Evidence of success in meditation (*bsgrub-pas rtags*) such as the mystic heat, visitation of deities, and ultimately Buddhahood, is described in the first section of these verses; the proofs of mastery (*grub-pa thob-nas grub-rtags*) demonstrated in her later life, like subjecting the Bonpo, hiding the terma, etc., and showing the eight great *siddhis*, etc., are alluded to in the second part.

2 *Zab-lam*: the profound path of co-incident Emptiness and pure pleasure (*bde-stong zung-'jug*) initiated by the Wisdom Empowerment.

3 *Byan-tshud-pa*: 'through a thorough and profound understanding to have complete facility in'; applied to oneself, with *rang* prefix, 'to know oneself inside out and to be in total control'.

4 *Ting-nge-'dzin gsum*: (1) wherein all is seen as magical illusion, or *maya*-vision *samādhi* (*sgyu-ma'i lta-ba'i*); (2) imperturbable vision, or *vajra*-vision *samādhi* (*rdo-rje'i lta-ba'i*) (see ch. 5, n. 18); (3) universal sameness free of evaluation and discrimination, the *samādhi* of sameness (*mnyam-nyid*) in which there is no good and bad, no acceptance and rejection (*bzang-ngan blang-dor-med-pa phyam-brdal-ba'i ting-nge-'dzin*). The three *samādhis* relate to the three modes of being (see ch. 4, n. 23). See pp. 78ff. for their practical application.

5 'Dzokchen's pure potential' (*rdzogs-chen bya-bral*) and 'all-pervasive Ati' (*ati khyab-gdal*) are aspects of the same ultimate reality. 'Ati' is here synonymous with primal purity (*ka-dag*) and space (*dbyings*)

which is the nature of the trek-cho (*mkhregs-gcod*) realisation, while spontaneous accomplishment (*lhun-gyis-grub*) is the result of togal (*thod-rgal*) practice.

6 *rTen-'brel zab-mo bsgrigs-nas yod*: See ch. 4, n. 60. Synchronicity is the circumstance that makes a situation portentous. Reading the ultimate (*zab-mo*) significance of omens, or intuiting the nature of the relative field of experience at any given moment, we realise that we *are* Buddhas and that we *do* fulfil the Bodhisattva Vow, or that we are *siddhas* and each moment is a miracle of our own creation.

7 Or, 'If you do not believe that Emptiness is the key to freedom from your neural disorders, you deny the manner of liberation (*thar-pa*) of the Buddhas (*rgyal-ba*) and the *mahāyāna dharma*.'

Chapter 7: Establishing, Spreading and Perpetuating the Teaching

1 *dGe-ba bcu*: abstention from killing, stealing, sexual misconduct (body); lying, slander, calumny and cursing (speech); and covetousness, malice and opinionatedness (mind).

2 *Zhang-zhung gsar-brgyud*. This must be a late appellation mimicking the terminology of the Tibetan reformers who depended upon the new translations of the Old School *tantras* and of new unknown scriptures from India. The followers of the New Zhang-zhung tradition (Zhang-zhung was the home and strong-hold of Bon) were called Inner, or Esoteric, Bon (*bon-nang-pa* or *nang-bon*) which I have translated as Reformed Bon; and the persecuted old-style Bon, the Outer Bon (*phyi-bon*), Causal Bon (*rgyu-bon*), etc., called by the Buddhists 'false Bon' (*log-bon*), etc., I have called 'Bon-shamans' or simply 'Bon' herein. I have distinguished between the priests of the old religion and Bon cult followers in general by calling the former 'Bon' and the latter 'Bonpos'.

3 *mTha'-thul dang ru bzhi*. To bind the demoness who is the body of Tibet, spread the *dharma* and civilise the people, Song-tsen built four major temples in the outer borderlands (*yang-'dul*), four in the provinces (*mtha'-dul*) and four in the Four Districts of central Tibet (*ru-bzhi*). (See M. Aris, *Bhutan*, pp. 1–43, for a very interesting account based on the *Ma-ṇi bKa'-bum*.) The Four Districts were the kings' administrative and military regions called 'wings' or 'banners' (*ru*): from east to west – Yuru (*gYon-ru*), Uru (*dbUs-ru*), Yeru (*gYas-ru*) and Rulak (*Ru-lag*, 'the reserve').

4 *Ci-yan-med-pa'i gnas, mtha'-yas-pa'i gnas, yod-min-med-min-gyi go-'phang*. These Bon heavens correspond to the upper reaches of the Buddhist realm of formlessness (*gzugs-med-kyi gnas*), and since this entire Bon eschatology employs Buddhist terminology it belongs to

Reformed Bon analysis. These three heavens must be the residences of the Bon gods, Mu (*dMu*), Cha (*Phywa*), and Yang (*gYang*), etc., reached by the rainbow *dMu*-cord that stretches like Jacob's ladder from heaven to earth.

5 *Khri-'khor bcu-gsum*: divisions of Tibet established in the thirteenth century by Kubilai Khan and 'Phags-pa during the Sakya ascendency.

6 Vimalamitra, Śāntigarbha and Nepali Hūṃkara (*Blue Annals*); Buddhaguhya (*Padma bKa'-thang*); Viśudhi Seṅge, Dharmakīrti, Jīnamitra and Dhanaśīla (*Red Annals*): these eight scholars, at least, probably taught at Samye at this time.

7 *Khyung-nag dgu-'gros*: although *khyung-po* is seen as Garuḍa, the *vahāṇa* of Vīṣṇu, he was a principal figure in the Bon mythology where he governed his 'white' creation in constant Manicheistic conflict with the 'black' *mKha'-lding*. Much of the rich Bon mythology has been forgotten by the Buddhists but *Khyung-po* is a direction-guardian on prayer-flags (*rlung-rta*).

8 *Lo-zad zla-zad*: lit. 'year-spent, moon-spent'.

9 *bDe-gshegs-kyi-gdung* and *chos-sku'i-tshab* are the *stūpa*'s *dharmakāya* designations, and *mchod-rten* is its *nirmāṇakāya* name.

10 *rGyal-po sku-rim*: (a) the ancient Bon rite affirming the contract between monarch and subjects; and (b) a Buddhist rite performed for the well-being of the king (or any layman).

11 The *rTa-mgrin gling* is probably in the east (see n. 36). The eight small temples representing the eight satellite continents in the *maṇḍala* of the universe lie one on each side of the four major temples in the four directions. The *Jo-mo gling* is unidentified.

12 *Shag-thong*: unexplained by Taksham, the nature and importance of this riddle contest remains unclear. The function of the Bon priests called *ldeu* centres around riddles; perhaps the riddle-priests were sooth-sayers or diviners. Riddles still appear in Tibetan culture on various occasions. See G. Tucci, *The Religions of Tibet*, p. 238.

13 Padma Saṃbhava is the Guru as a *paṇḍita*, a scholar, depicted wearing a pointed red hat and a simple robe. rDo-rje gro-lod is a wrathful deity, depicted riding a pregnant tigress, enhaloed in flame, carrying a *vajra* and scorpion. Both are counted amongst the eight names of the Guru (*Guru mtshan brgyad*).

14 *bKa'-'gyur ro-cog*: a canonic compilation of Śākyamuni's sermons.

15 *Sre-mo-gis spos thu/khyi kha-zan bor/mar-me khrag bsnub/ko mthu nag-po/btsan 'gyed dang/bdud 'gyed*. This could be Taksham's parody.

16 *Nga ni zag-med rdo-rje'i sku/rtsi-nyid rtsir gyur*. Here for the first time Tsogyel expresses her goal achieved. Through the alchemy (*bcud-len*) of extracting the absolute, pure essence (*rtsi-nyid*) from poison,

she has gained an immortal *vajra*-body. The impure, material body (*zag-bcas*) with the nature of primal purity (*ka-dag*) has dissolved into its own purity and has become immaterial (*zag-med*), outflows ceased.

17 *'Gro-don nus-pa.* Although *nus-pa* (*śakti*) can be rendered as 'ability' it is also the Ḍākinī's power to raise the Guru's *kuṇḍalinī*. Certainly this phrase means more than 'the ability to help others'.

18 *bKa'-brgyud.* At this time the kama (*bka'ma*) doctrines (pronouncements) would have comprised the mainstream tantric teachings transmitted from the Indian masters by Guru Pema, Vimalamitra, Sangs-rgyas ye-shes, etc. Both *bka'-brgyud* and *snyan-brgyud* are names of the school to which Marpa, Milarepa and Gampopa belonged.

19 *bsDu-ba bzhi* = *bsdu-ba'i dngos-po bzhi*: bestowing necessities, speaking sweet words, concurring in mundane matters, acting to benefit neophytes. Such actions bring the Guru disciples.

20 *Zab-la rgya.* This phrase, or *zab dang rgya*, is a formula indicating the *atiyoga* union of duality in the *dharmakāya*, Kun-zang yab-yum. It may be inferred here that the Word is to be embodied in the Ḍākinī so that she may reveal it to treasure-finders (*gter-ston*) when the time is ripe.

21 *bLa-ma dgongs-pa'i 'dus-pa'i dkyil-'khor.*

22 'Mind Accomplishment' (*thugs sgrub*) and 'Heart Drop' (*snying-thig*) texts are two widely discovered genres of terma. The former are mainly *Guru-yoga sādhanas*, texts of *mahāyoga* meditation liturgy, and the latter, belonging to the Dzokchen Nyingtik lineage, cover every aspect of theory and practice.

23 *Kha-byang, yang-byang, snying-byang, lung-byang*: types of terma manifests to assist tertons.

24 *'Phrin-las bzhi*: the Guru's Four Karmas or transformative activities: pacification (*zhi-ba*), enrichment (*rgyas-pa*), control (*dbang-ba*), and destruction (*drag-pa*).

25 If this date is not apocryphal, it is the tenth day of the tenth moon (Dec-Jan) of the year 790, or possibly 802.

26 *rDzogs-chen ati khyab-gdal-kyi dkyil-'khor.* Taksham does not describe this *maṇḍala*; he emphasises the dangers of the path.

27 *'Bras-bu chos-zad-kyi dbyings-su 'ub-chub bya-ba.* The adjective 'dynamic' (or 'pure' or 'inner') merely distinguishes this 'space' from interstellar space, or the interval between objects. *dbYings* (dhātu) can be conceived as a field of pure meaning or ultimate value, or the field of primal purity (*ka-dag*), or the sphere of Emptiness. Further, although 'continuum' is more precise than 'field' or 'sphere', experientially there is a sense of timelessness and stasis

in 'space' a sense of 'utterly pure and pristine from the beginning', although what defines space – illusory form – is in constant metamorphosis. But at least 'continuum' implies the indivisibility of 'space' from experience and being. Lastly, perhaps 'space' is best defined by paradox: 'the ineffable plenum of polar opposites united', 'the non-dual plenum of duality', 'the field of non-duality of *saṃsāra* and *nirvāṇa*'.

28 *Chos-nyid mngon-gsum*: the first of the four togal visions (*snang-ba bzhi*): (2) intensive visionary experience (*nyams-snang gong-'phel*); (3) optimal Knowledge (*rig-pa tshad-phebs*); and (4) reality extinguished (*chos-nyid zad-pa* or *chos-zad-chen-po*). These are four stages in the dissolution of the material body into light; four stages of increasing recognition of reality (*chos-nyid*) until finally there is no question of reality or non-reality – only Knowledge and Awareness.

29 *rDzogs-chen bya-bral thig-le ngang-du zhog*. This short, concise *mahāyoga* meditation liturgy of *Guru-yoga (Lama'i rnal-'byor)* results in rainbow body, Dzokchen's ultimate goal. Here reality is experienced as pure potential, or non-action (*bya-bral*), and as 'seed-essence' or 'cognitive seminal nuclei' (*thig-le*).

30 *Rig-'dzin Thing-'od 'bar-ma*.

31 In this list of highly auspicious ritual instruments, of those untranslated, *phems* could be a mis-spelling, tingcha (*ting-ting-shag*) is a small cymbal struck with a short horn, and war (*'ur*) tsel (*tshal*) and piwi (*phi-wi*) are instruments with onomatopoeic names.

32 *Zhal-chems dang-po*: the Guru's three testaments are not described. Such testaments are customarily verbal messages.

33 *'Das-rjes dang-po*: the Guru's three successive non-verbal legacies of his passing are the three essential experiences of his three modes of being.

34 *Yang-phur bsgrags-ma*. Consisting of a rite of confession before the *Yang-dag maṇḍala* and a rite of removing obstacles by rDo-rje gzhon-nu (Vajra Kumāra), a form of Phurba, this meditation re-establishes the integrity of the *samaya* of Guru and Ḍākinī.

35 *sTon-min, rtsad-min*: properly, *touen-men-pa'i* and *tsien-men-pa'i* (sudden and gradual schools), the Chinese faction of Hwashang Mahāyanā propagating quietistic *ch'an* and Kamalaśīla's Indian faction teaching the Bodhisattva's gradual path.

36 Since the *Byams-pa gling* (Maitreya Temple) was on the west side of the Samye complex, the *rTa-mgrin gling* (Hayagrīva Temple) was probably the *bDud-'dul gsang-sngags gling* in the east.

37 *sBas-yul brgyad*: these hidden valleys throughout Tibet (three in the Himalayas) were indicated by Guru Pema, and described by tertons, as places of refuge in the final conflagration of the *kaliyuga* and

other times of trouble. In the centre of each valley-*maṇḍala* is an indestructible *vajra*-spot.

38 *rDzong*: both an administrative district under a fort and the fort itself. In Bhutan the *rdzongs* are fortified monasteries.

Chapter 8: Fruition and Buddhahood

1 *bLa-ma bka'-gsang 'dus-ba, yi-dam dgongs-pa 'dus-ba,rdzogs-chen ati 'dus-ba.*

2 *Tshig bdun gsol-bdeb.* The Seven Line (or Syllable) Prayer, is at the essence of *Guru-yoga*. Its commentaries on three levels treat the entire *anuttarayoga-tantra*, but its plain exoteric meaning makes it a popular prayer for laymen.

3 *kLong* = *dbyings*, vast expanse, dynamic space. *kLong* can also be rendered as 'point-instant', since the centre of the *maṇḍala* can be anywhere, even on the circumference. This 'matrix' is also the manifestation since there is no coming into being or cessation in this reality. *kLong*, like *dbyings*, has no ontological status; it is indeterminable (*spros-bral*), incapable of definition by any of the eight classical 'extremes' of Buddhist ontology (*mtha'-brgyad*).

4 Sad-na legs: *sad-na* = 'on trial', or 'when tested', and *legs* means 'good', 'firm', etc. Thus KhrilDe-srong-btsan's common name means 'Strong-when-tested', etc.

5 *Zab-chos zhi-khro dgongs-pa rang-grol.* The principal of the *maṇḍala* of the Wrathful and Peaceful Deities is one of the Eight Logos Deities, Phurba or Chemchok (*Che-mchog*)

6 *Tshe'i 'di chos brgyad*: loss and gain, notoriety and fame, praise and blame and pleasure and pain.

7 *Chos thams-cad zad-par bya-ba'i ting-nge-'dzin*: in this final *samādhi* which induces the fourth of the togal visions, 'the extinction of all things (*dharmas*)', the final vestiges of the ego are destroyed, corporeality dissolves, and 'life' as we know it ends. Thus it is the ultimate metaphor for death.

8 Zangs-mdog-dpal-ri: Guru Pema's paradise afterwards created on the S.W. island continent of Nga-yab gling.

9 *Sems-can mi-rtag bya-ba gdul-bya'i mtshan-nyid. gDul-bya*: lit. 'what is converted or transformed' into Buddha, hence 'disciple', 'convert', or 'humanity'.

10 The three-fold Ati refers to the three incisive precepts (*Tshig-gsum-gnad-brdeg*) which follow (with the fourth, the goal); Vision (*lta-ba*) Meditation (*sgom-pa*), Action (*spyod-pa*). These precepts belong to *mkhregs-gcod* practice.

11 *dBang-bskur gong-ma gsum*: the Mystic, Wisdom and Word Empowerments.

12 *rTsa gsum*: *bLa-ma, Yi-dam, mkha'-'gro;* Guru, Deva Ḍākinī: the Buddha's three modes of being reified anthropomorphically. Experientially they are indivisible.

13 *gTor-ma, bali*: sacrificial cakes made of the five sacred ingredients offered to the deity as a representation of the deity and consumed to attain *samaya*, in separate rites, or as part of the *gaṇacakra*.

14 *Phar-bsre tshur-bstim gnyis-med klong/nyams-myong skyes-na*: in *atiyoga*, in order to achieve the resolution of duality, and consummation in an inconceivable field of space (*klong*), creative and fulfilment processes must be simultaneous, and radiation and re-absorption of light, efferent and afferent energies, must also be co-incident. The method given here is to watch the nature of the Lama's non-referential Knowledge (*rig-pa*).

15 *sPrul-pas khams dang skye-mched 'gyed/yang-sprul rten-'grel bcu-gnyis shar*. The elements of body-mind are the qualities of the five elements (solidity, fluidity, heat, motion and spaciousness) and the elements of perception (six consciousnesses, organs and sense-fields); the sense-fields are composed of the six internal and external sense-objects, and the twelve interdependent, functional elements of existence are ignorance, volition, consciousness, name and form, six senses, contact, feeling, grasping, clinging, birth, rebirth, old age and death.

16 *Ye-shes-chen-po, mahājñāna*: the cognitive primal purity of the mind, inseparable from phenomenal and noumenal appearances. The suffix *chen-po* (*maha*, 'great' or 'ultimate') makes 'Awareness' the all-inclusive, sole constituent of the unitary field of reality. It is represented as the *dharmakāya* Ḍākinī alone.

17 *bsKyed-rdzogs rdzogs-chen*: all three of these *yogas* (*mahā-*, *anu-*, and *atiyoga*) are formal meditation practices, but Dzokchen is the goal as well as a path, and, therefore, is experienced informally in the stream of existential praxis.

18 *Lhag-mthong, vipaśyanā*: the *yoga* of guarding the doors of the senses, taught by Śākyamuni and employed in various contexts in tantric practice.

19 Che-'jing mir-gan is probably the Mongol king Qoricar Mergan who lived *ca*. tenth century and whom the Tibetans considered an incarnation of Guru Pema (see *Blue Annals*, p. 57).

20 bDe-chen dbyangs-can ma: a name of Sarasvatī.

21 The text of the *mKha'-spyod sprul-sku snying-thig* is in three parts. The outer part conforms to the *sūtras*: *mkha'-'gro sku gsum rkyang-sgrub/spyod-yul 'dul-ba dkar-po/thog-'beb drag-spyod rnam-gsum/bla-ma sku*

*gsum rkyang-sgrub/byin-rlabs dbang-gi sgo-mo/gzer-'joms lta-ba cig-chod/ rtags-tshad so-pa dgu 'dres/gnad-kyi me-btsa' rnam-gsum/rdzas-sngags dmigs-yul brgya'-rtsa/rjes gcod lcam-bu gzer-them sogs spyi tshan bcu/*The inner part conforms to the *tantras*: *bla-ma mkha'-'gro zung-'jug-tu sgrub-thabs/bsgom-pa sgyu-ma 'phrul 'gros/rtsa-rlung 'gog-don /man-ngag gcig chog zab-mo/bsgyur-sbyang spel-ba rnam-gsum/mkha'-'gro'i bang-mdzod mig gcig/mkha' –'gro'i dmar-pa snying gcig/mkha'-'gro gnyer-po srog gcig/man-ngag sngags-kha gsum sprel/'od-zer zhags-pa rnam-gsum/dpa'-bo gyad stobs rnam-gsum spyi tsham bcu-gcig/*The secret part is like secret precepts: *bla-ma mkha'-'gro rang-lus dbyer-med-du sgrub-thabs/lta-ba phyag-rgya-chen-po/'bras-bu rdzogs-chen chig gchod/man-ngag gtum-mo sum sbrel/gdams-ngag thos chog rnam-gsum / nyams-len bsgom-pa rnam-gsum / gcig-chog mun chos rnam-gsum/las phran dgos-pa rnam-gsum/rten-'brel me-long rnam-gsum/rgyab-chos dgos-pa rnam-gsum/bka'-srung myur-mgyogs rnam-gsum/drag-sngags gnad-kha rnam-gsum sogs mthar-thug-pa'i chos sna bcu-gnyis sogs.* This sNying-thig text was one of Taksham's principal termas.

22 *mKha'-'gro-gling-gi nyal-le bcu-gnyis*: all the Ḍākinīs enumerated possess the 'wisdom heart' (*shes-rab snying-po*), but their forms and activities can appear fiendish. Tsogyel's wheel is an Ocean of Awareness, whereof the waves' appearances are both peaceful and wrathful.

23 *'Thung-spyod tshan-rdo-nye-ba'i gnas*. The 32 or 12 power places (*pīṭhasthāna*), places of pilgrimage and also focal points (*cakras*) and veins (*nāḍī*) in the human body, are divided into categories such as pīlava (*'thung-gcod*), chandoha, and upa-chandoha (*nye-ba'i* chandoha). These words appear to denote different kinds of meeting places but their meaning is obscure. See B.A. pp. 980, 983.

24 *mKha'-'gro gsang-ba'i brda'-dbang*. This initiation empowers the initiate to intuit the meaning of secret Ḍākinī languages (*brda'-yig*) and symbolic tantric terminology including the twilight language (*sandhyābhāṣā*).

25 *bLa-ma-thugs-kyi sgrub-pa 'bru'-gcig-gi dkyil-'khor.*

26 *Lung-byang-chen-mo.*

27 sMar Sa-skya senge and gYo Rin-chen 'byung-ldan were the two monks who fled from Tsang to Amdo *ca.* 840 during Langdarma's persecution and maintained the *mūlasarvāstivādin* lineage of ordination. The lineage was restored to Central Tibet by the Six Men of dbUs and gTsang a century later. The *Blue Annals* has three monks (*Bod-kyi mkhas-pa mi gsum*) fleeing for the East: gYar-stod Śākyamuni (gMar), gYo dGe-'byung of Drang-chung mdo (gYo) and Rab-gsal of Gya-rab in gTsang.

28 The chief disciple of the Abbot of Vikramaśīla, Atīśa, who came to

Tibet in 1042 to reform monasticism, was Dom-ton ('Brom-ston). He founded the reformed *bKa'-gdams-pa* sect, building sNye-thang and Rwa-sgreng monasteries, and he translated many texts with Atīśa. However, he was a monk and no mention of a consort, Jayākara, appears in the *Blue Annals*; but there was a Nepali scholar called Jayākara who translated in Tibet in the eleventh century.

29 'Sa' must refer to 'Phags-pa, the Sakya sect's hierarch (1235–79) who initiated Kubilai Khan and received Tibet as the initiation price. The hierarch of the eminent 'Khon clan who built the Sakya monastery was Kun-dga'-rgyal-po, a disciple of Drok-mi ('Brog-mi) who in mid-eleventh century was sent by the King of Ngari to Vikramaśīla. Drokmi was initiated into the *lam-'bras* system by Vīrupā and Doṃbi Heruka. *Lam-'bras* (The Path as Goal) is a non-dual system akin to *mahāmudrā*, an *anuttarayoga-tantra*, stressing the absence of a foundation to reality (*rtsa-ba-med-pa*); it is the Sakyapa's height of achievement.

30 'Phak's teaching' could indicate the precepts of the lineage of Vajra Vārāhī (Phag-mo), the Ḍākinī of Marpa, Mila, Gampopa and Phag-mo-gru-pa, or it could mean the teaching of the latter who was the Guru of the founders of seven of the eight Kahgyu sects including the 'Bri-gung (Dri), sTag-lung (Tak), Karma (Kar) and 'Brug-pa (Druk). Marpa Lotsawa's consort, the incarnation of Tsogyel, was named Dakmema (bDag-med-ma, Nairātmā); Gampopa (sGam-po-pa), born in sGam in Dwags-po (Dak), was Guru Pema's emanation.

31 'Karma' could refer to Karma Pakshi (1204–83), or Karmapa Rang-jung Dorje (Rang-'byung rdo-rje, 1284–1359), successive Karma Kahgyu hierarchs. While both were Old School initiates, the latter was a terton who meditated for a long time in Chimphu, and since Tibet was politically stable during Pakshi's reign, Rang-'byung rdo-rje is probably here intended.

32 The Virtuous Doctrine or Method (Geluk, dGe-lugs) is the name of the *bKa'-dams-pa* sect after Tsong-kha-pa reformed it. Its political power grew out of its allies, the Qosot Mongols, after the 3rd Dalai Lama converted Altan Khan and invited him to pacify strife-torn Tibet. Under the Great Fifth (1617–82), a Dzokchenpa and terton, Tibet was united with the aid of Guśri Khan, and the administration at Galden Monastery lasted until Mao's Chinese destroyed it. The Great Fifth's family had a link with the Zahor royalty.

33 'sBe Ye-shes snying-po, La-gsum rGyal-ba byang-chub (Atsara Sale) and rMa Rin-chen mchog will discover the *bsNyan-brgyud gong-'og* the *mKha'-'gro snying-thig* and the *mTsho-rgyal rnam-thar*s, extensive, condensed and concise, in later incarnations.'

34 This passage is an example of a condensed 'prophetic manifest'.

'rDo-rje of Lho-rong' is sTag-sham nus-ldan rdo-rje. The first in this list probably refers to Guru Chos-dbang (1212–70).

35 The great rDo-rje-ldan monastery of Ka-thog in Kham was founded by Dam-pa bDe-gshegs in 1039(?).

36 The blue eight-petalled lotus blossoms in the heart centre, and the red sixteen-petalled lotus in the throat centre.

37 *brTan-ma bcu-gnyis dang bcas-pa'i zhus-len lha-'dre'i lung-bstan.*

38 The sphere of blue light is not as significant for its shape as for what it contains; the sesame seeds are a metaphor for 'seed essence' (*thig-le*). None of the accounts of Tsogyel's *parinirvāṇa* speak of 'rainbow body' *per se.*

39 Ye-shes mtsho-rgyal-ma. rGyal-ma (Queen) can also be rendered Conqueror, a female Buddha (*jīna*).

40 sGrub-thabs: (1) a liturgical meditation text; (2) a cycle or regular and frequent practice, of any *yoga* or meditation; (3) aspiration, methods and experience of existential praxis – life is a *sādhana*.

41 The three Bodhisattvas, Protectors of the Three Doors (body, speech and mind), and in this context, Sangha, Dharma and Buddha, respectively, are also Protectors of Tibet.

42 At the end of each chapter are symbols in the Ḍākinī cypher (*mKha'-'gro brda'-yig*), Here four Sanskrit words can be discerned: *ithi* (thus), *guhya* (secret, mystical, *bhaga*), *evaṃ* (thus, in this way), *manda* (cream, liquor, essence) or maṇḍa(la). *Ithi* (ITI) and EVAṂ lend themselves to non-semantic interpretations; EVAṂ is a mantric word evoking the union of opposites – E is the Ḍākinī, perfect insight, and VAṂ is the Guru, skilful means. The Ḍākinī language functions chiefly on a non-discursive level; the intellectual scalpel destroys mantric efficiency, and analysis keeps the Ḍākinīs at bay.

43 On a mystic level, the evocation SAMAYA rGYA rGYA rGYA can be rendered: Union! Kun-bzang yab-yum are united in the *dharmakāya*; Hayagrīva and Vajra Yoginī are united in the *saṃbhogakāya*; and Guru Pema and Tsogyel are united in the *nirmāṇakāya*! On an internal level it may be rendered: I vow to practise the Guru's teachings with body, speech and mind! And on an external level it means: the word of the Guru is sealed with the three-fold bond of secrecy.

COMMENTARY

1

THE PATH OF THE INNER TANTRA

The Ḍākinī cypher and the Guru's *maṇḍala,* a lotus flower and a flaming *vajra,* a shooting star and a rainbow body: during this period of absorption in the Tantra, its terminology, premises and concepts should be taken to heart. In this semantic game of enlightenment, it is expedient first to clarify meanings and then to approach tantric formulae as if they represented absolute truths. There is little joy in the mere intellectual exercise of comparative study of meta-psychological systems, but a great deal to be gained by bathing the mind in a sublime vision that has a psychotropic effect. The purpose of this essay is to evoke a vision, the existential vision of the Inner Tantra (the Buddhist *anuttarayoga-tantra* consisting of *mahāyoga, anuyoga* and Dzokchen *atiyoga*), and further, to describe the methods of inducing this vision and the functions of the psycho-organism under its influence. This vision is not an escapist paradise or a means to obfuscate the harsh realities of a mean life, or to replace the vicissitudes of happiness and suffering by a narcotic hallucination; on the contrary, its core is the naked, basic fact of existence.

This vision is not only existential in so far as it pertains to existence; it accords in part with philosophic existentialism. Objective values are subjected to gnostic experience arising from within; the individual is recognised as master of his fate capable of casting off the ties that bind him in an authoritarian social and moral strait-jacket, and overcoming the intellectual and emotional obstacles that restrict knowledge of himself as a being capable of freedom of action and expression. Man's greatest potential for power, realisation and pleasure lies in the present moment, in his actual state of being; personal recognition of the human condition is the first step to potentiating the fullness of the moment. Suffering is accepted both intellectually and emotionally as an unavoidable fact, an integral part of life, to be used rather than avoided. Action is an absolute statement of being rather than a means to an end like behaviour conforming to social or moral mores or actions dictated by a manipulative ego. Thus this existential vision of the Inner Tantra is not merely a way of thought to be assimilated intellectually; it is a way of being aware that automatically affects thought-forms. Indeed it affects the full range of a human being's potential: his understanding of who he is and the world he lives in; his aesthetic appreciation and his communication with people and things; the breadth, depth and intensity of his awareness (consciousness); his moral being and his talent; and the motivation and efficacy of his activity from sex to singing a song. Although madness or a strange life-style may result from opening the doors of perception, there is not necessarily a radical external change in a person – it takes a Buddha to recognise a Buddha. And what or who is a Buddha? In the *mahāyāna*, Buddhahood is defined as the state of recognition of Emptiness in oneself and in phenomena. Thus recognition, an utterly intangible quality of awareness, is the key to tantric vision, meditation and action, and the means to attain this recognition is through initiation and sustaining the experience of initiation through *tantra-yoga* and meditation.

Formalistic exposition of tantric metaphysics and psychological description of tantric *yoga*s and practices are no aid to realisation of our Buddha-nature, neither is an explanation of the stages of the path relevant to an initiate's personal practice. The image of a ladder reaching from ignorance to wisdom can be a misleading idealisation. The mind will not follow the logical pattern of development laid out by optimistic guides. Even to generalise about methods of *yoga* practice can be counter-productive. Each individual has his own path, each mind its own peculiarities and needs, and it can be destructive to squeeze different minds into the same mould. Each mind reacts differently to the same stimuli; every individual has his own *karma*, and *karma* is so complex, its ramifications so diverse and subtle, that it is difficult to isolate clear-cut cases of moral cause and effect. The virtuous man, like the biblical Job, is often afflicted by unaccountable troubles, and the vicious man is often rewarded with wealth and sensual pleasure. The monk or *yogin* who practises the letter of the Buddha's law may become a stereo-typed religious fool, while the lay existentialist who maintains his tantric *samaya*s (vows) may fortuitously find himself a *siddha* or saint. Thus in this attempt at conveying the nature of the Inner Tantra, I have rejected the formalistic method; but by defining the concepts and elucidating aspects of the Tantra that arise in Tsogyel's *Life* and erecting sign-posts along her path of practice, I hope to have sketched a useful picture of the Inner Tantra and its processes and functions. In general, it is written from the standpoint of the Dzokchenpa, the *yogin* practitioner (*sādhaka*) of Dzokchen *atiyoga*; but it is a personal picture subject to the limitations of a personal understanding.

The practitioner of the most formless Buddhist practice, the Dzokchen *yogin*, travelling the fastest vehicle traversing the path to Buddhahood, will generally discipline himself in the practices of some of the eight lesser of the nine vehicles.[1] There is no contradiction here, as his sphere of activity is as broad as human experience. Since Tsogyel was to become a nun and teacher of both the theory and practice of many skilful means, before she received her tantric initiations she studied the rules of monastic discipline (*vinaya*), the *hīnayāna* and *mahāyāna* scriptures (*sūtra*s) and their commentaries, and metaphysics (*abhidharma*). If her philosophical studies were directed by Śāntarakṣita (the abbot of the newly erected Samye monastery) her tuition would have stressed the epistemology of the *svatantrika* branch of the *mādhyamika* school. But certainly she would also have studied the *yogācāra* Mind-Only (*sems-tsam-pa*) philosophy with its practical psychoanalytic terminology to which Nyingma tantric expression has some affinity, and also the dialectic of the *mādhyamika-prasaṅgika* school that was still a relatively new and vital philosophy in India. In particular she studied the concepts fundamental to all Buddhist thought, such as the notion of *karma*, the laws of causality in the moral and mental spheres: certain actions cultivate specific states of mind, and certain meditations produce specific cognitive modes and psychic powers. And the notion of Emptiness (*stong-pa-nyid, śūnyatā*), basic to the entire *mahāyāna*, is the crux of all theory and practice: through Emptiness all things have only a relative existence, and, therefore, individuals, gods and the universe itself is empty of a substantial, eternal principle of existence, such as a soul or the Judeo-Christian God.[2] Experientially, perception of Emptiness is co-incident with realisation of all phenomena as illusion. With the radically changed outlook that such perception implies, the priorities of being alive are revolutionised, and the conceptual function of mind arrested, the universe is perceived as light-form: thus, 'enlightenment'.

Apropos of Tantra *mahāyāna* is a rich well of ideas, metaphysics, *yoga*s and meditation practices that are adapted for use as skilful means in the pre-eminently pragmatic and syncretic tantric tradition. The theory and practice of *mahāyāna* provides the basis of practice of the Inner Tantra; the slow, graduated spiritual evolution effected by the *mahāyāna* primes the mind for the highly efficient means provided by the *tantra*s, which can effect Buddhahood in a single lifetime, although they do not provide a sudden method of release in principle. Thus in Tantra, the six perfections,[3] for instance, are given an added dimension. Generosity is the 'impartial dispensation of every requirement'. Morality is the automatic function of continuous, immediate Awareness 'free of public and private vows', though not, of course, free of the tantric *samaya* (see p. 227). Patience is the acceptance of the good with the bad, the *sādhaka* being based in the sameness of all experience. Perseverance is the 'flowing river *samādhi*', cultivating empty pleasure. Meditation is simultaneous creative and fulfilment processes of meditation 'with fixation upon *mahāmudrā*'. And perfect insight is inseparable from service to a consort of skilful means (for a *yoginī*). In that manner Tsogyel explained her practice to another of Guru Rimpoche's consorts, Śākya Dema, in Nepal (see pp. 54f.).

On the Bodhisattva path no Guru is needed, but as soon as the complex but enriching elements of enigma, paradox and twilight language (*sandhyābhāṣā*) enter into the expression of the *dharma*, the aspirant needs a Guru preceptor, a Lama, to make the appropriate meaning quite clear and to convey the empowering oral transmission and authorisations (*lung*). Although the *sādhaka* may be well aware of the multi-levelled possibilities of the injunctions implied in many passages of Tsogyel's *Life*, it is essential that he knows whether to practise a literal or figurative interpretation. The Lama's example and explanation will be quite explicit. Many traditional stories warn the neophyte of the karmic results of practising upon a level of interpretation in which he is unskilled or to which he is unsuited. The layman who received non-dual precepts such as the Twenty-five Branch Vows and practised fornication and killing, stealing and lying, was reborn as Rudra, the personification of egoistic immorality. For many other reasons, too, the Lama is the key to the Tantra. Since the 'real Lama', a fully endowed Buddha incapable of selfish motivation, an emanation of Guru Rimpoche himself, contains within himself the Three Jewels (Buddha, Dharma and Sangha), the three roots (Guru, Deva and Ḍākinī) and the Buddha's three modes of being (*nirmāṇakāya*, *saṃbhogakāya* and *dharmakāya*) he is considered to be an object of refuge superior to the Three Jewels themselves. In the basic formula of all tantric Buddhists' conviction – the refuge – the first line is 'I take refuge in the Lama'. The Lama's pronouncements and precepts *are* the *dharma*, and his word assumes the sanctity of absolute truth. In the maze of the mind after all supports have been discarded during the early phase of practice, some unfailing point of reference is needed: that touchstone is the Lama's precepts. This remains true even after the disciple has attained the status of Guru himself. Obedience to the Father-preceptor remains of primary importance even after the Guru's *parinirvāṇa*. So long as the *sādhaka* has a conditioned mind that can comprehend relative truth, so long is the Lama's word sacrosanct. Even when he reaches the level of realisation of the unconditioned Guru, and the Guru's word becomes the song of the birds, the tears of children, the wind in the trees, etc., the preceptor's word is still not superseded.

The importance of the Lama is succinctly expressed in the song that Guru Pema sings to Tsogyel upon her return from Nepal (p. 57). In the metaphor of the boat crossing the ocean of *saṃsāra*, the Lama is the captain of the boat called Oral Transmission; the great sail of secret precepts is provided by him; instructive advice received from the Lama is a guide to the other shore, like a land-bird sailing with the ship constantly seeking landfall; the Lama's example inspires the faith of fair winds; leaks in the *samaya* are plugged by the Lama; and the Lama (or the Ḍākinī Lama) gives maturity and release through post-meditation initiation and instruction. With the arsenal of techniques provided by the *tantras*, with judicious prescription the Lama can effect instantaneous release from *saṃsāra*. Even in Dzokchen where a basic precept is that nothing is to be added to, changed or eradicated in the mind, the single imperative factor is the Lama's introduction of the initiate to the inherent primal purity of his own mind.

Tsogyel's great devotion to her Lama, Guru Pema, and also her conviction that from the first the dynamics of Buddhahood have been functioning unrecognised, is expressed in her prayer in extremity when her practice of the austerity of bone ornaments has brought her close to death: 'From the first this body is the citadel of the Yidam; the nerves and energy flows are the Ḍākinī's courses; and seed-essence is the nature of the Sugatas – you know the entire nature of my being, Lama!' Two aspects of the Lama are implied here. The Lama is both the omniscient apparition, the incarnate Guru Pema (*rūpakāya*), and also his unconditioned, unstructured metaphysical body (*dharmakāya*). Faith in her Lama is the condition *sine qua non* of the success of her austerities. When Guru Pema is leaving for the South-West her emotional songs and histrionic antics, like rolling on the ground and banging her head against rocks, are indicative of her mountain-moving faith.

At this point it is necessary to explain the terms employed in the description of the Buddha Lama above. First, 'the Lama is the Buddha, Dharma and Sangha'. The Three Jewels need little explanation: the Lama embodies the Buddha, his Word and the Community. In so far as he is the Buddha, the Lama possesses the Buddha's three modes of being, the indivisible *trikāya* (three bodies). These three modes of being are essential, empty being (*dharmakāya*), visionary being (*saṃbhogakāya*) and apparitional being (*nirmāṇakāya*). There is a simple formula in *atiyoga* that defines these three modes: essence – empty; nature – radiant; compassionate manifestation – all-embracing.[4] They may be conceived as three interpenetrating spheres of being, or as three aspects of the Ineffable, as ice, water and steam are aspects or modes of H_2O. Although 'essential, empty being' is the totality, it is also individuated Emptiness, the empty primal space inherent in all sentient beings; in terms of the *maṇḍala* it is the all-pervasive centre; it is indeterminable because no proposition whatsoever can formulate its ontological nature; it is Emptiness because nothing substantial exists in experience of it; it is non-referential, non-dual awareness because no subject experiences it and no objective reference can be isolated in it; it is pure pleasure because it is known through ecstatic union with the Ḍākinī; it is personified as Kuntuzangpo or Vajradhara. 'Visionary being' is the radiant nature of the Buddha in variegated rainbow colours in meaningful patterns that instruct and delight; it is instructive because the Buddha's manifestations are intended only to lead beings out of *saṃsāra*; it is aesthetically delightful because it is completely free of emotional taint; it is consummate enjoyment because it is infinite and unimpeded; in terms of the *maṇḍala* it is the space between the centre and the circumference; it is the realm of the Five Buddhas – the Five Aspects of the Adi-Buddha – and the Wrathful Buddhas; it is the realm of the Yidam. 'Apparitional being' is the all-embracing sensibility of being manifesting compassion as illusory appearances in response to the need of all sentient beings; it is 'incarnate being' because the principal form of emanation is human form; it is all-pervasive because all of nature and all artefacts created by man are emanations of compassion; it is idealised human form because its phantom beings are characterised by the Buddha's eighty ideal marks and signs; in terms of the *maṇḍala* it is the circumference; it is represented by Guru Rimpoche in the robes of the nine vehicles.

The three roots are intimately related to the three modes of being. In fact they may be conceived as divine personifications of the three aspects of the Buddha's nature, of the Buddha's Body, Speech and Mind, and of the Buddha, Dharma and Sangha. The three roots are the Guru, Deva and Ḍākinī in Sanskrit, and the Lama, Yidam and Khandroma in Tibetan. In general, regarding the function of these three, the Lama confers empowering blessings, the Yidam bestows *siddhi* (power and realisation) and the Ḍākinī performs the Buddha's *karma*s (pacifying, enriching, controlling and destroying); the Lama bestows the Mind to Mind transmission of the Buddhas, the Yidam instructs through visionary forms and gives authorisation, and the Ḍākinī gives pleasure dancing the illusory cosmic dance. The relationship of the three roots differs according to the point of view. As essential empty being, the Lama may be conceived as the totality in which arises the instructive visionary realm of the Yidam and the apparitional realm of the Ḍākinī dancing the Lama's *karma*. The Lama and Ḍākinī may be viewed as a union of skilful means and perfect insight, while the Yidam is the product of their union. Each is also the totality of reality, and all three possess the three modes of being. The importance and nature of the Lama has been described already; the Ḍākinī is of no less importance, since she can perform the Lama's function as a preceptor when she incarnates like Tsogyel, and she can also be taken as a Yidam, a personal deity, guardian and instructor.

In translation I have preferred the evocative, mantric sound of the Sanskrit word 'Ḍākinī' to the Tibetan word Khandroma, although the latter contains more significant meaning. Khandroma (*mKha'-'gro-ma*) means Sky-goer or Sky-dancer. To the Old School, Ḍākinī is virtually synonymous with Tsogyel herself, for Tsogyel was the Consort of Guru Pema who is every Nyingma Guru. Every initiate of the Nyingma Inner Tantra takes Tsogyel as his Ḍākinī, so the nature of Tsogyel is the nature of every Ḍākinī. First, Tsogyel's empty being is the naked, blue Kuntuzangmo who is the personification of a plenum of Emptiness, Awareness, primal space and pure pleasure.[5] Secondly her body of aesthetic, instructive, enjoyment is Vajra Yoginī or Vajra Vāhāhī (rDo-rje Phag-mo) who with her hooked knife cuts away all ignorance and attachment, sometimes raging and sometimes benign. Kuntuzangmo's radiance may also take the form of Tārā, the compassionate Seven-Eyed Saviouress, whose instruction is to serve all creatures in every way necessary. In her previous rebirth Tsogyel was Sarasvatī, the goddess of learning and the arts, a celibate maiden but the Mother of the Buddhas. Thirdly in her apparitional form Tsogyel performs the deeds of the incarnate Buddhas, actions that release her from the wheel of rebirth and result in union with Guru Pema in the Buddha's essential, empty being. The nature of this union is lotus-light, where as Kuntuzangmo she emanates the apparitional forms of the world of sentient beings.

In her life as described herein, Tsogyel is Kuntuzangmo. 'Failing to recognise me, you objectify me as an external entity,' she tells her disciples. Believing each man to be an island, a discrete isolate, unable to see other people as incarnations of the Buddha's three modes identical to our own empty self, we make distinction between self and other, and the Ḍākinī appears to be an ordinary woman. Failing to see Tsogyel as Kuntuzangmo, failing to see the unity of absolute and relative, her disciples were in ignorance of the universal Ḍākinī projected in primal space as a field of Absolute Awareness (*mahājñāna*), a cosmic dance of pure pleasure, that operates through the delusory functions of mind.

After the refuge, the most important preliminary commitment is the Bodhisattva Vow (*sems-bskyed*), known otherwise as 'the thought of enlightenment' or 'production of an enlightened attitude'. Both formally in meditation practice, and informally on the path of personal evolution, the Bodhisattva Vow not only determines the aspirant's direction and motivation, but it reveals the well-spring of energy through which the goal can be achieved. The word that implies both motivation and energy is *bodhicitta* (*byang-chub-sems*), a key term in Tantra and on the Bodhisattva Path. In Tantra the Bodhisattva Vow can be defined as the will towards universal happiness, with the onus on 'will', because the energy of dynamic aspiration is employed in various tantric *yoga*s. This will is not a drive derived from the intellect that has concluded by deduction that one's own happiness is impossible amidst the suffering of others; it is not derived from altruistic sentiment; and it is not imposed by the Guru or the doctrine. Rather, it is life-force itself and the basic creativity of the mind, innate 'nuclear' energy released by the intuitive insight that the alienation of oneself from others is a function of karmic conditioning performed by a now redundant part of the mind. The greatest possible realisation of human potential is effected by the cultivation of this energy. The tantric texts are peppered with the word 'release'; it is this energy that is released. The Path should not lead to a quietist backwater where self-created visions can be enjoyed at leisure, or where various trance states can be indulged in at whim, although the temptation is strong to avoid the intensity of immediate experience and the Buddha's *karma*s and to take refuge in such paradisiacal pure-lands. The release of energy, which is dramatically and poetically described in Tsogyel's initiation and empowerment, is at once power and awareness.

In Tantra the word *bodhicitta* also denotes sperm and female juices, and the injunction to retain the *bodhicitta* for the sake of others therefore possesses a powerful dual meaning. 'The milk of human kindness' is one possible translation of 'white *bodhicitta*'. The power derived from retaining the *bodhicitta* and retracting it up the medial nerve is the power of the mind that permits the ambiguous facility of walking through walls, flying in the sky, chewing rock and other proofs of *siddhi* demonstrated by the Twenty-five Siddhas of Chimphu, and actual powers of shape-shifting, memory, concentration, verbal persuasiveness and physical prowess, etc. The Awareness which is concomitant with the release of energy will be examined below.

The source of this energy, however, is highly elusive. The selfless, altruistic will of the Bodhisattva, with which most human beings are familiar, comes and goes without rhyme or reason in ordinary minds. There are *yoga*s and meditations of many kinds to stimulate this energy. For instance, in the meditation upon the four stations of Brahmā,[6] which is a preliminary exercise in even the most advanced *yoga*s, the *sādhaka* will envision all beings as his mother and empathise with his enemies, etc., and the compassion that is effected is not so much pity for the less fortunate as an energy burst that is the driving force in the succeeding meditation activity. Meditation upon impermanence (*mi-rtag-pa*) is another stimulation of creative energy. If the mind is well-lubricated it is effective merely to recall that life is short, death may be imminent, minutes are passing, and that the enormous creative potential of 'the precious human body' can be the source of immense pleasure and power. If the mind is heavy and dull then a penetrating exploration to discover what appears to be the permanent basis of torpor and anxiety reveals the essential relativity of all states of mind, and if the analysis is thorough it can result in a great wave of creative energy and pleasure in the perception of Emptiness.[7] According to temperament and personality type, such discursive meditations, or simple breathing exercises, or both, will be effective in stirring the energy of the Bodhisattva Vow.

Samaya (dam-tshig) is of paramount importance. It lies at the heart of the tantric mysteries. It is the key to the mysteries. With the *samaya* we leave behind the firm ground of metaphysics and enter the realm of pure mysticism. Some Lamas will say that the *samaya* is the beginning and the end of the path; that seeking *samaya* and maintaining it is the entire *dharma*. Certainly nothing can be achieved without maintaining the *samaya*. So what is the *samaya*? The ultimate *samaya* is union with the Buddha Lama as the three roots: Lama, Yidam and Ḍākinī. Thus in the context of ultimate *samaya* it can be defined as 'union'. The union is achieved at the moment of initiation and is then sustained by the relative *samayas* which are the vows of Body, Speech and Mind. Thus in the context of the relative *samaya* it can be defined as 'vow', 'pledge' or 'commitment'. Tsogyel explains the vows that sustain the ultimate *samaya* in Chapter 4 (pp. 27f.). Indications that the *samaya* has been broken can be found in loss of integrity in fulfilment of the Bodhisattva Vow through selfishness; any loss of integrity in speech through failure to fulfil verbal commitments; and any loss of integrity in the non-referential non-dual Awareness of the Knowledge Holders through discrimination. Thus *samaya* may be defined as 'integrity'. When the *samaya* is complete it is the source of boundless and spontaneous energy capable of extra-sensory perception and certain spiritual powers (*siddhi*), and, indeed, Buddhahood itself. When the *samaya* is broken it can be restored through the remarkably efficacious ritual meditation called Kangso (*bskang-bsos*) which is a discretional part of the *gaṇacakra* rite. The principal function of the *gaṇacakra* offering ritual is to achieve union with the Lama, Yidam and Ḍākinī.

In the same way that it is counter-productive to follow moral laws blindly, performing 'good' deeds with hatred in the heart, it is futile to practise the relative vows and rules of the tantric *samaya* without ultimate *samaya*. The ultimate *samaya* gives meaning and purpose to the relative *samayas* and the relative *samayas* maintain the ultimate *samaya*. Different Lamas and lineages have different notions of the relative *samayas*. In Dzokchen some Lamas will reduce the vows to the maintenance of the Mind *samaya*. Some will make the relative *samaya* very simply, resting it upon a single Dzokchen precept that can sustain the ultimate *samaya*. However it is done, to do it is imperative. Not only is initiation the origin of the ultimate *samaya*, but *samaya* is the root of initiation and empowerment. Thus Tsogyel can say, 'Since I realised that initiation and empowerment are the key to the tantric mysteries and that *samaya* is the source of empowerment, I have maintained the *samaya* unbroken.'

The twenty-five branch *samaya*s can be the cause of dangerous misunderstanding and a demonic departure from the path. In the manner that they are set down by Tsogyel they need an explanation 'in the light of extended commentary from other sources'. Concerning the five actions that should be practised, for instance, it is imperative to recall that these actions are expressions of the relative *bodhicitta*, the will to universal happiness and the means of selfless service to others. Interpretation of these vows should come from a Lama, but, for example,[8] the vow to fornicate can imply constant maintenance of the congress of (male) immanent Knowledge and (female) *mahāmudrā*, resulting in a dissolution of obstacles into immutable bliss. 'Killing' may be practised in exceptional circumstances, when, for instance, the loss of one man's life may save the lives of many. The Buddha Śākyamuni's death by poison was caused by the karmic effect of the murder of a bandit chief about to slaughter a band of pilgrims. Also, 'killing' means 'to take the life' of dualistic conceptions with the Awareness implicit in Knowledge, and it implies arresting the karmic energies by binding them in the belly by means of the *yoga* of *kumbhaka*, etc. It is true that no action of body, speech or mind is categorically forbidden in practice of Tantra, but far from initiation offering a *carte blanche* to indulge in any whim or passion, every action is derived from the Bodhisattva's motive energy. On the other hand, no action of which human beings are capable is excluded from the *maṇḍala* of the Inner Tantras. Thus the tantric path is said to be superior to all other paths to Buddhahood in that it is the path of unlimited skilful means. Therefore, in theory, the Tantra offers a way of salvation to people involved in polymorphic perversion of any of the basic passions, no matter what degree of manifestation has been achieved. Further, since skilful means are infinite in quantity and quality, in so far as deities and their consorts represent a splendid diversity of conditions of being (male) and insight into their empty nature (female), the pantheon of the Tantra is at present immense and in the future capable of infinite expansion as existential modes of other cultures are assimilated.

Tsogyel's initiations are verbalised in the highly technical language of *anuttarayoga-tantra*. The mechanics of the lineal tradition of teaching do not allow the neophyte verbal definitions and explicit logical explanations. He or she is enjoined first to experience the results of meditation, and then, perhaps, he will study the literature and the conceptual vocabulary and symbolic imagery of the tradition in order to express realisation in mystic songs or to compose instructive works for students. As it is neither desirable nor necessary to examine in detail the nature of the meta-psychotherapeutic transformations effected by these initiations, I will classify the initiations and indicate some meanings that are not apparent in the translation.

The Inner Tantras are approached through four initiations: the Vase Initiation, the Mystic Initiation, the Wisdom Initiation and the Word Initiation. The first is also an initiation into the Outer Tantras; the other three are known as the superior initiations. Generally, I have translated the Tibetan word for initiation (*dbang-bskur*) as 'initiation and empowerment', for although the concept of a new-comer's 'initiation' into the mysteries is relevant, the Tibetan word means 'bestowal of power'. The Guru bestows the power to practise a certain *yoga* upon an initiate who experiences the climax of that *yoga*, in the Vase Initiation, in a rite that parallels the coronation of an Indian prince by his father the king. The Vase Initiation is an empowerment to practise *mahāyoga* and the creative process of meditation. The meditation to which Tsogyel is introduced transforms the dualistic universe, the prosaic environment inhabited by sentient beings, into a divine palace, an immeasurable abode of gods and goddesses, Ḍākas and Ḍākinīs. This is the sphere of apparitional being (*nirmāṇakāya*), the Guru's Body. The central concepts are 'the chalice' and its 'elixir', which bring to mind the Holy Grail and the elixir of Arthurian legend. The chalice is the inanimate world of appearances and the elixir is the life that it contains and which animates it. The essential transformation here is from a dualistic to a non-dual reality; a dualistic, egocentric world in which the 'knower' relates to his object of perception as a discrete isolate, is recognised as the Buddha's reality. In this universe the Ḍākinī's *maṇḍala* of Emptiness and Awareness (elixir-*bcud*) and the Guru's *maṇḍala* of form (*snang-ba*), sound (*grags-pa*) and mind (*thugs*) (the chalice-*snod*) form an integral unity (*zung-'jug*) and divine beings relate through *mudrā* (posture and gesture), *mantra* (the quality of sound) and *samādhi* (an intuitive understanding of their essential sameness).

The language Tsogyel uses to describe the mechanics of her initiation is called 'twilight language' or 'intentional language'. We do not know whether Tsogyel and her Guru are engaged in actual sexual dance and consummation or whether the sexual content is metaphor describing the symbiosis of polarised spiritual qualities and a subsequent blissful catharsis and inner transformation. There cannot, however, be any doubt as to the effectiveness of such language. Whether or not sexual congress is a part of tantric practice, it is the essential genius of Tantra that the most basic and most powerful of human instincts is used as a skilful means to stimulate, or expand, awareness and create insight into the nature of reality, and to generate the will to selfless service. In the Vase Initiation, at the height of sensual pleasure the red (female) and white (male) *bodhicitta*s interfuse, and retracted up the medial nerve in the spine, the focal points of psychic energy (*cakra*s) are charged; the sun and moon of each focal point is irradiated with light, and the entire psycho-organism is vitalised by a current of energy so strong that 'concrete reality', the product of our normal dualistic mode of perception, dissolves, and the vision which is described in terms of Mahāvajradhara, the Adi-Buddha, overwhelms the initiate in his gnostic trance. Mahāvajradhara is the Sixth Buddha; he represents a unitary field of non-dual perception of insubstantial appearances, a plenum of dynamic space in which phenomena float as gossamer light-form. The Five Buddha Aspects and their Consorts are contained within Vajradhara. They represent the five psycho-physical constituents (form, feeling, ideation, volition and consciousness), while their Consorts represent the phenomena of solidity, fluidity, heat, motion and spaciousness (earth, water, fire, air and sky) (Chapter 4, n. 14). This symbology of deities is an attempt with hindsight to analyse the unitary vision. At the moment of experience there is no analytic differentiation whatsoever; but by naming the deities, we are enabled to recreate the *maṇḍala* in subsequent meditation practice, and by recalling the nature of the initiatory experience it is possible to make that experience a continuous mode of perception.

When Tsogyel offered her 'mystic' *maṇḍala* to the Guru as the prerequisite of the Vase Initiation, initiation into the Outer Maṇḍala, the Guru's reaction is described in terms of the head centre. 'The radiance of his smile' destroys the defilements of the sensual realm. Thus whenever the Guru smiles his radiance (*mdangs*) can be understood as the pure-land of the head centre. When Tsogyel offers her mystic *maṇḍala* for initiation into the *mandala* of the Guru's Speech, the Inner Mandala, a *mandala* of pure vibration, sound and energy, the abode of the Yidam, the Guru's laughter (or resonance-*gdangs*) emanating from his throat centre purifies the realm of aesthetic form. While the Vase Initiation was received in an ambience of serenity and peace, the Mystic Initiation is charged with a ferocity that is no less terrible for the essential compassionate nature of Wongdrak Pema (dBang-drag Padma) Heruka, who is a form of the Yidam Hayagrīva representing the logos of the throat centre. Again the initiation is described as an immense orgasm that vitalises the five focal points of psychic energy. Each of the five centres is characterised by one of the five passions, and each of these mental poisons is realised as its own pure nature, which is an aspect of Awareness. Thus each union of Heruka and Ḍākinī (Hayagrīva and Vārāhī), one in each of the five focal points, represents a pure-land and an aspect of Awareness: jealousy becomes all-accomplishing Awareness; pride becomes the Awareness of universal identity; ignorance and sloth become Awareness of the nature of mind; lust becomes all-discriminating Awareness; and anger and hatred become the mirror-like Awareness. Tsogyel's song to the Nepali bandits elaborates the meditation which transforms the five passions into the *maṇḍala* of the Five Aspects of the Buddha and the five aspects of Awareness.

Since the Mystic Initiation empowers the *sādhaka* to practise *anuyoga*, which includes *haṭhayoga* practices to control the vital breath and the subtle psychic energies of the psycho-organism, the central concepts employed in elucidating these practices are 'psychic nerves', 'energy flows' and 'seed-essence' (*nāḍī*, *prāṇa*, *bindu; rtsa, rlung* and *thig-le*). These psycho-physical realities are defined, identified, and realised through visualisation, in certain fulfilment processes of meditation. The Mystic Initiation is an authorisation to practise fulfilment process *yogas*. Tsogyel however, has no need to perform the involved *haṭhayoga* exercises of fulfilment meditation because the results of such *yogas* are inherent in the accomplishment of non-referential, non-dual Awareness indicated by her identification with Vajra Vārāhī in union with Heruka. First: the karmic energies that are derived from mental impulses conditioned by past action are suppressed; the focal points of energy draw these karmic forces from the infrastructure of psychic nerves into the right and left nerves (*lalanā* and *rasanā*), and these in turn drain into the medial nerve, leaving the body in a state of divinity under perfect control and a highly tuned instrument to respond to the dictates of the Bodhisattva Vow. Second: each sub-centre (*rtsa-'khor*) in the system of psychic nerves, which is parallel to, though not identical with the system operated upon in acupuncture, is identified by a specific vibration represented by a seed-syllable (*yig-'bru*). After purification of the subtle body these syllables resonate to *mantra,* which is, therefore, the key to the control of this sheath of sound and vibration. Third: the level upon which seed-essence is described as *mahāmudrā* can only be penetrated by an intuition based in experiential understanding of non-dual reality. When there is complete absence of a sense of self, where the faculty of apperception is in abeyance and sense organ, object and consciousness are an integral unity, the field of sense perception is a field of Awareness composed of seed-essence (*thig-le*). This field of seed-essence is *mahāmudrā,* the female aspect of unitary Awareness.

The Vase Initiation has revealed Tsogyel's apparitional being; the Mystic Initiation has revealed her visionary being; with the Wisdom Initiation Tsogyel attains essential, empty being, the Pure Being of the Buddhas. The subtleties of the description of this initiation in *The Life* almost defy translation. It begins with light emanating from the Guru's heart centre purifying the formless realm, which indicates that Tsogyel is entering the *maṇḍala* of the Guru's Mind. The invocation RAṂ HAṂ dissolves propensities to think in logical and concrete terms; what we are accustomed to conceive of as an objective, stable and predictable external universe 'melts' and 'drips' into the all-consuming flame of Awareness, and the resultant mode of perception is defined in terms of Pure Being (*kāya, sku*) and Seed-essence (*bindu, thig-le*). The *yoga* implied by the two seed-syllables RAṂ and HAṂ is a simple fulfilment process of meditation complete in itself, and also a paradigm evocative of the succeeding practice. Then a key term is introduced that replaces the word *bodhicitta* that was used in the Vase and Mystic Initiations. The *maṇḍala* of Pure Being and Seed-essence is created by the infusion of the Ḍākinī's *maṇḍala* of dynamic space by the Guru's seed. 'Seed' is a translation of the Tibetan *dwangs-ma*. It denotes the distilled essence of a liquid (such as the spirit distilled from wine). The word is also used in descriptions of the alchemical process (*rasayana*) of distilling nectar from poison, and can be translated as 'essence' or 'juice'. Functionally, as the Guru's seed, it is the 'nuclear' energy that is released and suffuses the entire body at initiation, maturing and releasing the conditioned mind. It has also been rendered as 'radiation energy'.[9]

Before the complex universe of Pure Being and Seed-essence is described in *The Life*, Tsogyel excels herself in an ambiguous, witty vignette of an ideal tantric initiation. The translation fails to convey the sublimity of this encounter between Guru and Ḍākinī, which must be entirely free of any taint of gross human sexuality. The passage achieves its desired effect by mixing metaphysical and concrete imagery. The union of Tsogyel and her Guru creates the Maṇḍala of the Blazing Sun of Radiant Inner Space, which is a poetic synonym for the *maṇḍala* of mystic heat. Since this *maṇḍala*, both as an existential reality and a symbolic model, is a non-dual gnostic experience, the terms Pure Being and Seed-essence must necessarily refer to the 'male' and 'female' aspects of the same reality, for again we are looking at the 'internal' plenum of phenomena rather than a dualistic situation wherein a conscious sensor perceives an alienated 'other'. 'Pure Being' is the Buddha with four all-pervasive and interpenetrating existential modes described as the four pure-lands of the four Herukas of the four focal points of psychic energy. 'Seed-essence' is the self-aware, 'rainbow nuclei' of which these pure-lands are composed. Each light-seed has a constant centre (an inchoate plenitude) surrounded by four identical pin-points of light, and as such has a parallel in the atom with its fixed neutron and orbiting electron. Clusters of light-seeds form what are apparently concrete objects in ordinary consciousness. Each seed has a euphonic corollary in the form of a seed-syllable; the primal seed-syllable is A, while clusters of seeds resonate complex sounds. Thus seed-essence can be experienced as both light and sound. Perhaps the phrase 'molecular consciousness' is applicable to this mode of perception.

The dynamic of this *maṇḍala* is joy. As Tsogyel's joy increases through four levels the four focal points expand into complete *maṇḍala*s. In the meditation that this Wisdom Initiation empowers Tsogyel to practise, and in which she is instructed by her Guru after the initiation, joy is created by the ascent of the blended red and white *bodhicitta*s up the medial nerve from the sexual centre through the gut, heart, throat and head centres in turn (although the most intense feeling of joy is in the gut and the least intense in the head). The rising *bodhicitta* is *kuṇḍalinī*. Guru Rimpoche lays great stress on the necessity to retain the *bodhicitta* within the body – initiation is one of the few occasions when it is permitted to release the *bodhicitta*. Retention of semen is a *samaya* impressed as an imperative upon the neophyte in *anuyoga*. In Tsogyel's practice the motive force which drives the *bodhicitta* up the medial nerve is the desire riding on life-force (*srog-rlung*), stimulated by memory of her initiation; that desire is love, the after-glow of desire, renewed desire for consummation, all of which has been 'sublimated' into Awareness at the time of initiation. As the *bodhicitta* or Awareness ascends, a thorough process of purification occurs. In brief, the five stages of the path of the Bodhisattva (the path of accumulation, etc.), the ten levels of the Bodhisattva's progress to enlightenment, and the four levels of joy, are traversed as the *bodhicitta* rises through the eight focal points at twelve junctures or moments, purifying the five poisons, the twelve interdependent elements of existence, the three doors (body, speech and mind), the four impure states of mind (lust, sleep, dream and waking) and the five psycho-physical constituents (name and form, feeling, etc.), while the four colours, the four Herukas and their Consorts, the lotuses of varying numbers of petals, and the varying numbers of world spheres, are used to describe the Buddha's four modes of being which are the goal achieved. Precepts governing the *yoga* into which the Wisdom Initiation has given entry are given in Chapter 8 (pp. 155–7) and the zap-lam meditation, which is another name for this Third Initiation practice, is mentioned below (pp. 249f.).

The Word Initiation, the Fourth Initiation, is the third of the superior initiations. It empowers the *yogin* and *yoginī* to practise Dzokchen *atiyoga*, the highest of the tantric paths, and initiates them into the Buddha's fourth mode of being, which is 'self-existent being' or 'the existentiality of being' (*svabhāvika-kāya*). Guru Pema refused to initiate Tsogyel until he was about to depart, and even then, despite Tsogyel's obvious spiritual maturity, he was loath to do so, enumerating the dangers and inadequacies of such a path. Dzokchen practice is characterised by its formlessness, its speed of effectiveness, its need for a very solid foundation and its unique result, amongst many qualities that mark it as an extraordinary Buddhist vehicle. It belongs solely to the Old School although many great *yogin*s of other schools practise it, often in secret. The Dalai Lamas of the school most opposed to the Old School have held a Dzokchen lineage for generations and have often considered it with the same high esteem as the Nyingmapas themselves. It has been damned as a Hindu Śaivite school and as a Taoist school, a path of immoralists and heretics, but without doubt it contains the most potent and efficacious *yoga*s, precepts and metaphysical formulations, of the entire Buddhist *dharma*. Guru Rimpoche points out to Tsogyel that once Dzokchen initiation has been received and practice has begun, there is no way to prevent the inevitable result of dissolution of corporeality in a rainbow body or similar mode. If initiation and instruction had been given too early the relative *dharma*s of Tsogyel's austerities of teaching, service to others, etc. would never have been fulfilled. He enjoins secrecy upon her, and Tsogyel does not describe the Word Initiation.

The Dzokchen path has two stages, although these two stages can be practised as separate paths. These paths are trek-chod (*mkhregs-chod*) and Togal (*thod-rgal*). Trek-chod can be rendered as 'exploding solidity' or 'cutting through', and trek-chod precepts are given under the heads of Vision, Meditation and Action (p. 160), their capital letters indicating the highly specific, extraordinary qualities of these three terms. 'Primal purity' (*ka-dag*) and 'dynamic space' (*dbyings*) are the key-notes of the path: 'immersed in primal purity all things are dynamic space.' Togal can be translated as 'direct crossing'. Certain short-cut *yogas* accelerate experience of the four visions which Tsogyel seeks in her final periods of retreat. The keynote in togal is 'spontaneity' (*lhun-grub*). Its result is dissolution of corporeality and absorption in lotus-light. Besides the trek-chod and togal paths, the Mind, Space and Secret Precept (*man-ngag*) classes of precept represent three different approaches to Dzokchen, with slight differences in details of vision and in practice. Further, individual preceptors teach their own distinct methods transmitted by their lineages which cut through all formal categories. The spontaneity of the togal path does not imply that Dzokchen is a 'sudden school' like Zen, with which it is often compared. On the contrary Dzokchen *atiyoga* is pre-eminently the middle path which steers between the concepts of gradual and sudden schools. In so far as it is possible to say of Dzokchen that 'the starting point is the path is the goal' – the finger pointing at the moon is the moon itself – the concepts of gradual and sudden enlightenment do not apply.

The implications of the precept 'the starting point is the goal' are immense and profound. Extending the *mahāyāna* principle that the Buddha-nature is inherent in all sentient beings, in trek-chod Vision every human experience whatsoever is cognised as primal purity, and that includes mental events, suffering, emotion and conceptual and discursive thought, since defilements are not separate from their source. We are all emanations of Guru and Ḍākinī conceived in a Buddha-field; the Fourth Initiation introduces us to that Awareness, and thereafter the *samaya* is the key to sustaining it.

The good and the bad, pleasure and pain, all emotion and passion is the path itself. The greater the intensity of pain or passion the greater the potential of creative expression (*rtsal*) and pure pleasure (*bde-chen*); but although pain and passion are not to be rejected, neither are they to be cultivated. If excess is an individual's karmic destiny then the path of excess will surely lead to wisdom, not through an eventual understanding of passion's futility, or the hedonistic pleasure of indulgence, or the hiatus of exhaustion and childlike ingenuousness, or a reactive swing to puritanical repression, but through immediate, spontaneous Awareness. The traditional metaphor for this Awareness is a lotus redolent of compassion growing uncontaminated in a putrid swamp. The middle path is maintained in the experience of excessive passion and over-indulgence by practising the precept 'neither cultivation nor rejection but identification with the nature of being'. Such practice dissolves karmic propensities to passionate response, and keeps the *yogin* on the middle path of indeterminable 'suchness'. Likewise Tsogyel's austerities on the snowline, where for three winters she lives virtually naked and without food, is consistent with the middle path because she neither cultivates nor rejects her pain. She is not practising self-mortification or Calvinistic masochism out of guilt, a sense of sin and the hope of a happier hereafter. 'Turn whatever suffering arises into pure pleasure,' the Guru instructs her, and in the *yoga* of the mystic heat her physical pain is the causal means of her pure pleasure.

Thus, in general, the method of the Inner Tantras is not to suppress emotion (as in the *hīnayāna*) or to transform it into its opposite (as in the *mahāyāna*), but to transmute it into its real nature and use its inherent energy. When incisive insight into the nature of mind, from which emotion is inseparable, removes the sting of passion, passion becomes an inexhaustible source of energy, power and awareness. Following the middle path, emotional feeling is the *sādhaka*'s best ally. In Tsogyel's song to the punk Nepali youths who threaten to steal her gold she instructs them unambiguously upon using passion as the path. Jealousy, for example, the greener the better, must be cognised not by an objective examination of its marks and qualities, but by allowing the mind to relax and by identifying with the nature of mind that constitutes the syndrome. Then the greys of existence become scintillating rainbows and emotional energy becomes all-accomplishing Awareness. 'Perfect as you are' is the key precept, and denial, rejection or repression of any emotion cuts off an energy source. When Guru Pema finds Tsogyel close to death on the snow-line in her third year of solitary meditation he upbraids her for hypocrisy, pride and deceit. It appears that the *yoginī* was caught up in the vision of herself as a saintly nun and a disciplined ascetic unable to admit her human feelings, her pride and her desire; suppressing her emotion and thus breaking her *samaya*, she could not even keep herself warm. The Guru tells her to release her guilts, self-deceits, and hidden secrets, her passion and its accompanying neuroses that are the emotional rubbish, the flotsam and jetsam of the mind, so that it can be utilised on the path as a form of Awareness. Further, such 'hidden secrets' constitute a personality core with which one can identify, and with the dissolution of this 'ego' the sense of 'I' disappears. When the mind has been emptied of its secrets what is left is the naked, sky-blue Adi-Buddha Kuntuzangpo sitting in the heart centre.

Uncontrolled emotion (*nyon-mongs, kleśa*) and thought (*rnam-rtog, vikalpa*) are the *yogin*'s chief demons. We have seen how Dzokchen deals with emotion; thought is a different problem. Thought is the devil that distracts blissful concentration. Thought moves in peregrinations around and about objects hindering direct perception of them. Mixed with emotion it bombards us with poisonous, neurotic information which is the stuff of paranoid vision. Furthermore, although thought will finally lie down when it has exhausted its potential or when another powerful sensory stimulus has become the cause of another run of ratiocination, as premises, arguments and conclusions, preconception, belief and dogma, it will hide in the sub-conscious and repeat itself later, bringing its boring judgments and evaluations to bear on the same subject when it next arises. When thought is emotionally satisfying and, sometimes, logically sound, it will arrogate itself the status of conviction, and influence all other thoughts that arise. Such convictions have the tendency to become stronger and more assertive with repetition. The further thought extends from the existential reality at its inception, the more inflexible and dogmatic it becomes. Coupled with imagination or logic, thought is so subtle, potent and persuasive that 'thinking people' gain greater pleasure from it than from immediate sensual experience. Impregnated by mental constructs in childhood we are bound by the implications of such conditioning throughout our lives. Our concepts of 'truth' for example, are determined by conditioned constructs. Emotionally satisfying structures of speculative thought built upon these mental constructs can control our lives. *Anuyoga* in particular effects the eradication of mental conditioning, the destruction of systems of belief, the de-structuring of the mind, loss of conviction in relative truths, and finally the cessation of thought; in Dzokchen what thought remains is a Ḍākinī.

It is very difficult to stop thinking. However, suppression of thought is possible, and the meditation that induces thoughtless trance is called *śamatha* (*zhi-gnas*). Tantra spurns the condition of utter peacefulness, the paradisiacal trance, that *śamatha* induces; the life-style and concentration its constant practice requires are consistent with *hīnayāna* principles. In Dzokchen *atiyoga*, the Fourth Initiation introduces the *yogin* to the primal purity of all thought, and bound by *samaya*, thereafter, thought is a dance of the Ḍākinī – Awareness and pure pleasure. But uncontrolled, mental chatter, rigid convictions, deep-seated thought patterns, preclude the possibility of obtaining the Fourth Initiation, and some preliminary meditations and *yogas* are necessary to loosen the mind and slow down the pace of thought. An accomplished Guru can do much of the neophyte's work for him, but it is painful to have one's cherished beliefs demolished, and it requires a great deal of faith on the part of the disciple to permit the Guru to tamper with the thought that is inseparable from his ego. The Dzokchen Guru is the man or woman who with a word, a gesture, a game, or even a powerful *samādhi*, can induce his disciple to transcend his thought, to laugh at his projections and paranoias, to abandon his convictions, and then, either formally in a ritual situation or informally in direct rapport, introduce to him the nature of his own mind.

The ocean of consciousness that is the nature of mind is likened to a mirror, and thoughts to the reflections in a mirror. When the *yogin* is at one with the nature of mind there is no attachment to thoughts, they arise and fall like fishes jumping out of the ocean; and they leave no trace behind them, no residue in the sub-conscious to crystallise as preconceptions and karmic propensities. Thoughts are the mental counterparts of the karmic energies that run in the psychic nerves of the subtle body, and when thought has subsided after the cultivation of detachment, karmic energies are also less potent. Vice versa, when the *bodhicitta* is ascending the medial nerve, and when at each focal point of psychic energy all karmic energies are cut off, thought ceases. After the Fourth Initiation the practitioner of Dzokchen in meditation will watch thoughts arise: at first he will recognise the nature of the thought and greet it like an old friend, the thought immediately dissolving; second, the thoughts will release themselves like snakes uncoiling their knots; and finally, with application, thought arises like a thief entering an empty house. Even in Dzokchen thoughts are likened to thieves and snakes. However, these snakes and thieves are also Ḍākinīs, Ḍākinīs dancing in the unitary field of reality with the same inherent pleasure as the Ḍākinīs dancing in the visual field or the audial field.

Meditation upon pain, emotion and thought implies experiential knowledge of primal purity, which is virtually synonymous with Emptiness. To the epistemologist Emptiness is the quality of experience that gives perception its vivid, immediate, here-and-now flavour, provoking perhaps a frisson of delight or a touch of ecstatic omniscience, while for the ontologist it is primal space (*dbyings*), which is the all-pervasive, fundamental 'building block' of reality. It not only pervades all things as water pervades milk, but it *is* all things. There is nothing *but* space in our lived experience, according to the Vision of Dzokchen,and since its nature is radiance (*gsal-ba*), or clear light (*'od-gsal*), it is impossible to obstruct it. This is the reason that *siddha*s can walk through walls. Since primal space composes the unitary field of reality, it has an inherent cognitive capacity, and as such it is Knowledge (*rig-pa*). This Knowledge is non-referential; in other words it is not knowledge *of* something or *about* something – it is the Knowledge of the Buddha. Primal space, like Emptiness, cannot be separated from our sensory fields. A sensory consciousness, an organ of sense perception, and an object of perception, form a unitary field of primal space that is self-cognisant. Viewed as pure consciousness this field is Awareness (*ye-shes, jñāna*), a dance of the Awareness Ḍākinī; and for the sake of analysis, to pull apart an indivisible gnostic situation, the 'objective' element is Knowledge. Since Knowledge is ever non-referential and lacks the 'negative' association of Emptiness, critics have accused the Dzokchen metaphysicians of the heresy of eternalism. With 'Knowledge', they say, you are positing an eternal absolute, and because some of your *yoga*s are very similar to those of the Śaivites, you are actually Hindus masquerading as Buddhists. It is a moot point whether 'the middle' is an absolute or not, and indeed whether Emptiness itself is an immutable substance; this ontological question has been argued in debate for centuries and nothing that either proponents or antagonists have said has made the slightest difference to the efficacy of Dzokchen practice or to its outcome.

It is difficult to translate the Vision of Dzokchen into the English language. To do so the translator must endow ordinary English words like 'space' with profound meaning. 'Space' (*dbyings*) is not the interval between objects and it is not spatiality; it is better conceived as an all-pervasive, all-penetrating, sub-atomic plenum.[10] This notion is basic to the understanding of Tsogyel's *sādhana* (her spiritual practice). Her aim in life was to reduce, or rather expand, her reality to primal space. The four visions which she begins to cultivate after her Fourth Initiation refer to four degrees of increasing intensity and duration of the experience of primal space. Guru Rimpoche calls the goal, 'total immersion in the dynamic of empty reality where all realities are extinguished'. 'Total immersion' could be more loosely rendered 'stuffed head to toe', indicating a certain violence and directness to a process which is fraught with danger. The *yogas* that induce the vision of dissolution of corporeality into primal space are togal practices.

The four visions of togal are 'reality manifest', 'intensive visionary experience', 'optimal Knowledge' and 'all reality extinguished' (Chapter 7, n. 28). When the space in experience is intuited 'reality manifests'. As reality becomes increasingly illusory with the loss of any fixed point of reference, visionary and extra-sensory experiences occur. Unified on a psychic plane with other beings' minds and all natural phenomena, living in a dream-like state where the impossible is a matter of everyday occurrence, visionary experiences intensify. With the achievement of optimal Knowledge nothing arises in the mind, or in the sphere of the *yogin*'s activity, which is not cognised as primal purity. Individualised being is identified with universal being. In a state of complete equanimity where pleasure and pain are of one taste, and passions arise with only a distinction in their colour and the purpose for which they are intended, it would be a boring existence except for the feeling tone of pure pleasure which is likened to the quality of feeling in sexual consummation. When all reality is extinguished, corporeality has dissolved, and the *siddha* attains the capacity to manifest in whatever form is necessary – shape shifting; but Tsogyel's practice is consummate now, and at will she can vanish from the human world and become united with her Guru on the plane of lotus-light. Thereafter she can project emanations in human and inanimate form to enlighten others.

Tsogyel's secret precepts (*man-ngag*), given to Ma Rinchen Chok before she lost her apparitional reality and became Vajra Yoginī in visionary being, string together several metaphors descriptive of the togal visions. She begins by implying that the adept's recognition of Yeshe Tsogyel (the Ocean of Awareness) as the universal Ḍākinī, who lives in all our minds projecting the psycho-organism and the sensory fields, is like an initiation into this togal vision. 'The one naked mind arising from within, the absolute Awareness of primal purity (which is the sameness of all phenomena) is all-pervasive, and dammed like a lake the golden-eyed fishes of heightened perception multiply. Sustaining the consummation of visionary experience and pleasure, on the wings of perfect creativity, running and jumping in the meadows of visionary appearances, you fly into the sky-matrix and vanish. In the immense space of absolute Awareness the seed-essence of pure pleasure stands thick like a lake, Pure Being and Seed-Essence glisten and pulsate, and seed-syllables and light garlands sparkle and shimmer, the vision of reality manifest expands, intensive visionary experience increases and the castle of optimal Knowledge is finally seized.' This is not only a poetical expression of the four visions; it is a metaphysical statement, and also precise instruction on the practice. Unfortunately the precision of the terminology is lost in translation, as only the superficial meaning is rendered into English. It should be noted that there is no mention of extra-sensory perception and mundane *siddhi*. The purpose of practice is Buddhahood, gnostic perception and pure pleasure. Various powers may arise on the way, but they are incidental to the final goal.

In this description of togal visions our feet are no longer on the ground. Indeed, the ground has dissolved into space, our bodies are immaterial light-form, the laws of *karma* no longer apply, 'there is no good or bad *karma*, no superior or inferior beings, no youth or age, no acuity or dullness'; we have entered a mystical pure-land that is described in terms reminiscent of the ravings of an habitual user of the psychedelic LSD. Good *karma* may have given us glimpses of this pure-land at moments of extraordinary intensity, lucidity and concentration, or our meditation may have produced short periods of such heightened experience, but without doubt those who have experienced the effects of psilocybin, peyote and mescalin can find clear descriptions of their own 'trips' in the literature of Dzokchen. This reality is certainly far removed from our everyday experience, but it is the norm for the Dzokchen *yogin* and *yoginī*. As all appearances are transformed into light-seed, 'corporeality dissolves'. As dualistic perception becomes direct, immediate sensory awareness, 'the mind is extinguished'. As the intensity of gnostic awareness burns away all our habitual action patterns and thought patterns, '*karma* is exhausted'. When 'all reality is extinguished' there is no language left. When Guru Rimpoche exhorts Tsogyel to 'bathe in the seed-sphere of pure potential', he introduces the concept descriptive of the Dzokchen *yogin*'s mode of action, which is 'no-action'. But rather than employ the paradoxical term no-action, I have translated *bya-bral* as 'pure potential'. In the non-dual realm of Dzokchen Ati there is no 'birth or death', 'creation or cessation' 'beginning or end', and, further, there is no-action. This does not imply that there is no movement, and although it does imply that there is no busy-ness, involvement in worldly concerns and neurotic hassles, that is not the chief thrust of its meaning. Rather, the term suggests the transcendence of both action and stasis. Thus we have 'spontaneous no-action' in the Ḍākinī Sky-dancer's Paradise (*mKha'-spyod*), or better, 'spontaneous pure-potential'. Since nothing ever comes into being or ceases to be there is constant transformation of one form into another in a spontaneous movement of flux which is pure potential. The term 'no-action' is probably derived from the Taoist notion *wu-wei*; Taoist concepts arrived in Dzokchen metaphysics *via* the Chinese *ch'an* school.

Tsogyel's *parinirvāṇa*, her final release from the wheel of rebirth, is simultaneous with the dissolution of her corporeality and the attainment of her equivalent of rainbow body. At the *yogin*'s attainment of rainbow body, the body dissolves into light, and leaving hair, finger nails and the nasal septum behind, spirals up into the sky. This is the ultimate goal of Dzokchen. But she did obtain Buddhahood in her human form as Guru Rimpoche promised her. With 'the extinction of all reality' she was able to manifest in whatever form the needs of sentient beings required and still require. In *The Life* death is the metaphor for the attainment of Buddhahood. In Tantra *saṃsāra* and *nirvāṇa* are terms descriptive of the mind attached to its own forms, and the mind in a state of stasis respectively. *Mahānirvāṇa*, the Great Nirvāṇa, or the Ultimate Nirvāṇa, is the non-dual state which is the Dzokchen *yogin*'s aim. Tsogyel uses a variety of metaphors to describe *mahānirvāṇa*. She is absorbed into primal space, the omnipresent ground (*kun-gzhi*); her mortality has become immaculate (*zag-med*), or all her outflows have ceased; her illusory body has been transfigured into a body of light; she has melted into the primal syllable A; mother and son, the outside and inside, have finally united. Further, she has vanished into the lotus-light of the plenum of primal space (*dharmadhātu*); she has gone to the land of pure pleasure; she has passed into the sky; she has attained the 'white' evolutionary goal, united with Pema Jungne. Dzokchen *yogin*s and *yoginī*s all become one with Guru Pema and Yeshe Tsogyel respectively after attaining their goal. Thereafter, with the Guru and Ḍākinī, they manifest multiple apparitional forms in the continuous process of transforming, or converting, beings until all sentient beings have achieved Buddhahood and the Buddha's ultimate goal is attained.

Through the practices of togal we have arrived at the end of the path to Buddhahood. Trek-chod *atiyoga* practices alone can be the preliminary, purificatory stage on the path to rainbow body, but in most teachers' methods of approach to Dzokchen, *mahāyoga* and *anuyoga*, or one or the other, are essential preliminary *yoga*s. Both *mahāyoga* and *anuyoga* can take the *yogin* or *yoginī* to the end of the path, but usually they are practised in sequence. In general, the practice of the creative process of meditation is stressed in *mahāyoga* and the practice of the fulfilment process of meditation is stressed in *anuyoga*. In terms of the *maṇḍala*, an internal, ideal, three dimensional model of psycho-physical reality, creative processes cultivate centrifugal or efferent energy, and fulfilment processes cultivate and utilise centripetal or afferent energy. Centrifugal energy can be characterised as sexual energy in so far as it is creative desire; it tends towards structure, rigidity and concrete manifestation.

Centripetal energy is the dynamic of the 'death wish', tending towards inchoate essence, destructurisation and dissolution. In Dzokchen this duality is not tolerated, and rather than practise the cultivation of these energies in sequence they are practised simultaneously. Thus 'simultaneous creative and fulfilment processes' is an oft repeated precept in *atiyoga*. Likewise, referring to the creative process *yoga* of emanating and re-absorbing light, in Dzokchen, when the Lama is conceived only as the lucence of Knowledge, 'When the peak experience of vast space dawns, centrifugal diffusion and centripetal re-absorption are one' (p. 159). Such statements should clarify the relationship between *mahāyoga* and *anuyoga* on one hand and Dzokchen *atiyoga* on the other. However, *mahāyoga* contains elements of fulfilment processes and *anuyoga* contains elements of creative processes. For example, the rite of visualising a *maṇḍala* (creative meditation) concludes with dissolution of the *maṇḍala* into Emptiness (fulfilment meditation); and in the fulfilment process of realising the psychic nerves and energy flows, they must first be visualised in a creative process.

The creative process (*bskyed-rim*) consists chiefly in the creative visualisation and realisation of a *maṇḍala* with its principal deity and his entourage, and then modifying the *maṇḍala* in various ways to effect changes in the quality and form of the *yogin*'s psyche and perception. 'Approach' and 'identification' (*bsnyen-sgrub*) are two stages in the creative process. The deity is invited to approach and take his place in the *maṇḍala* by means of visualisation and recitation – visualisation of the deity's form and qualities and recitation of his *mantra*. *Mudrā*, *mantra* and *samādhi* co-operate to effect identification of the *sādhaka* with the deity. *Mudrā* implies certain ritual hand gestures, and also the posture of the body; *mantra* is the audial form of the deity; and *samādhi* is the empty state of mind. *Guru-yoga*, a liturgical ritual is included in *The Life* in Tsogyel's final instruction to her disciples, is a creative process *yoga*, involving invocation of the Buddha Lama, recitation of his *mantra* and identification with him. The basic practices of the Sublime Accomplishment of the Eight Logos Deities (sGrub-pa bka'-brgyad) are *mahāyoga* meditations in which the *maṇḍala*s of these deities are realised through the creative processes of visualisation and recitation.

The creative process rites of these deities are highly sophisticated.

Anuyoga and the fulfilment processes of meditation form a vast area of ignorance in academic study. *The Life* provides crucial clues and insights into the language of the *yoga*, its techniques and metaphysics. As little as possible should be said here to prevent preconceptions that would inevitably cloud the mind of a student approaching a Guru for *anuyoga* precepts. The following are some of the fulfilment processes of meditation (dzok-rim, *rdzogs-rim*): dream *yoga*, mystic heat, bardo *yoga*, *mahāmudrā*, apparitional body purification, resurrection, the clear light *yoga* and 'the seed-essence of empty pleasure'. Virtually all fulfilment processes involve visualisation of psychic nerves, energy flows and seed-essence, and some definition of this terminology will give perspective on *anuyoga*; and since the *yoga* of empty pleasure is Tsogyel's chief practice, an important approach to Dzokchen and the crux of sexual practice, something more should be said of it.

The system of nerves, energy flows and their focal points has a parallel in the body's physiology and also in the mental sphere, for the subtle, the gross and the mental inter-relate. The word for psychic nerves (*rtsa, nāḍī*) is the same as for veins and arteries, and for tendons and muscles. In Tsogyel's physical purification the gross body was to be brought into top condition in order for the subtle body to function effectively. Just as sinews, veins, nerves, and psychic nerves or pathways, are denominated by a single word, so wind, breath, vital energy, nervous energy, and mental energy are also implied by one word – *rlung*. Thus the term *rtsa-rlung* (the *yoga* of energy control, or *haṭhayoga*) does not specify whether the plane of 'pathways' and 'energies' indicated belongs to the physical, subtle or mental bodies. There are no single verbal equivalents of *rtsa* and *rlung* in English, so that when *rtsa* is translated as 'psychic nerves', and *rlung* as 'energy flows', it is important to remember that a whole spectrum of meaning may be implied; in particular *rlung* often implies both 'breath' and 'subtle energy', like the Sanskrit word *prāṇa*. The implications of the multi-levelled denotations of *rlung* are central to *anuyoga* practice: breathing controls subtle energy, and subtle energy controls thought; and conversely, when thought subsides, the physical body becomes an instrument capable of immense responsiveness.

The focal points of energy (*cakras*), the medial nerve, which is described as running down the spine, and also the left and right psychic nerves, the *rasanā* and *lalanā*, may be conceived as neuro-physiological phenomena that may be scientifically verified when science has improved its techniques. Undoubtedly *kuṇḍalinī* has a physiological aspect, as energy can be felt rising up the spine in *kuṇḍalinī yoga*; and in theory the principal glands can be related to the five or eight focal points of energy. But when in fulfilment meditation the *yogin* is directed to mix the psychic energies of his right and left nerves in the medial nerve and retract the red and white *bodhicitta* mixture up through the energy centres, his visualisation will function on a purely metaphysical level and the result will be unification of subjective and objective poles of his sense fields in a unitary plenum of reality. Moreover, no purpose is served by analysing and comparing different systems of *rtsa-rlung*, and attempting to formulate a coherent metaphysical system. Each *tantra* has its own correspondences and symbology, and often it is the relationship between symbols that is significant rather than the relation of the symbol to its meaning. To attempt to rationalise *anuyoga* precepts is to invite insanity, or, finally, to transcend conceptual thought and stop thinking. However, the fact remains that *anuyoga* precepts and practices are eminently efficacious; fulfilment process *yoga*s are a high-speed short-cut to Buddhahood.

The same qualities of supra-logic, multi-levelled meaning and effectiveness characterise precepts concerning 'seed-essence' (*thig-le, bindu*). The gross form of seed-essence as defined in *The Life* is 'lymph',[11] the clear white viscous liquid that in Tibetan medicine is considered one of the basic constituents of the body. Stored at the joints, when 'lymph' is purified it becomes the seed-essence that is to be conceived as particles, or *maṇḍala*s, of light and consciousness. Just as 'lymph' pervades the body, so seed-essence forms a dimension of Awareness (*ye-shes, jñāna*) inherent in the psycho-organism. Seed-essence (*thig-le*) is also *semen virile*, and purified 'semen' is Awareness. This following theory of the generation of semen and its concomitant gnostic awareness should be judged by its effectiveness in provoking recognition of the hierarchical relation of body and mind, the gross and the subtle, and the all-pervasive cognitive element in the nature of all things, and not as a scientifically verifiable medical thesis. 'The nutrition extracted from food in the stomach passes through the "vein which seizes the distilled essence" to the liver, where it is assimilated by bile, phlegm and air (the three humours). Refined nutrition forms blood, and refined blood forms flesh while the unrefined blood forms bile. Refined flesh forms fat, and unrefined flesh is excreted through the nine orifices. The distilled essence of fat forms bones, and unrefined fat forms grease and sweat. Refined bone forms marrow, and unrefined bone forms nails, teeth and hair. Refined marrow forms semen or menstrual blood (conceived as female creative seed), while the unrefined marrow forms the flesh around the anus. Refined semen is stored in the heart centre as "radiance", which produces long-life and gives a shine to the complexion. Unrefined semen is excreted during sexual intercourse and is, of course, procreative seed. The refined semen in the heart centre permeates the body as Awareness; "heart centre" is here a metaphor for the all-pervasive sphere of essential being (*dharmakāya*). Loss of semen, by any means, causes life-span to be shortened and causes a pallid complexion.'[12]

In *anuyoga*, though not in Dzokchen *atiyoga*, loss of semen is equated with killing a Buddha. Semen, seed-essence and *bodhicitta* are synonymous. After initiation, intensity of desire is essential to force the *bodhicitta* up the medial nerve; not only is desire vitiated by orgasm, but the will to enlightenment itself is temporarily lost. Once practice is perfected, and on the level of *atiyoga* the one value of all things (*ro-gcig*) is perceived automatically, retention or non-retention of semen is no longer a pertinent issue; but directly after the Third Initiation and immersion in practice, release of semen utterly destroys the *samaya*. 'Absorb yourself in desire,' Tsogyel instructs, 'for without it (this) Tantra has no meaning – desire as pure pleasure is the goal fulfilled.' Desire has become Awareness at initiation, and the feeling quality of Awareness is pure pleasure. Desire has lost its external reference and become empty desire and empty pleasure: thus 'the seed-essence of co-incident Emptiness and desire'. To understand the nature of the experience subsequent to initiation, as 'the *bodhicitta* rises up the medial nerve', it is essential to overcome the formal, conceptual limitation of regarding the 'medial nerve' merely as a tube connecting the genital centre to the fontanelle. The medial nerve is also a metaphor for individuated primal space, and as desire-Awareness intensifies it is a sphere that is increasingly pervaded by pure pleasure; or it could be likened to a balloon that is inflated as the *bodhicitta* ascends to the head *cakra* where it finally bursts, primal space dissolving into more primal space.

The particular fulfilment process *yoga* practised by Tsogyel in Bhutan with her two *yogin* partners, practised by Śākya Dema in Nepal, and stressed by Tsogyel in her final instruction to her disciples, is called 'the *yoga* of co-incident Emptiness and pleasure on the profound path'. 'Profound path' is zap-lam. It is also a practice on the 'path of skilful means', because sexual energy creates the motivation and supplies the wherewithal. Strip the *yoga* of its arcane terminology and there is a simple meditation technique: stimulate desire and then use it as the object of meditation and it becomes Awareness – a field of Emptiness and pure pleasure. From the Guru's point of view, the Ḍākinī herself is this dance of reality, both as an individuated being and as pleasure inseparable from gnostic awareness of phenomena. From the Ḍākinī's point of view all form is the Guru's Body, all sound is his Speech and all Mind is his Mind, and his Knowledge is Emptiness and pure pleasure. Whatever the denomination of the energy in the ascendant (*rjes-chags*), call it lust, love, the afterglow, or 'memory of desire', it is non-referential and therefore totally free from personal association; whether or not an embodied 'mystic partner' is present to intensify desire and stimulate the *bodhicitta*, there is no trace of hedonistic indulgence. Sexual pleasure as erotic play, intimate dalliance, orgasm or even *coitus interruptus* has no place in this *yoga*. The equation of sexual indulgence and the Buddhist Tantra has been formed by misguided, commercially motivated individuals pandering to the prurient neuroses of the sexually jaded seeking titillation in the arcane sex of obscure religious cults. 'Do not be loose with your sexual organs,' advises Tsogyel. 'Bind them fast.' And 'Preserve the seed of kindness for the sake of other beings.' No zap-lam sexual *yoga* can be accomplished without attaining control of energy on every level – a traditional metaphor compares the muscular control of a *yogin* or *yoginī* sucking up the blended *bodhicittas*, and retracting the elixir from the sexual centre, to a duck drinking water. If such proficiency is lacking the practice should not be undertaken.

In general, the precept governing sexual activity is the Bodhisattva Vow, the will towards universal happiness. Tsogyel married a leper and performed the duties of a model wife, and in so far as selfless sexuality and heightened sensory awareness are the keys to sexual satisfaction, and in so far as the female partner is a Ḍākinī, that leper must have been a very happy leper. We may all marry Ḍākinīs, and lepers; but aspiring to the reality of a Dzokchen *yogin* in which the one-taste of every sensual perception is pure pleasure, and no situation whatsoever has a higher Emptiness content than any other, to indulge in promiscuous sexuality is generally counter productive. The only motivations for sexual intercourse prescribed by the tradition are to project an apparitional being out of lotus light as an incarnation of Guru or Ḍākinī, to initiate a neophyte in the Third Initiation, or to effect certain other alchemical transformations that involve blending the white and the red *bodhicittas*.

A most remarkable example of the use of sex for the benefit of others is provided by Tsogyel when she initiates the rapists who successively abuse her. Much wisdom can be extracted from the song she sings to them (pp. 118–19). (1) In the first place, she shows what great power the Ḍākinī possesses over men, and in their dependence upon her how their need can be used for their own good. The desire that arises upon apprehending an attractive woman in the visual field can transform a man into a god if his desire is penetrated by insight into Emptiness; divine confidence creates a divine environment populated by gods and goddesses. The woman, or rather, the Ḍākinī, transforms the man who lusts after her into her Guru, the man of her dreams. (2) In this context, as in many other passages in *The Life*, *mahāmudrā* has a technical meaning distinct from its usage in the Kahgyupa School where it denominates the goal of practice synonymous with Buddhahood and virtually equivalent to Dzokchen. Here *mahāmudrā* indicates the totality of the unitary field of reality in its female aspect. (3) It is the Ḍākinī's nature of complete receptivity, empty space, that assuages male aggression; and it is the female organ's 'empty space' that is receptive to the symbol of his aggression. The *maṇḍala* is completed as the Yidam deity takes up residence in his palace; and joy and pleasure, serenity and peace, are the hallmarks of the Guru's experience of *mahāmudrā* after the Mystic Initiation. (4) Through 'involuntary exertion' ('no-action') desire reaches its climax, and it is at the moment of climax that pure pleasure is understood as Emptiness; insight into Emptiness is achieved in the union of the male and female aspects of the mind and of being itself. The experience of Emptiness is a function of the unitary field of reality, which in this case is a result of sexual consummation. (5) Even the uninitiated can gain intimation of pure gnostic awareness in the post-coitus hiatus, when our 'mystic partner' and all external phenomena seem to float in space, and sound has a clarity and timbre unrecognised in ordinary perception. The *samaya* of the Fourth Initiation is to sustain this experience of 'the natural purity in the world of appearances', and the *samaya* of zap-lam is to sustain recognition of the Emptiness in the desire that has been transformed into Awareness by the intensity of pure pleasure. Thus whatever arises in the fields of perception is cognised as primal space, and desire itself is the path so long as it is recognised as Emptiness: this is *Maha Ati*, Dzokchen, the starting point, the path and the goal.

In the final stanza of Tsogyel's explanation of the four levels of joy to the enlightened rapists, she stresses the crucial element of spontaneity in the initiation that they had just experienced. Seeking makes the path grow darker; trying to grasp the nature of mind stimulates conceptual thought; clutching at some little success it vanishes, and trying to perpetuate passing intimations of immortality in meditation guarantees the loss of them. Therefore, the only precept concerning Action in trek-chod practice is 'imperturbable relaxation', for in that lies the potential for spontaneity. 'Inasmuch as the Guru appears only for an instant, there is only an instant to enter the door of the mysteries,' the Ḍākinīs instructed Tsogyel in the pure-land of the Orgyen Ḍākinīs. 'In so far as we have obtained this precious human body for a moment, only a moment exists to celebrate the path.' In the transcendental metaphysics of Dzokchen a 'life' is also a moment, so the promise that the Inner Tantras will effect Buddhahood 'in this life, in this body' is given added meaning.

'Release from the wheel of rebirth' now implies that identification with the omnipresent, universal foundation (*kun-gzhi*), that is primal space, is achieved, and in every instant of existence there is spontaneous release from both *saṃsāra* and *nirvāṇa*. There is no possibility of deliberating upon the method and the aim, the mind is too slow, and therefore redundant. In each instant is a flash of spontaneous creativity emanating our personal reality in the form determined by *bodhicitta*. This vision depends upon the emphatic, basic premise of Dzokchen that all things are in reality dynamic space, primally pure from the beginning and through eternity. 'All things' include the rape of Tsogyel (and all rape in general), but it requires a Ḍākinī, or Guru, to initiate recognition of our premise existentially. Imperturbably relaxed, Tsogyel was capable of the requisite spontaneity.

Some brief description of the terminology of the fulfilment process and a general elucidation of zap-lam is all that can be included here of *anuyoga*. The practices of the creative and fulfilment processes of meditation are the result of the combined practical wisdom of generations of *yogin*s, scholars and monks of Greater India and Tibet, with some help from the Chinese, obsessively analysing human beings in the laboratories of hermitage and monastery, and through experimentation arriving at a transcendental psychology consistent with Śākyamuni Buddha's precepts and goal. A large descriptive and prescriptive literature, much of it translated from Sanskrit, elaborates this psychology, and liturgies of meditation (*sgrub-thabs, sādhana*) and manuals of *yoga* (*khrid*) elucidate the practices and formally re-state the oral precepts of the Guru. A tiny fraction of this knowledge has been translated into English and very few western practitioners have experience of fulfilment processes. At the moment it is impossible to evaluate comprehensively and objectively this science of the mind that has been formulated, refined and augmented by a hundred and eight Buddhas; but from Tsogyel's life, and from personal experience, it is clear that the meditations and *yoga*s of the Inner Tantra (*anuttarayoga-tantra*) comprise a vast wealth of psychotherapeutic technique that can provide the remedies to many of humanity's anxieties.

2

WOMAN AND THE ḌĀKINĪ

'Do not question woman. Adore her everywhere. In her real nature she is Bhagavatī Perfection of Wisdom; and in this empirical world Bhagavatī has assumed the form of woman.' Tantric metaphysics are derived principally from the *Prajñāpāramitā-sūtras*, and this *prajñāpāramitā sloka* clearly states the tantric view that there is no distinction between the ultimate metaphysical nature of woman and the relative human reality. Woman *is* the Ḍākinī and is to be worshipped as such. Further, the *Prajñāpāramitā* gave Tantra the concept of woman as the Perfection of Wisdom, perfect insight (*shes-rab, prajñā*), which is defined as 'awareness of all phenomena as Emptiness'. However, in Tantra, since 'Emptiness is not separate from form, nor form from Emptiness', this Awareness that is the Ḍākinī is the non-dual, gnostic awareness of which the male principle manifest as form is an aspect. Thus the totality of reality as Awareness can be represented by the Ḍākinī alone, or it can be indicated by the inseparable union of male and female principles. In the latter case the Ḍākinī's perfect insight into Emptiness is in contradistinction to skilful means (*thabs, upāya*), the Guru's ever-compassionate, dynamic motivation that manifests as phenomenal appearances. When the Dākinī alone is all-embracing Awareness (*mahajñāna, ye-shes-chen-po*), she is the blissful cosmic dance of illusion. The existential experience of the Ḍākinī is one, but the multiplicity of means to attain that experience,[1] and the different ways of conceiving the inexpressible, create a seemingly complex metaphysics.

After that attempt to clarify basic concepts, it is relevant to ask the question, has woman been arbitrarily assigned these existential values, or do Emptiness and Awareness relate to her essential nature? According to the metaphysical systems that frame the psychological insights of numerous ancient cultures, the physiological-sexual and psychological nature of woman is receptivity. The quality of receptivity, 'an enveloping openness', is evident in tantric symbols of the goddess: the lake, the well, the empty vase, and most graphically and ubiquitously, the *yoni* (vagina).

In so far as Tantra takes sexual processes as analogous to spiritual processes and relates sexual principles to mystical principles, if the essential nature of woman's anatomy and of her sexual response is receptivity, then receptivity can define the female principle. Receptivity is a condition of awareness of empty form. Practically, in the *yogin*'s meditation upon Emptiness, receptive relaxation is imperative; in total mental relaxation, consciousness perched at the doors of the senses achieves perfect insight into the forms of perception (*vipaśyanā* meditation). These forms of perception, into which perfect insight is achieved, are the compassionate forms of the Guru's skilful means. In the same way that the female's sexual receptivity invites the male's creative sexual activity, the Ḍākinī's mental receptivity facilitates her perfect insight into the Guru's dynamic forms, and the resulting union is of Emptiness and form, perfect insight and skilful means, Awareness and compassion.

Expressed in terms of receptivity, Awareness and Emptiness, the female principle may appear irrelevant to woman herself conscious of her human condition. But it cannot be sufficiently stressed that in the realm of tantric practice there is no distinction between woman in her everyday reality and the all-inclusive divine female archetype that permeates her being and dominates her mind (the Yidam Vajra Yoginī, for instance). Every woman *is* the Ḍākinī. Her third initiation is the empowering recognition of that fact, and her post-initiation practice is the *sādhana* (spiritual practice) of maintaining and substantiating the Ḍākinī's Awareness. Whether or not woman knows herself as the Ḍākinī, the Guru and *yogin* see her only in her divine form. A *yogin* can evaluate the maturity of his practice by judging the constancy and depth of his vision of woman as the Ḍākinī. That is not to say that he should see every woman as Tārā, the goddess of devoted service (although he should be able to discern that syndrome in every woman to some degree), for there are innumerable types of Ḍākinī, even as many as there are psychological types of woman. The tantric pantheon includes eldritch blood-sucking, flesh-eating and child-devouring Ḍākinīs, binding, beating and destructive Ḍākinīs, besides the sublime consorts of the Bodhisattvas. The constant in the adept's vision of them all is their empty dance of Awareness, whereas the mutable forms of their dances, and their functions, are like make-up and ornaments.

It is already clear that 'Guru' and 'Ḍākinī' are internal metaphysical realities. Evidently each human psyche contains both male and female principles; the male principle and its qualities are recessive in woman and the female recessive in man, even as the Ḍākinī's dominant Emptiness cannot be separated from the recessive skilful means, which is ever present but unstressed. In the symbology of *anuyoga,* both the white and red elixirs run in the psychic veins of both men and women, although the Guru's complexion is white while the Ḍākinī's is red. In *atiyoga,* when the recessive and dominant are nicely balanced, the elixirs are blended and the complexion of the Ḍākinī is 'blushing fair'. When an anchorite or a monk or nun describes his or her state of being as a union of Guru and Ḍākinī obviously there is no equation of Guru with man nor Ḍākinī with woman. But when *yogin* and *yoginī* are described as Guru and Ḍākinī cohabiting in perfect awareness and pure pleasure in a Buddhafield, this lay *tantrika* couple are projecting their recessive principles upon their partners. Or to formulate it in another way, when man and woman, *yogin* and *yoginī,* recognise he the Emptiness of her and she the compassion of him, their relationship is a union of Guru and Ḍākinī. The emotional vicissitudes of their personal relationship, the love and hate, the pride and jealousy, are the Ḍākinī's fine ornaments, while the gamut of response that she inspires in him are reflected in her face and in her stance.

In relation to the *yogin* practitioner the female principle may be conceived in four modes which are known as *mudrās*

(Chapter 4, n. 8). Maintaining the integrity of union with these four *mudrās* sustains the *samaya* of the Guru's Speech which is identity with the Yidam. These *mudrās* are best conceived as lovers with whom the *yogin* must retain an unbroken intimate, intense and true relation wherein no trace of doubt or infidelity arises. The first is the *samaya-mudrā*, the verbal promise to keep the root and branch *samayas*. The second is the Guru's Consort herself in whom is embodied the five Ḍākinī modes of Awareness. A consort is a Ḍākinī by virtue of her involvement in a moment, or rather an unbroken succession of moments, of integration and enlightenment. In fact, rather than define the Ḍākinī as a human being, she is better understood as a moment's intuition of the Emptiness and purity in passion when perfect insight and skilful means integrate. The third *mudrā* is hand gesture and posture, and the relationship with her is maintained by practising according to the Guru's instruction. The fourth is *mahāmudrā*; she is inconceivable, since she is an anthropomorphic representation of Emptiness – transforming, magical illusion, pure, all-inclusive sensual Awareness.

It can be useful here to distinguish between the *siddha*-adept's view of the Ḍākinī and the neophyte or *yogin*-practitioner's experience. To the former, a woman *is* the Ḍākinī, but even in a sexual situation she is of no higher order of Ḍākinī, or source of visionary instruction, than any other complex of sensory stimuli. This is no slur on woman but rather a manner of evincing the constancy of a *siddha*'s feeling tone of pure pleasure no matter what the content of his perceptual situation. There are no degrees of Emptiness for him. For the initiate on his way to the centre of the *maṇḍala*, however, a woman as a *karmamudrā* of Awareness is a guardian of the mysteries, a guide through the doors of the *maṇḍala*, a bestower of initiation, and the object of the initiation itself. She provides the first glimpses of a non-dual reality; she reveals what is the Emptiness of phenomenal appearances; she demonstrates the dance of magical illusion. Such experiences may be related to a particular woman until the initiation is complete, or knowledge of the Ḍākinī may be limited to a succession of encounters with many women, or the Awareness Ḍākinī may never embody herself in a human woman, and in the latter case experience of her need be no less intense or efficacious.

Thus it should be clear that although woman is the Ḍākinī, it is not woman as a discrete isolate in time and space. It is not the concept 'woman' that men usually project upon the Ḍākinī-woman who is a total experience of empty form, taste, touch, smell and sound. Due to our conditioned craving for the security of the concrete, our desire to possess something or someone tangible, and any of a welter of causes derived from uncontrolled emotivity, the mind fabricates an objective delusion and reifies it as woman, or at least all women are perceived through this screen of delusion. From the point of view of ignorance where the Ḍākinī is not recognised at all, woman is a symbol of the Ḍākinī, and further, if the aspirant cannot achieve the *samaya* of union with a Ḍākinī and know her directly he can project his vision of the Ḍākinī upon her and worship her, adoring her as a goddess. This last is the way of *kriyāyoga-tantra*, in the Outer Tantra.

Finally, in the non-dual reality of Buddhahood all phenomenal appearances are space and Emptiness on one hand and magical illusion, fairyland, and the reflection of the moon in water on the other hand. Understanding this, following Tsogyel, a *yoginī*-practitioner will know that her body-mind is empty of a substantial, discrete 'ego' and that her individual personality is an integral part of a dynamic field of relativity encompassing all living beings, embodied and disembodied, in all time and space. And detached from that field, identifying with the constant 'suchness' of experience, dynamic primal space, with Tsogyel she can then say 'I am the principal of the whole of *saṃsāra* and *nirvāṇa*. . . I live in the minds of all sentient beings, projecting myself as the elements of the body-mind and the sense-fields, and by secondary emanation projecting the twelve interdependant elements of existence' (p. 159). Or, identifying with the empty ground of her own being she discovers the universal ground of relativity that spontaneously emanates the universal illusion. This universal illusion is her Guru: his body is phenomenal appearances; his speech is all sound; and his Mind (*thugs*) all Mind.

These visions of Guru and Ḍākinī are quite different from the dictionary definition of Guru as a spiritual teacher, and the current occidental notions of a Ḍākinī as an embodied goddess, or as a nubile, sexually available cult-follower. The exoteric meanings and connotations of the word Ḍākinī in the common parlance of India, Nepal and Tibet cast another light upon her. Originally, it appears that the Buddhists borrowed the word from the *śāktas*, where in the cult of the Devī the Ḍākinīs were flesh-eating attendants of Kālī, who is the destructive aspect of Śiva's consort. In the Hindu Tantra Kālī vanquishes Śiva and consumes him; the inert *yogin* beseeches the Goddess to cut out his heart, representing his ego, and to unite with him so that his passive consciousness is vitalised by her power (*śakti*) and awareness. As a popular cult goddess Kālī bestows boons and favours upon those who make blood sacrifice to her; she is a blood-drinker. The fanatical devotees known as the *thugs* offered her human sacrifice until the Rāj virtually eradicated the cult last century. Thus from the beginning the Ḍākinīs were associated with the meta-psychotherapeutic function of ego destruction and the initiation of *yogins* into the *maṇḍala* of pure-being, consciousness and ecstasy (*satchitānanda*). Like the retinue of Kālī, Vajra Yoginī still carries the hooked knife (*gri-gu, karttari*) aloft in her right hand to cut away belief in an ego and to rend the blinds of emotivity. In her left hand she holds a skull-cup to catch the blood of her victims.

As embodied beings the Ḍākinīs were known as malicious witches performing no positive function, feared by all but *siddhas*. In contemporary India the word seems to be seldom used, and those who know it attach the same negative connotations. Similarly in Nepal, on the level of the uninitiated, the word *ḍāṅkinī* is used as an expletive or slur on a vile woman. It is also applied to a witch, an enchantress, a manipulator of the spirit world and a seductress who abuses her sexual powers. There are only a few Newari *vajrācāryas* who know the esoteric meaning of the word. In Tibetan the word Khandroma (*ḍākinī*) is reserved as an epithet for the consorts of Lamas, esteemed *yogins*' consorts or for realised *yoginīs* and tulkumas (female incarnations). In Tibet it is also a personal name.

A further important classification of Ḍākinī is the fourfold personification of the Guru's *karmas* (or functions). These four activities may be conceived as the functions of the Ḍākinīs in enlightening the initiate, in which case they may be performed by *karma* Ḍākinīs (mundane or human Ḍākinīs – *rjig-rten-kyi mkha'-'gro*), or they may be seen as the personifications of the

Guru's enlightening skilful means. These four activities are pacifying, enriching, controlling and destroying. These *karmas* are employed only for the conversion of sentient beings, in their spiritual evolution, and for spreading the tantric doctrines. Pacification (*zhi-ba*) implies the calming of aggression or anger. Enrichment (*rgyas-pa*), or growth, development, potentiating, etc., is a function of a woman's motherliness, and its effects are a sense of security, optimism, strength and confidence. Then control (*dbang-ba*) is the function of the wrathful Ḍākinī who firmly restrains futile emotivity and ratiocination. Destruction (*drag-pa*) may be performed by an aggressive woman who can undermine a *yogin*'s conception of an objective reality, destroy his fixed beliefs, eradicate his pride and even crush his ego so that his way of being is radically and irrevocably changed. Destruction can also imply death. But these powers are all relative *siddhis*; the *functions* of the Ḍākinī pall into irrelevance when compared to the intuition of her *essential nature* which leads to the ultimate *siddhi*, Buddhahood itself.

'Without *karmamudrā* no *mahāmudrā*.' The nature of the *yoginī* ideally suited as the Guru's consort is described by Guru Pema like this: 'she must be of good family, faithful and honour bound, beautiful, skilful in means, with penetrating insight, full of generosity and kindness; without her the factors of maturation and release are incomplete and the goal of tantric practice is lost from sight.' The phrase 'good family' may imply that this ideal Ḍākinī should belong to one of the five principal Ḍākinī families – lotus, jewel, *vajra, karma* or Buddha, rather than to a lower class of Ḍākinī, such as 'ashen' or 'flesh-eating' types. But it also implies that she should be of high caste, or, in Tibet, of high class. The ladies who accompanied the Twenty-five Siddhas of Chimphu in their principal initiations were all high-class women. This injunction that the *yoginī* should be of high caste conflicts with the prescriptions of some root *tantras*, and Indian practice, where low caste or outcaste women were preferred, a *Caṇḍālī, Ḍombhī* or *Śavarī*, etc. When the Indian initiate belonged to a twice-born caste there is obvious motive for the Guru to employ an outcaste woman in the initiation rite; destruction of social conditioning, reduction of pride and cultivation of the wisdom of equality may result from such an association.[2] But practical considerations also necessitated the use of low-caste women. Rigid caste rules chained all but the most karmically-favoured high caste women to orthodox Brahmanism, while the moral and sexual prejudices of high-caste girls ill-fitted them for the role of Ḍākinī in tantric ritual. On the contrary, outcaste girls were more promiscuous, uninhibited by Manu's laws, and further, since they would probably be of non-Aryan or Dravidian stock they could already be familiar with the Mother Goddess tradition from which Tantra sprung. In Tibet Tantra had the novel status of established religion, and was thus deprived of the negative social pressures that in India were conducive to the growth of the cult and the development of the individual.

Both in India and Tibet there was a custom for the initiate to offer the Guru a woman at initiation. Sometimes the woman would play a role in certain initiations.[3] For Nāropā the act of giving his woman to Tīlopā was in itself an act of self-denial, yet he said, 'Bliss is to offer unhesitatingly the *mudrā* as fee to the Guru who is Buddha himself.'[4] Here the act of offering the *karmamudrā* to the Guru is a skilful device provoking the emotional attachment that has as its real nature the discriminating Awareness of Amitābha. Figuratively, the initiate is offering the *karmamudrā* of perfect awareness of empty form to the Guru of skilful means to attain the bliss of spiritual wholeness. As the *yoginīs* sing to Tsogyel when she marvels at their apparent stupidity at offering their physical body to Vajra Yoginī, 'In so far as your perception of ultimate truth is instantaneous, it is as fast as a flash of genuine faith; if you fail to offer Awareness (the Ḍākinī) to the Guru the moment it dawns, procrastinating, merit is lost.' And, finally, the disciple is offering to his Guru what is most dear to him as an act of worship and a demonstration of his devotion, and also as some small recompense for the Guru's great generosity in bestowing the initiation upon him. Trisong Detsen gave Tsogyel to Guru Pema as part of the initiation price.

When Nāropā proves his blissful detachment to Tīlopā, Tīlopā praises him and then gives him instruction in *mahāmudrā*. 'You are worthy of eternal bliss, Nāropā, on the path of infinite reality. Look into the mirror of your mind, *mahāmudrā*, the mysterious home of the Ḍākinī.' Here the mirror of mind is the cognitive aspect of the universal plenum of non-dual reality, and the Ḍākinī is the flux of insubstantial reflection in the mirror. *Mahāmudrā* can be defined in the formula: non-dual Knowledge (*rig-pa*) and pure pleasure (*bde-chen*) in a primal existential state of being (*dharmakāya*). An instant's experience of that naked existential reality as instructive, visionary light-form is Vajra Yoginī (*saṃbhogakāya*); and if a *karmamudrā* embodies the experience, she is the apparitional body (*nirmāṇakāya*) of the Ḍākinī. Developing this thorough-going non-dual (*advaya*) analysis further, since union with the *karmamudrā* creates the pure pleasure of the *dharmakāya* and ultimately *mahāmudrā*, because all women are Ḍākinīs, an intense, integral sexual encounter or relationship is a means to attain *siddhi*. Then sexual practice is *tantra-yoga*.

After Guru Pema had accepted Yeshe Tsogyel from the King Trisong Detsen, she was thoroughly instructed in the ontology and epistemology of the *mahāyanā* before he initiated her into the Tantra. Before he bestowed the three initiations he explained the nature of his desire, 'I am free of every germ of desire whatsoever; the aberrations of lust are absent.' Another Dzokchen Guru, the first and greatest of the lineage, taught this precept and statement of the nature of his desire. 'Have no desire for what you see. Desire not; desire not. Desire; desire. Have no desire for desire. Have no desire for desire. Desire and freedom must be simultaneous.'[5] It is in the third initiation rite and post-initiation practice that the *karmamudrā* plays her part in formal tantric training; but in the space that the initiation reveals to the initiate, the nature of the Ḍākinī is equivocal and ambiguous, never localised as a woman as conceived in dualistic ignorance.

The treatment of woman as an object that can be 'used' in tantric practice, and 'given' by disciple to Guru, and vice versa, and the language that describes woman as 'an ingredient of Tantra', may appear inconsistent with the admonition to 'adore woman everywhere'. However, such phraseology is merely semantic convention and does not reflect the Guru's attitude. In fact the woman is worshipped as the Ḍākinī in rites in which she participates, and this worship should not stop when the rite is over. Lamas customarily treat women with great respect, in an exemplary fashion. Their treatment of women compares favourably with that of the *hīnayāna bikkus* who should disdain contact with women in obedience to their *vinaya* vows. Śākyamuni adamantly refused to ordain women until the last years of his life, fearing that they would bring the entire community into disrepute. His favourite disciple Ānanda, who consistently fought the women's case, finally persuaded him to establish an order of nuns; their disciplinary code was even more rigid and extensive than the voluminous strictures governing the personal and social behaviour of the monks. We can only surmise that it was the very quality that Śākyamuni felt to be an impediment on the nuns' path that Guru Pema considered a valuable aid on the path of Tantra when he said, 'The gross bodies of men and women are equally suited (as temples of the Yidam), but if a woman has strong aspiration her potential (for existential realisation) is greater' (p. 86). A woman's greater capacity for sensation and feeling, her innate receptivity and her greater powers of intuition are obvious qualities that can define 'greater potential'. If a woman has a strong karmic propensity to self-abnegation, or sufficient lust to overcome instinctual desire for security and motherhood, if her aspiration is clearly defined, strong and constant, her natural capacity for Awareness can be potentiated with less difficulty than a man's. Even though she limits her options by choosing motherhood, she can still utilise that karmic situation to attain the aim of Buddhahood; the stronger her attachment the greater potential energy to be directed as *śakti* (the energy that vitalises and galvanises the *yogin*'s *kuṇḍalinī*). Further, motherhood can quicken her social virtues (the four stations of Brahmā),[6] and cultivate compassionate skilful means, although in general, *anuyoga* characterises woman as passionate rather than loving, and it is a male Bodhisattva who symbolises compassion. Finally, in the *mahāyāna* it is said that woman should be considered pure as she is, and in the view of *anuttarayoga-tantra* both men and women are Buddhas from the beginning, through eternity; but with application of the Guru's skilful means, with a minimum of formal meditation, passively relaxing into her own receptivity, it is easier for a woman than a man to recognise our pristine existential condition: such is Guru Pema's implication.

Although the *yoginī* may possess a few constitutional advantages in the Tantra, she is constrained by some severe handicaps. Tsogyel begs her Guru for initiation into the Dorje Phurba *maṇḍala*, so that terrific deity may protect her from the stresses and strains, the demonic and aggressive forces, that her receptive nature naturally draws into her *maṇḍala*. Social disapprobation, thieves and fornicators are Tsogyel's bane. In eighth-century Tibet, Tsogyel would have been wandering in a predominantly Bon society, and it is certain that many Bonpos were hostile to the Buddhists. In Taksham's eighteenth-century Tibet, and throughout the sub-continent until the present day, hostility arose from disingenuous peasants incredulous of the nun or *yoginī*'s motivation, and believing that the robe was merely a cover for sloth and a trick to exploit hard-working people's charity. A Sanskrit adage has it, 'A woman is a thousand times more lustful than a man.' Consorting with her Guru, or a *yogin*, the *yoginī*'s motivation was in constant doubt, and ignorant of secret tantric *samaya*s but knowing that nuns were pledged to celibacy, and aware of the notoriety of some nunneries, the layman was quick to cast aspersions upon an indiscreet female *tantrika*.

There is little evidence of suppression of women in the period of the kings. In fact the palace women, the queens and princesses, appear to have carried some weight in politics, in which they played an active part. But in an era of heroic warfare it is easy to conceive of a degree of machismo prevalent in the menfolk. 'Even a woman can defeat you!' shouted the crowd at the Bon magicians after they had been discomfited by the Buddhists, Tsogyel amongst them. We do hear of Bon priestesses, however, and Tsogyel herself is proof of female participation in the most sacred and significant of her society's activities.

Tsogyel does not stress the danger of rape or theft, but like most *yoginī*s she was confronted by both in her lifetime. It would appear that these tribulations of *yoginī*s are universal and perennial. However, in Tantra personal vulnerability, such as that of a lone woman, presents important opportunities for exercising skilful means in conversion – pacifying, enriching, controlling or destroying. If a woman's rapists can be led to a profound recognition of their existential reality through the experience a woman gives them, there is no situation whatsoever that cannot be turned to advantage on the path. In this most poignant of all episodes in her life, Tsogyel not only demonstrates a valid and effective method of assimilating rape, but she shows how fortuitous sex can be an initiation with implicit formal stages. Tsogyel's method of making rape a positive experience was to accept the situation and then control it. Through visualisation identifying herself with Tārā, the Goddess of Service, who is willing to do whatever is necessary to serve the Guru who is all sentient beings, the victim was transformed into the Saviouress. Unfortunately not all women have the *śakti* that can raise a rapist's *kuṇḍalinī* and propel him through the levels of bliss in such a way as to give him total realisation. But just as all women become Ḍākinīs when relating to the Guru who sees them as such, here the rapists are transformed into the Ḍākinī's Gurus by force of her visualisation of them. The Ḍākinī sees all men as her Gurus; it is the sexual metaphor describing her lack of discrimination and her willingness to unite with all men that gives her a reputation for promiscuity. Lastly, confronting every situation on the path, both adversity and good fortune, with an equanimity that permits a spontaneous response free from fear and emotivity, seeing every moment through 'the third eye', the eye of non-dual awareness, the Boddhisattva Vow (*sems-bskyed*) automatically motivates the Ḍākinī's word and action.

The ambiguity of the word Ḍākinī is amply demonstrated above; perhaps there is error in attempting a too specific conceptualisation, for if the Ḍākinī is caught on the point of a nice definition she becomes a dead concept. She belongs to the equivocal language of the twilight world, where she can make a mind-changing verbal impact. The Ḍākinī remains a profound tantric mystery, an enigma that is only resolved upon initiation, when the *yogin* gains experiential understanding of her. In his introduction setting the stage for Tsogyel, Taksham is typically equivocal, 'It was this Buddha, then (Padma Saṃbhava), who served as skilful means to spread the Tantra. He had a greater number of accomplished mystical consorts than the number of sesame seeds (=*thig-le*, seed-essence) it takes to fill a room supported by four pillars (the four *kāya*s), and all of them came from the Highest Paradise ('Og-min), to inhabit the cremation grounds, the heavens, the human world, the great power places, the *nāga* realms and the realms of the celestial musicians. In this world of Jambudvīpa, . . . he had not less than 70,000 accomplished girls, and among them were the five (*nirmāṇakāya*) emanations of Vajra Vārāhī (*saṃbhogakāya*), the five from whom he was never separated: the emanation of Vārāhī's Body, Mandāravā, the emanation of her Speech, Yeshe Tsogyel, the emanation of her Mind, Śākya Dema, the emanation of her Quality, Kalasiddhi, the emanation of her Activity, Tashi Chidren (Khyidren),[7] and the emanation of her essential indefinable individuality, Khandro Wongchang (mKha'-'gro dbang-'chang).' These six were the six aspects of his apparitional being (*nirmāṇakāya*). We know too little of the actual life stories of Kalasiddhi, Tashi Khyidren and Śākya Dema, and nothing at all of Khandro Wongchang, while concerning Mandāravā there are several extant biographies and substantial mention of her in Guru Pema's own biographies. Here are brief sketches of the lives of the five.

Mandāravā is the daughter of the King of Zahor,[8] born into the royal family of a small but strategic Himalayan Kingdom in the middle of the eighth century. She is born an Awareness Ḍākinī (*ye-shes mkha'-'gro*) and a prodigy. At marriageable age, like Tsogyel, she refuses all attempts to marry her, but fails to convince her father that she is destined to take ordination as a Buddhist nun. She serves the flesh of a Brahmin's corpse to her father to eat – a heinous offence – and then she absconds from the palace, assuming beggars' robes. After she had been ordained by the Abbot Śāntarakṣita (also a native of Zahor), her father comes to terms with his daughter's predilection for the religious life, and provides a palace for her meditations.

When Padma Saṃbhava, the youthful prince turned ascetic *yogin*, appears in Mandi from Orgyen, Mandāravā is immediately entranced by him – she swoons as he floats up into the sky. As predestined, she becomes his disciple. But malicious gossip reports to the King that his daughter, the nun, is misbehaving herself with an unprincipled *tantrika*, and the outraged king is led to seize Guru Pema and burn him at the stake. The Guru is sustained by Ḍākinīs, and the fire is transformed into a lake that smokes for seven days. On the eighth day the King finds Guru Pema as an eight-year-old boy sitting upon a lotus in the middle of the lake.[9] Mandāravā has been thrown into a pit covered with thorns. Most thankful to find his daughter still alive, the King reunites her with Guru

Pema and worships them both. Until the Guru goes to Tibet it appears that he and Mandāravā are inseparable.

The Guru remains some time in Zahor, and after having converted the populace, he and his consort go to the Maratika Cave at Heileshe in Nepal (near Lamidada, east of Okhuldunga) where they practise the *yoga* of immortality in the maṇḍala of Amitāyus, Guru Pema attaining the level of Knowledge Holder of Immortality (*tshe'i dbang-la rig-'dzin*). From Nepal they travel to Baṅgala where Mandāravā is transformed into the Cat-faced Ḍākinī, and assists in the conversion of the country (early Pāla Bengal). Returning to his homeland, because no prophet is recognised in his own land, he is again burnt at the stake, this time with Mandāravā, and again they are unharmed. Thereafter Mandāravā becomes Queen of the Orgyen Ḍākinīs – Orgyen is the Pure-land of the Ḍākinīs, a *nirmāṇakāya* Buddhafield. Towards the end of Mandāravā's life she appears to Tsogyel while the latter is meditating at Phukmoche, and requests Tsogyel to teach her the twenty-seven secret precepts that Guru Pema had not taught in India, a rare admission that the Nyingma doctrines contained precepts that had no Indian antecedents.

The image of the fire and immolation appears twice in this legend. In the first instance, sustained by Ḍākinīs Guru Pema alone is rejuvenated; the fire of the Ḍākinī in the belly melts the concrete view of reality centred in the head, and in the lake of Emptiness that results grows the lotus of compassion wherein sits a resplendent, virgin youth embodying the miraculous psychic qualities of prepubescence. The essential existential cause of this transformation is the passion of the Guru's relationship with Mandāravā. In the meantime Mandāravā was sitting in meditation in a pit – a symbol of the universal *yoni*. In the second instance the Guru and Ḍākinī are burnt together. The fire of passion occurs repeatedly in tantric legend, signifying its important place in tantric practice. In general, the story of the *yogin* and *yoginī*'s perambulation about India is an oft repeated spiritual love story.

This context offers an excellent opportunity to present the facts of Tsogyel's existence from a radically different standpoint. Stripped of the hagiographical trappings, what do we know, or what can we infer, of Tibet's greatest female mystic? When

Tsogyel was about to leave this earth, asked by her disciples what they should tell posterity about her, she offers them some humanistic realism. First, she calls herself an 'unlovable spinster rejected by Tibetan men', and since the lack of physical attraction, real or imaginary, together with rejected love, are probably the two most common causes of women cloistering themselves for life, we are led to a possible inference that Tsogyel was only spiritually beautiful. Further, a sensitive young girl is wont to be resentful of being courted merely for her royal status and wealth. Rather than endure an arranged marriage she fled, an event not uncommon in contemporary India where the vision of nuptials with an unknown man inspires virgin horrors. Whichever way it was, we have Tsogyel fleeing to religion as an escape from a harsh world. She calls herself wanton, uninhibited, passionate and obstinate. Her wantonness is evinced by the quality of her erotic fantasies while in meditation at Nering in Bhutan, where she dreamed of verbal and physical seduction. But this should be considered normal for a nubile young woman deprived of all male company, and, likewise, the excessive sexual activity in which she indulged with three healthy young men in a further retreat is also a natural development. The purchase of a male slave smacks of Freudian fantasy. Her other sexual partners, the Emperor, who gave her a magnificent wedding, and the Indian Guru, were both much older than herself, and must have provided her with much mature experience. Her obstinacy and incorrigibility were probably her most unattractive qualities, but essential factors in her ability to endure three winters on the snow-line with only intermittent signs of success. It was a strong-willed adolescent who roundly cursed the minister Śāntipā as he performed his duty; and it was a mature woman who knew what she wanted and how to get it when she prevailed upon her Guru to give her the Dorje Phurba initiation after he had decided otherwise. Of her 'deceitfulness, propensities to intrigue and over-extend herself in power play', there is the evidence of the attempt upon her life and her subsequent banishment for causing conflict and schism within the government after the old king died, and the implications of her maintaining a relationship with the 'foreign devil-priest' against the wishes of the majority of ministers, and also of her evasion of the first sentence of banishment, with the connivance of the King, when she accompanied her Guru to Tidro. When the occasion demanded it she was quite capable of taking life while keeping her hands clean; the Bonpo leaders committed suicide at her behest. Towards the end of her life she succeeded in amassing a very large following and establishing several monastic establishments. She was the Emperor's priestess, the abbess of the principal monastic academies, and the Guru of many prominent figures in government. In the literary world she attained immortality by having a large proportion of Nyingma scriptures ascribed to her.

The above vignette, composed in *saṃsāra* of *saṃsāra*, is derived from internal evidence in *The Life*, which in general is written of *nirvāṇa* in *nirvāṇa*. The facts of Tsogyel's personal life are irrelevant; only her mythos has significance. Taksham's purpose was surely not to provide an objective statement of Tsogyel's life, but to use her life-story as a peg upon which to hang his purpose of throwing the reader out of his normal habits of thinking and being into a visonary realm of pure perception. Whether Tsogyel was a giant manipulative ego or a saint is irrelevant providing the reader gains some intimation of the Tantra (thread), in which moments of psychotropic experience are counted off like beads on a thread, each as a mystic union of Guru and Ḍākinī.

Śākya Dema, or Śākya Devī, is Guru Pema's first Nepali consort. He finds her at Sankhu in the north-east corner of the Kathmandu Valley on his way to Tibet. A *vihāra* of great antiquity, Sankhu sheltered pilgrims from Tibet en route to India. It was a *vihāra* of master bronze smiths who were creating some of the finest art of Licchavi Nepal about the time of Pema's visit. The shrine of Sankhu Bajra-Joginī is now dominated by a temple of Ugratārā called Khaḍga Joginī (the Yoginī of the Sword).[10] Perhaps the name Bajra-Yoginī had its origin in Śākya Dema's association with the establishment. A local queen dies in childbirth and her corpse is taken to the cremation ground with her new-born daughter. The baby survives, suckled by monkeys, and grows up with them; but her hands and feet are webbed for she is an Awareness Ḍākinī (*ye-shes mkha'-'gro*). Guru Pema finds her there and brings her to Pharping at the southern exit to the Valley, where at Yanglesho he performs his *mahāmudrā* meditation practice with her, utilising the *maṇḍala*s of Yangdak and Dorje Phurba. This is all we know of Śākya Dema except that when Tsogyel visits Yanglesho some years later, the Guru's former consort is still living there as a *yoginī*. The *yogas* which Śākya Dema relates to Tsogyel are the simultaneous creative and fulfilment processes of meditation that lead to *mahāmudrā*; the fulfilment process of 'burning and dripping'; the zap-lam *yoga* of co-incident pleasure and Emptiness; the togal *yoga* of the four visions leading to rainbow body; and sleep-*yoga*. A post-script to Śākya Dema's story is that some contemporary Tibetans believe that the Rāj Kumārī, the so-called Living Goddess of Basantapur Kumārī Bahāl in Kathmandu, is an emanation of the Goddess Śākya Dema.

Kalasiddhi is also born in Nepal. In ancient times Nepal was famous for its wool; Nepali blankets were sold in the market of Mauryan Paṭaliputra.[11] Kalasiddhi's parents are weavers. Her father and mother, Bhadana and Nāginī, name their child Ḍākinī. Like Śākya Dema she grows up in a place of the dead, her father having abandoned her in a charnel ground with her dead mother. Mandāravā, in the form of a tigress, suckles the child while keeping the mother's corpse warm so that the child will still cling to it. When Ḍākinī is old enough she spins cotton during the day and weaves it by night.[12] The fourteen-year-old Ḍākinī is found by Tsogyel on her second visit to Nepal, where she comes to teach the Guru's secret precepts. Tsogyel names her Kalasiddhi: *kala* is the name of the substrata of the elements of the human body (bile, phlegm, semen, etc.) or 'atoms', and since Kalasiddhi belongs to the 'Body' family (*kāyakula*) of Ḍākinīs (and specifically to the conch type of Ḍākinī, *Śaṃkinī*, which refers to the physical nature of the *yoni*), she will gain *siddhi* through realisation of the essential Emptiness of the 'atomic' structure of the body. In Mangyul, across the Tibetan border upstream of the Triśūli-kola, Kalasiddhi receives initiation into the Tantra Lama Maṇḍala (*gSangs-sngags bla-ma'i dkyil-d'khor*) and after extensive meditation she gains *siddhi*. She accompanies Tsogyel to Mutri Tsenpo's court at Samye and to the retreat centre at Chimphu where she meets Guru Pema. The Guru immediately perceives Kalasiddhi's potential as a *mudrā* in his practice to increase the Tantra in Tibet and asks Tsogyel to give her to him for that purpose. Very soon after, Guru Pema leaves for the South-west leaving Kalasiddhi in

Tsogyel's care. It is to Kalasiddhi that Tsogyel gave the detailed zap-lam instruction as her parting gift.

Tashi Khyidren of Bhutan is a well-known folk-figure in western Bhutan, where she is known as Bhutan's gift to the Great Guru in his work of propagating the *tantras* in Tibet. One Bhutanese source relates that she was the daughter of the legendary Sindhu Rājā, King of the Iron Palace (*lCag-mkhar rgyal-po*), who invited the Guru to Bhutan (the Bum-thang area) to cure his disease. Jamgon Kongtrul makes 'Tashi Khyeudren' (Khye'u-'dren – the preferred form of her name in Bhutan) and 'Tashi Chidren' two separate consorts of the Guru, informing us that the former was from Tsha-'og and the latter was the daughter of King Ha-mar or Hamra.[13]

The Life confirms that Tashi Khyidren was the daughter of King Hamra(s). At the age of thirteen she meets Tosgyel meditating in the Nering Drak Cave subjected to the wiles of the local spirits and demons. Full of admiration for the *yoginī*, from time to time she brings her milk and honey. After Tsogyel has succeeded in subjecting the spirits and also the hostile local populace, Khyidren's father comes to pay her homage, and Tsogyel asks him to give her his daughter. King Hamra(s) obliges, and Tsogyel changes his daughter's name from Khyidren to Chidren, although Taksham still uses her former name. Soon after, Khyidren accompanies Tsogyel to Womphu Taktsang in Tibet, where she meets Guru Pema. He asks Tsogyel to give him Khyidren to perform as his *mudrā* in the initiatory rites of Dorje Phurba, which he was to perform for the protection of Tibet. Khyidren plays an important role as the secondary consort of the Guru in this initiation. In the symbology of the *Phurba-tantra,* Khyidren is the tigress upon which Guru Pema and Tsogyel, as Phurba and Consort, ride to subject the gods and demons of Tibet. She remains a disciple of Tsogyel for the remainder of the Ḍākinī Guru's life. Khyidren is reborn as Machik Labdron's daughter.

Tsogyel lived during the climax of the Tibetan monarchy. Some years after her death there was a period of anarchy in Tibetan society out of which grew the roots of the theocratical system that was to develop and endure with various changes of direction until Mao's Chinese invasion. Despite the early political revolution there is little evidence of drastic social change in Tibet since Tsogyel's era. Except for some Indian, Mongol and Chinese influence, Tibet has remained socially isolated, and since Buddhism was assimilated underlying values have remained unaltered. The Buddhists (and Brahmins) teach the myth of an initial golden age, and a theory that recognises four ages, four stages in a process of inexorable decay from the glory of heaven on earth in the *dharmayuga* to the moral and physical corruption of the final cataclysmic *kaliyuga* in which we now find ourselves. These concepts imbue a profound conservatism and an intractable attachment to the *status quo*, so that the tendency is to conceive of any change as for the worse and to treat the past as a model for the present. After the end of the second period of propagation of the *dharma* (thirteenth century), the general bias was to consider foreigners, who inevitably brought new ideas with them, as harbingers of disaster. It was this xenophobic attitude, shared with the Chinese, that made Lhasa a forbidden city to the British Rāj and gave Tibet a further century of moribund social and political existence. But the very isolationism that protected Tibet from the British left the country hopelessly vulnerable to Mao's Chinese. Due to imperceptible social change in Tibet down the centuries, we can deduce the nature of eighth-century Tibetan womanhood from contemporary observation.

If we can judge from our contemporaries, the daughter of Tibet is a hardy soul by nature, physically strong, shrewd, stubborn, slow to burn but fierce and passionate when aroused; she is not devoted to a moral law, has little fear of the karmic repercussions of her acts, has complete faith in the power of her priests to ward off evil and to secure for her her desires. She is materialistic, but paradoxically she has implicit belief in the fierce and indiscriminately malicious world of spiritual powers surrounding her; she is highly superstitious but her faith in the efficacy of her charms and talismans, in the Lama's powers of sympathetic magic, and in the power and fidelity of her protecting gods, insulates her from morbid preoccupation with an evil spirit world. Unless she is educated in an exceptional nunnery she is illiterate, her sole source of learning being the classical epics, such as the epic history of Gesar of Ling and various religious legends, customarily sung around the fireside by a bard or her grandparents. She is eminently practical regardless of her class, and she will often trade or act as family banker, holding the purse strings for her husband; if required to strike a deal it will be a rare man who gets the better of her.

Marriage is not a sacred sacrament in her society, but if conjugal ties prove expedient she is likely to remain faithful to her husband. Polyandry allowed her to be married to two or three brothers simultaneously, but it appears that only the early kings practised polygamy. The Tibetan female is not of mystical bent, so that it is unlikely that she will enter a nunnery unless it is expedient in solving the problem of food, shelter and clothing. If popular anecdotes[14] reflect the reality, the nunneries were havens of frustrated women, with discipline lax and meditation an unusual concern. No doubt there were personal and institutional exceptions, periods of reform elevating the tone from time to time and always extraordinary Lamas must have inspired their disciples to practise *sādhana*. A woman with otherworldly propensities would have been well-advised to marry a Lama or a tantric *yogin* and thereby gain a very special status in society with many material fringe benefits.

Tsogyel was born into a hierarchical and patriarchal society, in which the clans were still the strongest social groupings. Taksham thought it of sufficient significance to mention that Bonpo fathers exchanged their daughters in marriage. From this can be inferred that marriage was a social device for strengthening political and economic ties within a clan or forming a beneficial alliance with another clan. Dowries were exchanged at marriages, which were celebrated by a secular feast. Arranged marriages were the norm in the upper strata of society, but the wishes of the girl seem to have been given consideration. A woman had certain rights of inheritance; Milarepa's mother, for instance, received land and property from her mother's family. Thus divorce for a woman was a simple matter of separation. Sexual morality seems never to have been puritanical or promiscuous; in general the Tibetans' sexuality appears well-balanced.

The status of women in the society into which Tsogyel was born, practically, could be said to be one of equality with men. True, it was a patriarchal society, but besides the basic power that resides in woman as mother and mistress, a power that unmarried feminists invariably underestimate in their evaluation of the status of woman, in every sphere of human activity women were active. In politics Trisong's queens' opinions carried significant weight, no doubt bolstered by the support of their powerful clans, and their prejudices changed the course of Buddhist history – Vairotsana's exile to Kham, engineered by a queen, carried Dzokchen to eastern Tibet, for instance. In religion the Bon gods were worshipped by priestesses besides male shamans, and in Buddhism Tsogyel herself was the best example of a woman reaching the apogee of attainment. This society was not highly sophisticated; but we need not envision feminine delicacy, intelligence and sensitivity oppressed in a tribal society of male warriors arrayed in skins with uncongealed blood still warm on their recently scabbarded swords. The cult of Avalokiteśvara had been propagated amongst a portion of the aristocracy for a century or more, and Bon-shamanism with its vicious gods and demons who demanded even human blood for their propitiation was on the defensive. It was probably the innately conservative women who were the principal votaries of such atavistic spiritual powers. In such a world Tsogyel shines 'like a star in the day-sky'.

To conclude this section on Woman and the Ḍākinī, the word Ḍākinī, or Khandroma, has introduced a valuable new concept to the western world. The value of the concept is in its very lack of precise definition; it embraces a range of meaning – the female principle, a moment of spiritual integration, the Guru's Consort, a female sexual partner – that adds up to an enigma and paradox. The image that 'Sky Dancer' conjures with its connotation of an immaterial, gossamer, shape-shifting goddess-Ḍākinī dancing in the empyreum is no less enigmatic. Such concepts as 'Ḍākinī' fulfil the needs of western *yogin*s trying to find expression of their experience in exploration of inner space. Discoveries on this re-found frontier, particularly experiences of gnostic sexuality, are not accommodated by western religious tradition with its equivocal dualistic concept of reality and strict compartmentalisation of sex and god. In the synthetic terminology and existential metaphysics of Tantra the word Ḍākinī is central, just as the experience of the Ḍākinī, by both *yogin*s and *yoginī*s, is central to the inner life.

3

THE NYINGMA LINEAGES

A spiritual lineage is an uninterrupted succession of Guru–*chela*, teacher–disciple, father–son relationships. The lineage not only carries the instructions and techniques of spiritual evolution and of attainment of *siddhi* from its originator, but through initiation it actually transmits the spiritual power of its original Buddha-Lama. Thus tantric rites invariably include a liturgy of praise, worship or supplication of the lineage. Indian Hindu *tantrikas* keep memory of their lineal antecedents alive in song, in liturgy and through didactic legend, and although Nepali *vajrācāryas* are notoriously ignorant of their original lineages, or their caste lineages, this could merely be a sign of decadence. The Tibetans, however, are deeply concerned with lineal purity. A text or doctrine is authenticated and given authority by the integrity of the lineage that transmits it. Proven lineal purity inspires the devotion that facilitates achievement of the lineage's *siddhi*, while it strengthens the lineage by reinforcing orthodoxy and thwarting deviant tendencies. Thus the Old School is highly sensitive to the reformed schools' allegations, though mostly unsubstantiated, that their early Tibetan lineages were adulterated by heresy, broken during the period of darkness between 840 and 950, or that they actually lacked authentic Indian antecedents. But to a large extent the terma theory of revelation provides a metaphysical support that displaces dependence on lineal purity.

The Old School lineages, specifically the lineages of

anuttarayoga-tantra, initiated their first Tibetan disciples in the latter part of the eighth century, although there are indications, but no proof, that tantric lineages had transmitted teaching upon Mahākaruṇika and Hayagrīva from the seventh century.[1] Quite distinct mainstream lineages carried the doctrines and empowerments of the three divisions of the Inner Tantra – *mahāyoga*, *anuyoga* and *atiyoga*; individual *tantra*s show similar but separate lineages. First, the *mahāyoga* lineage is said to have begun with the Eight Knowledge Holders,[2] who received the Eight Logos Sādhanas from the Ḍākinī's *stūpa* in the Śītavana Cremation Ground near Bodh Gaya. Each of the Eight received a single *sādhana*, but Guru Pema is credited with bringing all eight *sādhana*s to Tibet and teaching them to the Twenty-five Siddhas of Chimphu. Others of the Eight, Vimalamitra, and perhaps Dhanasaṃskṛta and Śāntigarbha, also taught *mahāyoga* to Tibetan disciples. The problem here is that the legend of the Knowledge Holders and the *stūpa* in Śītavana is partially, if not totally, apocryphal. Second, the *anuyoga* lineage originated in North-West India; King Dza[3] of Orgyen received the teaching from Vajrapāṇi himself. Transmitted by a line of *siddha*s that includes carriers of both *mahāyoga* (Hūṃkara and Prabhahasti) and *atiyoga* (Garab Dorje), and also links in the *mahāmudrā* lineage (Kukurāja and Lwa-ba-pa) of the *siddhācārya* tradition centred in the Pāla Empire, the *anuyoga* lineage was carried to Nepal by Dhanarakṣita, where Dharmabodhi, Vasudhara and Chetsan-kye the Sage of Gilgit, taught Nub Sangye Yeshe.[4] Vasudhara taught Tsogyel in the E Vihāra in Kathmandu and translated and taught at Samye.

Just as the Eighty-four Mahāsiddhas are the principal exemplars and the root of Marpa and Milarepa's *mahāmudrā* lineage, the Dzokchen *yogin*s of the Indian *atiyoga* lineage profoundly influenced the entire Old School tradition. Orgyen appears to have been the cradle of the Dzokchen lineage, and an examination of the origins of Dzokchen will provide ample evidence that North-West India was the sphere of activity of all the *siddha*s of *atiyoga*. Indeed, Dzokchen could be called the *dharma* of Orgyen. But before looking at the biographical legends of the Indian transmitters of *atiyoga* it is necessary to put the temporal lineages into perspective through an understanding of the transcendental origin of the Inner Tantra *dharma*, and the process of its direct transmission.

The time of the *dharma*'s teaching transcends historical time; the doctrine was, and is, taught at the time of 'changeless, ultimate sameness and primal purity'. The place of its teaching is the Buddhafield of Akaniṣṭha, the supreme pure-land of the *nirmāṇakāya*. The teacher is Kuntuzangpo manifesting as the principal deity of the *maṇḍala* of the particular *tantra* that is being taught, and the teacher's retinue of disciples are the deities of the teacher's *maṇḍala*. The *dharma*s that are taught are the *tantra*s of the Old School. Condensed into a transmittable, verbal form, the doctrine is taught by Kuntuzangpo in the *dharmakāya*, Vajrasattva in the *saṃbhogakāya*, and Vajrapāṇi (Guhyapati, Master of Secrets) and the Ḍākinī in the *nirmāṇakāya*. These same deities of the Buddha's three modes of being, and also the Five Dhyāni Buddhas, teach in the realms of the Ḍākinīs and of men.[5] The Dzokchen *siddha*s, and later many treasure-finders, received Mind to Mind Transmission of various *tantra*s directly from a transcendental source. Guru Pema himself received the Dzokchen transmission directly from *dharmakāya* and *saṃbhogakāya* deities, although he may have had human teachers also. Concerning the mainstream lineage of Dzokchen, Kuntuzangpo transmitted the teaching to Vajrasattva, who taught it to his *nirmāṇakāya* emanation Garab Dorje; Garab Dorje taught Mañjuśrīmitra, who taught Śrī Siṅgha, who taught Jñānasūtra and Vimalamitra, and Vimalamitra taught the Tibetan neophytes. Thus Vimalamitra is the principal transmitter of the lineal Dzokchen teaching to Tibet.

Garab Dorje[6] was born to a virgin nun in Orgyen. Wishing to live an unencumbered life she threw the child into a cinder pit. A week later she regretted her hastiness, and returning to the pit she found the child playing in a bed of ashes. She named him Rolang Dewa (Corpse of Bliss). Later, when the miraculous child had grown into a wise young boy, the King of Siṅghala (now Śrī Laṅka) called Mañjuśrīmitra, met him, and to him, his principal disciple, Garab Dorje taught a ninth vehicle to Buddhahood called 'how never to be wrong'. He taught this doctrine, *atiyoga*, to Mañjuśrīmitra in a temple in the middle of an island in the Dhanakośa Lake in Orgyen. This was the lake in which Guru Pema was born on the pollen bed of a lotus.

Here Garab Dorje taught Guru Pema the Dzokchen Nying-tik and the Space and Mind Classes of *atiyoga*.[7] Another source tells us that he taught Mañjuśrīmitra in the Śītavana Cremation Ground in Bodh Gaya, a location fraught with spiritual power and of enormous significance to the Nyingma lineage. At his death Garab Dorje appeared in a mass of light surrounded by a host of Ḍākinīs and presented his 'heart-son', Mañjuśrīmitra, with a golden box containing the complete Dzokchen scripture. This scripture was arranged by his disciples into the three sections of Dzokchen precepts: the Space Class (*klong sde*), Mind Class (*sems sde*) and the Secret Precept Class (*man-ngag sde*).

Mañjuśrīmitra's two chief disciples were Buddha Śrī Jñāna and Śrī Siṅgha. The latter was born in China, perhaps Chinese Turkestan (see p. 297), and studied in China at Wu t'ai shan before following the instructions of Avalokiteśvara to go to the Sosa-ling Cremation Ground west of Bodh Gaya if he wished to attain Buddhahood. In Sosa-ling the monk Śrī Siṅgha encountered Mañjuśrīmitra who gave him the entire Dzokchen message. Following his own Guru, Mañjuśrīmitra dissolved into a rainbow body at his death and presented his disciple with a casket containing his final testament.

In the next generation of the lineage we find the imposing figure of Vimalamitra. More than Guru Pema himself, Vimalamitra was responsible for the transmission of Dzokchen to Tibet. He was born in a house-holding family in western India at about the same time as his spiritual brother Jñānasūtra was born in another part of India in an outcaste family. When they were adults, Vajrasattva appeared to both Vimalamitra and Jñānasūtra and instructed them to go to a certain temple in China where they would meet their Guru. Taking his begging bowl Vimalamitra set off for China and discovered Śrī Siṅgha sitting under a Bodhi Tree. For twenty years his Guru taught him Dzokchen through the mouth-to-ear method, and then, finally satisfied, he returned to India. He found Jñānasūtra and taught him all he knew, but again feeling incomplete he accompanied Jñānasūtra back to China, where in a cremation ground they sat at their Guru's feet for a further twenty years. At the end of this period Śrī Siṅgha asked them if they were satisfied, and they both replied in the affirmative. 'But I have given you nothing!' the Guru exclaimed. Vimalamitra was not disheartened and returned again to India, but Jñānasūtra was enlightened by the Guru's remark, and having begged for the whole truth he was given the increasingly informal and formless (*spros-med*) initiations and instructions of Dzokchen. He meditated for sixteen years upon the highest precepts of *atiyoga* and was then given instruction upon meditation in action (*spyod-pa*). Invited by the King of Khotan to visit him, Śrī Siṅgha left Jñānasūtra. Some time later the disciple realised that his Guru had achieved *parinirvāṇa* when he appeared to him in a cloud of light to give him his final testament, which included direction to a certain Chinese temple where he would discover the complete Dzokchen Nying-tik scriptures. Jñānasūtra recovered these texts and returned to India to teach Ḍākas and Ḍākinīs in a cremation ground called Bha-sing. Vimalamitra in his turn was to find Jñānasūtra and ask his disciple, and now Guru, for the higher instruction that he had previously rejected. When Jñānasūtra died Vimalamitra received his final testament, which was the quintessential, ultimate meaning of Dzokchen.

After Jñānasūtra's death Vimalamitra wandered throughout India. He became priest of the King of Kamarūpa, he was patronised by the Pāla King of Baṅgala, he lived as a *yogin* in cremation grounds, he instructed the King of Orgyen, and he sojourned in Kashmir where he gained the epithet 'Sage of Kashmir' (*Kha-che pan-chen*). It was in Orgyen that he was approached by King Trisong Detsen's messengers (Nyang, Chokro and Kaba) begging him to come to Tibet. Much to the Orgyen King's chagrin he accepted the invitation. This offence to the King of Orgyen was to cause him much trouble in Tibet. According to Tsogyel's *Life* Vimalamitra arrived in Tibet in time for the great convocation after the completion of the Samye monastery and in time to take a leading part in the debate that resulted in the expulsion of the Bon-shamans from Central Tibet. But his Indian *yogin*'s appearance, the intrigues of the Orgyen king's spies and of the anti-Buddhist ministers, led to his impeachment, and he narrowly avoided exile. Since the period of persecution of the Buddhists was prior to the convocation, perhaps Vimalamitra arrived in Tibet earlier than *The Life* suggests. Certainly he enjoyed an extended stay in Tibet. To the majority of his disciples he taught simple, fundamental *dharma* – karmic cause and effect, the Four Noble Truths, etc., but to a few highly select disciples he taught *mahāyoga* and *anuyoga*, and particularly the Vimala Nying-tik. Together with his chief translator, Ma Rinchen Chok, he translated important Nyingma *tantras*: the *Guhyagarbha* (*gSang-ba snying-po – The Secret Heart*), and the *Guhyasamāja*, amongst many. Of the Eight Logos Sādhanas he taught the Dud-tsi Yonten, which he had received amongst the Eight Knowledge Holders in the Śītavana Cremation Ground. But unquestionably Vimalamitra's greatest contribution to the Nyingma *dharma*, perhaps the pinnacle of all Buddhist doctrines, was the Vimala Nying-tik, which is contained in the Secret Precept Class of the Dzokchen *atiyoga* scripture. Further, Go Lotsawa[3] maintains that Vimalamitra contributed thirteen of the eighteen chapters of the Mind Class of precepts. The principal recipients of his Dzokchen instruction were King Trisong Detsen himself, Nyang Tingzin Zangpo, Ma Rinchen Chok and Nyak Jñāna Kumāra. As the Guru of these four, from which all his Tibetan lineages sprung, he is the root of the most important Dzokchen *atiyoga* tradition. The ninth-tenth century period of persecution attenuated the Vimala Nying-tik lineage, as it did the entire Nyingma tradition, and the terma lineages were responsible for its continued vitality. In the fourteenth century Longchen Rabjampa blended the oral (kama) and revealed (terma) transmissions of the Vimala Nying-tik and produced his *Seven Treasures* (*mDzod-bdun*) which are exegesis upon the entire Nyingma tradition from the point of view of the adept of the Vimala Nying-tik. Finally, Vimalamitra left Tibet on pilgrimage to Wu t'ai shan, and he died in China. Among his later incarnations is Jamyang Khyentse Wongpo, the leading figure of the Khampa eclectic renaissance of the nineteenth century. His living representative is Dodrupchen Rimpoche of Gangtok, Sikkim.

Another of Śrī Siṅgha's disciples was a Tibetan monk, a man whose stature in the tradition is almost as great as Vimalamitra and Guru Pema, not the less venerated because he was Tibetan. His name is Vairotsana. When assembling the bright young men who were to translate the Sanskrit scriptures into Tibetan after the foundation of Samye, certain highly auspicious omens led Trisong Detsen to a place called Nyemo Jekhar in Western Tibet where he found the boy Vairotsana. Śāntarakṣita ordained him as one of the first seven probationary monks, and having become proficient in Sanskrit at Samye he was sent to obtain Dzokchen precepts from Śrī Siṅgha in Orgyen. In a nine-storied pagoda in a sandalwood forest near the Dhanakośa Lake Vairotsana found the 'Chinese' monk Śrī Siṅgha. Having proved himself to a Ḍākinī guardian, he begged Śrī Siṅgha for instruction. The Guru condescended to teach him, but only under the condition of rigorous secrecy, because the Orgyen King had proscribed Dzokchen. During the day Vairotsana received *mahāyāna* instruction while at night the Guru wrote down the eighteen chapters of precepts of the Mind Class in goat's milk ink on white paper, cypher that would become legible only when applied to smoke. He also obtained instruction on the Space Class of *atiyoga* precepts and the *tantra* section of *mahāyoga*. Śrī Siṅgha assured him that to understand one *dharma* was to understand them all, but the insatiable student went further into India after his departure from Orgyen, and in the Śītavana Cremation Ground he met Garab Dorje[9] who taught him the 84,000 Dzokchen Precepts. Only then did he return to Tibet.

In Samye he taught Trisong Detsen, Trisong's Khotanese Queen Li-za and Nyak Jñāna Kumāra, and he translated the Mind Class scripture. However, he could not escape the intrigues of the Bon ministers, the agents of the jealous Orgyen King and the Bon-po Queen Pong-za (whose deceits are recorded below). His exile to Tsawarong in Kham was profitable in so far as he established there a Dzokchen lineage that remains vital to this day. He taught on three notable occasions: to Gyelmo Yudra Nyingpo, who was to return to Samye and teach Nyak Jñāna Kumāra and others; to Nyang-ton Yeshe Lama; and to the ancient beggar Sangye Gompo, alias spang Mi-pham, who at the age of eighty-five meditated according to the Space Class of precepts, with the aid of a knee-belt and chin-rest, to attain great longevity. At the intercession of the Khotanese Queen, Vairotsana was recalled to Central Tibet, where he taught for the remainder of his life. His greatest contribution was the Mind Class of precepts; but he also taught the Space Class precepts; he taught Pang Mi-pham the *Vajra Bridge* (*rDo-rje zam-pa*), an important *anuyoga* text; and he translated a commentary upon the *Guhyagarbha-tantra* on *mahāyoga*. Vairotsana was one of the Twenty-five Siddhas of Chimphu, and his principal meditation was upon the Drek-ngak *maṇḍala*. He was one of the privileged few who concealed texts that would become part of the terma transmission.

Then what of Guru Pema himself? It was inevitable that western scholars should attempt to demythologise Tibet's Great Guru.[10] But after the profound layers of myth and legends have been stripped away scholars have found little of substance remaining. Without doubt, they say, Guru Pema was a great exorcist, but it was unlikely that he brought more than the *mahāyoga* Eight Logos Sādhanas with him to Tibet and perhaps only some of those. The amount of indisputable, scientifically verifiable 'fact' we have relating to the early history of the *dharma* in Tibet is minuscule. While we have volumes of myth and legend concerning Padma Saṁbhava, the chronicles are silent and facts are few. But like any founder of a great religious cult, Guru Pema's significance lies in his mythos, in what people believe, not in forgotten fact. The principal fact of the Guru's life is that he had such an impact upon the Tibet of Trisong Detsen that he became the focus of a cult that considered him a Buddha whose teaching was more profound, or certainly more relevant to Tibet, than that of Śākyamuni himself. The cult, of course, evolved later, and the legends accrued later, but can we doubt that the Guru's activity was exemplary, that he was the *vajrayāna dharma* embodied, and that it was his power and realisation that gave the dead scripture existential meaning? Guru Pema was an exorcist and Jesus Christ a carpenter; and no doubt they were both masters of their crafts. There is no proof that Guru Pema initiated the Dzokchen Nying-tik lineage, but on the other hand there is no evidence refuting the later lineal tradition, and, further, there is no good reason to cast doubt on the purity of the lineage.

There is no need to resume the events of Guru Pema's life here. Although there is as yet no satisfactory translation of the Guru's biography available, his career is sufficiently well known. *The Life* is surprisingly short on description, and weak on emphasis, of the part that he played in the unfolding drama of Tsogyel's life. These are the main scenes in *The Life* in which he takes centre stage:

1. His arrival and the foundation of Samye;

2. the initiation of the King and his gift of Tsogyel;
3. Tsogyel's initiations and meditation instruction;
4. The King, Queen and courtiers' initiation into the *sādhanas* of the Eight Logos Deities;
5. the Dorje Phurba initiation, and subjection of gods and demons;
6. the inauguration of the Buddhist-Bon debate and the sentencing of the Bon;
7. hiding the terma;
8. The Guru's testament and his departure for the South-West;
9. Tsogyel's Dzokchen initiation;
10. his appearance in visions at Boudha, Karchung, Tidro etc.

During the forty years, including seven years of exile, that *The Life* implies that the Guru stayed in Tibet, he appears to have spent much of his time in meditation in various caves and meditation centres: Chimphu, Tidro, Womphu Taktsang and Drakmar. Other sources stress his activity of subjecting gods and demons and converting the Bon in the provinces. The Guru is invariably portrayed as a supernal being, a Buddha transcending mortality, and no distinction is made between his corporeal existence and his appearance in vision; indeed, according to the metaphysical view of Dzokchen his ontological status is identical in both forms of being.

Guru Pema's disciples are called 'The Twenty-five Siddhas of Chimphu' or 'The Twenty Five: King, Consort and Subjects' (*rJe-'bangs nyer-lnga*), but different sources vary in their lists of the twenty-five. *The Life* gives these twenty-one names of subjects (or 'courtiers') who received the *mahāyoga* initiation at Chimphu together with the King and the Guru's Consort:

Chogyel Trisong Detsen.

Kharchen-za Yeshe Tsogyel.

Nub Namkhai Nyingpo, or *Lho-drak* Namkhai Nyingpo because he was exiled to Bum-thang for many years, or *Gelong* Namkhai Nyingpo because he was a monk, and possibly one of the first seven probationary monks; he was also a teacher of Tibetan *ch'an*.

Nub Sangye Yeshe, the principal recipient and transmitter of *anuyoga;* a disciple of Vasudhara and Dharmabodhi in Nepal, and Vairotsana in Tibet; the author of the *bSam-gtan mig-sgron;* a concealer of terma.

Nanam Dorje Dunjom, a concealer of terma.

Dre Gyelwa Lodro or Dre *bande*, a minister and perhaps one of the first monks.

Khung-lung Gyelwa Chokyang or Ngan-lam Gyelwa Chokyang, a master of the *Hayagrīva-tantra;* one of the first monks.

Denma Tsemang, a minister and important translator.

Vairotsana, transmitter of the Mind Class of Dzokchen precepts from Śrī Siṅgha; a principal translator and one of the first probationary monks.

Kaba Peltsek, an important minister, messenger and translator; murdered by Langdarma.

Odren Wongchuk, not to be confused with Odren Zhonnu.

Nyak Jñāna Kumāra, a great translator who combined all the Dzokchen lineages, particularly those of Vimalamitra and Vairotsana.

Sokpo Lhapel Zhonnu, sometimes confounded with the other Uigur, Sokpo Yeshe Pel.

Lhalung Pelgyi Senge, or Pelgyi Dorje, who assassinated Langdarma and fled to Kham in AD 842; Trulzhi Rimpoche of Jumbesi is his contemporary tulku.

Chokro Lui Gyeltsen, minister and Kawa Peltsek's associate and co-translator and revisor of the old *tantra*s in Repachan's reign.

Rinchen Zangpo, perhaps Atsara Rinchen (=dbUs Ratna?) one of the first monks.

Nyang Tingzin Zangpo, Trisong Detsen's trusted minister and messenger; guardian of the boy Senalek; Abbot of Samye; proponent of *ch'an;* disciple of Vimalamitra.

Langdro Konchok Jungne, an important translator; reincarnate as Tinle Jampa Jungne in the 19th c.

Lasum Gyelwa Jangchub, Atsara Sale, Tsogyel's yogic partner and editor of *The Life* (= Dre Atsara Sale?).

Drenpa Namkha Wongchuk, great *siddha,* translator and Bonpo scholar; author of the *gZer-myig.*

Drokben Khyeuchung Lotsawa, an important translator;

reincarnate as Ratna Lingpa, and at present Dunjom Rimpoche.

Ma Rinchen Chok, a minister, messenger and great translator; one of the first monks; Vimalamitra's chief translator and disciple.

Gyelmo Yudra Nyingpo, received Vairotsana's precepts in Kham and taught in Samye.

Two other siddhas, mentioned in *The Life* as demonstrating *siddhi* at the Bon debate, Tsang-ri Gompo (?) and Odren Zhonnu Pel, complete the list of twenty-five. Dunjom Rimpoche's *History of the Dharma* and other sources list these *siddha*s amongst the twenty-five: Atsara Yeshe Pelyang (= Nyen Pelyang), Yeshe De, Drok Pelgyi Yeshe, Kharchen Pelgyi Wongchuk (Tsogyel's brother), Nanam Zhang Yeshe Dorje and Shubu Pelgyi Senge (a minister and messenger and Tsogyel's disciple). Dunjom Rimpoche also gives a list of seventeen Ḍākinīs, ladies of high rank, who were initiated with the twenty-four *yogin*s at Chimphu.

Tsogyel's eleven root disciples are named in *The Life* as Be Yeshe Nyingpo, Ma Rinchen Chok, Odren Zhonnu Pel, Langlab Gyelwa Jangchub Dorje, Lasum Gyelwa Jangchub (Atsara Sale), Darcha Dorje Pawo, Ukyi Nyima (Surya Tepa), Monmo Tashi Khyidren, Kalasiddhi, Li-za Jangchub Dronma (Trisong's Queen), Shelkar Dorje Tsomo and Kharchen Zhonnu Drolma. Also mentioned as her disciples are King Mutri Tsenpo and his son Murum Tsenpo, and Murum's wife Ngang-chung Pelgyi Gyelmo; her Nepali disciples, Jila Jipha, Vasudhara and Śākya Dema; Gelong Namkhai Nyingpo who Tsogyel taught in Bhutan; and the *yoginī* Demo who she found in Bhutan and who is variously called Dewamo, Chonema and Dechenmo; and Selta and Lodro Kyi who she initiated in Mangyul. It may be inferred that all these disciples lived through Mutri and Murum's reigns and some into Repachan's era.

Śāntarakṣita does not belong to the *anuttarayoga* tantric lineages, but since his significance in the Tibetan tradition can be considered more fundamental than Guru Pema himself, because he introduced the monastic lineage to Tibet, without which there is no *sangha*, his importance should not be overlooked. Known as Khempo Bodhisattwa (the Bodhisattva Abbot) to the

Tibetans, he was born in the Kingdom of Zahor and became Abbot of Nālandā University. First and foremost of the *paṇḍitas* invited to Tibet, he arrived when the Bonpo ministers were still too powerful, and he was forced to retreat to Nepal after strongly advising the King to invite Guru Pema to exorcise the country. After his return to Samye he ordained the seven probationary monks, about whose names there is no unanimity.[11] Through this first ordination in Tibet Śāntarakṣita instituted the *Mahāmūlasarvāstivādin* ordination lineage, which remains unbroken until this day. His *mahāyāna* philosophical views have had a powerful impact on all Tibetan thought. He belonged to the *svatantrika-mādhyamika* tradition,[12] but he was of a syncretic turn of mind, strongly influenced by the dialectics of Dingnāga and Dharmakīrti. He wrote several works which had a formative influence on Tibetan thought and were of major import in the development of Indian Buddhist philosophy. His principal Indian disciple was Kamalaśīla, who was to be invited to Samye to defend his school's position against the quietist Chinese *ch'an* masters, should the need arise. The need arose. Śāntarakṣita probably returned to India to die before AD 790.

A part of the reformed schools' compendiums of Indian scripture called the *Kanjur* and *Tenjur* were translated from Sanskrit to Tibetan during the early period of propagation of the doctrine in Tibet. The *Kanjur*, containing the *hīnayāna tripiṭaka*, the *mahāyāna sūtras* and the *tantras*, which comprise the Buddha Śākyamuni's corpus of teaching, and the *Tenjur* containing exegetical works of Indian scholars, saints and *siddhas*, are of great importance to the Old School, but the works omitted from the *Tenjur* by its fundamentalist compiler, Buton, are of even greater importance because they comprise the bulk of *anuttarayogatantra* texts and the works of Guru Pema, Vimalamitra and their lineage holders. These texts were collected and collated into two major collections: the *Nyingma Gyud-bum* (*The 100,000 Nyingma Tantras*) and the *Kama Canon*. *The Nyingma Gyud-bum* was collected by Ratna Lingpa in the fifteenth century; the *Kama Canon* consists of the literary forms of the orally transmitted pronouncements of the Dzokchen Gurus. The principal collection of termas is the *Rinchen Terdzod*, a compendium of selected termas edited by Jamgon Kongtrul and Jamyang Khyentse Wongpo in the nineteenth century.

In general, the teaching of the kama and terma are identical in substance; the entire corpus of literature explains the metaphysics, and instructs in the practical techniques, of the Inner Tantras – *mahāyoga, anuyoga* and *atiyoga* (although some space is given to the Outer Tantras). The major difference between kama and terma lies in the manner of transmission of their substance. The kama is transmitted by the 'long lineage' (*ring-brgyud*), indicating temporal extension of the lineage from a moment in time prior to Guru Pema's birth to the present day. The terma lineages are 'short' or 'direct' lineages (*nye-brgyud*), where 'short' means emanating directly from the extra-temporal sphere, or originating with the discoverer to be transmitted by a short lineage. Although some terma lineages extend back to the early Sovereign Tertons[13] of the later period of propagation of the *dharma* in Tibet, usually the termas the practitioner uses are those of his Guru or of his Guru's Guru. Specifically, there are three kama lineages, each defined by its method of transmission ('transmission' is used here as a synonym of 'lineage'). These three methods of transmission are the Buddhas' Mind to Mind Transmission (*rgyal-ba dgongs-brgyud*); the Knowledge Holders' Symbolic Transmission (*rig-'dzin brda'-brygud*); and the Individual's Whispered Teaching Transmission (*gang-zag snyan-brygud*). Since termas are in essence concealed, and rediscovered, kama teaching the entire Nyingma *dharma* originated, and continues to emanate, through one of these modes of transmission. Capable of different levels of interpretation the relevant level is determined by the interpreter's didactic purpose. One important purpose is to endow kama and terma texts with authority, and another is to provide a metaphysical basis for the doctrine of direct revelation of 'mind-treasures'.

The Buddhas' Mind to Mind Transmission is taught unremittingly by Kuntuzangpo in the *dharmakāya*. The *yogin* who accomplishes the *dharmakāya* immediately receives the totality of Kuntuzangpo's transmission. In the *saṃbhogakāya* the same message is transmitted by the Five Dhyāni Buddhas as light-form. In the *nirmāṇakāya* the supernal Bodhisattvas – Mañjuśrī, Avalokiteśvara and particularly Vajrapāṇi (Guhyapati) – transmit Mind to Mind to those beings who transport themselves through meditation practice to the Bodhisattva's own Buddhafield. In short, the Mind to Mind Transmission is effected by the *yogin*'s accomplishment of the three modes of Buddha's being.

The Knowledge Holders' Symbolic Transmission can be defined by distinguishing between two forms of transmission – 'word transmission' and 'meaning transmission' (*tshig-brgyud* and *don-brgyud*). Transmission of meaning is affected by a Knowledge Holders' intentional disposition of Body, Speech and Mind as a free-play of Knowledge (*rig-pa*) in a form determined by the spiritual potential of the recipient, and understood by him as a blessing (*byin-brlab*) or 'wave of grace'. The 'word transmission' is Vajrapāṇi or Vajrasattva's transmission of verbal symbols that contain the condensed content of a text or doctrine. For example, Vajrapāṇi transmitted symbols containing the verbal key to the *sPyi-mdo dgongs-'dus*, an *anuyoga sūtra,* to a group of Knowledge Holders, one of whom, a Rakṣasa, translated the symbols into manuscript form.[14] The Knowledge Holders played an important role in revealing the kama scriptures.

The Individual's Whispered Teaching Transmission is a temporal lineage founded by a *nirmāṇakāya* incarnation who has received the essence of the doctrine through Mind to Mind Transmission from a Buddha, or as a symbolic transmission from the Knowledge Holders. Taking the Dzokchen *atiyoga* lineage of whispered teaching as an example, Garab Dorje received the doctrine from Vajrasattva in direct Mind to Mind Transmission. The teaching was then passed down from mouth to ear as the essential Dzokchen precepts. These precepts were written down by Garab Dorje, Vimalamitra and Vairotsana and have come down to us as the kama texts of the Mind, Space and Secret Precept Classes of Dzokchen precepts. But notwithstanding the lineage's attenuation at the time of Langdarma's persecution it is taught that the oral transmission has also been transmitted vocally from Garab Dorje's time to the present day and constitutes the oral commentary given by the initiate's Dzokchen Lama on the kama texts. Thus kama can be defined as the original word, logos, or pronouncements of the Indian Gurus of the Inner Tantra, transmitted orally or written down in a literary form in India and translated during the early period of propagation of the *dharma* in Tibet, or written down directly in Tibetan during the same period. Since all terma was derived from kama, kama can be viewed as the 'mother' lode and termas as the 'son' caches.

The reformed schools considered the kama texts to be spurious scripture; they doubted that any Sanskrit originals ever existed. The implication was that Guru Pema, Vimalamitra, Vairotsana and Sangye Yeshe in particular were heretics, that their realisation was not of the order of King Dza (Indrabhūti), and that their oral transmission was invalid. Literary reasons were also given for rejecting translations made in the early period, but essentially Buton was prejudiced against any Old School doctrine that was even remotely tainted by the ideas that Kamalaśīla reputedly refuted in the Great Debate of Samye. This prejudice resulted in exclusion of some of the most profound tantric texts from the great *Kanjur* and *Tenjur* collections, texts that had their genesis in Kashmir, Orgyen, Gilgit – North-west India – where Chinese influence was strong.

The kama texts are subsumed conventionally under three heads: *sūtra*, *māyā* and mind (*mdo-sgyu-sems gsum*). *Sūtra* refers to the *anuyoga* literature, and means 'tantric exposition'. The *sPyi-mdo dgongs-'dus* (*Chido Gong-du*) is probably the most famous of these *sūtra*s. *Māyā* refers to the *mahāyoga* Net of Illusion (*sGyu-'phrul dra-ba*) cycle of *tantra*s. The *Guhyagarbha* is the most important *tantra* in this cycle. 'Mind' indicates the three classes of *atiyoga* precepts – Mind, Space and Secret Precepts. As noted above, the termas are highly practical applications of the kama doctrines. The kama tradition is still alive, but in general practitioners use terma texts for their daily ritual meditation and for every exceptional occasion such as rites of passage and advanced *yoga* practices.

The notion of terma is not an original Tibetan idea. The first termas were the *Prajñāpāramitā-sūtra*s which the Buddha Śākyamuni had hidden in the *nāga* realms until the time propitious for their propagation, and which Ārya Nāgārjuna discovered in the second century AD. The canonical *tantra*s 'discovered' in the Orgyen Ḍākinī Paradise (*Orgyan mkha'-'gro gling*) and those relating to the south of India (Dhānyakaṭaka) are also termas of a kind.[15] In Tibet termas were concealed by Guru Pema and Tsogyel, by Vairotsana, Sangye Yeshe, Namkhai Nyingpo, Jñāna Kumāra, Dorje Dunjom, Tingzin Zangpo and others during the latter part of the eighth century and the early ninth. Undoubtedly more were hidden during the following period of political turmoil. Two hundred years later these termas began to be rediscovered. Sangye Lama (1000–1080) is remembered as the first treasure-finder. Innumerable termas were discovered by many tertons during the later period of propagation of the doctrine in Tibet, and the period up to the end of the fourteenth century was the great period of discovery. Even Atīśa himself, the reformer of the monastic tradition who abhorred 'loose' tantric practices, discovered a chronicle (*dkar-chag*) in a pillar in the Rasa Trulnang Temple in Lhasa.

It will be useful first to make a superficial distinction that is often ignored by the Nyingmapas themselves, between those sacred artefacts – images, *stūpas*, *vajras*, *phur-bas*, and most important, manuscripts – that have been actually concealed by human hands in caves, in temple walls and other places of safe keeping during times of persecution, and those artefacts and books that were, and are still, discovered as pure creations of an enlightened spirit. But these categories overlap. First, both categories of artefacts are said to have been consciously hidden by Guru Pema and his contemporary *siddhas*; second, many literary termas are inspired re-editions of ancient termas; third, tertons often appended apocryphal colophons to their works to give them the authority exerted by the doctrine of revelation, thereby obscuring the texts' origins. To the *yogins* of the terma lineage, all termas have the same status, no matter what their origin or whether the discovery was made in the earth or in the sky; but a sceptic who demands the authority of Indian origins attached to his texts will look askance at the cryptic label *dgongs-gter* ('mind-treasure') in the colophon of a manuscript. In the largest category of terma, liturgies of ritual meditation (*sgrub-thabs*), there have been no major departures in metaphysical thought or technique since the eleventh century; the same structural formula is evident today no matter what the text's origin. The literary historian has a difficult, complex task in determining a terma's origin; but for a *yogin* the source is largely immaterial.

The nature of termas is highly complex and ambiguous; it can be defined in terms of the three different methods whereby the terton is empowered to reveal termas, three different terton lineages. These three lineages are the 'short' or 'direct' lineage of transmission as distinct from the 'long', or temporal, kama lineages. The first of these three is the Lineage of Command and Authorisation through Prophecy (*bka'-babs lung-bstan brgyud*), command that may have issued from Guru Pema in a vision or from a prophecy contained in the scriptures. The ninety-third chapter of the Guru's biography called the *Padma bKa'-thang Shel-brag-ma* gives prophecies of fifty tertons, most of whom had lived or who subsequently appeared. The second lineage is the Transmission of Initiation and Empowerment through Aspiration and Resolution (*smon-lam dbang-skur brgyud*); the prayer of a Buddha in the *dharmakāya* has sufficient force to empower his *nirmāṇakāya* emanation as a terton. To the third lineage belong those tertons to whom specific termas are entrusted by Ḍākinīs (*mkha'-'gro gtad-rgya brgyud*); the archetypes of this lineage are the Eight Knowledge Holders who were entrusted texts by the Ḍākinī Pleasure Power,[16] removing them from the *stūpa* in the Śītavana Cremation Ground (the *stūpa* is a representation of the *dharmakāya*). One branch of this lineage is Transmission through the Yellow Parchment Cypher Lineage (*shog-ser tshig brgyud*) – an Awareness Ḍākinī entrusts a sealed scroll to the appropriate terton. The nature of the cypher on the parchment may be Sanskrit or Apabhraṃśa; it may be the language of Orgyen, from which Orgyen Lingpa, for instance, translated the *Sheldrakma*; or it may be the Ḍākinī cypher itself (*mkha'-'gro brda'-yig*). When a terton has difficulty in translating a cypher he will reconceal the terma.

The Ḍākinī cypher, says the Lama, can be understood only by initiated tertons, and this initiation is one of the deepest mysteries of the Tantra. Yeshe Tsogyel wrote many termas in the Ḍākinī script; this script may be understood as a highly condensed symbolic language. The few symbols deciphered to construe an entire chapter of a terma often preface that chapter. Some texts Tsogyel reduced to a single cypher and then concealed them in one of the five elements, in earth, rock, water, trees, fire, wind or sky, etc. The terton versed in the interpretation of such cypher expands the original single hieroglyph into the Ḍākinī language and then into an extended manuscript form in Tibetan. Such termas are called 'earth-treasure' (*sa-gter*), 'fire-treasure' (*me-gter*), 'wind-treasure' (*rlung-gter*), etc. Thus the ripples of a lake, the glyph formed by the bark of a tree, a constellation of clouds, may be the original seed-cypher. If a terton reveals such a treasure and finds the time is unpropitious he will reconceal it, and it may be re-discovered later as a 'twice-revealed treasure' (*yang-gter*). Ḍākinī cypher revealed as 'mind-treasure' (*dgongs-gter*) or 'profound treasure' (*zab-gter*) may be conceived in this manner: The Adibuddha Kuntuzangpo is the indeterminate ground of all being and experience, and his three modes of being embrace all things under the sun. Every entity of existence, or synonymously, every point-instant of experience, is a divine cypher of the totality of being in the same way that each point of light in a hologram contains the entire hologrammic vision, or each cell of the body contains in potential the entire psycho-organism. A point-instant of experience is an emanation of Kuntuzangpo, a cypher of Kuntuzangpo, but its form is heterogenous and enigmatic, analogous to an apparently meaningless, unique Taoist magical diagram. This cypher is described in terms of its universal, metaphysical infrastructure that is represented in Tantra by a complex *maṇḍala* of Buddhas loaded with intentional significance. When a terton 'discovers' a particular cypher that is the key to a disciple's realisation of Buddhahood, or to the attainment of a certain *siddhi,* it is in terms of a *maṇḍala* of Buddhas that he translates it into a descriptive *tantra,* or liturgical manuscript form. But only tertons can read the language of the Ḍākinīs, and without the Ḍākinī's initiation into her mystic language (*mkha'-'gro gsang-brda'-i dbang*) we fumble in the dark.

The most convenient categorisation of terma is three-fold: 'earth-treasure', or ancient manuscripts discovered by human hands; 'twice-revealed treasure', which includes terma from every source, not excepting terma of dubious origin; and 'mind-treasure' that is the prerogative of the visionary. In general, the manuscripts that were hidden in the eighth and ninth centuries were discovered during the following few centuries, and there have been fewer and fewer ancient texts coming to light since – the Tun Huang stash discovered by Sir Aurel Stein in 1907 is an important exception – and no doubt ancient manuscripts can still be found in caves, *stūpas*, and temples in Tibet. In the nineteenth century the Old School eclectic masters of the Kham renaissance left the defensive in the centuries-old battle with the reformed schools' insistent, uncompromising demand for proven Indian origin of didactic texts and propounded an unequivocal doctrine of mystical origin of their 'mind-treasures'.[17] Most termas discovered these days are mind-treasures.

Two important conditions govern the moment of revelation of a terma. First, a terton must have realised the spiritual potential necessary to propagate the apocalyptic message contained in the terma; and secondly, since every terma is designed to benefit a certain person, a group of disciples or the entire community, according to spiritual, political or social need, at a specific point in time, suitable recipients must be waiting at a propitious juncture. Treasure-finders are invariably emanations (*sprul-pa*) of Guru Pema or emanations of his emanations (*yang-sprul*). United with his consort in fields of lotus light (the clear light of the *dharmakāya*), the Guru projects emanations in the *nirmāṇakāya* to perform the terton's bodhisattvic activities. These tertons need only to understand their origin and purpose to realise their power and fulfil their functions as tertons. Illiterate tertons are not unknown. Immediately transferred to the realm where the truths of the Guru's doctrines are self-evident and the meaning of the Ḍākinī cypher is naturally apparent, the immense and profound self-confidence inherent in the recognition of himself as a tulku-terton goes far to explain the prolific production of some tertons.

The Life stresses the importance of the termas and of Tsogyel's chief *raison d'être* as concealer and custodian of the apocalyptic literature, but the text passes all too quickly over the practical details of concealment and discovery. Tsogyel was a human being with a phenomenal memory which permitted her total recall of all her Guru's discourses and precepts; but she was also an Awareness Ḍākinī, and the personification of the wisdom (*prajñā*) that is the 'meaning' of all scripture, and also the embodiment of all Awareness Ḍākinīs who would present yellow parchment scrolls to tertons of the future. Namkhai Nyingpo, Denma Tsemang, Atsara Pelyang, Chokro Lui Gyeltsen, Yudra Nyingpo and Vairotsana are mentioned by name as her assistants in writing down the termas, although all twenty-five of the Siddhas of Chimphu were involved. The termas were written in Sanskrit, Newari, the languages of Gilgit and Orgyen and in various Tibetan styles of writing, in the Ḍākinī script and in letters of fire, water and air. The texts were then 'collated' according to manifests (*kha -byang*) of various types. The simple manifest is a list of texts; the concise manifest (*snying-byang*) is a short cryptic list; lists of termas to be reconcealed (*yang-byang*) anticipate discovery at an unpropitious moment; and extensive prophetic catalogues (*lung-byang*) give cryptic indications of discoverers' names, the circumstances of revelation, the name of the text and its whereabouts – the manifest in the *Sheldrakma* foretelling the tertons of undisputed pre-eminence is of this nature. *The Life* makes clear that the function of these manifests is to inspire trust and confidence, to imbue a terton's discoveries with the authority of the Guru.

Before *The Life*'s explicit description of the manner in which the termas were concealed, a crucial statement is made identifying Guru Pema and Tsogyel as Kuntuzangpo and his Consort Kuntuzangmo. Guru and Consort indivisible they are 'co-extensive with all-pervasive space'; they are the union of ideal cognitive fields (*ye-shes, jñāna*) and ideal spatio-temporal fields (*dharmadhātu*); their apparitional bodies (*nirmāṇakāya*) are the nature of all phenomena, and their Speech (*saṃbhogakāya*) is the nature of all sound. With this realisation we can then read how Guru and Consort wander throughout the ethnic Tibetan world, from power place to power place, blessing the ground, praying for the success of *yogins* who meditate there, exhorting protectors (*gter-skyong*) to guard the terma, concealing the termas themselves and hiding the manifests, sometimes with the caches of terma and sometimes without, until 'not a sod of earth lacked blessing'. The entire passage in *The Life* treating terma (pp. 122–4) is a fine example of the way in which realistic analogue and metaphysical dogma is mixed in tantric literature; it has the effect of breaking the readers' habit of critical, judgmental thought (*rnam-rtog*), transporting him into a mystical universe where there is no distinction between fact and fiction, 'reality' and 'illusion'.

As to the content of the termas, *The Life* identifies the methods of accomplishing the Lama's Mind (*thugs-sgrub*) and similar ritual meditation liturgies (*sgrub-thabs*) belonging to the heart-drop cycles (*snying-thig*) as the most profuse. Together with the meditation rites of Lama, Yidam and Ḍākinī (*rtsa gsum*) these texts originate from the *sādhana* section of *mahāyoga* in the kama lineage. The major tertons discovered *sādhanas* that give their disciples entrance to the *maṇḍala*s of Lama, Yidam and Ḍākinī, most drawing upon the Eight Logos Deities for a Yidam. The *sādhana* section of the *Rinchen Terdzod* collection of termas is by far the largest of its sections. Besides root *tantra*s, exegetical works, and books of precepts for all kinds of *yoga*s, the biographies of Guru Pema (*Guru rnam-thar*) and other legendary works are highly significant termas, and another large class of terma, a genre omitted from the chief collections, consists of texts propitiating local spirits and gods and demons, exorcising them or invoking them to fulfil purposes of a lower ethical order. To be cynical, one could say that if an author wishes to endow his work with the authority of the tradition he declares himself a terton and his work a terma no matter what the content of the text. Indeed, down the centuries periodic rashes of spurious termas treating low-level magic and its rites have appeared, the products of bogus tertons acting through self-initiation.

The subject of terma is vast and deep and these remarks have merely scratched the surface of the matter. However, it should be evident that the doctrine of revelation is far more than a skilful means of keeping the *dharma* out of the hands of scholarly morticians by constantly revivifying the lineages with texts fulfilling contemporary need. *Anuttarayoga-tantra* offers initiation into lineages that provide direct access to the Buddha-nature (*tathāgata-garbha*) and to the pure inspiration that is capable of creating 'treasures' of value equal to Guru Pema's own teaching. The ramifications of the terma doctrine sharply define the difference between the Old and the New Schools. The Old School has little respect for the authority of Indian texts *per se*; the spirit is more important than the letter. The genius of Tibet and its mystics is the mainspring of the Old School's tradition; Śākyamuni belonged to another time and place. Guru Pema, the Second Buddha, is more important than the first both as an exemplar of Buddhahood and as a fount of meditation teaching. Finally, since initiation can be had from internal, transcendental sources, and Guru Pema, Guru Rimpoche, is every Lama and accessible to all, there is a tendency towards an independence that leads to true spiritual anarchy and personal freedom, militating against communal religion, institutionalisation and establishmentarianism.

Although several of the Dalai Lamas have been covert practitioners of Dzokchen (the Great Fifth was a terton) the notion that Dzokchen was tainted by non-Buddhist and heretical schools at its inception has always persisted. Several distinguished Yellow Hat pundits have stooped to most undistinguished invective and vilification of the Old School. The historian Sumpa Khempo is one such eighteenth-century scholar who became emotionally involved in this purely academic debate. It is difficult to understand why companions on the same path should curse each others' techniques of endeavour; but it certainly happened in Tibet, and it is still happening in refugee communities and even amongst Western converts to the Tantra. But after extracting the invective there does seem to be some truth in Dzokchen's detractors' claim that nascent Dzokchen was influenced by hetrerodox schools and perhaps by Śaivism. Because these influences have made Dzokchen what it is, and because elements of the original synthesis are still affective, it is interesting to examine the ground in which the lineage took root.

Ch'an bloomed in T'ang China. The missions arriving in Central Tibet from China during Trisong Detsen's reign were probably practitioners of *ch'an*. The *ch'an* master Hwashang Mahāyāna taught at Samye for some years.[18] One of the accusations levelled against Dzokchen is that it was heavily influenced by heretical *ch'an*. Certainly there are superficial similarities between Dzokchen and *ch'an*: they both claim to be short-cut paths to Buddhahood; both employ *yoga*s derived from non-Buddhist traditions (Śaivism and Taoism); both lay strong emphasis upon the importance of the Guru; both employ paradox and *koan* as skilful means. Then on a deeper level: both stress the immanence of Buddha-nature; both maintain the view of all phenomena and existence as pure from the beginning, *ab initio, ab aeterno*; both use undiscriminating activity as a fast method of personal evolution; and both are non-dual schools. Although Dzokchen employs a more rigorous, non-dualistic dialectic than *ch'an*, unequivocally maintaining the middle path, rejecting the concepts of both 'sudden' and 'gradual' awakening, in practice the methods that the tradition uses in common with *ch'an* produce a sudden awakening; spontaneity (*lhun-grub*) is the key work in Dzokchen togal, and the Tibetan names for the adherents of the Dzokchen Nying-tik (*snying-thig-*

pa) and *ch'an* (*chig-car-pa*) are virtually synonymous. Further, some *ch'an* hierarchs were also links in the Dzokchen lineage and vice versa. Namkhai Nyingpo was an initiate of both schools, and Aro Yeshe Jungne was the seventh link in both the Tibetan *ch'an* and the Dzokchen lineages,[19] founding a Dzokchen school in Kham. Then dissimilarities should be noted: the salient 'quietist' aspect of *ch'an* is not stressed in Dzokchen theory (although in practice some Dzokchen lineages insist upon years of total sensory deprivation); *ch'an* emphasises 'suppression of thought', while the Dzokchen precept is 'without acceptance or rejection', 'without suppression or cultivation'. Explicitly, Dzokchen allows entry to the *maṇḍala* through any door and every door, whereas *ch'an* insists upon its narrow quietist methods.

There is not sufficient evidence to prove that Dzokchen was derived from *ch'an*, but it is reasonable to assume a strong formative influence. Although some Dzokchen lineages may have assimilated some techniques and modes of expression from the Tibetan *ch'an* of Hwashang Mahāyāna and his lineage, it is probable that basic Dzokchen texts (particularly of the Vimala Nying-tik) had become virtually inviolable by the time they were taught in Tibet, and thus they had become impervious to Chinese influence. *Ch'an*'s formative influence would have been effective in the land of Dzokchen's birth, Orgyen, and through the 'Chinese' Guru Śrī Siṅgha and his disciples. Orgyen lay on the southern branch of the silk route that passed over the Hindu Kush and into Chinese Turkestan. The silk route was the great ancient highway that facilitated cultural intercourse between China and India, and in the eighth century China sent *ch'an* to North-west India with the pilgrims who passed through *en route* to Āryāvarta and with the scholars who came to study in the academies of the area. In the eighth century Kashmir was experiencing the climax of its creative cultural efflorescence. It was the most vital of the four great Indian centres of Buddhist learning;[20] it was creating incomparable art; and it produced the non-dual school of Kashmiri Śaivism with which Buddhist Tantra had an important creative interaction. The pre-Muslim history of both Kashmir and Orgyen is obscure, but it appears that they were both Śāhī kingdoms[21] with a shared culture, if not political ties; their bronze casting provides sufficient evidence of their cultural alliance. Thus we assume that students of Orgyen and Kashmir studied with visiting Serindian teachers of *ch'an* who were eager to propagate their vital doctrine, and, thereby, *ch'an* became known to the *yogins* of the Indian North-west.

As for Śrī Siṅgha we have no evidence that he was an adherent of *ch'an*, and again we can only posit assumptions that appear reasonable and fit the facts of legend. There is no evidence that Śrī Siṅgha was an ethnic Chinese; but he was a Chinese citizen, living in Turkestan or Kansu, trained in the Buddhist disciplines current in Chinese monasteries, which included Taoist tainted *prajñāpāramitā* and *ch'an*. Śrī Siṅgha is not a name that could have been translated from Chinese, and it is a name that would be congruous amongst the names of the indigenous Indo-Iranian inhabitants of the oasis city states of Turkestan. The towns associated with Śrī Siṅgha, Tashi Tigo and So-khyam, are probably to be found in Turkestan (or possibly Kansu), for no better reason than if they were located in southern China, as some have suggested, the Guru and his disciples would have spent more time on the road travelling to and from India than practising yoga.[22] We may speculate that the Wut'aishan where Śrī Siṅgha studied was Khotan, which was a centre of Mañjuśrī's cult, a drained valley-lake surrounded by peaks, and one of the few places in T'ang China where it was possible to study the *tantras*. Both before and after King Trisong invited him to Tibet, the pre-eminent proponent of Tibetan *ch'an*, Hwashang Mahāyāna, lived in a *ch'an* community in Tun Huang where certain of the school's texts were written down; thus indisputably *ch'an* flourished in Turkestan. Śrī Siṅgha died on his way to visit the King of Khotan to whom he was known. If the religious life of North-west India and Chinese Turkestan, its neighbour, were inter-related and *ch'an* was known in both areas the source of the *ch'an* influence on Dzokchen is self-evident.

That Orgyen was the cradle of Dzokchen is indisputable, and more specifically, the Dhanakośa Lake has the same relation to Dzokchen as Bodh Gaya has to *hīnayāna* and Gṛdhrakūta to the *mahāyāna*. Vajrapāṇi taught Dzokchen to the Knowledge Holders at Dhanakośa;[23] Garab Dorje taught Mañjuśrīmitra there; Śrī Siṅgha taught Vairotsana near the lake; Garab Dorje was conceived by a virgin in Orgyen, and Padma Saṃbhava was born in the pollen bed of a lotus on the lake; Vimalamitra was born in 'Western India' and was discovered by Trisong's messengers at the King of Orgyen's court; he was known as the Kashmiri Paṇḍita. Indrabhūti (King Dza), the initiator of the *anuyoga* lineage, was King of Orgyen. Several *tantras*, including the *Guhyasamāja*, were revealed there. Orgyen was an important power place (*pīṭhasthāna*) amongst the twenty-four spots sacred to the practitioners of the *Cakrasaṃvara* and *Hevajra-tantras* and also to *śāktas* worshipping Mahādeva and Ūmā. The Chinese pilgrim Huan Tsang records observing many *yogins* covered in ashes or wearing bone ornaments only in Orgyen.[24] It was in Orgyen, then, that Garab Dorje had Dzokchen revealed to him, and where he formulated its expression using the literary modes available to him and employing whatever *yoga* techniques proved efficacious regardless of their origin. A thorough study of Kashmiri Śaivism would probably reveal loans to Dzokchen other than certain togal *yoga* exercises. The contribution of *ch'an* with its Taoist-flavoured paradoxical elements, meditation techniques, and perhaps the books that Jñānasūtra brought back from China, may have been assimilated further down the lineage. But primarily Dzokchen is the quintessence of the Indian Buddhist *tantras*, and it had lain incipient in the great root *tantras* awaiting the genius of Garab Dorje to distil it and dispense with the dross.

Another school which claims to teach the quintessence of the *tantras* was in the process of glorious conception in the same century as Dzokchen. The *adi-guru* of the *mahāmudrā* lineage riding the 'vehicle of spontaneity' (*sahajayāna*) to imminent Buddhahood was the Great Brahmin Saraha, who lived in the latter part of the eighth century.[25] Some features of *ch'an* were also traits of this *siddha* tradition: anti-scholasticism, anti-monasticism, use of *haṭhayoga* techniques, and use of paradox as skilful means (although the *siddhas'* mystic teaching-songs, the *caryāpādas*, contain a notion of the absurd quite distinct from that of the Chinese). Many of the *mahāmudrā siddhas* were well grounded in the scholarship that they abandoned, and because they never departed from the Bodhisattva path they avoided conflict with orthodox mahāyānists. The metaphysical, didactic *dohākośas* of Saraha, Vīrupā, Tīlopā and Nāropā[26] translated into

Tibetan in part by Vairotsana, is *mahāmudrā* instruction (*upadeśa*) that could be accepted *in toto* by Dzokchen *yogins*, particularly the expression of vision (*lta-ba*). Was there mutual exchange of ideas between two independently arisen *siddha* schools, Mahāmudrā and Dzokchen? Or was Orgyen the source of the quintessential *vajrayāna* doctrines, ideas that were to spread gradually across northern India to Bodh Gaya, Nālandā and Vikramaśīla, carried by wandering *siddhas* from the western Himālayas? The *mahāmudrā* lineages of the Eighty-four Mahāsiddhas include some *yogins* who were born or operated in the North-west, and some of these (Lwa-ba-pa, Indrabhūti, Kukurāja) belong to the *anuyoga* lineage. The spheres of activity of the two schools of *siddhas* would have overlapped in Bodh Gaya, where Dzokchen was taught in the Śītavana Cremation Ground.

Finally, the Reformed Bon believe that Dzokchen had its genesis in Tibet, and that the Bon Master, Shenrab, is the *adi-guru* of the Dzokchen lineage. According to Bon texts, Shenrab was a native of Western Turkestan (Tazik),[27] west of the Pamirs, and he made only one or two visits to Zhang-zhung in western Tibet where he taught his Dzokchen doctrines. Shenrab is believed to have taught in Tibet long before the seventh-century King Songtsen Gampo's reign. After their assimilation in Zhang-zhung his doctrines were taught in Central Tibet, where in the reign of Trisong Detsen they were systematised, using a *vajrayāna* framework and *vajrayāna* terminology, as the Bonpo Dzokchen of the *A-khri* and *Zhang-zhung snyan-brgyud* lineages. In this case the metaphysics and *yogas* that would have impinged upon nascent Dzokchen would have been those of Central Asian Manichaeism, Zhang-zhung Bon, the Buddhist Tantra and Kashmiri Śaivism. It should be noted that Shenrab's native country, Tazik, is contiguous to North-west India, and to refrain from dismissing the Bonpo claim peremptorily, it is possible to posit a common origin of Buddhist and Bon Dzokchen doctrines. The Bonpo theory gives more power to the Tibetan people and disdains the possibility of an Indian provenance of their most exalted *yoga*. It is also the most extravagant conjecture in a welter of unfounded conjecture about the origin of Dzokchen.

One final flight of fancy: if the Dzokchen texts were not in an immutable form when Vimalamitra taught in Tibet, we can imagine a metaphorical scenario during Trisong Detsen's reign wherein mystics of genius and high existential praxis and realisation belonging to the Orgyen Dzokchen, Tibetan *ch'an*, Mahāmudrā and Reformed Bon schools gathered in Samye from China, Turkestan, Kashmir, Orgyen, Nālandā, Nepal, Baṅgala, Zhang-zhung and Central Tibet, and in an ambience in which the spirit of the *dharma* prevailed over the letter they crystallised the *atiyoga* incipient in all their traditions creating a ninth vehicle to Buddhahood. Both kama and terma texts would have been the outcome, written down by Vairotsana, Jñāna Kumāra, Ma Rinchen Chok and others. Regarding its two aspects, metaphysics and *yoga* techniques, Dzokchen's non-dual metaphysics are then the distilled essence of many Buddhist schools' doctrines; and as for Dzokchen's *yoga* techniques, their heterogeneity is explained by the diversity of foreign *yogin*s in Samye. Such a congress of *yogin*s would have been orchestrated by Guru Pema himself. This hypothesis would support the Old School belief that Guru Pema alone formulated the doctrines that were to be hidden as terma, the Dzokchen Padma Nying-tik, a system parallel to the Vimala Nying-tik. But to answer those critics who believe that the Guru taught only *mahāyoga* precepts in Tibet, he must have been aware of the dynamic new *yoga* emanating from his homeland of Orgyen, and after instruction by *dharmakāya* or *saṃbhogakāya* deities he could have achieved Dzokchen realisation with or without instruction from a lineal Guru before arriving in Tibet. Thus he could have taught the Eight Logos Sādhanas of *mahāyoga* within a Dzokchen framework.

The Reformed Bonpos' claim to be the originators of Dzokchen was probably motivated by a defensive chauvinism provoked by the zealous and highly successful Buddhist missionaries. Undoubtedly the Reformed Bonpos borrowed shamelessly from the Nyingma *tantra*s, working on the principle 'If you can't beat them, join them'. But the movement from Buddhism to Bon was by no means a one-way flow. By the end of the period of the later spreading of the doctrine the Old School had absorbed important elements of the Reformed Bon tradition. The liturgical forms of various Bonpo rites had been absorbed through Bon termas hidden at the time of Trisong

Detsen's persecution. Some Dzokchen doctrines were reabsorbed in the same way. Peculiarly Tibetan concepts had been assimilated, including numerological devices: the sacred Bonpo numbers 9 and 13 were employed by the Old School. Bon rites propitiating or exorcising local deities were given a Buddhist tantric framework. Guru Pema had subjugated the entire Bon pantheon, and Tibetan gods and demons were now considered at best as protectors of the Buddha *dharma* and at least as servants of the tantric *yogin*. The Nyingma *yogin*-priest, the ngakpa (*sngags-pa*), appropriated many of the functions of the Bon-shaman, satisfying the religious needs of ordinary people concerned with rites of passage, exorcism and prognostication. Eventually there was little practical difference between Reformed Bonpo and Nyingma ngak-pas, both wandering magician-priests performing ritual magical functions.

Two important rites containing elements of the indigenous Tibetan religion are the Long-life Empowerment (*tshe-dbang*) and death rites (rites of the *bar-do*). The former is, in essence, a eucharistic sacrament, and it has been suggested that the Nestorian Christians brought its antecedent ritual to Tibet – there was a sufficient number of Tibetan Christians to merit a Nestorian Bishop of Tibet. 'Bread' and 'wine' are sanctified by the power of the principal of the *maṇḍala* disclosed for the purpose – Amitāyus, Avalokiteśvara or Dorje Phurba are commonly invoked – and then the consecrated 'host' is distributed and consumed by the communicants who thus gain longevity. On an esoteric plane, the *yogin* is initiated into the state of the Immortal Knowledge Holder (*tshe-yi-dbang-la rig-'dzin*), and substantiating that power through *yoga* techniques he attains control over his life-span. The Bonpo bardo rites that guided the soul (*bla*) as it winged its way through the phantasmagoric realms of the spirits to the heavens of Mu, Cha or Yang, influenced the Buddhist *tantrikas*' guide to 'the principle of consciousness' (*shes-pa*) striving to attain a pure-land. The forty-nine day journey in the tantric rite is structured according to the process of efflorescence of the *maṇḍala* of the Wrathful and Peaceful Deities (Zhi-khro lha), which is a specifically Nyingma *maṇḍala*. On an esoteric level, the bardo rite is a *mahāyoga* ritual meditation for attainment of Buddhahood here and now. *The Tibetan Book of the Dead* (*Bar-do thos-grol*),[28] which contains these rites, is a terma which like many other termas (including *The Life*) is probably edited from lost sources, in this case both Indian Buddhist and Reformed Bonpo.

Together with these rites the Nyingma *yogin*s borrowed several very important ritual instruments from the Bonpos. The large two-faced drum is well-known in Siberian shamanism where it is used for conjuring spirits, inducing trance and for transportation into spirit realms like the broomstick of a witch; it is used by Buddhist *tantrika*s to invoke raging deities, and gods and demons. The phurba (*phur-bu* is the diminutive form), or magical dagger, is of immense importance to the Nyingma *yogin*, and although it was known in India its close association with the shamanistic world compels the conclusion that the Bonpos also wielded a magical dagger, though not the 'dagger of Emptiness'. There is no representation of the phurba in Indian stone or bronze art, and there is no mention of it in the legends of the *Mahāsiddha*s or in their songs: it would have been the *siddha*s who carried it. In the *Saṃbara-tantra* guardians of the *maṇḍala* are armed with the phurba to transfix evil spirits who trespass into the magic circle, but here it is the unique weapon of insignificant protectors.[29] On the contrary, in the Bonpo world the demon-transfixing phurba is ubiquitous and of central importance. Both Buddhist and Bon ngakpas always carry one in their belts. King Mutik-tsenpo (early ninth century) went into battle with a cohort of phurba – wielding officers on his left hand.[30] When Guru Pema arrived in shamanistic eighth-century Nepal he exorcised and subjected a class of demons called Phurba Protectors (*Phur-srung*);[31] this is, perhaps, a reference to a local class of shamans who used the phurba. Even today every Nepali *jaṅkri* (healer and exorcist) must carve his own wooden phurba (in Newari *forba*) as an initiatory exercise, and the Buddhist Tamangs, ethnic Tibetans who are believed to have entered Nepal in the seventh century, employ *jaṅkri*s called *bon* who use the phurba in their rites of healing. Little is known of the early history of the phurba, but a close study of old Bonpo texts would probably reveal the Bonpos' independent, pre-Buddhist, use of it.

The origin of the phurba is closely associated with the origin of the *Dorje Phurba Tantra*; Dorje Phurba is one of the Eight Logos Deities and the most popular Nyingma Yidam. Guru

Pema brought the *tantra* to Tibet after he had received initiation from several sources: he was initiated directly by deities of the Phurba *maṇḍala;* the Nepali Dhanasaṃskṛta gave him the whispered transmission and initiation into the lineage of King Dza of Orgyen;[32] Prabhahasti, one of the Eight Knowledge Holders, sent him the compendium of Phurba texts called the *Phurba Byitotama* when spirits obstructed his *mahāmudrā* meditation at Yanglesho in Nepal,[33] texts that he had received from the Ḍākinī-guarded *stūpa* in the Śītavana Cremation Ground. Prabhahasti hailed from Zahor, King Dza lived in Orgyen and Dhanasaṃskṛta was Nepali: these three *siddhas* all lived in sub-Himalayan, shamanistic kingdoms (if Prabhahasti's birthplace is Mandi rather than E. Bengal). Some critics denied that the Phurba Tantra was an authentic Sanskrit *tantra;* but Śākya Paṇḍita discovered a short Sanskrit version of a Phurba *tantra* in the thirteenth[34] and Buton included this text in the *Kanjur.* The most important caches of Phurba termas were discovered at Senge Dzong Sum and Taktsang in Bhutan. Although Guru Pema's Dorje Phurba scriptures were translated into Tibetan in the eighth century, the phurba was probably known already through tantric practices relating to Hayagrīva, in which the phurba with the horse's head above its *vajra*-hilt is used. Hayagrīva, the Horse-necked Deity, was perfectly suited to the horse-worshipping, horse-dependent Tibetans with the finest cavalry in Asia; their god-king, Songtsen Gampo, was known as 'Exalted Horse' (rTa-mchog). It seems quite plausible that the Tibetan *tantrikas* harnessed the horse to their sacred phurba. This would be one of the first cases of Bon's amalgamation with Buddhism, and that would have been in the seventh century at the time of Thon-mi Sambhoṭa.

This space devoted to speculation upon formative influences upon the early Nyingma lineage may appear irrelevant to readers who have taken up *The Life* in order to gain insight into the principles and practice of Tantra. But apart from the hedonistic pleasure gained from tantric archaeology and the excavation of mystical Tibetan literature, since religion cannot evolve in a vacuum and is always a human response to a specific political, cultural and geo-physical environment, the purpose of this digression is to prevent mistaking the wood for the trees when approaching Tantra, to identify, even if only by conjecture, some of the factors that have made Tibetan Buddhism what it is. Guru Rimpoche may have been born spontaneously upon a lotus, and Garab Dorje may have been born to a virgin nun, but Tibetan mysticism was not a product of spontaneous combustion in the psyche caused by such factors as oxygen starvation of the brain or over-exposure to ultra-violet rays. Much as Tibet's art is a blend of foreign influences in a Tibetan mould so its religion, and particularly the unreformed schools' religion, is a melding of heterogenous inspirations.

4

THE HISTORICAL BACKGROUND

Yeshe Tsogyel lived during the heroic period of Tibetan history. The Tibetan Empire was at its height, and Tibetan military power was feared throughout Central Asia. The princes of the obscure Tibetan province of Yarlung had become masters of an Empire larger than the Indian sub-continent, and this sudden widening of the horizons of the people of Central Tibet was co-incident with an implosion of knowledge from India and China. Perhaps because it contained the highest knowledge and was the most dynamic religion of the day, and perhaps because the Tibetan temperament demanded such an abstract expression of spirituality, Buddhism was the form of knowledge that filled the vacuum in the minds of the Tibetans, the nobility in particular. But Buddhism was not unopposed; Tibet's first Buddhist king, Trisong Detsen, championing the Buddhist cause, provoked a storm of protest amongst the priests of the old religion and conservative clan leaders, and the politics of the early period of Tsogyel's lifetime is primarily the power play of Buddhists and Bonpos. Concerning foreign affairs, an intermittent war was in progress with China on the eastern frontier; but although a war involving tens of thousnds of Tibetans, and perhaps hundreds of thousands if we are to believe the legends, must have had a profound effect on family life when fathers and sons were absent, gone to war, the Buddhist histories mention the effects of war and Trisong Detsen's campaigns only in passing.

There are innumerable sources for the history of this period, but only two or three are authoritative and reliable. Two of these are the so-called Tun Huang chronicles and Tun Huang annals, and the third is the Chinese *T'ang Annals*, which was translated into Tibetan and incorporated into the fifteenth-century *Red Annals*; even the *Red Annals* is not totally reliable. Otherwise, there are several Tibetan histories which give detailed accounts of the period, but unfortunately these accounts conflict, often in statement of crucial facts. The authors of these histories relied upon ancient texts, but in weaving their stories their didactic purpose overwhelmed any concern for an objective truth that anyway had become distorted by the bard or the clan story-teller by the time it was first written down. The period of political and social turmoil unleashed by Langdarma in the ninth century had an incalculable, disastrous effect upon cultural continuity; it formed a hiatus in the history of Tibet, and but for the three sources mentioned above we would be dependent upon legend for a history of the period of the kings. This is to omit one other source: terma.

Termas form the link between the early and the later periods of the spreading of the *dharma* in Tibet, and for Tibetans, particularly the Nyingma school, a perfectly valid and adequate link. But for Western historians termas are anathema; undoubtedly there is much authentic historical fact in, for instance, the *Five Classes of Legend* (*bKa'-thang sde lnga*), which relate history concerning Guru Pema, the King, his queens, his ministers and the savants, but the separation of fact from didactic legend, parable and metaphor is fraught with difficulty. Indeed it is only possible when it is evident that a terma is composed of sections edited from various sources, some of them ancient and authentic, and when such historically valid sections can be easily isolated. One such section is the few folios in Tsogyel's *Life* that describe in a style and language inconsistent with the main body of the text the nature of a Bon blood sacrifice. Many of the historical termas are evidently compilations of old texts; our own manuscript is a fine example. So that although Taksham Nuden Dorje 'discovered' the text as late as the eighteenth century, it contains historical material of great import to a study of the Tibet of Guru Pema. This is not to deny the original authors' work or to treat the theory of revelation with scepticism; there is no contradiction of the metaphysical theory of terma in the statement that the terton combined a rediscovered biography of Tsogyel, written by Gyelwa Jangchub and Nankhai Nyingpo, with other relevant material to form a composite narrative inspired by union with Tsogyel's *maṇḍala*, emotional, metaphysical, spiritual, sexual and social. The essential characteristic of a terma is that the terton's vision of it and the dynamic of its creation originates in a mind that can be described as 'an emanation of Guru Pema and Yeshe Tsogyel in fields of lotus light'; the texts are quite clear that the contents of a terma can originate in many different ways. There are many different kinds of terma. If a Tibetan scholar had discovered the Tun Huang cache of manuscripts he could have edited the Tun Huang chronicles himself and produced an historically authentic terma, although his didactic treatment of it would not, perhaps, coincide with a Western scholar's view of what was scientific scholarship.

Thus the story which forms a temporal background to Tsogyel's timeless *sādhana* in *The Life*, the political drama enacted during her lifetime in Tibet, can be sifted for new historical data and for evidence to support existing hypotheses; it can also be enjoyed simply as historical legend. Although the temporal theme is of secondary importance to the principal purpose of *The Life*, which is to instruct and inspire in the Tantra, in so far as a religion or *yoga* is a function of the needs of a human community at a specific time and place, knowledge of social institutions, the politics and economics of that time and place provide insight into the purpose of religious modes and their evolution. The method that I have adopted here is to summarise a passage from the text and then to comment upon it.

> King Nyatri Tsenpo was a scion of the Śākya Clan of Śākyamuni Buddha. He patronised the Bon who practised exorcism and propitiation of spirits. The last in his line was King Lhatotori, in whose reign the basic doctrines of Buddhism were introduced into Tibet, particularly the ten virtues (abstention from murder, theft, fornication, etc.) and also in whose reign the Bon Master Shenrab's Reformed Bon became popular. The doctrines of the Reformed Bon were consistent with the *Buddha-dharma*, and painted scrolls

were created depicting Śākyamuni and Shenrab as forms of the same essence (Chapter 7).

The legend has it that in the far distant past some tribal inhabitants of the Yarlung Valley of Central Tibet discovered an Indian refugee belonging to the Śākya Clan of Northern India descending their sacred mountain, and being mightily impressed by him they carried him down on their shoulders and made him their king, calling him 'Neck-enthroned King' (Nyatri Tsenpo). Early inscriptions identify the father of the royal clan as Ode Pugyel.[1] This first king patronised the indigenous shamanistic religion. It was during the reign of Lhatotori Nyentsen, the third-century king of a later dynasty, that a box of apocalyptic treasures fell upon the palace roof (Om-bu lhakhang), the chief of these treasures being a *sūtra* in Sanskrit called the *Karaṇḍavyūha*.[2] No one was able to read this scripture, but a prophecy accompanied it predicting that it would be translated after five generations. It is quite conceivable that wandering Buddhist monks found their way to Yarlung in the third century and that the Tibetans gained their first intimation of the *Buddha-dharma* from them; but it was only in Songtsen Gampo's reign, five generations later, that a civil code based on the ten Buddhist virtues was promulgated.

The early history of Bon is lost in legend, and there is no early literature to shed any light upon it. The Bon themselves ascribe Shenrab a very early birth, so that Reformed Bon is flourishing in Lhatotori's time. This implies Buddhist influence encroaching from the west into the old Bon kingdom of Zhang-zhung.[3] Most Western historians like to think that Reformed Bon was an eighth-century phenomenon because in earlier times the Tibetans were simply incapable of the subtle and complex metaphysical thought that assimilated Buddhist doctrines into Bon. Zhang-zhung apart, it is unlikely that Central Tibet was culturally evolved before the seventh century when Chinese, Kashmiri, Zhang-zhung and Nepali cultural influences penetrated deeply; the Chinese saw Songtsen Gampo as a barbarian nomad warrior king leading a fearsome host of untamed montagnards out of the back of beyond.[4]

Namri Songtsen was the last of Nyatri Tsenpo's line to rule as an equal of six other Tibetan princes. His son, Songtsen

> Gampo, unified Tibet and the other princes ruled at his sufferance. Songtsen's reign was characterised by religious tolerance. The Rasa (=Lhasa) Trulnang, Ramoche and Trandruk temples, besides 108 smaller temples throughout Tibet and the borders, were constructed. Images were imported for these temples, and Nepali and Chinese artisans built them. A civil code based upon the ten virtues was promulgated. Tonmi Sambhoṭa translated the *Mahākaruṇika-tantras* and 'King, Queen, ministers and subjects lived according to their commitments and pledges to *Mahākaruṇika*' (Chapters 4 & 7 pt 1).

The reign of Songtsen Gampo was a period of immense achievement. Father and son transformed the small principality of the Yarlung kings in the Yarlung Valley, south of the Tsangpo (Brahmāputra) to the south-east of Lhasa, and one of seven Central Tibetan principalities, into the heart of an empire including most of the Tibetan ethnic world, plus Nepal and parts of Central Asia and China. Namri began by conquering the neighbouring states of Dakpo and Phenyul, and Songtsen took the culturally superior Bon state of Zhang-zhung to the west, Kham and Amdo (Azha, the area around lake Kokonoor) to the east, parts of Kansu and Chinese Turkestan to the north, and Nepal to the south. Thus the Tibetans gained unrivalled military supremacy in Central Asia. As political influence flowed out of Yarlung, cultural influences flowed in. Namri is said to have studied medicine and astrology in China; certainly these sciences were introduced into Tibet during his reign. Songtsen married a Chinese princess who brought Chinese scholars, artisans and monks to Lhasa with her. His Nepali wife brought Nepali painters and sculptors, and no doubt his third wife, from Zhang-zhung, was accompanied by Bon priests and bards. Queen Bhṛkutī, the daughter of the great Nepali king, Aṃśuvarman, had the Rasa Trulnang Temple built to house the image of Akṣobhya she brought from Nepal; and the Ramoche Temple was built by Wen-cheng Kong-jo to house the dowry of her father, the T'ang Emperor T'ai-tsung; his dowry was an image of Śākyamuni Buddha that had been presented to the Chinese Emperor by a Buddhist king of Bengal. These two temples with their images remain Tibet's most sacred shrines to this day. The third of Songtsen's temples was the Trandruk Temple built around a self-manifest image of Tārā. The 108 border temples, testifying to the Emperor's ardent faith, bound the supine demoness who is the body of Tibet to the *Buddha-dharma*. Many of them still stand today.[5]

These achievements in art and temple building, however, are overshadowed by the genius of one man whose attainment is unique in the annals of mankind. Tibet has nurtured several men of immense intellectual stature, men like Longchen Rabjampa and Tsongkhapa, but Tonmi Sambhoṭa was the first and perhaps the greatest of them. He contrived an alphabet (probably from the Western Gupta script) and a grammar and syntax, and then, creating a new technical vocabulary, he proceeded to translate into this new language complex Sanskrit works. The *Mahākaruṇika-tantra*s and the *Karaṇḍavyūha-sūtra* were only a part of the corpus of his translation. Chinese works on astrology, geomancy and medicine, and Zhang-zhung Bon works, were also translated during Songtsen's reign. Although legend has no doubt exaggerated Songtsen's achievements and the extent of the penetration of Buddhism, certainly the foundations of modern Tibetan culture, both religious and secular, were laid at this time.[6]

> Twenty-five years after Songtsen's death the Buddhists and Reformed Bon were persecuted. Temples were destroyed and the faithful banished. Bon-shamanism corrupted the country, and when Trisong Detsen was enthroned the *dharma* was barely alive (Chapter 7, pt 1).

There is little evidence of persecution of Buddhism twenty-five years after Songtsen's death. However, Songtsen's grandson Dusong was enthroned just twenty-five years after the great king's death, and this would have been an ideal opportunity for reactionary forces to counter Buddhist advances. The Bon opposition to the Buddhist kings of the eighth century was led by *zhang* ministers, who in *The Life* are virtually identified with the Bon ministers. The *zhang* ministers seem to have been hereditary officials belonging to the clans from which the kings' wives were chosen, and thus, strictly, were the kings' maternal uncles. Their great power lay in their apparent right to govern during a young king's minority, and since there is evidence that

Tibetan kings assumed the throne as soon as they could ride a horse, around the age of thirteen, their fathers abdicating, and perhaps in the distant past being sacrificed, the *zhang* ministers held power potentially equal to the king himself.[7] Their politics were naturally conservative in order to maintain their tenuous traditional rights; and in so far as the abdicating kings may have been 'buried alive', that is to say, sent to live in the area of the tombs reserved for the 'living dead', the Bon priests whose territory that was, and for whom funeral rites were an important source of power, were their natural allies. Thus it is quite possible that as regents during Dusong's minority the *zhang* ministers persecuted the Buddhists, as they were to do when Dusong's son, Me Aktsom, died leaving the thirteen-year-old Trisong Detsen in the power of the *zhang* minister regents.

If Dusong neglected Buddhism, MeAktsom patronised the new faith, founding temples, and in his marriage to a Chinese princess he was instrumental in bringing Chinese missions to Central Tibet.[8] The missions sent by the Chinese Emperor probably consisted of *ch'an* monks. When Trisong was aged thirteen his father was assassinated, possibly by the *zhang* minister faction. Led by one Ma-zhang Trompa Kye the anti-Buddhists indulged in an orgy of persecution for about five years. The Rasa Trulnang Temple was boarded up and obscene graffiti scrawled upon its walls, and the Chinese Hwashangs (monks) were expelled. Between the ages of seventeen and twenty, having spent some time on the frontier with his army, Trisong experienced a conversion and came into his own. The Buddhist legends would have us believe that this incarnation of Mañjuśrī was thereafter bent on transforming Tibet into a Buddhist Elysium, but even *The Life* exposes the King as somewhat equivocal in his support of the *dharma* until much later in his life. Taksham may have projected Ma-zhang's persecution back to Dusong's reign to whitewash Trisong's reign.

> Trisong Detsen's first act was to send for Śāntarakṣita to teach, translate, ordain and to build him a great *vihāra*. But the opposition was still strong, and to exorcise the country and to quieten the Bon, Śāntarakṣita insisted that the King invite Guru Padma Saṃbhava to Samye where the foundations of the temple had been laid. Guru Pema was

> immediately successful, and the Samye temple-monastery and ritual abode of the King was constructed without hindrance. The translators were assembled, together with candidates for ordination. Thirty-three hundred monks were ordained and the translators began their work. But again political opposition interfered; intrigue caused the exile of translators and work was halted thrice. The King was forced to accord Bon privileges equal to the Buddhists, permitting the construction of a Bon Samye (Chapter 7, pt 1).

The above passage summarises the entire twenty-year period between the King's Buddhist awakening and the great convocation and the consecration of Samye. Śāntarakṣita's enforced return to Nepal is omitted. The Bon opposition delayed Samye's construction for a decade or more, but in *The Life* the 'demon ministers' (Ma-zhang's role is played by Takra and Lugong, who are sometimes confounded in *The Life*) are not so successful. Other sources describe malice, treachery and betrayal as the ethic attendant upon the establishment of Buddhism in Tibet. The story of Ma-zhang's death illustrates this. Buddhist ministers bribe an oracle to demand human sacrifice to avert calamity befalling the King and the country. The ministers Go and Ma-zhang are chosen as the honoured victims, and they are incarcerated alive in a tomb. Go, however, has a means of escape prepared, and using it he leaves Ma-zhang to his fate.[9] Another source tells of the same bribed oracle, but describes how two junior ministers first volunteer as victims and how Ma-zhang and Lugong are forced to overrule them in order to maintain face. Here they do not die, but become 'living dead', living amongst the tombs, denied all intercourse with the living.

Ma-zhang's death barely affected the strength of the opposition to the King, but Trisong felt sufficiently confident to recall Śāntarakṣita from exile, and only then did construction of Samye begin. *The Life* is not explicit as to when Samye was consecrated, but it implies that it was at the time of the great convocation of translators and *paṇḍitas*. In that case the abbot Śāntarakṣita ordained the first seven probationary monks and thirty-three hundred novices, and translation of Sanskrit texts began, before the consecration. The work of translation, an immense undertaking involving two Tibetans and one Indian or Chinese *paṇḍita* for each of hundreds of lengthy texts, was slow, intrigue causing the exile of principal Tibetan translators. Vairotsana, for instance, is accused by Indian *tantrikas*, agents of the King of Orgyen, and some Bon ministers, of bringing spurious *dharma* back from India. The King is forced to pretend that he has had Vairotsana executed, but actually he has hidden him in an isolated temple, where a jealous queen notices the King's frequent visits. The queen, Tsepong Za, seeks Vairotsana's downfall and attempts to seduce him, and provoked by her failure, in a popular Indian scenario, she rends her clothes and rushes to the King accusing Vairotsana of raping her. The King is not convinced, but he is forced to exile his favourite to Kham. Namkhai Nyingpo was also banished due to intrigue and the King's weakness in believing poisonous lies; the Gelong Namkhai Nyingpo was sent to Kharchu in Lhodrak, north of Bumthang in Bhutan, where he was successful in influencing the Bhutanese.[10] The King's faith weakened by the opposition's persistent and often successful intrigue, he attempted a policy of reconciliation and appeasement. He was reconciled to the Bonpos and permitted them to build their monastery, sensing perhaps that confrontation and a religious division between clans, and in families, would sap the nation's strength; later events proved such a notion only too true. It was unexpected events at the annual assembly for worship of the king and the translators' and *paṇḍitas*' uncompromising stance that forced him to stage the unwanted final confrontation.

> Tsogyel was born princess of Kharchen. Kharchen was one of the seven Central Tibetan principalities subjected by Songtsen Gampo. Courted by princes of two other kingdoms, Kharchu and Zurkhar, Tsogyel would have neither and absconded to Womphu (the valley in which one of the three Taktsang power places is located). Finally, the Emperor married her when she was twelve or thirteen years old (Chapters 2 & 3).

> Guru Pema was exiled to Turkhara (in Turkestan) for seven years. When he returned his enemies were still thirsting for his blood, and two attempts were made upon his life while he was living at the hermitage village of Chimphu,

> near Samye. The King was ensconced in the Samye monastery itself. While the Bon ministers sought the Guru's life, the King begged for initiation into the Tantra. Guru Pema insisted that Trisong Detsen wait a year for his initiation, and during that year the King married Tsogyel. Thus when the King again asked the Guru for initiation, he could offer Tsogyel along with his Empire as the initiation price (Chapters 2 & 3).
>
> The empire that Trisong Detsen offered his Guru included China, Jang (south of Lithang), Kham, Jar, Kongpo, Bhutan, Purang, Mangyul, Guge, Hor, Mongolia and the Northern Plains (Jang-thang) (Chapter 3).

In 763 Tibetan armies gained their greatest success. Marching and riding rapidly from the area of Kokonoor (Azha), rolling all opposition before them, they seized the imperial capital of Ch'ang-an. They installed an emperor of their own choice in place of the T'ang Emperor, T'ai tsung, who had fled, and exacted a heavy tribute before retreating. During the next two decades Tibetan armies rode with impunity throughout Central Asia. In 783 a peace treaty with China formally ceded Azha and Chinese Turkestan to Tibet. Thus Trisong was not boasting when he offered a part of China and Jang to his Guru. Nepal is notably absent from the list; a revolt in 704 had freed the Nepalis from their pledge of tribute. Purang and Guge are later names of southern parts of the old kingdom of Zhang-zhung, with its capital at Khyung-lung to the west of Mount Kailāś. Zhang-zhung had rebelled twice since Songtsen had first conquered it, but it was now an integral part of Tibet (*Bod*). Later, in 790, Tibetan armies marched to the River Oxus in northern Sassanid Persia, but thereafter an alliance between the Arab Caliph Harun-al-Rashid and the Chinese checked Tibetan expansion in the west. The Chinese were later to regret their assistance to the Muslims, for the Tibetans were one of the few powers that could arrest the advance of the victorious Muslims in their great march for Islam across Asia. Another military feat relevant here as evidence that the King's *maṇḍala* offering was no fiction, is his cavalry's ride to Bodh Gaya for relics to enshrine in a *stūpa* at Samye. The Tibetans left an iron pillar engraved with details of their prowess on the banks of the Ganga, and a certain clan was left behind to guard it. The pillar has disappeared, but scholars claim evidence of a village in South Bihar where Tibeto-Burman racial features are evident. But the size of the empire changed almost daily. Limited in human resources, unused to garrison duty in hot lands, after the cavalry had won their battle those nomad horsemen would exact their tribute and move on, the defeated soon returning to the *status quo*.

> At the age of sixteen (*ca.* 773) Tsogyel received initiation. The King's admission that he had given his queen to the 'vagrant sadhu' was the cause of a raucous quarrel in council between the Buddhist and the Bonpo factions. The senior ministers Lugung Tsenpo and Takra Lutsen were the most active opponents of the King. Mama Zhang (Ma-zhang) was also present in council but played no part in the dispute. The King felt sufficiently strong to decree the building of monasteries and hermitages, and that any opposition to himself or the Guru would be punished. The violent reaction of the Bon ministers caused the King to compromise – both Guru Pema and Tsogyel would be banished. However, with the King's connivance, they went to Tidro to meditate (Chapter 4).

It is significant that the Bon ministers were provoked to the point of open rebellion by the King's gift of Tsogyel to the Guru. It was no doctrinal issue and no political or economic defeat that incensed them, it was the King's violation of tradition, his trampling on social convention, that outraged their conservative sense of propriety. Tradition was sacred; only universal honouring of accepted social forms stood between them and anarchy – and the loss of their authority and privilege. With hindsight it is evident that the old order was fighting for its very existence; but it was not possible for them to see that the monasteries, the first of which was still in the process of construction, would eventually appropriate a virtual monopoly of authority, property and wealth. Not long after their defeat they were paying increasingly heavy taxes to support the nascent monasteries.

Taksham makes two men out of other sources' one. While ignoring Ma-zhang Trom-pa Kye, he mentions Takra Lutsen (sTak-ra klu-btsan) and Lugung Tsenpo (gLu-gung btsan-po) as the two principal Bon ministers.[11] Takra Lugong is the Bon minister who is known to have been an opponent of the King and who was eventually banished. This minister should not be confused with the Takdra Lugong who was a loyal servant of the King, saving his life when his father was assassinated and leading the military campaign that reached the Chinese capital, and who modestly recorded his services in the Zhol Pillar inscription below the Potala in Lhasa.

The King's council meeting offers some insight into the nature of government and its processes during the period of the Buddhist kings. It is immediately apparent that the king has no absolute authority. On the contrary it appears that a crude form of parliamentary government is operative, comparable perhaps to the Anglo-Saxon witan, 'a supreme council composed of king, lords, elders, ecclesiastics and the king's friends and dependants'. Go the Elder, possibly the Chief Minister during Trisong's early reign, acts as a parliamentary Speaker, calling order and governing procedure, but he also appears to possess prime-ministerial powers such as the power of veto and the power of decision and execution, as for instance when he sent the religious quarrel to court. In the council described in *The Life* both the King and ministers agree that their power is mutually dependent, and that issues should be resolved by 'wise and civilised discussion'. As proved by the council's ability to force the king to compromise his evangelical fervour, the council acts as a check upon him, but he still wields the ultimate power of decree. Trisong's decrees are made in spite of the ministers and sometimes appear as weapons to curb them. Three of Trisong's decrees are mentioned in *The Life*: the first made in council, decreeing the propagation of Buddhism and protection for the Guru; the second after a later council, decreeing the procedure and judgment of the trial; and after the trial a third, decreeing that the Bonpos should be outlawed. These three decrees were aimed at the *zhang* and Bon ministers rather than at the common people whose religious activity was virtually ungovernable. There is no intimation of the judicial system operative throughout the empire; but other sources assert that the empire was divided into military districts each governed by a general, and it is to be assumed that the general would implement the king's decrees and apply rough and ready justice. Concerning the manner of effecting decrees: the second decree was made law after it had been read nine times by the ministers reading from a law scroll (*khrims-yig-ring-mo*) and nine times by the King. And one further remark: it is evident from this description of the council meeting that if the king is weak a numerically superior opposition with an eloquent spokesman can control him and render him politically impotent, while if the king has charisma and popularity he can dominate the council and wield absolute power.

After the council Guru Pema and Tsogyel are banished. But they do not go to their respective places of exile; they go together to meditate at Tidro. We need not wonder at the ease with which they evaded the law. The population of Tibet was probably the same in Guru Pema's time as it is today – about four million souls – since the king was able to martial an army of perhaps hundreds of thousands. There was a relatively large sedentary population of clans in the villages of the fertile valleys who considered themselves culturally superior to the nomad pasturalist clans who wandered in the northern plains and the eastern hills. There was no machinery of central government and the provinces were to all intents and purposes independent. The king governed by moving his mobile capital of tent-palaces from place to place, making his presence felt wherever it was needed. In such an environment it would have been very easy for the Guru and Tsogyel to avoid human contact.

> After a period of meditation, Tsogyel was instructed to go to Nepal to find her partner in *yoga*. Nepal was the Kathmandu Valley (Bal-yul). In Nepal she visited Khokhomhan, the Boudhnāth Stūpa, the E Vihāra and Yanglesho. In Khokhomhan she found her consort, who was a slave, and bought him from his owners. She met Śākya Dema, Vasudhara and Jila Jipha (Chapter 4).

The glimpse of eighth-century Nepal provided by *The Life* doubtless contains eighth-century elements, but there is no certainty that it was not derived from Taksham's own personal observation in the eighteenth century.[12] However, all the sites visited by Tsogyel in the eighth century should have existed then. The Newars believe that the Boudhnāth Stūpa was built in the fifth century by the Licchavi King Mānadeva, while the Tibetans project its origins back into the distant past to the era of the

Buddha Kāśyapa. The Tibetans believe that the E Vihāra was the original building that stood upon the site now occupied by the great Kaṣṭhamaṇḍapa temple-cum-resthouse in Durbar Square in Kathmandu. From 1143 until recent times, this so-called Maru Sattal was occupied by Śaivite *yogins*, but there is evidence to indicate that before the great building was constructed out of its single tree trunk a Buddhist *vihāra* stood on the site; a local *guṭhi* (coven of *tantrikas*) still performs ancient Buddhist rites there. At Yanglesho near the Śeṣa Narayāṇ Temple, and above it at Asura, are the caves in which Guru Pema performed his *mahāmudrā* retreat and gained his ultimate enlightenment through the efficacy of the Dorje Phurba *maṇḍala*; to the Nyingmapas it is more sacred than Bodh Gaya. There is no reason to doubt that this is the actual place of Guru Pema's meditation. Khokhomhan is usually identified with Bhaktapur, but in early texts it appears to indicate the capital town of the Valley rather than Bhaktapur specifically. Thus in Tsogyel's time Khokhomhan may have denoted the town in the area of the fabulous Kailāśakuta Bhāvan, that had been built by Aṃśuvarman only a hundred and fifty years before. Whatever the location of Khokhomhan, slavery existed there, as indeed it has done in Nepal until recent times. And even today sadhus have a reputation as child thieves, the sadhu's garb being a convenient disguise.

Concerning the devotees she met, both Jila Jipha and Vasudeva are described as kings (*rgyal-po*). It is probable that 'king' signifies *kṣatriya*, a man belonging to the ruling, warrior caste. Vasudeva is an important link in the Tibetan tantric lineage of *anuyoga*, and Śākya Dema is an emanation of Vajra Vārāhī in Guru Pema's mind.

> Tsogyel returned from Nepal to Tidro, where she met her Guru and began her practice of the Third Initiation *yoga* with Atsara Sale, her consort. Then the King's speed-walkers, the ministers and translators Shubu Pelseng, Gyatsa Lhanang and Ma Rinchen Chok, arrived at Tidro to invite the Guru to initiate the twenty-one (or twenty-five) disciples. Takra Gungtsen was sent to welcome the Guru from afar. After initiation the disciples dispersed to practise in retreat (Chapter 4).

Speed-walking was the Tibetan equivalent of the American pony-express; trained messengers were capable of walking, or rather loping in a trance over vast distances without respite.[13] It is curious that Takra Gungtsen is sent as envoy of welcome to meet the Guru. Either reconciliation had effected a change in his heart for a time, or in the confusion of identity of this man the loyal minister of the Zhol Pillar, Takdra Lugong, was intended. It was the Tibetan, and also the Chinese, custom to send an envoy of welcome, and if the visitor was to be greatly honoured two or three different envoys, to meet a guest at varying distances from his destination. A similar custom governed departure; it is a mark of respect for a Tibetan to accompany his departing guest some distance from his house.

An indication of the lull in political infighting is the willingness of the King to permit his ministers, his brother-disciples, to disperse to practise their meditation. The twenty-one or twenty-five Siddhas of Chimphu (the Twenty-five: King, Queen and Courtiers – Jewong Nyer-nga) were the cream of the Buddhist aristocracy, the privileged and educated, and their consorts ladies of high birth. Although the twenty-four were the King's ministers and supporters in council they were probably quite young, their fathers still alive; many of them were able to participate in Repachan's revision of the canon (Ma, Shubu, Chokro, etc.).

It is possible that the lower orders of society had been influenced, if not converted, by very early Buddhist missionaries to Tibet, but during the period of the Buddhist kings it was the upper classes who received Buddhist education and initiation. With the edict prohibiting the practice of Bon rites the peasants and nomads may have been touched by Buddhism, but it is difficult to see how any but the nobility could have been forced to abstain from the practice of Bon rites and relinquish their attachments to the clan deities, the local spirits and demons, the earth-lords, personal gods and protectors and the war-gods, etc. It is improbable that the nomads and peasants could comprehend the nature of the abstruse metaphysical deities of Buddhism. In theory Buddhism is the most democratic of religions since no priest-mediator is necessary for the devotee to practise his religious observances, but in Tibet, from the first, *dharma* was seized upon by the educated social and political elite, who through their economic power then gained control of the monasteries. Since initiation was obtained by a substantial offering of gold to the teacher, the rich had an advantage, and later the tulku system was corrupted to assure certain families' hegemony of power in the monasteries. Thus a self-perpetuating theocracy arose, in which the ecclesiastical sons of the political and economic aristocracy were worshipped by the peasants like a pantheon of gods. This system had the great redeeming feature of permitting upward social mobility through academic achievement; if a novice showed great promise he could usually obtain the funds necessary to complete his education, and then he could aspire to the position of 'abbot' (khempo) or an administrative position. Otherwise, he could practise meditation, and if he had the karmic potential he could become a 'naljorpa' (*yogin*), a 'gomchen' (master of *yoga*), or a ngakpa (a wandering 'magician'). In many ways Tibetan Buddhism was similar to the medieval European Church; the Church, however, lacked any institution with a procedure of selection of its functionaries comparable to the method of choosing the tulku, the titular head and ultimate spiritual authority of a monastery. From a social standpoint the discovery of a tulku in a peasant or nomad family had the effect of raising the tulku's family from the bottom to the top of the social hierarchy; this was, and still is, a common phenomenon, since the process of divining a tulku's rebirth is often performed without prejudice.

> Tsogyel spent six years in meditation at Tidro and in Bhutan. Then she returned to Womphu and received the Phurba initiation from Guru Pema, during which the Guru projected 'killer' forms of Dorje Phurba to eradicate or subject the gods and demons of Tibet. A single demon escaped from the Mānasarovar Lake, at the foot of Mount Kailāś, and in the form of a red ox was given sanctuary by King Trisong Detsen at Samye (Chapter 5).

This story can be interpreted as a political parable. The Lake and the Mountain, universal symbols of fertility and virility, are the spiritual home of Bon and the chief power places of the ancient kingdom of Zhang-zhung. As noted above, Zhang-zhung had been conquered by Songtsen in the seventh century, and thereafter marriages between the royal families of Yarlung and Zhang-zhung had maintained the tie. But Zhang-zhung had risen twice in revolt, and Trisong was forced to have the Zhang-zhung king assassinated. The story of the King giving sanctuary to the Red-ox Demon, Guru Pema's castigation of the King for this seemingly charitable act and his inauspicious prognostication predicting disaster out of all proportion to the cause, possibly indicates that Trisong compromised fatally in his treatment of the Zhang-zhung Bon. Falling between two stools – the short-term political security of an important province and the long-term survival of Buddhism in Tibet – he assassinated the king but cherished the Bon snake that eventually turned upon his grandson and destroyed all that he had sought to build. The Zhang-zhung Bonpos must have been staunch supporters of Langdarma the Apostate.

> When Tsogyel had concluded her meditation practice, she found that the King had been reconciled to the Bon faction and that a peace treaty had been sealed with the Chinese Emperor (in 783); King Trisong Detsen's aspirations seemed close to fulfilment. The building of Samye completed, the King convoked a great assembly. Translators were recalled from exile; twenty-one *paṇḍitas* were invited from India, amongst them Vimalamitra; Bon sages and shamans were called from Zhang-zhung and other Bon centres, two magi named Tongyu and Tangak in particular; in a category of his own was Drenpa Namkha, the Bon scholar and shaman turned Buddhist *siddha*; Guru Pema and Tsogyel were escorted from Womphu Taktsang; and three thousand candidates for ordination were assembled from all over Tibet. The convocation took place on the Yobok Plain outside Samye (Chapter 7, pt 1).

Regarding the chronological succession of events, *The Life* is not authoritative; there is, however, a certain logic in the sequence of the convocation, the consecration of Samye, the quarrel at the Annual Worship of the King, the contest in magic and debate between Bon and Buddhist, and the edict establishing Buddhism as the state religion and abolishing Bon. The possible dates of these events will not be discussed here. In *The Life* the Tibetan Buddhist representatives are usually referred to as 'translators' (lotsawas); this does not limit them to the function of translation. The translators are also the Siddhas of Chimphu; they are *yogins*, saints, magicians (*siddhas*) and the root-gurus of many Old School lineages, besides being scholars and translators.[14] But the Tibetans lay greatest emphasis upon their achievement as translators, emphasis commensurate with the enormous and profound respect that they feel for the scriptures, which are identified with the Buddha's Word or logos. Two periods of translation can be discerned during the early dissemination of the *dharma*: the first begins before the consecration of Samye, and ends when the pressure on the Chinese schools hardens and the Indian schools begin to dominate. The later period begins with the defeat of Hwashang Mahāyāna and ends with Langdarma's persecution. In the former period the translation of Chinese texts took priority, the majority of Tibetan translators working with Chinese. In response to Trisong's request the Chinese Emperor, T'ai tsung, returned to Tibet the Chinese *ch'an* mission banished by Ma-zhang. Further, after the Tibetan army took Tun Huang in the eastern Tarim Basin in *ca.* 782 the *ch'an* Master Hwashang Mahāyāna and some of the *ch'an* community with whom he lived were invited to Samye, where they assisted in translation. The Sanskrit scholars, though fewer, translated many texts of great importance to the Nyingma School. Vimalamitra from Kashmir translated his Dzokchen texts and Guru Pema and Vairotsana also translated Dzokchen texts together with some *tantras*.[15] Perhaps because of the greater facility, exactitude and literality with which Sanskrit rather than Chinese could be translated into Tibetan, or because of the greater capability of the newly arriving Indian *paṇḍitas*, it became evident that higher standards of translation could be achieved and that standardisation of terminology was required. After completion of the *Mahāvyūtpatti* and other glossaries and lexicons, during Repachan's reign revision of the earlier translations assumed high priority, and whereas in the earlier work there was concern for essential meaning and cogency, the revisers eschewed paraphrase and suffered stilted grammatical exactitude. The *Padma bka'-thang Shel-brag-ma* gives extensive lists of Nyingma *sūtras* and *tantras* translated in this early period, as does a catalogue of the Tibetan books in the royal library of Samye, called *lDan-dkar-ma*, prepared perhaps in 788 and revised later.[16] The early translations omitted from the *Tenjur* and *Kanjur* are to be found in the *Nyingma Gyud-bum* and other collections.

Invited with special honour by Trisong, Drenpa Namkha Wongchuk[17] was also present at Samye. He seems to have been a man of towering intellect and magical power. He bridged the gap between Buddhism and Bon, and if he did not initiate the process of Bon's assimilation of Buddhism he assisted in the process. His termas were to be discovered in the eleventh century and after, when Reformed Bon appeared in Nyingma guise. The Bonpos maintain that he was Buddhist only in Body and Speech, his Mind remaining committed to the *swastika*. There appears to be admittance of some deceit in this statement; if not for his significant work for Buddhism, Drenpa Namkha could be seen as a Bon infiltrator of Nyingma tantric lineages, achieving the Promethian task of stealing the tantric fire.

> The period of harmony between Buddhist and Bonpo was short-lived. After the convocation came the Annual Worship of the King (*rgyal-po sku-rim*) at the new year festival. The Bon were contemptuous of images and image worship and *stūpas*, of the Indian element in Trisong's religion. In the Bon Kurim the *swastika* Gods, Cha and Yang, were invoked and propitiated by immense animal sacrifice; the King's longevity, good fortune and prosperity were contingent upon these gods' satisfaction (Chapter 7, pt 1).

Annual and grand triennial rites in which king and subjects were bound by oath to mutual loyalty were attended by sacrifice of animals including horses and dogs as witnesses and protectors of the vow. The sacrifice also instilled the fear by which the imprecation 'May all vow-violators come to a similar end!' was rendered more effective. It seems probable that the description of the Bon Kurim, which in its style, vocabulary and syntax betrays its ancient provenance, portrays the triennial oath of loyalty rite.[18] This rare glimpse of an unreformed Bon-shaman rite (although Buddhist influence may have eliminated human sacrifice) introduces Cha and Yang. Essentially, these *swastika* Gods are sky-gods who like Mu (dMu) reign over their celestial paradises, heavens reached by the rainbow-like mu-cords by the early kings, and later by *yogin*-adepts. On a popular level, where Cha has come to mean 'chance', 'omen', or 'luck', they are virtually synonymous as the metaphysical powers of prosperity and fortune. The priests who propitiate these gods are called Bon in the limited sense of adept officiants in rites of exorcism, invocation, etc.; both Bon and Shen (*gshen*) can be translated as 'shaman', and in 'Tomb Bon' (the shamans who perform funeral rites) and 'Cha Shen' (soothsaying shamans) 'Bon' and 'Shen' have the same value.

In a broad sense 'Bon' denotes not only a practitioner of the pre-Buddhist religion and a devotee of Reformed Bon, but the indigenous Tibetan religion itself. At this point the difference between Bon-shamanism and Reformed Bon should be clarified. We have very little evidence of the nature of ancient Bon-shamanism; thus the importance of the Kurim passage in *The Life*. Taksham's description of Bon-shaman metaphysics is obviously of Buddhist-influenced doctrines, but from other sources it is clear that the Bon priests were primarily involved in rites of exorcism, divination and death. Exorcism is to be understood as manipulation of noumenal powers, and thus includes the expulsion of 'black' spirits from impure locations (such as a diseased body or a haunted house), and the invocation of 'white' spirits for the purpose of destroying the black, or to fulfil the desire of an adept, or his client, for success in any enterprise. In short, the Bon-shaman controls the spirit world; he balances the forces of good and evil, harmonises the spirit world with the human world, and attempts to influence the phenomenal world through his control of noumenal forces. Divination and funeral rites are applications of his skill in manipulating spiritual forces.

As in animistic, sub-Aryan India the universe is conceived in three planes: the heavens, the earth and the subterranean realms. The heavens are the stratified abodes of the sky-gods such as Mu, Cha and Yang. The shaman may send his soul on journeys to these heavens for various purposes. The Tomb Bon leads the soul through the 'intermediate space' by means of the *bar-do* rites when the time is ripe for the soul to leave the body; or the shaman-healer may chase an elusive soul that has been frightened out of its residence by a spirit of disease, in order to return it to its body. The middle plane, the earth, is populated by gods associated with human existence: the personal gods who inhabit various parts of the body, the 'energy gods' who fight evil, and the war gods, etc. and spirits that exist in the environment as extensions of the mind – the animistic gods of nature, the earth-lords (*sa-bdag*) who dominate specific locations, the spirits of power-places, the elemental spirits that inhabit the elements *per se* and whose imbalance causes disease, spirits of specific diseases identifiable with viruses, bacteria, etc. These gods, demons and spirits are subject to sympathetic magic – charms, amulets, talismans, imprecations, music, dance, song, drugs and potions – and direct supplication through trance, hypnosis and sophisticated ritual psychoanalysis; the shaman has a large arsenal of weapons with which to control them. The subterranean world is inhabited by serpents – *nāga*s – who are the guardians of wealth; minerals are their province, gold in particular, and also the element water. In general all these gods and demons, and sometimes spirits, are anthropomorphic in that they are capable of good and bad, but they are not merely projections of a human mind that determines their nature; they exist as extensions of the mind in so far as all experience occurs on planes comprising the mind, but they possess *karma*s of their own determined by their function in a universal order, or chaos, galvanised by the eternal, antagonistic play of light and darkness. In short, relative to the ego, gods and demons exist as discrete entities, but if the individuated mind is identified with the universal mind they exist as a part or 'projection' of the *yogin*-shaman's mind. But the shaman's philosophical idealism is animistic in origin, and has no causal relationship with Buddhist mentalistic philosophy. 'The universe was held to be immaterial mindstuff in the form of gods and demons, so that whatever the mind conceived was a god or demon' – this statement is probably derived from a rationalisation of a shaman's experience rather than from a coherent metaphysical system, which the Bon-shamans lacked. Indeed Bon-shamanism appears to have been an eminently practicable corpus of psycho-therapeutic and mystical ritual devices, largely free of scriptures, although legends and the liturgies of ritual may have been written down in the Zhang-zhung language. The innumerable methods of divination; the cult of the dead, employing vast tumulus-like tombs; the *swastika*, the drum and the phurba; the bards and the riddle-priests:

all excite the imagination, and deserve extensive discussion, but there is no space here.[19]

The very fact that the Bon *dharma* was transmitted by bards as creation myth, parable and heroic legend, demonstrates the weakness that betrayed it when it was confronted by the systematic and highly sophisticated metaphysics of the Buddhists. But regarding the early history of Reformed Bon, while the traditional Bon view is that Buddhism modified Bon as early as the third century and that by the time of Trisong Reformed Bon was already highly evolved, some scholars now suggest that the originator of Reformed Bon, the Master Shenrab, was a mythical creation of a Bon genius, or a group of highly motivated and intelligent men, defending the indigenous religion in the eighth century. Shenrab, the Bon tradition tells us, was a native of Tazik, probably the area around Samarkand, and he visited Tibet only once, to spread his doctrine in Zhang-zhung. His doctrines consisted of much material consistent with the Buddhist Tantra, while some scholars have found traces of Śaivism, Manichaeism, Nestorian doctrines and elements of other faiths of the sphere of Persian cultural influence and of North-West India.[20] Until original texts in the Zhang-zhung language have been discovered and original Bon doctrines have been culled from Reformed Bon manuscripts, the origins of Reformed Bon will remain a mystery. As it is, Reformed Bon appeared like a phoenix in the eleventh century, almost indistinguishable from the Old School, an intimate mutual exchange having caused a close superficial similarity. The lower four of the Nine Ways of Bon, comprising the shamanistic techniques of healing, divination, exorcism and propitiation, and attainment of the devotee's well-being, are known to the Nyingma ngak-pa, but not practised by the Nyingma *bhikṣu*. The upper five of the Nine Ways of Bon are modified paths of the Nyingma Tantra; in the ninth vehicle for instance, the Way of Dzokchen, the Bon Dzokchen Atri and Zhang-zhung Nyen-gyud systems are reflections of the Dzokchen terma and kama traditions of the Old School. It appears that since the upper five Bon paths are saturated with Old School terminology and concepts they were directly derived from the Nyingma Tantra, while the practices of the lower four Bon vehicles were borrowed by the Nyingmapas.[21]

> The Bon's contempt for Buddhism, and their blood sacrifice, caused the *paṇḍitas* and translators to revolt and demand the disestablishment of Bon. The King equivocated, wishing to avoid a confrontation within his council that would inevitably result in civil war, and the King conducting a campaign to suppress the Bon. The issue was decided, however, by the acquiescence of all parties to a suggestion of Chief Minister Go that a debate and contest in magic should resolve the problem for all time, the losing faction accepting compulsory banishment. The contest had three parts: a contest in riddles, a doctrinal debate and a contest in magical power. The Bon were defeated, but refusing to accept their exile an extremist faction made a final militant stand, only to be destroyed by Tsogyel's ritual magic. Takra and Lugong (*sic*) were amongst her victims. The Bon of Central Tibet were then concentrated at Samye, and maltreated, it is implied. Guru Pema's sentence liberated the Reformed Bon followers of Shenrab, their books being hidden as terma, while the *swastika* Bon, the Bon-shamans, were banished to Mongolia (Sog-po) and their books burned. The King then promulgated his second decree binding all Tibetans to refrain from Bon-shaman practices and to practise only Buddhism (Chapter 7, pt 1).

The historicity of these events is doubtful, but not disproven. Where the Tun Huang chronicles may have mentioned such a debate the manuscript has a lacuna. The debate is ignored in many early historical works. But whether or not the events occurred as described above, the Bon surely lost the eighth-century political and religious struggle with the Buddhists, the result being their exile from Central Tibet and the destruction or concealment of their texts. Until 1959 there was only one Bon monastery in Central Tibet,[22] and we know that the Bon texts appeared later as terma. The debate serves as an excellent subject for dramatisation, but something can be learned of Tibetan justice in the eighth century. The procedure of counting pebbles (*rdeu*), either black or white, is mentioned only in passing, but it may indicate an ancient Bon method of reckoning justice. The contest in riddles is precisely what it implies, but for the Bon riddles had an esoteric meaning and function which is obscure.[23] It is improbable that the Tibetans had a tradition of debate before the Buddhists brought it from India; 'by metaphysics shall you be judged' casts doubt upon the authenticity of the account, and would certainly have sounded the death knell of the Bon. More significant than their superiority in debate was the Buddhists' superiority in magic; Guru Pema's magical subjection of Tibet's gods and demons, like Milarepa's defeat of the Bonpo in a contest in magic on Mount Kailāś, looms large in the popular legends that convince the people of the *Buddha-dharma*'s greater power. Finally, if the Bon-po-Buddhist debate is a figurative description of actual events then the legend of the other Samye Debate, that between the Indian and Chinese factions of Buddhism, could also be a metaphor.

> After the annihilation of the Bon the way was opened for the unobstructed propagation of the *dharma*. Another convocation affirmed the triumph of the King; the *paṇḍita*s were liberally rewarded and the King begged them to stay to teach and translate. During the next few years many monks were ordained and many monasteries were constructed; specifically mentioned are the tantric meditation centres (*sgrub-grwa*) of Chimphu, Yang Dzong and Yerpa, and the academies (*shes-grwa*) of Samye, Lhasa, and Trandruk. Some years later all the *paṇḍita*s except Guru Pema, Śāntarakṣita and Vimalamitra returned home, their work complete. Satisfied, the great Buddhist King, the incarnation of Mañjuśrī, Trisong Detsen, abdicated in favour of his son, Mune Tsenpo, and died soon after (Chapter 7, pts 1 & 2).

Trisong Detsen's reign saw the *Buddha-dharma* firmly established in Tibet. The first great monastic centre and several other academies and meditation centres were built, thousands of monks were ordained and a large portion of essential scriptures was translated. The Bon-shamans had been banished from Central Tibet and the Reformed Bon impregnated with Buddhist doctrines. However, the seeds of the *dharma*'s destruction had been set by the physical and social violence of the means employed to establish it.

> Mune Tsenpo was poisoned by his mother shortly after his enthronement. Mune was succeeded by his brother Mutri

> Tsenpo. Tsogyel healed a schism in the Community and an edict prohibited schism by law. The anti-Buddhist queens responsible for the schism banished Tsogyel to Tsang, and after an attempt was made upon her life by a Bon priestess she journeyed to Tsang and Nepal to meditate and to preach (Chapter 7, pt 2).

Mune reigned for as few as three months or as many as twenty-one months, according to different sources.[24] He is credited with three attempts at egalitarian reform, but even twenty-one months seems too short a period to implement, and fail in, a policy of redistribution of land. Guru Pema's comment upon land reform provides a basis for the ethical attitude that not only may rationalise Mune's failure, but also justify the hierarchical social system, kick-the-dog social values, and the feudal system that characterised Tibet down to modern times and in the end, perhaps, destroyed the old order: 'The rich are rich and the poor are poor on account of their generosity, or lack of it, in past lives; both are reaping the rewards of their karma.'[25] We are told that Mune was killed by his inordinately jealous mother, Margyen Tsepong Za, out of spite for her daughter-in-law, Phoyongza Gyeltsun, a younger queen of Trisong – she deprived her of her greatest pleasure. But in so far as *The Life* asserts that she was an inveterate supporter of the Bon faction, voting against her husband in council, and also causing Vairotsana's banishment, it is credible that she acted as an agent of her clansmen, the Tsepong *zhang* ministers, in the assassination of her communistic son. She may also have been instrumental in the schism; there is no mention of it in other sources. It is interesting to note that the *swastika* Bon Princess who attempted to kill Tsogyel was denominated a Bon-shaman in the passage describing her magical battle with Tsogyel, but that now she is described as an Esoteric or Reformed Bonmo. No doubt many Bon-shamans converted to the reformed sect to avoid exile.

With Trisong's death we enter a very confused period of chronology. Almost all the events of Tsogyel's phase of service to the *dharma* and sentient beings fall into the reign of Mutri Tsenpo, but Mutri's reign is relatively short. Problems of chronology will be discussed below (see pp. 338ff.).

Legend has associated Tsogyel's name with several places of

pilgrimage in Central Tibet; the caves at Tidro where she practised meditation and where an anchorite's cave is named after her; Tidro Peak where she practised her austerity; Zapu Lung where she meditated and finally passed on; Tsogyel Dragmar, where a temple is attributed to Trisong Detsen; the Nyingma monasteries of Womphu Taktsang, Drak-dar, Samye Yamalung, Zapu and others associating her name with their establishments; and the Senge Dzong Sum and Nering Temples in Bhutan, both of which are sources of termas relating to Dorje Phurba. But her name is chiefly associated with Western Tibet (gTsang), where she roamed during her period of exile. She gave her name, or rather her title 'Jomo' (Lady), to Kharak Gang and to the monastery she established there, Jomo Kharak, and also to Jomo Nang. She also visited Sangak Ugpalung, Shampo Gang, Zurpisa, and Pema Gang in Shang; she taught in Mangyul, which lies north of the Nepali town Triśūli and has contemporary Kyirong as its capital. Tradition associates her with many of the cis-Himalayan areas of Nepal, particularly Yolmo (Helembu) where lies the Gung-thang cave, today called Tsashorong, in which she received her Dzokchen initiation, and also with the power places of Sankhu, Yanglesho and the E Vihāra in the Kathmandu Valley.

> Invited to return to Samye by Mutri Tsenpo, Tsogyel found Śāntarakṣita dead, and she mourned before his reliquary *stūpa*. Then she spent some time with her Guru, and having written down his termas she travelled with him throughout Tibet. Because the termas were hidden wherever they set foot, they were known as 'foot-termas' (*zhabs-gter*). The Guru then departed for the South-west (Chapter 7, pt 2).

It is possible that Śāntarakṣita left Tibet to die in the land of his birth before the Samye Debate in 792, and that the Samye *stūpa* enshrines token relics. The date of Guru Pema's departure will be discussed below. Some scholars have attempted to identify his destination, Ngayab Ling; but undoubtedly Ngayab is a mythic island, the sub-continent that lies to the south-west of Jambudvīpa. In the island's centre stands Zangdokperi, the Copper-coloured Mountain in the form of the Guru's *maṇḍala*, and outside the *maṇḍala* live demon-savages (sinpo) who can be either humans or spirits.

> After the Guru's departure Tsogyel lived at Chimphu (the Samye retreat centre situated about 40 miles north-east of Samye itself), where she taught many monks recently ordained by the newly appointed Abbot of Samye, the Indian *paṇḍita* Kamalaśīla. During this period a dispute erupted between the Chinese faction in Samye called the Tonminpa (adherents of the 'sudden' school) and the Indian faction called the Tseminpa (adherents of the 'gradual' school). The former led by the Chinese monk Hwashang Mahāyāna held the western area of Samye and the Jampa Temple, while the Indian Abbot Kamalaśīla held the Hayagrīva Temple. It appears that violence was resorted to. Tsogyel descended from Chimphu, and although she was disobeyed initially, she eventually healed the schism. A decree established Kamalaśīla's doctrines as the only path, while Hwashang Mahāyāna was sent home with honour (Chapter 7, pt 2).

The Samye Debate, whether the traditional account is interpreted literally or figuratively, was one of the most important events in the history of Tibet during Tsogyel's dramatic life. It determined that Tibet would turn away from China for both religious and cultural sustenance, and away from *ch'an* quietism, and follow the Indian Bodhisattva path. Taksham deals with it cursorily. Although Indian, Chinese and Tibetan sources describe the debate, none are authoritative, for almost every source has an axe to grind. Kamalaśīla's *Bhāvanākrama*[26] uses the debate as a peg on which to hang an exposition of Bodhisattva philosophy, idealising the debate and ignoring the opposition; the earliest and oft-quoted Tibetan account, Buton's *History of the Dharma*, is uncomfortably biased in the Indian's favour; amongst the amazing treasures of Tun Huang were several texts, some complete and some fragmentary, describing the doctrines of Hwashang Mahāyāna's *ch'an*, including an account of the debate by a disciple of the master, a writer who was probably present at the event.[27] The Nyingmapas are strangely quiet about the debate, but it is highly significant that a very early source makes the Chinese the victors. Indeed, we cannot be certain that the result was clear-cut, and it is indisputable that Hwashang Mahāyāna's influence continued to be felt in

Tibet through the Old School's lineages, and that Buton served a vested interest by reporting Kamalaśīla's absolute victory and by pouring scorn upon the Chinese.

The reformed schools influenced by Atīśa continued and developed the 'gradual' school methods of Śāntarakṣita and Kamalaśīla, sustaining the prejudices of the Indian party at the Samye Debate against *ch'an* and the Chinese. China enjoyed a cultural influence in Tibet during the T'ang dynasty that it was never to attain again; China was to become the enemy in Tibetan history. Since Songtsen Gampo had married a T'ang princess, Chinese social and cultural mores held an exemplary sway at the Tibetan court. The Tibetan nobility learnt Chinese, rather than Sanskrit, to educate themselves in the important sciences of medicine and astrology; Chinese tea and music became fashionable. The Tibetan army absorbed Chinese culture directly, through social intercourse. Before envoys invited Śāntarakṣita to Samye, Trisong's father had sent Ba Selnang and 'Sang-shi'[28] to the Imperial Court to gather books. These two roving ambassadors were taught *ch'an* while in China and brought back texts that were hidden as terma due to Ma-zhang's unexpected ascendancy. But the *ch'an* monks invited by Trisong's father to Central Tibet had great success in their conversion of Tibetans. Expelled by Ma-zhang they returned in strength to participate in translation and propagation of the *dharma*, and they accrued a library of translations larger than the Sanskritists. The most prominent of the Chinese *ch'an* monks (*ho-shang*, corrupted to *hwarshang* by the Tibetans) was Hwashang Mahāyāna.

Thus the Chinese had achieved a powerful political and religious position by 792; the majority of Buddhist converts in Central Tibet belonged to the *ch'an* schools. There was ample reason for the Indian party to fear them and for Tibetans to involve them in their politics. But besides political considerations there were important doctrinal differences at issue. To be brief, Kamalaśīla taught that Buddhahood can only be attained by practice of social virtue and personal discipline, and that *mādhyamika* dialectics are essential to condition the mind gradually to the reality of Emptiness and the futility of discursive thought. Practice of virtues and selfless acts throughout aeons of rebirths slowly but surely cultivate a Bodhisattva's *karma*, so that when enlightenment is finally achieved Buddha activity spontaneously arises. Traversing the paths and climbing the levels of a Bodhisattva's career, through persistent meditation upon the peaceful centre of the mind while guarding the doors of the senses, and practising giving, patience, moral discipline, etc., one's own purpose and the good of others are served simultaneously, and gradually *saṃsāra* is transcended and *nirvāṇa* attained. Solitary meditation with the aim of attaining gnosis alone, betrays the *mahāyāna* ideal 'for the good of others' and smacks of *hīnayāna* self-preoccupation; and anyway ordinary human beings are incapable of sustaining the thought-free *samādhi* (*nirvikalpa-samādhi*) by which the Chinese were obsessed. On the contrary, Hwashang Mahāyāna taught that not only are human beings perfectible but that they are perfect as they stand, and they need only an instant of that realisation to take hold of the root of their being to effect a turning around in the seat of consciousness and to transform them suddenly into Buddhas. Thus virtue is irrelevant and quietistic meditation is all. Rejecting academic and monastic discipline, logic and dialectics, good works and persevering piety, the *ch'an yogin* is concerned only with the suppression of thought, with the elimination of all mental activity whatsoever, so that he may enter the thoughtless trance that reveals the ultimate nature of reality. Taoist techniques had been borrowed, and new methods evolved, to effect that trance; *prāṇayāma, koan, za-zen,* and the soteriological psychotherapy of the master were some of the methods that achieved a sudden awakening to Buddhahood. This doctrine was heresy for the Indians, who accused the *ch'an* school of ignoring skilful means (*upāya*), one of the twin pillars of *mahā-yāna* metaphysics and religious practice; transcendent awareness, or gnosis (*jñāna, ye-shes*), was stressed to the exclusion of skilful means, the expedient form of response by a high receptive sensibility that is always a form of compassion (*karuṇā*).

In the orthodox account of the debate the existential Chinese poet-mystics lost to the erudite Indian scholars; like the Bon-shamans defeated by Buddhist scholars they were at a disadvantage in the sphere of formal logic. But disregarding any weakness in Hwashang's formal presentation, if the result rested purely upon doctrinal considerations – and the King pronounced *mādhyamika* the superior *dharma* – certain Indian *siddhas* and Dzokchen *yogins* should have been saddling their horses at the same time as the banished Chinese. What were the political factors that militated against the Chinese and exculpated the Indian *siddhas*? What made a Buddhist doctrinal controversy into a violent feud? Although the politics of the period were Byzantine in complexity, an effect heightened by the lacunae in our knowledge of the period and the multiplicity of conflicting sources, it appears that the old struggle between the *zhang* and Bon ministers and the king was now translated into a purely Buddhist conflict between the king's pro-institutional party supported by the Indians and the more anarchic, non-institutional faction supported by the old order and the Chinese-oriented majority. Ba Selnang, now ordained as Yeshe Wongpo and the successor to his mentor, Śāntarakṣita, as Abbot of Samye, seems to have initiated the conflict by attempting to arrogate to his own position greater status and dignity than the *zhang* and Bon Ministers possessed. Opposed successfully by Nyang Tingzin Zangpo, a Dzokchenpa and confidant of the King, who was to become the tutor of Tride Songtsen (Mutri-Tsenpo in *The Life*), Yeshe Wongpo was banished to Kharchu in Lhodrak, Ba Pelyang replacing him as Abbot. Although Pelyang sat with Kamalaśīla at the debate (according to Buton's prejudiced account) he seems to have had close associations with Myang Tingzin and the Chinese; and it seems more than coincidence that immediately after the debate the King endowed Samye with a large benefice in perpetuity and allocated the receipts of a tax on householders to monks and *yogins*, as if the defeat of the Chinese faction had eliminated obstacles to the strengthening of Samye economically and politically. Thus it is plausible that the Chinese downfall was necessary to establish an Abbot in Samye sympathetic to the King's objectives, and also that it was the King's prejudice tied to the minority Indian party's superior skill in dialectics and logic that effected Hwashang Mahāyāna's defeat, rather than a deficiency in doctrine or practice.[29] As regards doctrine the King was probably equivocal; he was an initiate of Dzokchen, but marked by social and socialising doctrines and demanding a strong centralised monastic institution Kamalaśīla's Bodhisattva School must have had greater appeal to him than the anti-institutional, mystical, *ch'an* school.

In the aftermath of the debate, some say that the Chinese committed suicide, unable to bear the loss of face; reformed orthodoxy maintains that Kamalaśīla had his legs broken, or was murdered, by avenging Chinese. As regards Hwashang Mahāyāna, *The Life* reflects a current of Nyingma belief that the Chinese were lauded as worthy opponents, even if their leader was not loaded with gold at his departure; Hwashang Mahāyāna probably retraced his steps to the Tun Huang area to compose his *apologia*.

> In the Kharchung Dorying Temple Tsogyel initiated King Mutri Tsenpo and his son Mu-rum (or Mu-rub), who was named Senalek by Guru Pema who appeared in a vision. Amongst Senalek's sons were Repachan and Langdarma (Chapter 8).

The Kharchen Dorying Temple in the Yarlung Valley contains an inscription attributing the construction of the temple to Senalek, who enjoined respect for the *dharma* upon his successors. According to *The Life* Senalek gained his name, which means 'successful on trial', after his successful attempt at reforming a prodigal period of youth. It would take too much space here to unravel the tangled problem of succession after Trisong's death. *The Life* gives Trisong's eldest son, Mune, a very short reign, Mune's brother Mutri a very long reign, while Murum-Senalek's reign is not mentioned; Tsogyel died at the beginning of Repachan's reign. Although no line of succession has been established definitively this thesis is quite plausible: Trisong had four sons, Mutri, Mune, Murum and Mutik; Mutri died young; Mune reigned 797/8; Murum was banished to Bhutan for killing a minister and then recalled to reign as regent (798–804) until his brother, Mutik (Senalek), came of age to reign for ten years (804–15).[30] Apart from the difference in names the most significant departure of *The Life* from the above lineage is Senalek's relationship to his predecessor, that of son rather than brother.

> Repachan's first decree assembled all those associated with Tsogyel's *parinirvāṇa* in order to establish the precise nature of that event (Chapter 8).

Assuming that Repachan's first decree occurred during the first fourteen years of his reign, the year of Tsogyel's death can be fixed as the first bird year of his reign, which is the year AD 817.

> A summary of the prophecy concerning the assassination of Repachan by his brother Langdarma's henchmen, and the aftermath, given in the *Lungjang Chenmo*: King Triral (Repachan) will accede to the throne as Vajrapāṇi (the last of the three Bodhisattva Kings) and he will be murdered by Langdarma with the connivance of his ministers. Langdarma will be a paradigm of evil 'who will erase even the memory of monasteries and scriptures, establishing a law inimical to the *Buddha-dharma*. . . . The most devout will be killed, the lesser will be banished and the least enslaved. But the tantric *vajra*-brothers of the villages will keep the *dharma* alive. Lhasa and Samye will be despoiled and fall into ruin. When Pelgyi Dorje remembers his Guru's injunction he will assassinate the diabolic king and flee towards Mekham' (Chapter 8).

> Guru Rimpoche prophesied to Mutri Tsenpo that his grandson's appearance would herald the loss of the throne of the Yarlung kings. A cause of this disaster is Mutri's failure to wear the cloak of devotion lightly (Chapter 8).

> To Trisong Detsen, Guru Pema predicted that the Red-ox demon to whom the King had given sanctuary would reincarnate in the third generation, kill his brother and establish an iniquitous government (Chapter 5).

In these prophecies references consistently affirm Senalek as the son of Mutri; Repachan and Langdarma are Trisong's great-grandchildren and Mutri's grandchildren. The prophecies were accurate. Langdarma may have resisted his most reactionary ministers initially, but very soon (*ca.* 840) persecution became severe. Buddhist monks were given the choice of marrying, or becoming hunters, or Bon priests, who would advertise themselves with small bells, like lepers. Many Buddhists felt that this was no choice and, like Nyang Tingzin, Ma Rinchen Chok, and, perhaps, Vairotsana, were executed. After Pelgyi Dorje shot Langdarma in the eye with an arrow, the kingdom fell into chaos; the provinces became independent, and the empire was lost before the end of the century. But in Central Tibet, and perhaps Zhang-zhung, as Tsogyel predicted, ordained monks were all killed or converted, and the *tantrikas* of the villages who lived as householders sustained the tradition. Further it is improbable that a few pockets of monks did not survive in the border areas; but it was in Kham that the lamp of *dharma* burned until the second half of the tenth century, when devotees from Central Tibet received ordination there and brought the *vinaya* back with them.

Langdarma's successful reaction should not lead to doubt of the extent to which Buddhism had permeated the country. However, it is true that Buddhism had been imposed by foreign priests under the patronage of a charismatic king upon an unwilling aristocracy, who felt rightly enough that its traditional authority was being undermined by the new political forces, and that its ageless religion was in peril. Unable to adapt with alacrity, its ancient institutions were endangered. No doubt the proud Tibetans were humiliated by a large number of foreign priests who failed to conceal their disdain for the 'demon-worshipping' Bon; and no doubt many people were unable to understand Buddhist metaphysical concepts and the nature of the foreign deities and liturgies. Mystical, supra-rational *ch'an* appealed to the people more than *mādhyamika*, which required a subtle, analytical brain and a sophisticated moral sensibility.

Although the hard-core Bon were frenzied by jealousy and some segments of society and individuals were alienated by the *Buddha-dharma*, there must have been an unbending nucleus of sympathetic support for Buddhism from converts unwilling to renounce their vows; Guru Pema's success in assimilating Bon deities and spirits by subjection, and converting village shamans in the process, was of enormous importance when the *dharma* was threatened. Langdarma destroyed the monasteries with ease and the lineage of ordination was eradicated; it was in the villages that the *dharma* survived, the villages where Guru Pema had roamed for years. He had subjected the local demons and spirits and taught Bon-shamans how to control and manipulate spiritual forces, removing the fear from the minds of people who had previously propitiated demonic powers in terror. The converted Bon-shamans were the '*vajra*-brothers of the villages' who survived the persecution, who virtually deified Guru Pema for opening to them the doors of perception, and who foiled Langdarma's intention. Thus, according to the Old School legends, although Langdarma was successful in cutting off the head of Buddhism he failed to destroy its heart; although the seeds of Trisong's violent and destructive treatment of his opposition finally bore fruit in surgent reaction, Buddhism had been so successful on a grass-roots level that its eradication was impossible.

THE CHRONOLOGY OF THE PERIOD OF TSOGYEL'S LIFE

A study of the chronology of the period leads into an interminable maze, and the game is barely worth the candle. A plethora of sources exists, each with its own integrity, but none offer sufficient evidence to invite credence. Neither the generally authoritative *T'ang Annals* nor the Tun Huang chronicles provide much assistance. Again it should be emphasised that attempting to derive history from legend is to treat an orange as if it was an apple. The dates arrived at by Professor Tucci[31] are as precise as can be ascertained at this stage: to the undisputed date of Trisong's enthronement, 755, he adds 775 as the year of the foundation of Samye, 779 as the year of ordination of the probationary monks, and he accepts 792–4 as the date of the Samye Debate. The year of the King's death is 797. *The Life*'s only contribution to chronology is to imply that Tsogyel lived from 757 to 817, despite her own claim to have lived 214 years. The only other date mentioned is the well-known year of the Guru's departure for the South-West – the monkey year. Although *The Life* reinforces some less credible legendary sources' views and can add little to an understanding of the true sequence of events and their dates, a hypothetical chronology based on *The Life* is contrived here for purposes of comparison and to assist the reader in placing the events of Tsogyel's life in an historical perspective. Events the dates of which have been established within the bounds of probability are italicised.

742	*Trisong Detsen born*
753	*Tride Tsugtsen dies*
753–765	*Bon ministers in control*
757	*Tsogyel born*
764	Śāntarakṣita arrives in Tibet

765	Guru Pema arrives in Tibet
	Foundation of Samye
ca. 766–770	Pema banished (for 7 years?)
769	Completion of Samye
770	Tsogyel marries Trisong
772	Tsogyel offered to Guru
773	Tsogyel initiated
774	Dispute in council
	Pema and Tsogyel banished to Tidro
775	Tsogyel in Nepal
776	Pema returns to Samye
	Initiation of the 25 Siddhas of Chimphu
776–785	Tsogyel's *yoga* practice
786	*Paṇḍitas* and translators assemble
	1st convocation at Samye Yobok
787/8	The Bon Kurim
	The Buddhist–Bon Debate
	Exile of Bon-shamans
	2nd convocation at Samye
783–797	Period of teaching and construction
796	*Trisong abdicates*
797	*Mune enthroned*
	Trisong dies
798	*Mune is assassinated*
	Mutri enthroned
800	Schism healed by Tsogyel
	Tsogyel banished to Tsang
802	Śāntarakṣita dies
803	Tsogyel returns to Samye
803–4	Termas written and hidden
804	Guṛu Pema departs for the S.W.
ca. 805	Kamalaśīla Abbot of Samye
ca. 808	Samye Debate
805–815	Kharchung Dorying built
	Mutri dies
	Murub enthroned, reigns and dies
815	*Repachan enthroned*
817	*Tsogyel dies*

Although an exhaustive discussion of this chronology of what is essentially legendary material would be futile, some important points should emerge from a closer look at some topics.

Trisong Detsen

Concerning the great King's regnal dates, 755–97, the first is undisputed. He was probably born in 742[32] and assumed the throne at the customary age of thirteen. The first years of his reign were dominated by the Bon ministers, and he came into his own only after achieving a religious awakening, similar to that of Aśoka, between the ages of seventeen and twenty[33] while fighting on the empire's frontier. He could only invite Śāntarakṣita to Tibet after the demise of Ma-zhang and Takra Gungtsen. The end of his life is fraught with mystery. Why do the *Blue Annals* and the *Red Annals* give such early dates for his death (780 and 787 respectively)? Why does the *Sheldrakma* claim that he was given a magical extension of life in the 780s? Why do other sources claim that his death was kept a secret for a number of years? The *T'ang Annals* give 797 as the year of his death.

Mune Tsenpo

Although Mune's regnal dates are uncertain there is unanimity that his reign was short (except in the *Blue Annals* where it is claimed that he succeeded Trisong in 780). He was poisoned by his mother in his late twenties in 798 or 799.

Mutri Tsenpo

There is confusion in the name of Mune's successor, who was undoubtedly another son of Trisong. Following the *T'ang Annals*, the *Blue Annals* names him Ju-tse btsan-po; this is the Mutik of the *Sheldrakma* and the Mutri of the *Ladakhi Chronicles*. He may have been the brother banished for killing a minister and recalled to reign as regent for his son (or younger brother) Senalek. He reigned from 798/9 to 804.

Senalek (Tride Songtsen)

The *T'ang Annals*, *Blue Annals* and *Ladakhi Chronicles* all agree that Senalek was his predecessor's son. He is called Murum or Murub in *The Life*. There is no reason to doubt the *T'ang Annals'* 804–14 for his regnal dates. *The Life* is extremely vague about the reigns of the kings succeeding Mune Tsenpo; perhaps Taksham's sources conflicted.

Repachan (Tritsuk Detsen)

Repachan was Senalek's son and the brother of his fratricidal successor Langdarma. He was enthroned 814/15, but there is no agreement about the year of his death. The *Red Annals* supposes as late as 852, but the *T'ang Annals'* 838 is probably correct.

Śāntarakṣita

The orthodox legend records that Śāntarakṣita, the Bodhisattva Abbot of Nālandā and then Samye, made a short unsuccessful visit to Central Tibet after Ma-zhang and Takra Gungtsen's demise, when he advised Trisong to invite Guru Pema to Tibet. If Samye's foundation was in 775 Śāntarakṣita must have arrived in Tibet a year or two previously. *The Life* seems to maintain that he came to Tibet in the early 760s and remained continuously. As for the end of his life, it appears uncertain whether he died in Tibet or returned to India to die;[34] but at least there is a *terminus ante quem* established by the Samye Debate. Before his death, or departure, he foresaw the coming schism and advised the King to invite Kamalaśīla to defend his school. If the debate occurred 792–4 then Śāntarakṣita would have been absent from Samye after ca. 790. *The Life* has him die in Samye *ca.* 802 in Mutri's reign and, again, before the Samye Debate. A *stūpa* at Samye enshrines all or some of the great abbot's mortal remains.

Guru Pema

Neither Tibetan nor Chinese political records give any indication of Guru Pema's movements. *The Life* maintains that he arrived early in Trisong's reign soon after Śātarakṣita, was banished for seven years, returned, was banished again with Tsogyel for a year or so, before returning again and remaining until after Trisong's death. But if the Abbot did not arrive in Tibet until 773/4 it is probable that the Guru's arrival was *ca.* 774, just before the Samye Temple was begun in 775. However, it appears that the Guru's most important work was performed while he roamed the villages in Central Tibet and on the borders, and perhaps as far away as Kham, 'subjecting demons' and converting the Bon-shaman priests into '*vajra*-brothers'. The termas claim he performed this mission before arriving to exorcise Samye; he may have continued during his period of exile, as it is unlikely that he ever went to Turkhara. Wishing to minimise his importance, some sources claim that he stayed only a few months in Tibet, others a few years; but it is improbable that he could have created in so short a time the impression upon which a great cult was built. It cannot be established how long he stayed in Tibet. According to *The Life* he departed in the monkey year after Trisong's death; if Trisong died in 787 the Guru left for the South-West in 792, and if he died in 797 the Guru left in 804.

The Foundation of Samye

The termas (*Zanglingma, Sheldrakma, The Life* and others) unanimously proclaim that Samye was built early in Trisong's reign; *ca*. 762 is indicated, after rationalisation, for its foundation, and 766 for its completion. But as in *The Life* consecration is often indicated as late as 785, fifteen years later. The Tun Huang chronicles imply that building started in 775, although the Samye pillar proclaims a Buddhist Tibet by *ca*. 779–82. Without bias it can safely be stated that works such as *The Life* underestimate the political difficulties of Trisong's early years. The King spent several years fighting with his army in China, while at home the Bon ministers controlled the state. 77 is an acceptable date for the foundation of Samye.

The Samye Debate

It is difficult to dispute the dates 792–4 for the Samye Debate, for the Tun Huang chronicles, a contemporary source, are clear in their implication. However the sources are in such conflict that the inscrutable subject of the debate lends itself to endless speculation. How could the *Ladakhi Chronicles* and *The Kings' Genealogy* (*rGyal-rabs gsal-ba'i me-long*) claim that it was Senalek who invited Kamalaśīla to Samye? Was this a second visit for a similar purpose? And how is it credible that Trisong gave unequivocal support to the enemies of his *vajra*-brothers who were initiates into his own Dzokchen lineages, those of Vimalamitra and Guru Pema, besides the lineage of Hwashang Mahāyāna whose doctrinal stance was close to that of the Dzokchenpas? Can we safely ignore the orthodox account of Buton who considered the single debate to have been won outright and conclusively by Kamalaśīla and that the Chinese faction was then silenced forever? If Buton's orthodox account is, indeed, suspect, Tsogyel's conflict could have been a later confrontation, if it is not a spurious account inserted into *The Life* to prove Tsogyel's orthodox affiliations. One further point: the long reign assigned to Mutri and the occurrence of the Samye Debate in Mutri's reign are two of several indications in *The Life* supporting an early death for Trisong.

Yeshe Tsogyel

In order to establish the bird year of Tsogyel's birth as 757, it is necessary to reject the happy fiction that all opposition had been overcome, that the light of the *dharma* shone unshadowed throughout Tibet, and that Samye was completed, when Tsogyel was born. Even if Samye was completed by 769, the alternative bird year of Tsogyel's birth, she would have been too young to take initiation with the Siddhas of Chimphu in 776. Thus Guru Pema was probably not present in Tibet at her conception, and at that early stage he could not yet have been banished to cavort with the Ḍākinīs in Orgyen Khandro Ling. Also, in order to give credence to her life in an historiographical context, the biographical information she gives her disciples just before her death at the age of 214 must also be ignored; a numerological investigation of it may be rewarding. Atsara Sale, the writer of *The Life*, informs us that she died on Zapu Peak in Central Tibet on the 8th day of the bird month in a bird year before Repachan's first decree. Since Repachan was enthroned in 814/15 and the next bird year, the year of her death, was 817 there can be no doubt as to the date of her death. She was 60 years old. The only other source to mention a date for Tsogyel's birth or death is the *Sheldrakma*, which gives the wood-bird year, 745, for her birth. This would make her too old for initiation as a sixteen-year-old virgin by Guru Pema if the Guru did not arrive until ca. 774; but the *Sheldrakma* mentions the fire-bird year (757) as the date of meeting of Guru and Consort. Thus the element part of the Tibetan year indicator must be ignored, as it always must be ignored in order to render this terma's dates useful, and a measure of agreement with *The Life* is discovered.

Indeed, it is conceivable that the *Sheldrakma* was one of the sources that Taksham drew upon when writing *The Life*. There is no other source to corroborate or refute the dates given in *The Life*, and since they accord with those dates incontrovertibly affirmed, until new evidence appears they must be accepted.

NOTES TO THE COMMENTARY

1 The Path of the Inner Tantra

1 *Theg-dgu*: see p. 192, n. 4. The Dzokchen *atiyoga* tradition is complete in itself in so far as it provides both external and internal preliminary practices (*sngon-'gro*). The lesser vehicles may also be considered as preliminary purification practices suited to different personality types.

2 Precise phraseology is important here. Although the word Emptiness is frequently used as if it denotes an ontological absolute, the Old School, unlike the other sects, stresses that ultimate reality is only *empty of* defilements, etc. (the *gzhan-stong* formula) and not Emptiness itself (the *rang-stong* formula). The problem is not only semantic; by implying that Emptiness can be experienced divorced from phenomenal appearances there is danger of the *yogin* striving for other than what is here and now, or for utter cessation, as in the *hīnayāna nirvāṇa*. The relative world is not to be shunned for a pie in the sky; the absolute (*don-dam*) *is* the relative (*kun-rdzob*), and the male and female principles (*upāya* and *prajñā*, *yab* and *yum*) are always in indivisible union.

3 *Pha-rol-tu-phyin-pa drug*. At the outset of the Bodhisattva Path the six perfections are practised conscientiously to condition generosity, moral behaviour, etc. Tsogyel defines them as spontaneous reflexes of her own being, which bound by her *samaya* automatically manifests these perfections.

4 *Ngo-bo stong-pa, rang-bzhin gsal-ba, thugs-rje kun-khyab*. 'Essence' is misleading if it is conceived as something apart from the whole: it is the whole. 'Existentiality' is an alternative rendering of *ngo-bo*

(*svabhava*). The definition of *nirmāṇakāya* (*sprul-sku*) does indicate that no specific apparition is implied; rather it is a principle, or mode of being. 'Manifestation' is by definition 'compassion' (*karuṇā*); the creative act is an act of love, and only our confused notions and emotions corrupt it. Unveiled, a kettle or a gun no less than the Ḍākinī herself are manifestations of the Guru's compassion.

5 *sTong-pa-nyid* (*śūnyatā*), *ye-shes* (*jñāna*), *dbyings* (*dhātu*) and *bde-chen* (mahāsukha). These four are indivisible; it is impossible to experience one without the others, but in different contexts the Ḍākinī may represent only one or another.

6 *Tshangs-pa'i gnas bzhi* (*caturbrahmāvihāra*), the Four States of Purity, or *tshad-med bzhi*, the Four Immeasurables: loving kindness, sympathetic joy, compassion and equanimity.

7 See K. Dowman, *Calm and Clear*, pp. 67–71, for Mi-pham Rimpoche's incisive instruction on the analysis of impermanence.

8 This explanation is based on the *Lam-rim ye-shes snying-po grel-ba* of bLo-gros mtha'-yas, f. 102ff.

9 See H. Guenther, *Kindly Bent to Ease Us*, pt 2, p. 113, n. 13.

10 *dbYings*, *dhātu*: the Dzokchen equivalent of *chos-dbyings* (*dharmadhātu*).

11 *Chu-ser*, lit. 'yellow water'. At death the red corpuscles sink in the organism leaving a clear serum in the capillaries which gives pallor to the corpse – this is *chu-ser*; the clear serum that a wound exudes for protection and to form new skin is *chu-ser*; the lubricant of joints is *chu-ser*. Despite an alternative medical theory that makes marrow the origin of semen, *chu-ser* becomes semen (*khu-ba* = *thig-le* = *semen virile*) after its purification.

12 Summarised from the *bShad-rgyud*, ch. V: *Tibetan Medicine*, p. 44, trans. Rechung Rimpoche.

2 Woman and the Ḍākinī

1 *Mahāyoga*, *anuyoga* and *atiyoga* may be classified as father, mother and non-dual *tantra* and the respective views of reality of these classes of *tantra* are iconographically represented by the Guru, the Ḍākinī and the Guru and Ḍākinī united.

2 See J. Robinson (trans.), *Buddha's Lions* (*The Legends of the Eighty-four Mahāsiddhas*); the legend of Darikapa, p. 236.

3 See C. George (trans.), *Caṇḍamahāroṣana-tantra*, p. 55.

4 See H. Guenther (trans.), *The Life and Teaching of Naropa*, p. 80.

5 W. Evans-Wentz (ed.), *The Tibetan Book of the Great Liberation*, p. 133.

6 *Tshangs-pa'i gnas bzhi* (caturbrahmāvihāra): loving kindness, sympathetic joy, compassion and equanimity.

7 bKra-bshis spyi-'dren; but Taksham prefers Khyi-'dren. Other sources have Khye'u-'dren.

8 Without unanimity Tibetan and Western scholars identify Za-hor as the Kingdom of Mandi at the head of the Kangra Valley, Himachal Pradesh, India. Mandi is not far from the Jālandhara pīṭhasthāna. Probably the Great Fifth Dalai Lama's family and Prabhahasti came from Mandi where Guru Pema and Mandāravā lived, while Atīśa (as the Gelukpas believe) and Śāntarakṣita were born in E. Bengal, probably in the Vikramapur District. See G. Tucci, *Tibetan Painted Scrolls*, p. 736.

9 mTsho-padma, Rewalsar, located approximately 10 miles south of Mandi.

10 See K. Dowman, 'A Buddhist Guide to the Power Places of the Kathmandu Valley', *Kailash*, Vol. VIII (2–3).

11 Kautilya's *Arthaśastra*, quoted in D. Regmi, *Ancient Nepal*, p. 41.

12 See K. Douglas and G. Bays (trans.), *The Life and Liberation of Padma Sambhava (Padma bka'-thang shel-brag-ma)*, hereafter *Sheldrakma*, p. 300f. Also W. Evans-Wentz, *The Book of the Great Liberation*, p. 146.

13 For the Sindhu Rāja legend and sKong-sprul's reference taken from a very short chapter of his *gTer-ston-kyi rnam-thar*, f. 31b–34b called *Guru Rin-po-che'i thugs-kyi gzungs-ma lnga'i rnam-thar*, see M. Aris, *Bhutan*, p. 298, n. 11.

14 See Rinjing Dorje, *Tales of Uncle Tomba*.

3 The Nyingma Lineages

1 Such texts as the *Karaṇḍavyūha-sūtra*, the *sPyan-ras-gzigs-kyi mdo rgyud* and *The 108 Names of Avalokiteśvara* (the last two translated by the Nepali Śīla Mañju) introduced Tibet's protector, Avalokiteśvara, to the Tibetans, and his lineage was sustained until Pema's arrival. *The Kings' Genealogy* (*rGyal-rabs gsal-ba'i me-long*), f. 32b, describes Hayagrīva as Song-tsen's protector, and the *Maṇi bKa'-'bum* describes a visitation of Hayagrīva to the King. But there is no record of a sustained lineage until Trisong received the initiation from Guru Pema.

2 *Rig-'dzin brgyad*: Vimalamitra (western India), Hūṃkara (Nepal), Mañjuśrīmitra (Siṅghāla), Nāgārjunagarbha (Baṅgala?), Padmasaṃbhava (Orgyen), Dhanasaṃskṛta (N.W. India?), Rong-bu Guhyacandra (Rong-bu is in Western Tibet), and Śāntigarbha. These eight are known to have taught Tibetans *anuttarayoga-tantra* they may all have been Dzokchenpas.

3 King Dza (Sanskrit: Ja) is identified with King Indrabhūti I of Orgyen who originally received the *Guhyasamāja-tantra*. See Trinley Norbu Rimpoche, *The Small Golden Key* (privately published, based upon Dunjom Rimpoche's *Chos-'byung*), p. 4.

4 The Indian *anuyoga* lineage is fascinating but complex, and various sources conflict. The names King Dza (Indrabhūti of Orgyen), Gaga-siddhi of south-eastern Western Turkestan, the Sage of Bruśa, Che-btsan-skye (G. Roerich *et al.* has Bruśa as Gilgit, but Snellgrove and Richardson identify it as Hunza), Hūṃkara and Vasudhara (from Nepal), relate the Tantra to the Himālayas, particularly the North West. See Dunjom Rimpoche's *History of the Dharma* (*Chos-'byung*), f. 56a–60a; and 'Gos Lotsawa's *Blue Annals* (*sDeb-ther sngon-po*, hereafter the *Blue Annals*), p. 159.

5 See Dunjom Rimpoche, *gNam-leags spu-ti*: *Lo-rgyus chos-'byung*, f. 2a. The five graces (*phun-sum-tshogs-pa lnga*) are time, place, teacher, teaching and retinue.

6 Sanskrit: Ānandavajra or Prahaśavajra. Ro-lang-bde-ba = Vetālaśūkha.

7 These legends of the Dzokchen *atiyoga* Gurus are based upon Dunjom Rimpoche's *History of the Dharma* f. 60a–69a except where indicated. The preceding part of this paragraph is derived from K. Douglas and G. Bays (trans.), *The Life and Liberation of Padma Sambhava* (*Padma bka'-thang shel-brag-ma*, hereafter *Sheldrakma*), p. 183. Garab Dorje and Guru Pema were not contemporaries. Lineal history is complicated by Tibetan commentators who neglected to indicate whether transmission of precepts from a deceased Guru was transmitted through vision, a Ḍākinī, or an incarnation, etc.

8 *Blue Annals*, p. 107; see p. 191ff. for the sNying-thig lineage.

9 Perhaps transmitted by Garab Dorje in a vision; see n. 7 above.

10 See Eva Dargyay, *The Rise of Esoteric Buddhism in Tibet*, p. 31ff. Here the author perpetuates prejudices that have bedevilled inter-school politics for centuries. Since it is impossible to either prove or disprove the assertions of the lineage concerning its origins, better let sleeping dogs lie. Recounting the tradition uncritically whenever possible maintains its integrity; it is contrary to certain tantric vows to undermine the faith of devotees.

11 *Sad-mi mi bdun*. Sources differ, but the so-called *Samye Chronicles* (*sBa-shad*) is probably the most authoritative: Pa-gor Vairotsana, Ngan-lam rGyal-ba mchog-dbyangs, rMa Rin-chen-mchog, 'Khon kLu'i dbang-po, gTsang Legs-grub, mChims Sa-skya lta-ba, dbUs Ratna. The first three are commonly corroborated; other possible names are gNam-mkha'i snying-po, sBa gSal-snang, rGyal-ba'i blo-

gros. See G. Tucci, *Minor Buddhist Texts*, p. 324 for comparative lists.

12 The essential beliefs of the *yogācāra-mādhyamika-svatantrikas* are that (a) external objects do not exist apart from the mind that perceives them; (b) ultimate reality is what is directly perceived in gnostic awareness and (c) the phenomenal aspect of this Awareness is non-delusory; (d) conventional reality is either illusory like a lake or delusory like a mirage; (e) only six types of consciousness are valid (omitting *alaya-vijñāna* and *kleśa-vijñāna*); (f) a Bodhisattva is free of delusion; (g) a Buddha ceases to be a sentient being because he has no mind to perceive himself or phenomena as discrete entities. See H. Guenther, *Buddhist Philosophy in Theory and Practice*, p. 131ff.

13 *gTer-ston rgyal-po lnga*: Nyang-ral Nyi-ma 'od-zer (1124–92), Guru Chos-dbang (1212–70), rDo-rje-gling-pa (1346–1405), Orgyan Padma-gling-pa (1450–?), mKhyen-brtse-dbang-po (1820–92). Rig-'dzin rGod-ldem-can (1337–1409) initiated *byang-gter* lineages that are still vital.

14 See Trinley Norbu, *The Small Golden Key*, p. 4.

15 The *Guyhasamāja-tantra*, etc. discovered in Orgyen and the *Kālacakra tantra* taught at Dhānyakaṭaka could be considered 'mind-treasures' (*dgongs-gter*) or 'profound treasures' (*zab-gter*) since they were revealed by Guhyapati, Śākyamuni, etc.

16 bDe-ba rtsal. But in Dunjom Rimpoche's *History* it is Las-kyi dbang-mo who delivers the *mahāyoga* texts to the Eight Knowledge Holders and in Padma dKar-po's *History* it is Rig-'dzin rDo-rje Chos.

17 In his *History of the Dharma* Dunjom Rimpoche's amazing summary of Khyentse Wongpo's secret biography, an exposition of Khyentse's fulfilment of the Seven Mandates (*bKa'-bab bdun-ldan*), is an uncompromising acceptance of the terma doctrines, and it reveals the essential Old School spirit. Khyentse revitalised innumerable dormant terma lineages and edited their texts for inclusion in the *Rinchen Terdzod*. The Seven Mandates are empowerment to intuit the meaning of symbolic language (*brda'-i dbang*), to recover earth-treasures (*sa-gter*), twice-revealed treasures (*yang-gter*), treasures of Buddha's profound dynamic mind (*zab-mo dgongs-pa'i gter*), memory-treasures from past lifes (*rjes-dran gter*), vision-treasures (*dag-snang gter*), and treasures of the audial lineage (*snyan-brgyud*).

18 Hwashang Mahāyāna, the 7th and last *ch'an* patriarch, fled from the Emperor's persecution to Tun Huang from whence he was invited to Samye after the Tibetans captured the area. The Tun Huang Buddhist community had strong ties with Tibet during the seventh (?) and eighth centuries. He returned to Tun Huang after

the Samye Debate (794). Hwashang Mahāyāna is counted amongst the eighteen ārhats.

19 See *Blue Annals*, p. 167. Phag-mo-gru-pa received precepts from Aro's school called 'Dzokchen according to the Kham method' and commented that they were nothing but *śamatha* precepts.

20 (1) Kashmir and Orgyen, (2) Southern Bihar – Nālandā, Vajrāsana and Oḍantapuri (Bihari Sharif?), (3) East Bengal – Vikramaśīla, (4) Andhra – Dhānyakaṭaka, Śrī Parbhat.

21 Śāhī, or Śāhīyas, were families descended from Śāka tribes that invaded the North-West *ca.* first century BC.

22 See Eva Dargyay, *op. cit.*, p. 18, 23ff.

23 See Dunjom Rimpoche's *History of the Dharma*, f. 60a.

24 See S. Beal, *Chinese Accounts of India*, Vol. I, p. 118.

25 See R. Sanskrityayana, *Dohākośa* (Hindi), p. 9ff.

26 *Dohā mdzod bdun* (*Treasury of the Seven Dohās*), published in Rumtek, Sikkim. Technically a *dohā* is a metrical form, but it has come to mean a genre of song sung by the Indian *siddhas*, the content of which is *mahāmudrā* precepts or *anuyoga* instruction in twilight language.

27 See T. Skorupski, 'Tibetan gyung-drung Bon Monastery', *Kailash*, Vol. VIII 1–2, 1981.

28 The *Bar-do thos-grol* is a terma of O-rgyan-gling-pa (*ca.* fourteenth century).

29 See Kazi Dawa Samdup (trans.), *Śrīcakrasaṃbara-tantra*, p. 13ff; translated from Sanskrit in the fourteenth century at Swayambhu, Nepal, 'at 'Phag-pa's command'. Within the encircling *vajra*-wall of the *maṇḍala* stand protecting deities carrying phurbas (*kīlas*) and clubs in their left and right hands respectively. Their function is to transfix black spirits through the head with the phurba while the initiate attains Buddhahood. But these phurbas were probably the simple 'nail' or 'peg' type daggers rather than the elaborate, unmistakable dagger forms of the Bonpo phurbas.

30 See Gedun Choephel, *The White Annals*, p. 30, quoting the *rGyal-po Thang-yig*, a terma of Orgyen-gling-pa based on ancient sources.

31 Dunjom Rimpoche, *Guru rnam-thar Yid-kyi mun-sel*, f. 366.

32 See Dunjom Rimpoche, *gNam-lcags spu-ti: lo-rgyus chos-'byung*, p. 2b. Kun-tu-bzang-po to rGyal-ba rigs lnga and rDo-rje gzhon-nu and Vajrapāṇi, to rGyal-ba rigs bzhi, to Guru Pema. Also, Kun-tu-bzang-po to rDo-rje gzhon-nu, to the Brahmin Kapālika and Prabhahasti and Guru Pema. And, Indrabhūti to Dhanasaṃskṛta to Guru Pema and Vimalamitra and the Nepali Śīla Mañju.

33 K. Dowman, *The Legend of the Great Stupa*, 'The Life Story of the

Lotus Born Guru' (Chos-gling's *Guru rnam-thar dpag-bsam ljon-shing*), p. 78.

34 See *Blue Annals*, p. 103. Sakya Panchen translated the *Vajramantra-bhīrusandhi-mūlatantra*. The *Vajrakīla-mūlatantrakhaṇḍa* is also included in the *Kanjur* (*Blue Annals*, p. 106).

4 The Historical Background

1 O-lde pu-rgyal may have been Pu-lde gung-rgyal, son of King Gri-gum of the second dynasty, who was the first king to be buried rather than ascend to heaven via the *dMu*-cord. See *Maṇi bka'-'bum* f. 100a, and H. Richardson, *Ancient Historical Edicts at Lhasa*, P.P.F. Vol. XIX. The early legends are also retold in *The Genealogy of Kings* (*rGyal-rabs gsal-ba'i me-long*) ch. VII, the *Red Annals* and the *Blue Annals*. See also G. Tucci, *Tibetan Painted Scrolls*, pp. 727–34, and *The Religions of Tibet*, p. 226ff.

2 A *mahāyāna sūtra*, very popular in Licchavi Nepal, describing the blessings of Avalokiteśvara and the significance of his *mantra*, etc., translated by Thon-mi Sambhoṭa and known as the *Za-ma-tog*.

3 It is by no means improbable that Indian Buddhist missionaries had succeeded in influencing the Tibetans as early as the third century or even earlier. A legend that an Indian sadhu brought the *Karaṇḍav-yūha* to Yarlung could indicate early Buddhist influence in Central Tibet, also. However, it would have been in Zhang-zhung where Shenrab taught that Buddhist influence would have been strongest; but it is unlikely that Buddhism had any radical reforming effect on Bon until the seventh or eighth centuries.

4 'How can we give the contents of our classics to these barbarian enemies of the west? . . In what way would this differ from giving weapons to brigands or one's possessions to thieves?' Snellgrove and Richardson, *A Cultural History of Tibet*, p. 31.

5 See M. Aris, *Bhutan*, pp. 3–33.

6 See *Maṇi bKa'-'bum*, chs XII–XXII for the most extensive catalogue of Songtsen's achievements. Although a late terma, undoubtedly the *Maṇi bKa'-'bum* was based upon ancient sources.

7 See H. Richardson, *ibid.*, pp. 5–6, and B. Laufer, *Bird Divination Amongst the Tibetans*, p. 103ff. Also R. Stein, *Tibetan Civilisation*, pp. 94ff. and 99ff.

8 See A. Chattopadhyaya, *Atīśa and Tibet*, p. 217.

9 Recounted in *The Samye Chronicles* (*sBa-bzhad*), a very early and credible work; see W. Shakabpa, *Tibet: A Political History*, p. 35.

10 See M. Aris, *Bhutan*, p. 72.

11 See H. Richardson, *ibid.*, p. 1ff.

12 For historical references to Nepal see K. Dowman, 'A Buddhist Guide to the Power Places of the Kathmandu Valley', *Kailash*, Vol. III (2–3), 1981.

13 Although speed-walking is one of the eight great Buddhist *siddhis* this reference indicates that it was also a Bon *siddhi*.

14 The principal Tibetan translators were Vairotsana, Ma Rinchen Chok, Kaba Peltsek, Chokro Lui Gyeltsen, Drok-ben Konchok Jungne, Drenpa Namkha, Namkhai Nyingpo, Yudra Nyingpo and Nyak Jñāna Kumāra.

15 See Ch. 7, n. 6.

16 See *Sheldrakma*, p. 414ff., 504ff., and G. Tucci, *Minor Buddhist Texts*, p. 356, n. 1, for an interesting account of the *lDan-dkar-ma*.

17 See T. Skorupski, 'Tibetan g-Yung-drung Bon Monastery at Dolanji', *Kailash*, Vol. III (1–2), p. 33.

18 See R. Stein, *Tibetan Civilisation*, p. 200.

19 Tucci gives a comprehensive account of Bon and the folk religion in *The Religions of Tibet*, chs 6 & 7, and in *Tibetan Civilisation* R. Stein includes many interesting details from more limited sources; but much work remains to be done on the history of Bon.

20 See G. Tucci, *The Religions of Tibet*, p. 214ff.

21 See D. Snellgrove, *The Nine Ways of Bon*.

22 In fact Bon has only been recognised by the Tibetan theocratic establishment since the recent foundation of the Dolanji Monastery, near Simla, India. See T. Skorupski, *op. cit.*, p. 40.

23 See G. Tucci, *The Religions of Tibet*, pp. 232, 238. Along with the Bon (priests and *dharma*) and the bards (*sgrengs*), the riddle priests (*ldeu*) were considered one of the three supports of society.

24 Buton's *History of the Dharma* (*Chos-'byung*) gives twenty-one months, and Dunjom Rimpoche quotes unidentified sources in his *Yid-kyi-mun-sel* giving three and six months.

25 *The Genealogy of Kings*, f. 102a. Whether moral cause and effect is a psychological law or an expedient though baseless theological premise (both Christian and Buddhist) belief in it negates the hypothesis of the social equality of man. However it may be argued that social inequality is the most profitable condition for personal evolution since it accelerates exhaustion of *karma* on the direct path and provides for passive acceptance or the attainment of merit on the gradual path.

26 See G. Tucci, *Minor Buddhist Texts*. Introducing the *Bhāvanākrama* in Tibetan, Sanskrit and English, Prof. Tucci gives an invaluable résumé of our knowledge of the Samye Debate and its political and religious background, and also of several basic Dzokchen texts.

27 See P. Demieville, *Le Concile de Lhasa*, Introduction. The terma that claims that the Chinese were the victors is the *bLon-po thang-yig*.

28 Sang-shi or Shang-shi is the Tibetan transliteration of *ch'an-shih*, translated as *bSam-gtan mkhan-po* (master of *ch'an*). The identification of Sang-shi is discussed in G. Tucci, *Minor Buddhist Texts*, p. 333ff.

29 Another factor determining the King's anti-Chinese bias was the Chinese betrayal of the peace treaty signed in 783.

30 See M. Aris, *Bhutan*, p. 73.

31 See G. Tucci, *Minor Buddhist Texts*, p. 336ff.

32 Confirmed in the Tun Huang chronicles.

33 The *Sheldrakma* gives his age as seventeen and the *Zanglingma* as twenty.

34 In A. Warder, *Indian Buddhism*, p. 480, his presumably Indian sources imply that Śāntarakṣita returned to India to die.

INDEXES

Index of Tibetan Words

This index is ordered according to the Tibetan alphabet. It includes the phonetic forms of Tibetan words found in the text. It does not include notice of every passing reference to common terms. Sanskrit, transliterated, phonetic and synonymous terms within the brackets may refer to additional entries. Ch. = Chinese; pr. = pronounced.

Index of Sanskrit Words

This index is alphabetised according to the Sanskrit alphabet. Passing references to common words have been omitted. Tibetan equivalents in brackets refer to the Tibetan word index. N. = Newari.

Index of Texts

This list includes the Sanskrit and Tibetan texts and collections of texts mentioned in both *The Life* and the Commentary.

Index to Place-Names

This list includes the dwelling-places of both men and Buddhas. Prov. = province; dist. = district.

Index of Men, Buddhas, Gods and Demons

After the headword, within the brackets, the transliterated form is given together with the Sanskrit or Tibetan equivalents and any alternative names included within the index that carry additional references. Ch. = Chinese.